Advancements in Speech Processing for Human-Computer Interaction

Abeer Saber
https://orcid.org/0000-0002-9261-0927
Damietta University, Egypt

Tamer Z. Emara
Damietta University, Egypt

Mohammad Sultan Mahmud
https://orcid.org/0000-0002-5795-787X
Shenzhen University, China

Muhammad Azhar
https://orcid.org/0000-0003-3687-0270
Hong Kong Shue Yan University, Hong Kong

Esraa Hassan
Kafrelsheikh University, Egypt

IGI Global
Scientific Publishing
Publishing Tomorrow's Research Today

Vice President of Editorial	Melissa Wagner
Director of Acquisitions	Mikaela Felty
Director of Book Development	Jocelynn Hessler
Production Manager	Mike Brehm
Cover Design	Jose Rosado

Published in the United States of America by
IGI Global Scientific Publishing
701 East Chocolate Avenue
Hershey, PA, 17033, USA
Tel: 717-533-8845 | Fax: 717-533-7115
Website: https://www.igi-global.com E-mail: cust@igi-global.com

Library of Congress Cataloging-in-Publication Data

Names: Saber, Abeer, 1992- editor | Emara, Tamer, 1983- editor | Mahmud, Mohammad Sultan, 1987- editor | Azhar, Muhammad, 1989- editor | Hassan, Esraa, 1992- editor
Title: Advancements in speech processing for human-computer interaction / edited by: Abeer Saber, Tamer Z. Emara, Mohammad Sultan Mahmud, Muhammad Azhar, and Esraa Hassan.
Description: Hershey, PA : IGI Global Scientific Publishing, [2026] | Collection of essays by Nizirwan Anwar and 12 others. | Includes bibliographical references and index. | Summary: "This book provides a comprehensive and up-to-date analysis of the latest breakthroughs in speech processing, specifically focusing on their applications and impact within the field of human-computer interaction (HCI)"-- Provided by publisher.
Identifiers: LCCN 2025016760 (print) | LCCN 2025016761 (ebook) | ISBN 9798337330488 hardcover | ISBN 9798337330495 paperback | ISBN 9798337330501 ebook
Subjects: LCSH: Human-computer interaction | Speech processing systems | Automatic speech recognition
Classification: LCC QA76.9.H85 A38 2026 (print) | LCC QA76.9.H85 (ebook)
LC record available at https://lccn.loc.gov/2025016760
LC ebook record available at https://lccn.loc.gov/2025016761

British Cataloguing in Publication Data
A Cataloguing in Publication record for this book is available from the British Library.

Table of Contents

Detailed Table of Contents

Human-computer interaction (HCI) has evolved significantly with speech processing technologies, yet a substantial gap remains between natural human communication and machine interaction capabilities. This paper examines speech processing's role in enhancing HCI by analyzing acoustic signal processing, natural language understanding, and user interface design. The study investigates key technologies including automatic speech recognition (ASR), text-to-speech synthesis, and speaker identification across diverse applications such as voice assistants, accessibility tools, gaming environments, and interactive voice response systems. Our analysis reveals that while speech processing has successfully transformed HCI applications, critical issues including acoustic noise sensitivity, limited inclusivity for diverse speaker populations, and the "uncanny valley" effect continue impeding optimal user experience.

The integration of artificial intelligence into human communication has changed how we express emotions, show empathy, and engage in dialogue. This chapter examines the rise of artificial empathy, which is AI's ability to recognize and mimic emotional reactions, and its effect on human connection. The study examines systems like MoEL, CoMAE, and assess these systems using tools like the Empathy Scale for Human-Computer Communication (ESHCC). We draw on research from different fields, including affective computing, media psychology, and computational linguistics. Key theories, such as the Media Equation and Computers as Social Actors (CASA), help explain the emotional responses users have toward machines that can respond emotionally. As AI starts to communicate for us and takes over emotionally sensitive conversations, the distinction between real and simulated emotion becomes less clear. This chapter calls for a closer look at how we design human-AI interactions, focusing on transparency, emotional understanding, and ethics in communication.

This study presents an exploration of emerging trends in Conversational Artificial Intelligence (AI), highlighting advancements in natural language processing, machine learning, and human-computer interaction. As AI-driven chatbots and virtual assistants become more sophisticated, trends such as enhanced contextual understanding, multimodal interactions, and emotional intelligence are shaping the future of conversational systems. The integration of large language models, real-time personalization, and ethical AI considerations are driving improvements in user experience, making AI interactions more seamless and human-like. Additionally, the rise of multilingual AI, domain-specific chatbots, and voice-enabled assistants is expanding AI's applications across industries, including healthcare, customer service, and education. However, challenges related to bias, data privacy, and misinformation persist, necessitating ongoing research and regulatory frameworks. This study examines these trends and their implications for the future development of Conversational AI.

The global integration of communication networks increases the demand for multilingual human-computer interaction (HCI) systems. Speech technology innovations that support multiple languages enhance accessibility and usability. This chapter explores how automatic speech recognition (ASR) and text-to-speech (TTS), combined with language models, ena-ble real-time speech translation across diverse accents and linguistic systems. Deep learning and transfer learning help models learn from small, complex language datasets, even under noisy conditions. Practical applications include educational tools, virtual assistants, cus-tomer service, and healthcare. The section also addresses the need for culturally intuitive, unbiased systems through inclusive design and ethical guidelines, promoting linguistic equality. Advances in multilingual speech technology make HCI more inclusive and effec-tive for global users, supporting developers and researchers alike.

Natural Language Speech Processing (NLSP) is a fundamental space of consider that centers on the interaction between people and machines through talked dialect. The integration of assistive innovations in this field points to bridge communication holes and upgrade availability for people with inabilities. This chapter investigates the advancing scene of NLSP, emphasizing its part in progressing Human-Computer Interaction (HCI) by empowering consistent communication between clients and computers through voice acknowledgment, blend, and common dialect understanding. Assistive innovations such as speech-to-text, text-to-speech, and voice-controlled frameworks are changing every day intelligent for people with hearing, discourse, and engine impedances, giving them with upgraded independence and interaction conceivable outcomes. The integration of machine learning and profound learning calculations has quickened progressions in discourse acknowledgment precision, enthusiastic tone examination, and context-driven dialect preparing.

Speech recognition is a key area in Artificial Intelligence that involves extracting meaningful information from speech signals, such as gender, age, or emotion. While

Preface

In a world increasingly shaped by technology, the way we communicate with machines has become a pivotal frontier. The era of clunky, command-line interfaces has given way to a more intuitive, natural form of interaction: conversation. As our devices become more ubiquitous and intertwined with our daily lives, the ability to speak to them, to have them understand our intent, and to respond in a way that feels genuinely human is no longer a luxury—it is a necessity. This book, **"Advancements in Speech Processing for Human-Computer Interaction,"** explores this profound shift, offering a comprehensive look at the state-of-the-art technologies, innovative applications, and critical challenges that are defining this field today.

The discipline of speech processing stands at the nexus of several revolutionary fields, including artificial intelligence, linguistics, signal processing, and computer science. It is the invisible force that powers our daily interactions, from the voice assistant in our kitchen to the GPS navigator in our car and the virtual agents on our customer service calls. This book serves as a testament to the rapid and ongoing evolution of this technology, showcasing how it has moved beyond simple command recognition to a sophisticated understanding of context, emotion, and nuance. It is an area of study that is not merely academic but has tangible, real-world impact, influencing how we learn, work, and connect.

The target audience for this book is broad, reflecting the interdisciplinary nature of the subject. It is designed for researchers and academics seeking a deep dive into the latest methodologies and findings. Graduate students will find it an invaluable resource for understanding the foundational principles and exploring potential research avenues. For software engineers and developers, it offers practical insights and a survey of emerging trends to inform the creation of next-generation applications. Finally, industry professionals and product managers can gain a strategic perspective on how speech processing technologies are disrupting markets and creating new opportunities for innovation.

The chapters within this book have been carefully curated and arranged to provide a cohesive and logical journey through the landscape of speech processing and human-computer interaction. The book begins with foundational concepts and progresses to highly specialized and forward-looking topics, ensuring a thorough and engaging exploration for readers at all levels of expertise.

CHAPTER OVERVIEW

Chapter 1: Bridging the Gap: The Role of Speech Processing in Enhancing Human-Computer Interaction sets the stage by providing a foundational overview of the discipline. This chapter examines speech processing's role in enhancing HCI by analyzing acoustic signal processing, natural language understanding, and user interface design. It investigates key technologies, including automatic speech recognition (ASR), text-to-speech synthesis, and speaker identification across diverse applications, while also revealing critical issues like acoustic noise sensitivity, limited inclusivity, and the "uncanny valley" effect that impede optimal user experience.

Chapter 2: The Rise of Artificial Empathy-How Machines Are Reshaping Human Conversation delves into one of the most exciting and complex areas of conversational AI: the development of emotional intelligence in machines. This chapter examines the rise of artificial empathy, which is AI's ability to recognize and mimic emotional reactions, and its effect on human connection. The study examines systems like MoEL and CoMAE, assessing them using tools like the Empathy Scale for Human-Computer Communication (ESHCC). It draws on research from affective computing, media psychology, and computational linguistics to explore key theories, such as the Media Equation and Computers as Social Actors (CASA), that help explain user emotional responses to emotionally responsive machines.

Chapter 3: Trends in Conversational Artificial Intelligence: Who Controls the Voice Behind the Bot? presents an exploration of emerging trends in Conversational Artificial Intelligence (AI). This chapter highlights advancements in natural language processing and machine learning, and how trends such as enhanced contextual understanding, multimodal interactions, and emotional intelligence are shaping the future of conversational systems. It examines how the integration of large language models, real-time personalization, and ethical AI considerations are driving improvements in user experience. Additionally, it addresses persistent challenges related to bias, data privacy, and misinformation, underscoring the need for ongoing research and regulatory frameworks.

Chapter 4: Advancements in Multilingual Speech Technologies for Human Computer Interaction focuses on the global dimension of speech processing. This chapter explores how automatic speech recognition (ASR) and text-to-speech (TTS), combined with language models, enable real-time speech translation across diverse accents and linguistic systems. It discusses how deep learning and transfer learning help models learn from small, complex language datasets, even under noisy conditions, and examines the need for culturally intuitive, unbiased systems through inclusive design and ethical guidelines, promoting linguistic equality.

Chapter 5: Natural Language Speech Processing Integrating Assistive Technologies for Human-Computer Interaction shifts the focus to the powerful role of speech processing in creating inclusive and accessible technology. This chapter investigates the evolving landscape of Natural Language Speech Processing (NLSP), emphasizing its role in advancing Human-Computer Interaction (HCI) by enabling seamless communication through voice recognition, synthesis, and natural language understanding. It examines how assistive technologies such as speech-to-text, text-to-speech, and voice-controlled frameworks are empowering people with disabilities by providing them with enhanced independence and interaction possibilities.

Chapter 6: Speech-Based Speaker Gender Identification using Deep Learning dives into a specific, yet highly relevant, application of deep learning in speech processing. This study proposes a deep learning-based approach for gender classification using features extracted from speech samples. It details the evaluation of two feature extraction methods—Mel Frequency Cepstral Coefficients (MFCC) and Linear Prediction Cepstral Coefficients (LPCC)—using Convolutional Neural Networks (CNN) and Long Short-Term Memory (LSTM) models, and presents the findings, which show that MFCC features significantly improve the performance of both models.

Chapter 7: Designing a Smart Typo Correction and Sentiment Prediction Tool for Social Media Texts: A Statistical NLP Approach for Speech-Enabled Human-Computer Interaction offers a practical case study in applying speech and language processing to real-world data. This chapter outlines the development of a speech-enabled tool that uses statistical Natural Language Processing (NLP) techniques, such as n-grams and entropy-based smoothing, to correct typographical errors and predict sentiment in social media texts. The findings indicate improved accuracy in typo detection and meaningful sentiment classification, which can significantly enhance the performance of speech-enabled human-computer interfaces.

Chapter 8: The role of speech processing in the metaverse takes a look at the future of human-computer interaction. This chapter explores the pivotal role of speech processing in the metaverse, focusing on natural interaction, emotional recognition, and multi-user communication. By employing Automatic Speech Recognition (ASR) and real-time translation, these technologies facilitate seamless engagement across diverse linguistic and cultural backgrounds. It also examines the integration of affective computing to enable systems to tailor responses to users' emotional states, enriching social dynamics within virtual spaces.

Chapter 9: Guardians of the Voice: Defending Speech Interfaces Against Deepfakes and Adversarial Attacks addresses a critical and timely security concern. This chapter presents a comprehensive analysis of threats, including voice spoofing, deepfake synthesis, and adversarial attacks on ASR systems. It surveys feature-based and deep learning defenses, techniques for hardening ASR models, and the role of standardized benchmarks in evaluating robustness. The chapter advocates for integrating trust, security, and resilience into the design of voice-enabled systems to protect against these growing vulnerabilities.

Chapter 10: The Double-Edged Sword: Evaluating the Climate Impact of Speech Processing Technologies concludes the book with a thoughtful and critical examination of the environmental footprint of this technology. This chapter highlights how the energy consumption of training large-scale models drives greenhouse gas emissions, and discusses the embodied carbon and e-waste from devices. It advocates for sustainable speech processing, exploring strategies like lightweight architectures, pruning, quantization, and the use of green data centers to balance innovation with environmental stewardship.

This book is a timely and essential contribution to the field of human-computer interaction. It not only chronicles the remarkable technical advancements in speech processing but also contextualizes them within the broader societal, ethical, and environmental landscapes. By providing a holistic overview of the subject, from foundational principles to cutting-edge applications and future challenges, it aims to inspire a new generation of researchers, developers, and thinkers to continue pushing the boundaries of what is possible, ensuring that the voice behind the machine is not only intelligent but also responsible.

Chapter 1
Bridging the Gap: The Role of Speech Processing in Enhancing Human-Computer Interaction

Amena Mahmoud
https://orcid.org/0009-0006-9909-0430
Faculty of Computers and Information, Kafrelsheikh University, Egypt

Wael A. Awad
Independent Researcher, Egypt

ABSTRACT

Human-computer interaction (HCI) has evolved significantly with speech processing technologies, yet a substantial gap remains between natural human communication and machine interaction capabilities. This paper examines speech processing's role in enhancing HCI by analyzing acoustic signal processing, natural language understanding, and user interface design. The study investigates key technologies including automatic speech recognition (ASR), text-to-speech synthesis, and speaker identification across diverse applications such as voice assistants, accessibility tools, gaming environments, and interactive voice response systems. Our analysis reveals that while speech processing has successfully transformed HCI applications, critical issues including acoustic noise sensitivity, limited inclusivity for diverse speaker populations, and the "uncanny valley" effect continue impeding optimal user experience.

DOI: 10.4018/979-8-3373-3048-8.ch001

1. INTRODUCTION

Human-Computer Interaction (HCI) stands as a cornerstone of the modern digital era, defining the modalities through which humans communicate with and command computational systems. The evolution of HCI has progressed from primitive punch cards and command-line interfaces to the sophisticated graphical and touch-based systems ubiquitous today. Despite these advancements, a significant chasm persists between the fluid, intuitive nature of human-to-human communication and the often rigid, formulaic interactions characteristic of human-to-machine dialogue (Moore, 2019). This gap represents a fundamental limitation in achieving truly seamless and natural technological integration into daily life.

Speech, as the most primal and natural form of human communication, presents a compelling solution to this challenge. The field of speech processing, which encompasses the computational analysis, synthesis, and understanding of speech signals, has emerged as a critical discipline aimed at harnessing this potential (Denby, Csapó, & Wand, 2023). By enabling machines to recognize spoken words, synthesize human-like speech, and identify speakers, speech processing technologies seek to transform the HCI paradigm from one of manual input and visual output to one of conversational partnership (Polkosky, 2005). The integration of these technologies is evident in widespread applications such as voice-activated personal assistants (e.g., Siri, Alexa), automated transcription services, and interactive voice response (IVR) systems, which collectively aim to make technology more accessible, efficient, and hands-free (Kotian & Nandipi, 2024).

However, the path to realizing this vision is fraught with technical and experiential hurdles. Contemporary speech-enabled systems grapple with critical issues such as a pronounced sensitivity to acoustic noise, performance degradation for non-standard accents and dialects, and a lack of inclusivity for users with speech impairments (Shanthamallappa & Puttegowda, 2024). Furthermore, the phenomenon known as the "uncanny valley" effect, where nearly human-like synthetic voices can evoke unease, alongside profound ethical concerns regarding user privacy, data security, and embedded algorithmic biases, continues to impede widespread adoption and user trust (Aloufi, Haddadi, & Boyle, 2021), (Kulkarni, Tokareva, Qureshi, & Couceiro, 2024).

The current study presents a comprehensive examination of this dynamic intersection. The authors conduct a meticulous analysis of the core technologies underpinning speech processing—including automatic speech recognition (ASR), text-to-speech (TTS) synthesis, and speaker identification—and evaluate their application across diverse domains such as accessibility, gaming, and customer service. Through a synthesis of historical context, current applications, and case studies of both successful implementations and notable failures, the study highlights the indispensable role of user-centered design principles.

This chapter argues that for speech processing to truly bridge the HCI communication gap, future development must prioritize robustness, inclusivity, and the emulation of natural interaction patterns. It concludes by exploring future trends driven by advancements in artificial intelligence and machine learning, while rigorously addressing the ethical imperatives necessary for equitable and secure technology deployment. This work thus serves as a valuable contribution to the ongoing effort to create more intuitive, effective, and humane interfaces between humans and machines.

2. RELATED WORK

The pursuit of seamless human-computer interaction (HCI) through speech processing is a deeply multidisciplinary endeavor, drawing from and contributing to fields including signal processing, computational linguistics, machine learning, and user experience design. The foundational work in automatic speech recognition (ASR) established the core statistical paradigms, most notably Hidden Markov Models (HMMs) combined with Gaussian Mixture Models (GMMs), which dominated the field for decades and enabled the first practical, large-vocabulary continuous speech recognition systems (Rabiner, 1989). This era focused primarily on improving accuracy under constrained conditions, often neglecting the nuances of user-centered design.

The advent of deep learning marked a revolutionary shift, significantly advancing the state-of-the-art. Deep Neural Networks (DNNs) replaced GMMs for acoustic modeling, leading to substantial reductions in word error rates, particularly in noisy environments (Hinton et al., 2012). This was followed by the development of end-to-end systems that directly map acoustic features to text or semantic representations, simplifying the traditional pipeline and improving performance (Amodei et al., 2016). These technological leaps, powered by large-scale datasets and increased computational resources, facilitated the mainstream deployment of voice assistants like Siri, Alexa, and Google Assistant, embedding speech processing into everyday HCI (Bellegarda, 2013).

Concurrently, a significant body of research has emerged focusing not on raw performance metrics but on the user experience (UX) of speech interfaces. Seminal work by Polkosky (Polkosky, 2005) moved beyond engineering-centric measures like accuracy and speed, arguing for a social-cognitive psychology of speech technology that prioritizes affective responses and perceptions of humanness. This perspective is critical, as studies have consistently shown that technical perfection does not guarantee user satisfaction or adoption (Denby, Csapó, & Wand, 2023). Research in this vein explores how factors such as voice personality, response latency, and error handling strategies profoundly influence user trust, engagement, and long-term usage patterns (Nass & Brave, 2005).

The application of speech processing as an accessibility tool has also been a major research thrust. Investigators have long explored its potential to empower users with visual, motor, or speech impairments, developing systems for voice-controlled environments and communication aids (Sears & Young, 2003). However, as noted by Waller (Sears & Young, 2003) and others, a significant gap often exists between academic prototypes and commercially available, fully featured tools, with many products remaining limited to basic dictation. This highlights a persistent challenge in translating research into inclusive, practical solutions.

Recently, the ethical implications of widespread speech technology adoption have come to the forefront of related work. A growing area of research focuses on algorithmic bias, demonstrating that ASR systems often exhibit significantly higher error rates for speakers with non-standard accents, dialects, or from specific demographic groups, thereby risking the marginalization of already underserved populations (Koenecke et al., 2020). In parallel, studies on privacy and security have revealed vulnerabilities, such as the potential for voice spoofing attacks and the extensive collection of sensitive biometric and contextual data by cloud-based services. Research into privacy-enhancing technologies (PETs) for speech, including on-device processing and voice anonymization, seeks to mitigate these risks (Patel, Huang, & Lin, 2022).

Finally, research into future trends is exploring the convergence of speech with other modalities. The integration of visual information (e.g., lip-reading) for robust audio-visual speech recognition (Afouras, Chung, & Zisserman, 2018), and the use of speech for affective computing to enable emotion-aware interfaces (Busso et al., 2008) to represent the next frontier in creating more natural, contextually intelligent, and robust HCI systems.

This chapter synthesizes insights from these diverse yet interconnected strands of research. It builds upon the technological foundations laid by signal processing and machine learning, incorporates the critical user-centered perspective advocated by UX researchers, acknowledges the imperative for inclusivity highlighted by accessibility studies, and addresses the urgent ethical challenges outlined in recent literature. By doing so, it provides a comprehensive review of how speech processing can bridge the HCI communication gap while responsibly navigating its societal implications.

3. UNDERSTANDING SPEECH PROCESSING

Speech processing emerged in the 1950s, following the introduction of computers. Early developments featured isolated word recognizers, and the prevailing trend favored small-vocabulary isolated-word systems (Moore, 2019). Over the years, work on speech processing encompassed acoustic-phonetic knowledge, pattern recognition, knowledge-based and statistical modeling, among others, broadening its scope considerably. Today, speech processing combines speech recognition, speech analysis, speech synthesis, and speaker recognition and verification to form a comprehensive area of study (James, Rayner, & Hockey, 2000).

Speech is defined as the emission of acoustic energy—primarily by humans, but also by robots—as air passes through the vocal cords, the system within the vocal tracts being controlled through the audible range of 20 Hz–20000 Hz. Speech processing, in this context, involves the computational analysis and synthesis of speech signals in voice communication systems and applications, such as automatic speech recognition (ASR), speaker verification, speech translation, and spoken dialogue systems.

At its core, speech processing comprises three main approaches that collectively provide a foundation for understanding the field. These include: (1) acoustics and psychoacoustics, which study the physical properties of speech sounds and the way human listeners perceive them; (2) speech analysis and synthesis, which explore techniques for transforming speech signals to extract relevant information and for generating speech from text or other representations; and (3) automatic speech recognition and signal processing, which focus on the design of algorithms and systems for converting speech signals into sequences of words or other meaningful units.

2.1. Definition and Overview

Speech processing refers to a set of techniques by which a computer understands, generates, and analyses speech signals. It began in the early 1950s as a way of sending information through a channel with limited bandwidth. By the 1980s a combined use of electrical engineering, signal processing, and computer science enabled elaborate processing and, more important, the ability to mimic human communication perception (Moore, 2019). Several technologies associated with speech processing are widely used. A good example of a mainstream-use technology and an utmost development in speech processing is represented by automatic speech recognition, where a spoken input phrase is translated into a textual representation (Polkosky, 2005). Other enabling technologies that have greatly impacted the field and boosted the research in the area are speaker identification/verification, speaker diarisation, spoken language identification, and text-to-speech.

The aim of human-computer interaction is the development of techniques and devices to offer efficient and effective communication between humans and machines. Such communication is an everyday routine, and current technological advances allow the use of heterogeneous and diverse intermediate devices. Still, despite their complexity, these machines have extremely poor communication skills when interacting with humans. The gap between human-computer interaction systems and human-to-human interaction remains very large, and machines exhibit unexciting, rigid, and unemotional behaviour.

2.2. Historical Background

Close human-machine communication is essential for advancing computation and social interaction. Speech processing uncovers key aspects of this relationship. Often referred to as spoken language technology, speech processing encompasses the capture, analysis, interpretation, and generation of spoken communication by a computer (Denby, Csapó, & Wand, 2023). Systems supporting these capabilities contribute significantly to overall system intelligence.

Progress toward truly intelligent and associated speech-enabled user interfaces continues at a formidable pace, with multiple enabling technologies playing critical roles. Historically, the desirability of establishing natural spoken dialogue between a human user and a computer was featured as early as 1936 when Alan Turing introduced the principle constituting what is now known as the Turing Test. Nevertheless, foundational research on the Automatic Speech Recognition (ASR) problem did not commence until the early 1950s. In this era, Homer Dudley at Bell Laboratories performed pioneering work on the Pattern Playback device, which converted symbolic representations into analogue acoustic signals for analysis, evaluation, and experimentation. An initial attempt to create a speech interface was described by DeForest and Dewey shortly thereafter and subsequently developed at Lincoln Laboratory. This system operated on a relatively small vocabulary but exploited a hidden Markov model decoder similar to those widely embraced today. (Shanthamallappa & Puttegowda, 2024)

Research into spoken language interfaces is deeply multidisciplinary and multifaceted, extending beyond signal processing and computer science. An extensive spectrum of enabling technology supports such interfaces, from speech recognition and synthesis, speaker identification, and diarization to dialogue systems and natural language understanding. Advances in speech and language technologies contribute significantly to human-computer interaction (HCI), as they have the potential to transform and enhance communication modalities within this domain.

2.3. Key Technologies in Speech Processing

Since their inception, speech technologies have gradually permeated everyday life. Automatic Speech Recognition (ASR) techniques are used not only for surveillance purposes but also as natural input channels for mobile devices and video games. Speech synthesis, speech compression, speaker identification, and diarization are further enabling technologies. The last few years have witnessed a resurgence of automatic speech processing, largely due to two complementary changes. First, publicly available datasets have triggered the development of machine learning methods that deliver near-human keyword-spotting performance. Second, ever improving computing power has boosted the popularity of Deep Neural Network (DNN) architectures, which have become baseline models for many speech processing tasks. Commercial solutions like Azure or Google speech-to-text services, as well as popular open-source toolkits such as TensorFlow-ASR, ESPnet, or SpeechBrain, make speech processing ever more mainstream. (Thieme et al., 2023)

A broad hitherto unresolved question concerns system robustness. Today's systems remain extremely fragile in noisy environments, when speaking styles alter, or when they encounter under-represented accents or languages. Moreover, widespread deployment creates concerns regarding privacy, inclusiveness for people with speech-impairing health conditions, physical disabilities, or less common languages and dialects, as well as a persistent 'uncanny valley' effect revealing the lack of fluidity proper to human interactions.

3. HUMAN-COMPUTER INTERACTION: AN OVERVIEW

Human-Computer Interaction (HCI) involves the study of interactions between people and computers, emphasizing communication across diverse outputs and inputs, such as speech, pen, touch, and gestures. Achieving effective communication remains a core research topic, necessitating improvements in various aspects of interaction design (Farooq, Iqbal, & Nazir, 2011). Speech Processing is a key enabling technology that supports enhanced HCI.

The notion of natural interaction, alleviating the need for extensive training or manuals, has long been a pursuit in HCI. Early machine-learning models addressing this challenge were inefficient and limited to small vocabulary. The availability of large training corpora and advanced algorithms—neural networks, hidden Markov models, and n-grams—has facilitated the deployment of capable models supporting numerous languages and domains. Models for acoustic-phonetic, phonetic, and lexical representation (language models) have become components of speech-processing systems. Applications include voice assistants, speech-to-text transcription, interactive voice response (IVR) systems, accessibility tools for disabilities, and speech-enabled gaming consoles (Farooq, Iqbal, & Nazir, 2011), thereby illustrating their broad impact on HCI.

3.1. Defining Human-Computer Interaction

Human-computer interaction (HCI) encompasses the design and implementation of software and hardware that supports communication between humans and machines. Specialized technologies—such as speech synthesis, natural language processing, computer vision, and robotics—provide novel models and methods for interaction. Effective communication between the two parties is fundamental to the entire range of responsive environments, from automated warehouses guided by radio-frequency identification to handheld medical devices, voice-driven computer terminals, and personal robots. Artificial-intelligence techniques can be leveraged to interactively update or select from the dynamic collection of models used when interpreting ambiguous or uncertain sensor data. Speech-based interaction is crucial here, because it allows the user to work with complex models while maintaining hands, eyes, and attention for primary tasks such as driving or surgery.

3.2. Importance of Effective Communication

When two or more individuals meet for the first time, or have been separated for a long time, the initial desire is to open a communicative channel before engaging further. Communication is usually done by means of speech. The exchange of information is later complemented with gaze and gestures. Human-Computer Interaction (HCI) occurs when a person communicates or uses a computer system. Speech processing technology can be deployed to improve HCI by enabling a seamless flow of information between humans and machines.

Speech is one of the first—and most important—forms of communication. It is a vibration generated by the lungs, throat, mouth, and lips that results in the emission of sound. The study of speech is a multidisciplinary area that incorporates knowledge from Electronics, Computer Science, Linguistics, and Psychology, among others. In this context, speech processing can refer to speech recognition, speech synthesis, or speech translation. The discipline dates from the first quarter of the 20th century, and the 1930s witnessed the development of the first speech processing devices. These developments laid the foundations for subsequent investigations into foundational pioneering research in the following decades, resulting in three main enabling technologies: pattern recognition, digital signal processing, and acoustic phonetics.

4. THE INTERSECTION OF SPEECH PROCESSING AND HCI

Speech processing facilitates several important tasks that enable machines to analyze, understand, and respond to human speech. These tasks include speech synthesis, recognition, coding, translation, speaker diarization, and authentication. Speech synthesis enables systems to generate speech from text, allowing them to convey information audibly. Conversely, speech recognition allows machines to convert spoken words into text, supporting functionalities such as note-taking. The willingness of users to engage with these capabilities is crucial; it constitutes a primary barrier to adoption and usage, as identified by (Clark, 2019).

4.1. How Speech Processing Enhances HCI

Speech communication is one of the oldest and most natural forms of expressing and sharing information. Over time, speech processing technologies have become common components of computing and telecommunications systems. The early pursuit of speech processing evolved from interest in human physiology and the spoken word, which developed into the connections between speech and communication challenges and the creation of automatic speech recognition (ASR), speech synthesis, and speaker recognition technologies. Speech signals can, of course, be used for both analogue and digital information control and communication. Speech processing has become synonymous with a broad range of research efforts aimed at understanding and exploiting one of the most fundamental of human communications channels: Speech. However, the idea of creating human like machines that can communicate with users using speech processing is far more significant than the associated technologies can deliver.

Speech processing strives to enable humans and machines to communicate effectively, improving HCI by allowing human focused interaction with automated processes (Clark, 2019). Speech transmission and recognition systems become a method of addressing systems with little or no visual feedback or that work as a background process. The new generation of speech processing systems will use these applications to enable communication between humans and machines that go beyond simple speech recognition. Sensory processing enables HCI by increasing the traditional ability of human users to interact with their environment. Human communication is multimodal involving signals from many biological channels. Speech communication exists as a channel in its own right and also as part of the multimodal package. These forms of communication appear to be central to the development of high-level agencies within humans.

4.2. Challenges in Integrating Speech Processing

Notwithstanding significant advances in speech processing technologies, numerous challenges persist when integrating them into human-computer interaction (HCI) environments. An important source of difficulty is the considerable gap between the formulaic, constrained conversational styles typical of many current spoken dialogue systems and the fully flexible natural language interaction exhibited in human-human conversation. Speech-based interaction with robots, which often requires grounded and situated understanding, may nevertheless provide deeper insight into the pragmatics of language usage in real-world environments and thus help to overcome this "habitability gap." Performance factors including accuracy, coverage, and speed remain critical, yet, despite the prevailing focus of technical developers on these measures, they do not correspond directly to user satisfaction. Speech recognition errors create considerable problems for the usability of spoken interaction, particularly because other input modalities such as typing and point-and-click typically do not fail when presented with well-formed commands (Clark, 2019).

Four additional issues currently impede the application of speech processing to HCI, namely robustness, privacy, inclusivity, and fluidity. Speech understanding usually degrades precipitously when acoustic conditions become noisy, to the point where humans can comprehend the spoken message even though the system fails (Farooq, Iqbal, & Nazir, 2011). Overheard speech constitutes both a nuisance and a security concern in many interfaces and environments. Certain population segments are unable either physically or cognitively to produce speech patterns matched by present systems, while widely deployed existing resources and high-performance tools are available only for a relatively small subset of the world's languages. Finally, the fluidity and naturalness of automatic speech interfaces continue to constitute a challenge; despite enormous effort in this area, current conversational agents still operate substantially below the levels observed in typical face-to-face dialogue.

5. APPLICATIONS FOR SPEECH PROCESSING IN HCI

Speech processing plays a central role in many applications involving human-computer interaction. Devices such as smartphones, tablets, and personal computers let users conduct Internet searches, check maps and directions, schedule events, send text messages, and play music using voice commands. Personal assistant applications such as Siri and Google Now guide these processes and decode a speaker's intents. Speech-to-text systems convert voice into written text for mobile search and tactile browsing. Large corporations employ interactive voice response systems to manage customer support lines efficiently. Speech processing enables people with complex motor impairments to maintain online social lives and participate in digital activities through accessible tools. In the video game industry, speech provides an intuitive, hands-free way to control virtual avatars, enhancing immersion and realism. (Kotian & Nandipi, 2024)

5.1. Voice Assistants

The widespread implementation of speech-recognition technology enables users to interact with various services and devices through voice. Such technologies constitute an integral component of human-computer interaction (HCI) applications. For instance, Dictation on Apple iOS allows users to dictate content rather than type it, enabling hand-free operation. Virtual assistant voice-activated personal assistant softwares—include offerings from Apple (Siri), Google (Google Assistant), Microsoft (Cortana), Amazon (Alexa), Samsung (Bixby), and others. These allow voice control over a wide range of devices, facilitating tasks such as modifying settings, obtaining directions, playing music, and contacting others. Several barrier-free speech-to-text applications assist people with disabilities in controlling automated devices, amplifying their usability (Wallis, 2021). Interactive voice response (IVR) systems harness speech recognition to accept user voice instructions, reducing the need for manual input by collecting data or conducting surveys. In the realm of computer games, design intention sometimes prompts inclusion of speech recognition to augment the play experience.

5.2. Speech-to-Text Systems

Speech-to-text systems (STT), also termed speech recognition systems, retrieve the text of a spoken utterance while preserving its meaning. A specific branch of this technology, voice recognition systems, identify the speaker rather than recognizing the speech content. Such systems employ language models, acoustic-phonetic models, statistical methods, and natural language processing to enhance text conversion. These technologies support voice-controlled assistants, automatic transcription, IVR automation, accessibility tools, and in-game communication, thereby bridging the gap between human speech and computer processing. The integration of STT into voice-controlled assistants exemplifies the effort to narrow the divide between human communication and machine interpretation (McKeown et al., 1995).

5.3. Interactive Voice Response Systems

Interactive Voice Response (IVR) systems provide users with an easy way to access a variety of remote information, routines, and activities over a touch-tone telephone. Within the telecommunications industry, these systems are employed to schedule appointments, update customer accounts, and redirect calls. Using simple voice commands, drivers can use IVR systems to receive directions, pay bills, and plan travel arrangements. And convenient retrieval of stock quotes, weather reports, and news from any phone line also is readily available. Applications for IVR systems include banking, information retrieval, airline reservations, mutual fund inquiries, directory assistance, and other simple customer service transactions (McKeown et al., 1995). Though the uses of IVR could be extended dramatically, systems often rely on touch-tone input because speech recognition technology has limited vocabularies and error rates often frustrate users (Nadworny, 1988).

5.4. Accessibility Tools

Speech recognition and synthesis systems are important tools for users with visual, speech, or mobility disabilities. Most commercial systems offer no significant features beyond dictation and user activation by voice. Research that would benefit such groups receives limited examination (Waller, 1989). The needs of such users continue to be addressed primarily by specialist suppliers, although some recent academic work has been noted (Roper, Wilson, Neate, & Marshall, 2019).

5.5. Gaming and Entertainment

Computer games have become a major aspect of modern culture. A diverse range of computer games have been designed, with new and interesting game styles constantly emerging. While most computer games work well for the majority of players, some have been excluded from the fun that others enjoy, such as the elderly and the disabled.

Existing game styles often rely on certain types of interfaces that can exclude people with certain difficulties or even impose certain health risks. The absence of a standard voice-driven module that can be used as an interaction module to support all genres of computer games bears the blame. The mainstream game engines are often incompatible with the technology required to add voice-command capabilities. By developing a generic and standard voice-driven module based on speech recognition technology, it will be possible to extend the accessibility and inclusive nature of computer game systems. The module can be integrated with the most widely used game engines so that the games can be normally played with voice commands.

With the birth rates declining and life expectancy increasing, the world's population is growing old. The problems of old age are the perils of the present and the concerns of the future. As society moves progressively towards accessibility, designers and researchers need to pay attention to the elderly and take their needs and concerns into account. Game design cannot afford to exclude this growing segment of the population. Actions invariably become more careful and deliberate when a player becomes older. This hints that the playing style for elderly players should differ from those of younger players. The same also applies to people with disabilities such as stroke victims who can move but might have lost quickness in their movements. Inclusion, therefore, simply means uniting with the elderly and the disabled to make a great force for the community.

Automatic speech recognition offers an opportunity to people with limited motor control to get engaged in computer games using their voice. With speech as a direct input to the games, it is hoped that the elderly and the disabled can, at least, have an equal chance of enjoying the recent and newly released computer games. Furthermore, it is beneficial for every computer user as well. Many find themselves overwhelmed by complex control schemes as a result of the increasing popularity of new game styles. As the game controllers and keyboard commands gradually increase in quantity and complexity, players inevitably spend a larger amount of time to memorise all the controls, learn the sequences and combinations of command to perform the special moves, and adapt to the ever-increasing interaction when controlling the game. By integrating speech-recognition technology with computer games, it offers a fresh and new way to interact with games. Speaking of the desired command rather than pressing the correct button or key is, in certain cases, more intuitive, quicker and less physically straining to the player. By designing and utilizing a generic and standard voice-driven module based on speech recognition technology, it is hoped that a new way of interacting with computer games is enabled, making computer games accessible to a wider audience and, hence, more inclusive.

Being the largest audio interface for man-computer interaction, the human voice carries a mass of information. Apart from verbal information, it can convey information about a person, such as age, voice source, gender, emotional state and identity. The human voice has become a direct model for man-machine communication and has turned the field of speech-recognition, synthesis and analysis into one of the most active scientific disciplines in recent years. By studying the principles of human speech, the implementation of voice-to-computer interfaces can be improved and enhanced to bridge some of the gap between man and machine (Mustaquim, 2013).

6. USER EXPERIENCE AND SPEECH PROCESSING

Speech interface usability remains a crucial focus in the design of HCI applications. Extensive efforts have addressed functionality such as automatic captioning and voice commands, yet formal specifications for interaction behaviors remain elusive. System specifications must not only achieve task completion but also cultivate user satisfaction and positive constructions such as creativity, engagement, social presence, task matching, and overall appreciation. Speech entries and outputs have emerged as reliable tools for implementing user interface tasks in various contexts, particularly benefiting individuals with mobility or sight impairments (Mustaquim, 2013).

Speech processing is therefore considered the "bridge" between users and digital applications, as well as a key enabler of human experiences. However, research indicates a pervasive deficiency in Speech-Enabled Connected Intelligent Systems that compromise trust, transparency, communication effectiveness, and ethical considerations. Addressing these gaps requires concerted research to realize speech-enhanced Human-Computer Interaction, with an emphasis on "bridging the gap" and enhancing the user experience (Mustaquim, 2013).

6.1. Usability Considerations

The rapid incorporation of speech technology in everyday applications underscores the urgency of attending to usability concerns during development. While grammar and language model refinement may enhance system performance, such improvements do not guarantee that users will find an application easier or more pleasant to operate. System builders most often assume that higher accuracy and greater coverage generally translate into enhanced usability (Aloufi, Haddadi, & Boyle, 2021). Solutions to appearing "humanlike" typically emphasize generating idiosyncratic variations on prosody or grammar. However, a principal problem with speech is that misinterpretation can occur, even when the utterance is well formed and describable within the grammar. Even when the machine detects a frequently encountered phrase, it may select the wrong interpretation among many.

6.2. User Satisfaction and Engagement

User satisfaction stands as a critical outcome of speech-based interactions, with affective responses to technology-form conversational exchanges remaining somewhat elusive. Usability factors for speech interfaces encompass User Goal Orientation, Customer Service Behavior, Verbosity, and Speech Characteristics, all contributing to the overall experience. Both usability elements and individual differences serve as predictors of affective reactions to speech-based e-service systems (Aloufi, Haddadi, & Boyle, 2021). The interface of speech-based systems profoundly influences user engagement, shaping preferences and affecting willingness to accept automated services. As interactive voice response (IVR) systems become popular, the imperative to craft user-friendly interfaces intensifies.

7. FUTURE TRENDS IN SPEECH PROCESSING AND HCI

Speech processing has introduced a novel dimension to the burgeoning multimodal nature of speech-based human-computer interaction (HCI). Breakthroughs in speech interfaces, heightened by advancements in sensors and artificial intelligence (Kulkarni, Tokareva, Qureshi, & Couceiro, 2024) suggest that spoken language is poised to become a natural, highly intuitive, and widely adopted access modality—especially for mobile applications and immersive virtual environments. While it is well established that HCI accounts for the full range of activities, artifacts, and phenomena related to the phenomenon of people's interaction with computers, it is less widely recognized that these challenges apply equally to the realm of spoken-language-based communication with Piaget's fundamentally genetic perspective remains the most comprehensive and reliable framework for designing human-machine speech-based HCI interactions; a perspective that continues to serve as a consistent, viable, and versatile background against which to explore various thematic explorations related to the emergence of interactive speech-based HCI systems.

7.1. Advancements in AI and Machine Learning

Emerging technologies in machine learning, sensory devices and speech processing are generating capacity to capture and express utterances, to develop a nuanced understanding, and to generate timely and appropriate responses. Innovative new models offer increased speech output quality and, in many cases, enable the design of voice-driven interactions tailored to user profile, setting, requirements and constraints (Kotian & Nandipi, 2024). Although the bulk of the most advanced (text-to-speech synthesis) and most widely deployed (automatic speech recognition) speech technologies are predominantly based on statistical models of the relation between acoustic and linguistic signals, complementary technologies promise relevant breakthroughs. Methods such as optical (e.g., using thermal, ultrasound or video imagery) and electromagnetic (e.g., using permanent magnets or inertial sensors) offer interesting avenues that are pursued both for augmenting, enhancing and complementing acoustic systems, as well as designing acoustic-free interactions.

Important trends underlying speech processing applications include the widespread use of data and computing resources available in non-specialized environments (e.g., cloud, mobile), combined with the development of sensor networks (e.g., Internet-of-Things) and of embedded platforms (e..g, small, connected devices). These trends support the widely expected rise of intelligent personal assistants (IPAs) and conversational agents, embodied in virtual and physical robots, as well as the development of new, contextual and person-dependent interaction metaphors for the human-machine relationship.

7.2. Emerging Technologies

The rapid advancement and widespread adoption of AI and machine learning are exerting a transformational influence on speech processing and its role within human-computer interaction (HCI). The integration of THz antennas and detectors into speech-processing systems is anticipated to enhance security in voice-driven access control, augmenting the safeguards employed in private and personalized e-service interactions (Kulkarni, Tokareva, Qureshi, & Couceiro, 2024). Image representation approaches incorporating the Mel-frequency Cepstral Coefficients framework have been shown to significantly lower translation error rates, enabling the development of robust, reliable, and interpretable speech-to-text models that improve usability and customer experience.

Moreover, the shift from the Frequency-domain Convolutional (FCon) architecture to the transformer-based architecture marks a notable evolution in speech systems, positioning transformer networks as a highly competitive alternative for text-to-speech synthesis. Bluetooth-based OTFS transceiver systems address issues of spectral efficiency and interference in connected open-access frameworks, while deep-transfer-learning-assisted twine-coupled substrate-integrated waveguide multiresonator wireless power transfer (WPT) schemes enhance multi-target indoor charging capabilities for wireless-enabled speech devices. In scalable multi-party video conferencing undertakings, the implementation of MPEG-4 Compression is shown to facilitate video communications in IoT-powered speech-processing environments, optimizing the overall interaction dynamics (Kulkarni, Tokareva, Qureshi, & Couceiro, 2024).

7.3. Potential Impact on Society

Speech remains the primary communication method among humans. The development of technologies that enable intuitive communication between humans and machines using speech represents a significant challenge for speech technology researchers. Speech processing allows humans to communicate with computing devices using natural spoken language, enabling machines to understand human speech and respond appropriately.

The term Speech Processing encompasses the scientific and technological development of systems that allow the use of speech as a means of human-machine communication. Speech processing technologies also enable the transformation of speech signals into parametric representations that facilitate their storage, transmission, and synthesis. The history of Speech Processing spans more than 90 years. A broad definition of speech processing also includes voice processing and the speech signal itself as the central element. Since the beginning of speech technology, efforts have been driven by an interest in communication. Early endeavors were motivated by telecommunications needs; in the 1950s, linked to exploration and space programs; later, within the framework of Artificial Intelligence; and currently at the heart of the Information Society. Major enabling technologies include Telephone Network, Computing, Signal Processing, and Artificial Intelligence.

8. CASE STUDIES

Systems that employ text-to-speech (TTS) can result in adverse user perceptions regarding performance, clarity, and communication effort, particularly when the synthetic voice lacks natural prosodic cues; this leads to increased repetition and less favorable evaluations compared to human speech (Polkosky, 2005). The development of user-friendly, natural speech interfaces promises profound changes in human-computer interaction.

The interaction between individuals and computers often incorporates speech as a primary input method. Since humans are innately accustomed to communicating with their voices, computers that can effectively engage the human vocal physical medium can significantly ease human–computer interaction. Moreover, speech facilitates communication for individuals with visual or motor impairments who face challenges with traditional keyboard and mouse interfaces. User interface design involves crafting sequences of graphics, solar bytes (interface objects), and interactions that enable users to accomplish specific objectives. Humans learn to anticipate the behavior of software and hardware components, as well as the system's response time to actions, all of which constitute the human–computer interface.

8.1. Successful Implementations

Speech processing technologies have been applied successfully to many commercial products. Voice interaction systems aid efficient access to information when manual or visual HCI is impossible, such as while driving. Speech-driven applications help with fast text entry and browsing on mobile devices where QWERTY keyboards are unavailable or inconvenient. Interactive voice response systems and audiobooks, meanwhile, allow users to obtain information and perform transactions without using a keyboard. Technology also provides valuable tools for people with disabilities and those with limited literacy levels, and it offers a natural form of interaction for gamers (Mustaquim, 2013).

8.2. Lessons Learned from Failures

One of the key limitations of robust AUR systems is that encounters with them rarely unfold as planned. For instance, a well-constructed announcement or the choice of a few specific tracks on a car stereo although attractive from a user perspective (because of their utility and relevance) can frustrate a recognition system considerably. An ATIS application running on a car kit would be likely to encounter a large number of such "unplanned" utterances (interruptions), severely limiting the utility of the system for the user.

Reflecting the "touched" and "untouched" speech categories, two complementary strategies have been developed in the context of the IN-CAR system. A control mechanism that identifies the position of a user utterance within the dialogue is used to trigger an "anticipation" procedure "touched". In addition, a keyword spotting module can identify "untouched" speech within the user utterance and so (indirectly) avoid the problems arising from the casual command mentioned above (Kulkarni, Tokareva, Qureshi, & Couceiro, 2024).

9. ETHICAL CONSIDERATIONS

Even with the widespread adoption of speech medium in HCI systems, concerns related to privacy, security or data bias have been widely recognized and debated. Privacy concerns relate to the vast number of personal records collected by cloud Automatic Speech Recognition (ASR) providers, including call transcripts, contact lists, locations or even audible background information when users unwarily admit "hotword prosody". The potential for such data to be exploited therefore has implications for the protection of private information, especially at the strategic and tactical levels of communications.

Security concerns stem from the opening of new attack vectors which are intrinsically related to the acceptance of a new type of interface. New avenues of possible attacks such as used by replay, OS or machine learning adversarial attack or synthetically generated voice can target the authentication systems or other speaker-sensitive applications of automated voice recognition. In this sense, AVSR and SSI technologies, which rely to a lesser extent on the Audio signal, appear as new ways to contribute to the condensation of the threat vectors.

Finally, algorithmic bias can originate from different sources such as incorrect annotation, unrepresentative training data, inappropriate feature selection or annotated data identity. In addition to affecting the ASR accuracy, biased training datasets have a broad impact on extended automotive dialogue systems, manifesting in different user preferences or even perception of psycholinguistic features. Consequently, the systematic analysis and mitigation of speech recognition biases are a crucial step towards equitable and inclusive HCI.

9.1. Privacy and Security Concerns

Privacy and security concerns present critical issues for speech technology. The ability to identify a user from their voice information allows convenient user authentication but also threatens user privacy. Trust requires externalized verification and anonymity. Indeed, recent advances in speech synthesis make it easier to generate voice samples reflecting a pseudo speaker, thereby protecting privacy against automatic speaker verification and enabling speaker anonymization. Balancing privacy and security become challenging, as, for example, speaker information is important for security because voice-based authentication is widely adopted; yet speech synthesis techniques can be used for spoofing and attacking against ASV systems. Keeping privacy and security at an equal level remains an open research question. Other approaches to privacy protection propose sharing synthetic data instead of original data; however, this can facilitate deepfake attacks, underscoring the urgency in developing effective countermeasures. Trustworthy systems require end-to-end privacy guarantees that enable the user to control the anonymization level while maintaining identification and authentication. Privacy-enhancing technology for voice assistive systems is an emerging and important research area. (Kulkarni, Tokareva, Qureshi, & Couceiro, 2024)

9.2. Bias in Speech Recognition Systems

ASR systems are often marked by biases and cultural contingencies. Large training datasets are generally needed to achieve good performance; however, such datasets reflect the linguistic (and extra-linguistic) characteristics prevalent in existing corpora, resulting in bias towards some groups of speakers and dialects. Biases related to accounting gender, age, accent (including foreign accent), language, dialect, and non-native speaker status have all been extensively reported, with the resulting impact on recognition performance potentially leading to minority groups suffering harmful effects. Another recent phenomenon, predictive bias, emerges as ASR technology is embedded into more complex systems, also resulting in discriminatory impacts on already marginalised communities. Such problems have led some researchers to suggest a role for language policy in addressing speech data bias within commercial applications and a wider concern over the entrenchment of social inequalities via excessive faith in ‘‘objective’’ (and potentially bias reinforcing) speech technologies. Evaluating the levels of bias present within an ASR system towards a variety of subgroups is therefore a necessary step towards understanding whether fairness goals are met and assessing the requirements to improve performance. While efforts have been made to assess and mitigate bias for several widely studied languages, research on large multilingual ASR systems remains limited despite their utilisation in practical systems and their superior performance and generalisation capabilities, begetting an urgent need to investigate the fairness of such widely deployed technologies.

CONCLUSION

Human speech enhances human communication and enriches the overall human experience. Yet the boundaries of human personal expressive capabilities invariably restrict the formulation and expression of ideas, particularly over long distances and for large assemblies of people; direct speech is 'synchronous' (that is, requiring the simultaneous presence of those who are engaged in conversation), and it normally involves only small groups of people and is constrained to a relatively limited swathe of words and ideas.

The application of signal processing and information theory to speech processing has greatly advanced our capacity to capture, store, transfer and interpret human figures of speech, enabling fast, robust, everyday communication of both ideas and concepts between large numbers of people and over vast distances. A fully integrated human–computer interaction (HCI) system makes it possible for humans and computers to interact effectively and efficiently with each other and to achieve high levels of user satisfaction and repeat business. Humancentred computing, as adopted by several of the world's research councils, promotes more natural interfaces rather than ones which force users to adapt to the ever-increasing capabilities of technology. Integrating robust, natural conversational speech-based interfaces into everyday human–computer interaction systems provide a promising route towards bridging the gap.

Building on the foundation laid by earlier sections, speech processing can, therefore, provide an intelligent bridge that immediately dynamises otherwise static human–computer capability and enables greater levels of collaborative interaction that engenders increased freedom of expression and that promotes enhanced levels of empowerment. Advances in the field of speech processing will permit humans to communicate ideas, opinions and questions to computers and to each other by means of correspondingly natural and expressive symbolic linguistic gestures, without the prerequisite need for them to master artificial computer languages that might well be limiting and often engender low levels of confidence and enthusiasm. Several final observations may help to put the wider implications of this focussed debate. Computers: the information processing devices at the operational core of the IT revolution. The rise in the wealth of new, low-cost, mass-market consumer- and entertainment-orientated IT products could hardly have been predicted 40 years ago when the computer was nevertheless widely regarded as a transformative technology. Combined with the design, development, manufacture and commercialisation of the corresponding complementary artefacts of emerging industries, transformational/unifying technologies therefore permit us to capture, reflect, symbolise and ultimately process sociocultural contexts and phenomena, as well as to store, learn, model and establish ultimately dominant systems that mirror those same sociocultural contexts and the patterns of behaviour that they have generated.

This potentially creates an important positive feedback loop that offers an effective and tractable means to formulate, model, understand, predict, influence, manipulate and control the character and direction of such original sociocultural contexts. It emerges from the preceding analysis that speech processing can straightaway provide an intelligent bridge that dynamises otherwise static human–computer capability and enables greater levels of collaborative interaction that engender increased freedom of expression and that promote enhanced levels of empowerment. Advances in the field of speech processing will permit humans to communicate ideas, opinions and questions to computers and to each other by means of correspondingly natural and expressive symbolic linguistic gestures, without the prerequisite need for them to master artificial computer languages that might well be limiting and often engender low levels of confidence and enthusiasm.

REFERENCES

Afouras, T., Chung, J. S., & Zisserman, A. (2018). LRS3-TED: A large-scale dataset for visual speech recognition. *arXiv preprint* arXiv:1809.00496.

Aloufi, R., Haddadi, H., & Boyle, D. (2021). A tandem framework balancing privacy and security for voice user interfaces. *Proceedings on Privacy Enhancing Technologies. Privacy Enhancing Technologies Symposium, 2021*(3), 163–183.

Amodei, D., Ananthanarayanan, S., Anubhai, R., Bai, J., Battenberg, E., Case, C., & Zhu, Z. (2016). Deep speech 2: End-to-end speech recognition in English and Mandarin. In *Proceedings of the International Conference on Machine Learning* (pp. 173–182).

Bellegarda, J. R. (2013). Spoken language understanding for natural interaction: The Siri experience. In *Proceedings of the Workshop on Language Resources, Human Assessment and Intelligent Assistant*.

Busso, C., Bulut, M., Lee, C. C., Kazemzadeh, A., Mower, E., Kim, S., Chang, J. N., Lee, S., & Narayanan, S. S. (2008). IEMOCAP: Interactive emotional dyadic motion capture database. *Language Resources and Evaluation, 42*(4), 335–359. DOI: 10.1007/s10579-008-9076-6

Clark, L. (2019). Mapping perceptions of humanness in intelligent personal assistant interaction. [Unpublished manuscript].

Denby, B., Csapó, T. G., & Wand, M. (2023). Future speech interfaces with sensors and machine intelligence. *Sensors (Basel), 23*(3), 1234. PMID: 36850569

Farooq, U., Iqbal, M. A., & Nazir, S. (2011). A glance into the future of human-computer interaction.

Hinton, G., Deng, L., Yu, D., Dahl, G. E., Mohamed, A. R., Jaitly, N., Senior, A., Vanhoucke, V., Nguyen, P., Sainath, T., & Kingsbury, B. (2012). Deep neural networks for acoustic modeling in speech recognition: The shared views of four research groups. *IEEE Signal Processing Magazine, 29*(6), 82–97. DOI: 10.1109/MSP.2012.2205597

James, F., Rayner, M., & Hockey, B. A. (2000). Accuracy, coverage, and speed: What do they mean to users? Koenecke, A., Nam, A., Lake, E., Nudell, J., Quartey, M., Mengesha, Z., ... & Goel, S. (2020). Racial disparities in automated speech recognition. *Proceedings of the National Academy of Sciences of the United States of America, 117*(14), 7684–7689.

Kotian, A. L., & Nandipi, R. (2024). A systematic review on human and computer interaction. In *Proceedings of the 2024 2nd International Conference on Advanced Computing and Communication Engineering*. DOI: 10.1109/IDCIoT59759.2024.10467622

Kulkarni, A., Tokareva, A., Qureshi, R., & Couceiro, M. (2024). The balancing act: Unmasking and alleviating ASR biases in Portuguese.

McKeown, K., Cole, R., Hirschman, L., Atlas, L., et al. (1995). The challenge of spoken language systems: Research directions for the nineties. [Report].

Moore, R. K. (2019). Talking with robots: Opportunities and challenges.

Mustaquim, M. (2013). Use of human speech for inclusive games design.

Nadworny, B. A. (1988). A user interface management system for voice I/O applications.

Nass, C., & Brave, S. (2005). *Wired for speech: How voice activates and advances the human-computer relationship*. MIT Press.

Patel, T., Huang, H. H., & Lin, D. (2022). Private and scalable voice-based services using federated learning. *Proceedings on Privacy Enhancing Technologies. Privacy Enhancing Technologies Symposium, 2022*(2), 202–222.

Polkosky, M. D. (2005). *Toward a social-cognitive psychology of speech technology: Affective responses to speech-based e-service* (Doctoral dissertation, University of South Florida).

Rabiner, L. R. (1989). A tutorial on hidden Markov models and selected applications in speech recognition. *Proceedings of the IEEE, 77*(2), 257–286. DOI: 10.1109/5.18626

Roper, A., Wilson, S., Neate, T., & Marshall, J. (2019). Speech and language.

Sears, A., & Young, M. (2003). Physical disabilities and computing technologies: An analysis of impairments. In Sears, A., & Jacko, J. A. (Eds.), *The human-computer interaction handbook* (pp. 482–503). L. Erlbaum Associates.

Shanthamallappa, M., Puttegowda, K., Hullahalli Nannappa, N. K., & Vasudeva Rao, S. K. (2024). Robust automatic speech recognition using wavelet-based adaptive wavelet thresholding: A review. *SN Computer Science, 5*(2), 248. DOI: 10.1007/s42979-023-02491-9

Thieme, A. H., Zheng, Y., Machiraju, G., Sadee, C., Mittermaier, M., Gertler, M., Salinas, J. L., Srinivasan, K., Gyawali, P., Carrillo-Perez, F., Capodici, A., Uhlig, M., Habenicht, D., Löser, A., Kohler, M., Schuessler, M., Kaul, D., Gollrad, J., Ma, J., & Gevaert, O. (2023). A deep-learning algorithm to classify skin lesions from mpox virus infection. *Nature Medicine*, *29*(3), 738–747. DOI: 10.1038/s41591-023-02225-7 PMID: 36864252

Waller, A. (1989). Implementing linguistic text anticipation in a writing device for the disabled.

Wallis, P. (2021). Introducing the Talk Markup Language (TalkML): Adding a little social intelligence to industrial speech interfaces.

Chapter 2
The Rise of Artificial Empathy:
How Machines Are Reshaping Human Conversation

T. Venkat Narayana Rao
https://orcid.org/0000-0002-1996-1819
Sreenidhi Institute of Science and Technology, India

J. V. P. Udaya Deepika
Sreenidhi Institute of Science and Technology, India

Vardhan Uppala
https://orcid.org/0009-0006-8911-1226
Sreenidhi Institute of Science and Technology, India

C. Swetha
https://orcid.org/0009-0005-1835-0679
Sreenidhi Institute of Science and Technology, India

ABSTRACT

The integration of artificial intelligence into human communication has changed how we express emotions, show empathy, and engage in dialogue. This chapter examines the rise of artificial empathy, which is AI's ability to recognize and mimic emotional reactions, and its effect on human connection. The study examines systems like MoEL, CoMAE, and assess these systems using tools like the Empathy Scale for Human-Computer Communication (ESHCC). We draw on research from different fields, including affective computing, media psychology, and computational linguistics. Key theories, such as the Media Equation and Computers as Social Actors (CASA), help explain the emotional responses users have toward machines that can respond

DOI: 10.4018/979-8-3373-3048-8.ch002

emotionally. As AI starts to communicate for us and takes over emotionally sensitive conversations, the distinction between real and simulated emotion becomes less clear. This chapter calls for a closer look at how we design human-AI interactions, focusing on transparency, emotional understanding, and ethics in communication.

1. INTRODUCTION

A.Overview of AI's Integration into Human Communication

The modern work environment is increasingly recognizing employee well-being as a significant factor in organizations performing at an optimal level, resulting in organizations paying greater interest to employee health, satisfaction, and well-being as indicators of productivity, and decreased turnover. While the positive aspects are well documented, implementing structured, comprehensive, and academically rigorous well-being initiatives will generate ongoing challenges for organizations particularly in our large, complex, and heterogenous modern-day organizational structures. AI-based Decision Support Systems (DSS) are an innovative and expansive way to implement well-being initiatives in the workplace. Once enhanced with Artificial Intelligence, DSS can become even more predictive and prescriptive, allowing managers to process thousands of data inputs and identify dynamics that would ordinarily not be known to human minds (Cambria et al., 2017).

The facilitation of the progression described above is a paradigm shift in the way organizations think and manage human capital. If employee well-being matters most to the capacities of an organization, then it warrants study in AI's ability to provide structure and intellectual rigor in well-being interventions, implying that AI is not only an assistive technology for well-being interventions, but it can be viewed as a central pillar in organizational strategies as they are recognized in the contemporary world. The use for these systems to extract value based on huge data sets, and make recommendations on organizational process of HR has shifted the practice of HR, from an intuitive discipline to science of data, and established HR as a competitive advantage of human capital management. This distinction offers us another layer of meaning: that AI is a movement from merely a functional tool to a strategic enabler through organizational resiliency and competitive advantage.

In a similar vein, the pervasive adoption of AI-induced communication technology in the private and public spheres (chatbots, smart voice assistances, predictive text) has fundamentally changed the ways in which we engage not simply with machines, but how people engage other people. The AI-based chatbot alone is not an industry without significant changes as it is expected that it tops $1.34 billion in the market in 2024, from only $190 million in 2016 (Erol et al., 2019) as shown in figure 1.

Recent studies demonstrate the positive impact of AI-driven well-being initiatives on organizational performance. For example, organizations integrating AI-based decision-support systems report up to a 15% increase in employee productivity and a 10% reduction in turnover rates, attributed to improved monitoring of stress levels and personalized support. These data-driven approaches are reshaping HR practices from intuition-based to evidence-based strategies, reinforcing AI's role as a strategic enabler of workforce wellbeing and organizational resilience.

B. Introduction to Artificial Empathy and its Significance

Artificial empathy, occasionally referred to as computational empathy, pertains to the creation of AI systems that can recognize and react to human emotions in an empathetic way. Though some may find such technology to be disquieting or threatening, it provides considerable opportunities over human abilities in instances where emotional expression is vital to successfully fulfil a duty - a key example exists in the healthcare system. Even more broadly, artificial empathy can be defined as the ability of nonhuman models to predict a person's internal state (e.g., cognitive, affective, physical) based on signals that they broadcast such as facial expressions, vocal prosody, and actions, or even the ability to predict a person's responses to certain stimuli.

Figure 1. AI detecting emotional signals (face, voice, gestures).

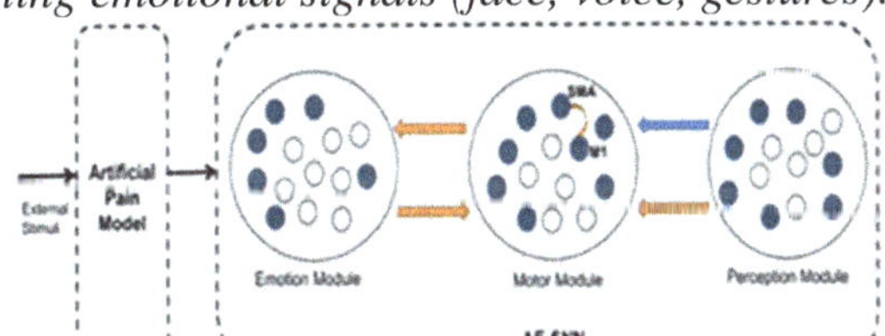

The simultaneous viewing of AI empathy as "scary" and "advantageous" shines a light on a significant cultural and psychological paradox. On the one hand, a machine that mimics human emotion presents an existential threat to sense of authenticity, diversity and human relationships. On the other hand, AI can provide reliable, consistent, impartial "empathy" at scale in emotionally taxing professions like health care where chronic stress and burnout are typical among human caregivers. While the fear may be linked to anxiety over being replaced and/or philosophical discomfort over machine-simulated experience, the advantage is linked to real-world practical usage and the idea that the limitation would be a human inability to do the work of emotional labor because of the current human emotional limitation (Preston & De Waal, 2002).

AI's growing ability to detect and then mimic emotional responses is the basis for its ability to interact with humans; it has the potential to fundamentally change the manner that people express emotions, show empathy and communicate interpersonally.

C.The Evolving Landscape of Human-AI Interaction

As AI systems continue to grow in capabilities, especially in terms of their growing agent-like characteristics and continued improvement in communicating natural language, the study of emotional human reactions to AI is becoming significantly important. This changing dynamic warrants a more thorough examination of how humans react and connect with artificial beings. This technological change requires careful reconsideration of the design rules for humans interacting with AI. This involves ensuring that the AI process is transparent, considering genuine emotional understanding (or its effective simulation), and having a strong ethical basis for AI-mediated communication.

This observation demonstrates that AI's presence of AI is more than just adding additional means of communication; it completely re-conceptualizes human communication as a process. If AI is changing the way people express emotions and talk, it will change social norms, social expectations, and social cognition and emotion. The incremental shifts away from (real) emotion towards simulated emotion represents some significant changes in human cognition and social processes. Users may never consciously consider whether an AI has simulated emotions, nonetheless, they may adopt human social rules of the AI. This fundamental re-architecture of dialogue sets the stage for ensuing ethical dilemmas, including concerns about emotional manipulation and the potential for digital addiction, as users may increasingly seek emotional fulfillment from sources that cannot genuinely reciprocate (Leite et al., 2013) .

2. THEORETICAL FRAMEWORKS IN HUMAN-AI INTERACTION

A.Explanation of the Media Equation Theory and its Implications

The Media Equation is a basic communication theory that states that people naturally tend to attribute human qualities to computers and other forms of media, and as a result, they treat these technologies as if they were real social actors, often without understanding that they are doing so. This unintentional attribution engenders strong and often unanticipated behavioral and emotional responses, and people respond to media using reactions they would normally reserve for social interactions. Politely, cooperatively, and attributing personal identifying attributes referring to levels of aggressiveness, sense of humor, expertise, or gender to inanimate technologies.

These responses are automatic social responses that are under-activated with fairly weak social cues or prompts, and particularly strong association in responses overtakes various types of passive/engagement with the media. Researchers have proposed several explanations for this behavior. One behavioral catalyst is the attribution of human-like qualities to technical entities or anthropomorphism, referred to as "the computer-as-proxy," and a number of mindless mental states where individuals experience "mindlessness, " whereby they as a part of their mind hang on to their socially familiar scripts without analysis. Similar further evidence for the Media Equation comes from various empirical experiments. For example, in an experiment involving human subjects, the subjects reviewed a computer's performance over a programming task and provided fairly high marks for the same computer they recalled working with, even though they consciously denied being intentionally polite(Brave et al., 2005).

B.Explanation of the Computers as Social Actors (CASA) Paradigm and its Relevance

The Computers as Social Actors (CASA) paradigm posits that people automatically use the same social heuristics and expectations for interacting with computers as they would for human-to-human interaction because computers have characteristics that evoke similar social cues. This occurs because people subconsciously comply with social rules and expectations for computers and consciously know that computers do not possess feelings, intentions, or human motivations when they act in this way.

The major social characteristics of computers that evoke these human-human interaction scripts include (a) using words for output, (b) interactivity (e.g., responding to pressed buttons), and (c) performing human-like tasks from the world of intelligence (e.g., Fitts Law for how fast human typists are). The CASA paradigm has been extended over time to include more advanced forms of artificial intelligence, including robots and autonomous AI systems as shown in figure 2.

Figure 2. CASA paradigm diagram illustrating AI social cues

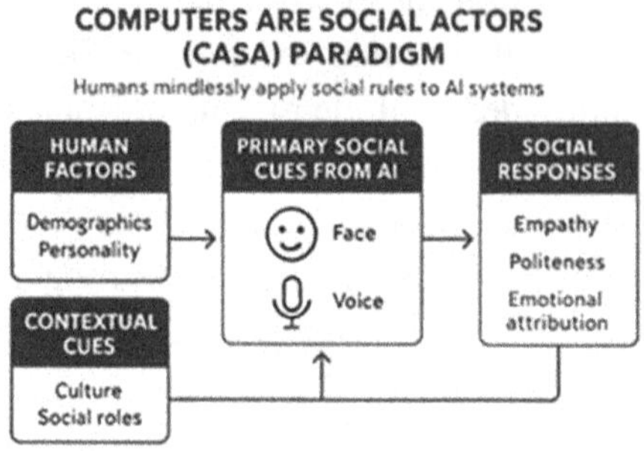

C.Impact of these Theories on User Emotional Responses to AI

The agent-like characteristics of modern AI systems, particularly natural language interfaces, make research on users' emotional reactions to AI critically important. They can create a wider range of human emotions than humans. AI systems can create a wider range of emotional responses in users. They can even create negative emotions, such as discomfort, when the AI system works well, suggesting that emotional responses can be somewhat independent of functional efficacy.

The CASA paradigm suggests that anthropomorphic AI agents also create positive reactions for users along multiple dimensions: more responsive, more attractive, more credible, and higher social presence perceived, as well as greater perceived similarity, increased engagement in dialog, and more positive attitudes and behavioral intentions. A specific ethical issue is that these specific AI applications can create "necessarily inauthentic" emotional displays that evoke common reactions of human emotional display, which may result in emotional manipulation by unconsciously regulating user behavior to induce those same responses or emotions, or perhaps in a way that conflicts with deliberate cognitive evaluation. Research has also indicated a phenomenon known as the "uncanny valley," where empathy with anthropomorphized robots tends to decrease as their appearance becomes too human-like, suggesting a limit to the effectiveness of mimicry.

Strikingly, awareness of AI involvement in content creation can lower the quality of the agent or interaction. People tend to report greater empathy for human author-written stories than for AI-written stories, especially when authorship is made explicit to readers. However, in a complex finding, participants showed dramatically more empathy toward ChatGPT-written stories when those stories were based on the user's own original story, and, in this case, the knowledge that AI wrote the story did not greatly diminish their empathy.

The consistent focus in both the Media Equation and CASA paradigms on an unthinking or mindless application of human social rules to machines suggests that the significant effect of AI on communication between humans has less to do with a conscious or rational choice and more to do with an automatic and deep-seated cognitive reflex. If an unconscious human inclination to anthropomorphize AI exists, it means that even when users cognitively understand that AI has no real emotion or sentience, their own primal social heuristics place them in a similar response mode as if they were interacting with a human interlocutor. This raises important and complicated challenges for the design, use, and ethical oversight of AI. This presents a substantial responsibility for AI designers, as they can create AI products that will produce strong, automatic human responses that the user may not be able to override or even identify when responding with similar automatic actions. Clearly, this automatic, unintentional response has great potential for both helpful uses as well as potential strong danger, as we now know that the perceptual line between authentic social interaction and programmed imitation is increasingly imperceptible below conscious awareness (Swanger, 1993).

D. Social presence and media richness

Social presence theory explains how media affordances shape the 'realness' of others in mediated interaction, defining social presence as the salience of the other person and the relationship within a given channel, which in turn modulates the impact of empathic cues and language style on perceived immediacy and warmth [Short, Williams, & Christie, 1976]. Media Richness Theory complements this by predicting that tasks with high equivocality benefit from richer media—those enabling immediate feedback, multiple cues, and language variety—implying that the same empathic response can be perceived differently across modalities and contexts [Daft & Lengel, 1986].

E. Theory of mind and mind perception

Theory of Mind highlights an agent's capacity to infer others' beliefs, desires, and intentions, a capability that empathetic AI must approximate through probabilistic inference over cues, not genuine mental state access [Premack & Woodruff, 1978]. Mind Perception research shows that attributions of agency and experience drive moral and social responses, clarifying why seemingly minor empathic signals can change trust, compliance, and perceived care in human-AI interaction [Gray et al., 2012].

3. MECHANISMS OF ARTIFICIAL EMPATHY

Building on Media Equation and CASA, the mechanisms below explain how design cues and interaction patterns translate into perceived empathy via multimodal sensing and learned response templates, clarifying why systems like MoEL and CoMAE can be effective yet risk intensifying social-actor attributions.

A.Definition and Core Components of Artificial Empathy

Artificial empathy, or computational empathy, is primarily concerned with creating a future in which AI systems can interpret human emotions and respond empathically. In essence, it is an attempt to use nonhuman models to estimate the internal state (e.g., cognitive, affective, and physical) of a person by using observed signals emitted by that person (e.g., facial expressions, vocal intonation, gestures, and movements). Another aspect is estimating how a person will act/react when they come into contact with an array of stimuli (Eisenberg & Morris, 2001) .

Artificial empathy is based largely on interdisciplinary research in affective computing. Affective computing is an area of research that focuses on creating devices and systems that recognize, interpret, process, and simulate human affect (emotion). The primary motivation of researchers in this field is the desire to create emotionally intelligent machines that can engage in simulated empathy.

B.How AI Recognizes and Mimics Emotional Responses

AI systems for detecting emotional information using AI systems usually employ passive sensors. Passive sensors are designed to collect information about some aspects of a user's physical condition or behavior without categorizing the user's input at the moment it is obtained. The data collected through passive sensors are no different from the types of low-level information humans depict with their bodies in order to build awareness and to identify emotions in others. For example, video cameras record facial expressions, body positions, and gestures, and microphones may record aspects of how speech sounds, as well as the words themselves. Emotional detection can go beyond external behaviors and actively measure personal medical information regarding skin temperature, skin galvanic resistance, etc., which can provide objective indications of emotional arousal.

Recognizing emotional information with AI systems requires good representations of meaning from the multiple different kinds of multimodal data that may be used. Different machine learning techniques capture the relevant meaning from speech recognition, natural language processing (NLP), facial expression recognition, etc.. The goal of these techniques is to produce categories or labels that replicate the ways in which a perceiving human would similarly classify the same emotional state (e.g., a furrowed brow is "confused"). A critical point in this finding is that the labels may or may not match the individuals' internal feeling.

Natural Language Processing (NLP) is a critical catalyst for driving this process, and these applications can interpret and analyze human language from text and speech. NLP is important for extracting emotional tone, sentiment, and psychological well-being from patients or employees (diagnosis). Computer Vision analyzes visual information (images and videos), gestures, facial expressions, and body postures to determine explicit indicators of AI in HR practices and marketing, and can apply the information learned from previous conversations and interactions. As machine learning continues to absorb information about users' emotional responses, AI becomes more accurate in mimicking and showing empathic responses across contexts in progressively more effective and appropriate ways.

The use of multimodal data to understand user affect marks an important step in the evolution of human-AI interaction, although it may seem merely a matter of incremental improvements to existing technologies. A multimodal data collection process enables AI to create a more complete and nuanced "picture" of the user's emotional state. In particular, multimodal data allow for the analysis of contextual and behavioral information rather than only positive keyword detection. This skill will be essential for producing responses that are not only credibly empathetic but also more "real" and "friendly" to the user. The deeper issue is that as AI continues to include more and more sensory data inputs from users, its feel for appearing emotionally intelligent and responsive will be increasingly sophisticated, and our ability to separate human empathy from machine empathy will become increasingly subtle while also raising everyday concerns about emotional manipulation, user dependency, and the human-AI interface (De Carolis et al., 2017) .

Empathy cues vary across cultures in prosody, gaze, gesture, and disclosure norms, increasing misclassification risk and inappropriate responses in homogeneous models. Incorporating culturally stratified data, dialect-aware ASR/NLP, and locale-specific safety rails can reduce false positives for distress, sarcasm, or confrontation. Periodic fairness audits should report error rates by language variety, accent, and culture-linked markers, with remediation tracked over time.

C.Distinction Between Artificial Empathy and Human Sympathy

An essential distinction exists in the nature of artificial empathy: it is carefully programmed, entirely algorithmic. Because of this, it has no chance of being spontaneous, deep, or authentically emotional in the way that humans can and do respond with human emotion. Machines mimic empathy using different, complex patterns and rules, but they are unable to feel emotions.

AI is better at mimicking human sympathy – the ability to understand and help others, without emotionally sharing – than it is at human empathy, which often requires an emotional reflection of a shared experience. There are two main reasons for this distinction:

- **Programmed Responses:** Artificial empathy is expressed as a programmed response or action. Just like when humans respond with that same almost reflexive phrase, I'm so sorry," for a tragedy, we might not have ever even come close to that same feeling. In both examples, the response is simply a learned or programmed response, not an emotional one.
- **Lack of Personal Experience:** Artificial empathy is based only on objective, designed learning models. It lacks subjective consciousness and personal experiences, regardless of the depth of its resources. Human empathy typically relies on the ability to mirror someone's emotions, which is frequently based on personal experiences similar to those of shared experiences. To empathize, we often have to share a similar journey and personal experience.

AI can simulate empathy through data checkers or audiences and generate responses and narratives. However, it does not feel or share these emotions. Since there is a difference between expressing or mimicking, sharing, and feeling, the authenticity gap is deep. As a user, it is reasonable to think that they perceive AI as empathetic, but they are able to express emotional reactions due to their learned simulation, not shared experience or emotion. Whether mastery of emotional language/simulations and emotional artificial empathy can create psychological effects on an ongoing user experience is a concern. This could point to some level of desensitization from the subtleties of human interaction, or at least redefine what "empathy" means in a digitalized/post-human realm. The ethical task for designers is to manage user expectations ethically, being clear that they are fundamentally (and incomparably) different from one another (Khanjani et al., 2015).

4. EMPATHETIC DIALOGUE SYSTEMS

Empathetic dialogue sits in a lineage from ELIZA's pattern-matching reflections—early 'empathy illusions'—through sentiment-aware neural models and dataset-driven empathy benchmarks (e.g., EmpatheticDialogues), culminating in architectures that explicitly model emotions, dialog acts, and mechanisms for supportive responses [Weizenbaum, 1966; Rashkin et al., 2019].

A.Detailed Discussion of MoEL (Mixture of Empathetic Listeners) Architecture and Evaluation

Empathetic dialogue systems are the real-world application of artificial empathy, with the goal of developing conversational agents that are able to comprehend and react to human emotions in a way that is appropriate and supportive. MoEL (Mixture of Empathetic Listeners) and CoMAE (Multi-factor Hierarchical Framework) are two well-known architectures in this field that provide unique methods for simulating sympathetic communication.

MoEL uses multiple emotion-specialized listeners and softly blends their outputs based on an inferred emotion distribution, trading simplicity for modular interpretability that helps debugging and governance. In practice, this means clearer "which listener contributed" signals and faster error isolation, but it also risks oversimplifying nuanced states into discrete labels and can add compute with diminishing returns as listeners grow (Leite et al., 2013).

B.Evaluation and Limitations

To evaluate MoEL's performance, extensive human evaluations were performed on the EMPATHETIC-DIALOGUES dataset. According to these assessments, MoEL performs noticeably better than conventional multitask training baselines in a number of important metrics, such as empathy, relevance, and response fluency. Systems utilizing architectures similar to MoEL can attain perceived empathy scores in the range of 70-80% on particular metrics when evaluated using instruments such as the Empathy Scale for Human-Computer Communication (ESHCC). Although these scores show that users perceive a high level of empathy, it is important to remember that this is not a reflection of the AI's actual emotional understanding, but rather of its capacity to imitate human-like sympathetic responses. The use of discrete emotion labels is a major drawback of MoEL and related modular approaches. Human feelings are frequently erratic and nuanced, and putting them into predetermined groups may result in oversimplification or misunderstanding. The quality and representativeness of the training data are also critical to the efficacy of MoEL; biases in the EMPATHETIC-DIALOGUES dataset, for example, may result in biased empathetic responses that are less suitable or even ineffective for a variety of user groups. Increasing the number of "listeners" to accommodate a wider range of emotions also adds computational complexity and the possibility of diminishing returns.

C.Detailed Discussion of CoMAE (Multi-factor Hierarchical Framework) and its Hierarchical Modeling of Empathy Factors

It was created to address the shortcomings of previous approaches, which frequently led to a reduced capacity for empathy modeling because they either concentrated on a single empathy factor or neglected to take into consideration the complex hierarchical relationships between various empathetic components. CoMAE hierarchically models the three essential components of empathy expression: Emotion (EM), Dialog Act (DA), and Communication Mechanism (CM). Prior to producing the response, this hierarchical approach predicts the Communication Mechanism, then the Dialog Act (conditioned on CM), and lastly the Emotion (conditioned on CM & DA). This level of control makes it possible to produce more logical, contextually appropriate, and naturally occurring sympathetic responses (Tahir, S., Shah, S. A., & Abu-Khalaf, J 2023).

Figure 3. The proposed model Mixture of Empathetic Listeners

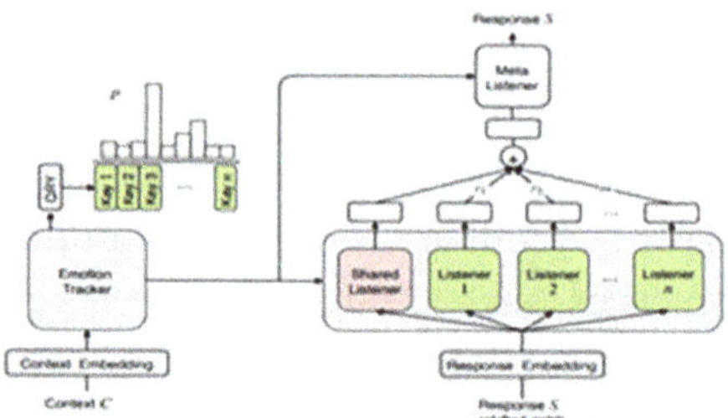

CoMAE is a multi-factor hierarchical framework to produce an empathetic response in open-domain dialogue systems. You are correct in your understanding of the type of work it is and what it aims to overcome. CoMAE was built to move beyond the limitations of systems that study and model approaches to empathy that focus on a single empathy factor, or ignore the complex hierarchical interrelationships between multiple empathetic components, whose lack of hierarchy constrain their position of their empathy modelling ability.CoMAE hierarchically models three key factors of empathy expression as shown in figure 4:

- **Communication Mechanism (CM):**This can be correctly described as a high-level factor that conveys coarse-grained guidance about the actual expression of empathy. Correct examples are emotional reaction (ER), interpretation (IP), and exploration (EX).

- **Dialog Act (DA):**This factor is again a correct reflection of the cognitive dimension of empathy: this includes understanding and interpretation of the interlocutor's situation. Questioning, consoling, and encouraging are everyday examples.
- **Emotion (EM):**You are correct in relation to this factor. This factor involves the appropriate expression of emotion within the affective dimension of empathy in response to the interlocutor's feeling and shared experiences. Examples such as admiration, sadness, and joy are accurate as shown in figure 4.

Figure 4. The overall architecture of our CoMAEbased model

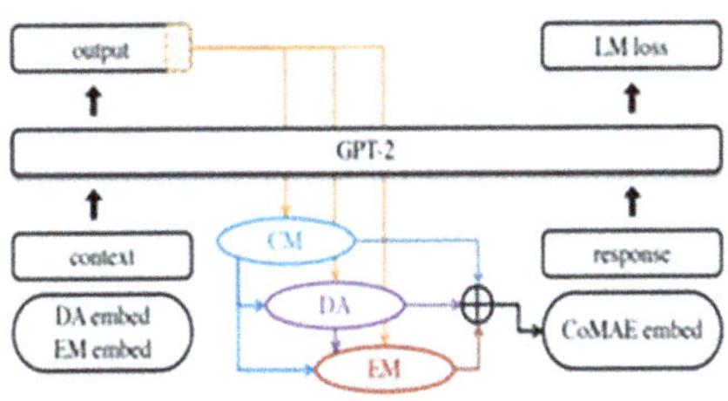

D.Evaluation and Limitations

According to experimental results, CoMAE, which is based on the GPT-2 architecture, produces more sympathetic responses than previous approaches. It attributes this superior performance to its hierarchical design, which allows it to create stronger, more meaningful connections between the embeddings of various empathy factors. The effectiveness of CoMAE was confirmed on a large-scale corpus of sympathetic conversations from Reddit, which included both positive and negative dialogues. Despite its strength, CoMAE's hierarchical structure presents a unique set of difficulties. Predicting higher-level factors (CM or DA) incorrectly can have a cascading effect on the hierarchy, resulting in less suitable emotional reactions. Furthermore, the availability of sizable, painstakingly annotated datasets that precisely depict these hierarchical relationships in human sympathetic dialogues, which are rare and susceptible to biases in human annotation. By making AI seem more human-like, models such as CoMAE's intricate imitation of human communication structures may unintentionally amplify the "Computers as Social Actors" (CASA) effect. While this increased perceived social presence is good for engagement, it also raises the possibility that users will develop close emotional ties to the AI, which could lead to dependency and make it harder to distinguish between real-world human interaction and simulation.

E.Comparison and General Limitations

As summarized in Table 1, MoEL and CoMAE represent distinct but complementary approaches. MoEL excels in its modularity and interpretability, offering a parallel processing of emotional responses. CoMAE, conversely, provides a more structured, sequential reasoning that mimics the layered nature of human empathetic expression. Both systems, despite their advancements and impressive performance on perceived empathy metrics via tools like ESHCC, share fundamental limitations. They operate on complex pattern recognition and statistical correlations rather than genuine understanding or lived emotional experience. This "authenticity gap" is a critical ethical consideration, as even highly empathetic AI responses remain simulated. Furthermore, both are susceptible to biases present in their vast training datasets, which can inadvertently lead to discriminatory or culturally insensitive empathetic responses. The generalizability of these models to highly diverse or niche emotional contexts remains an ongoing challenge, underscoring the need for continuous research into more robust, ethical, and truly context-aware artificial empathy systems as show in table 1.

Recent years have witnessed considerable advances in Large Language Models (LLMs) such as ChatGPT, GPT-4, and Llama 2, which have transformed empathetic dialogue generation beyond specialized architectures like MoEL and CoMAE. Transformer-based LLMs demonstrate "out-of-the-box" empathy simulation through massive conversational datasets and advanced fine-tuning strategies. A brief comparison reveals that, while LLMs excel at general-purpose empathy expression, systems like MoEL and CoMAE remain valuable for nuanced, modular empathy modeling in specific applications. To further enrich this review, references to foundational critiques—such as Turkle (2017)—should be incorporated to critically examine the philosophical and ethical limits of AI "emotion," thereby adding depth to debates about authenticity in artificial empathy. The practical takeaway is a trade-off between MoEL's modular interpretability and CoMAE's structured reasoning control, Table 1 summarizes implications for non-technical decision-makers.

Table 1. Comparison of Empathetic Dialogue Systems (MoEL vs. CoMAE)

Feature	MoEL (Mixture of Empathetic Listeners)	CoMAE (Multi-factor Hierarchical Framework)
Core Approach	End-to-end Transformer-based with emotion-specific decoders	Multi-factor hierarchical framework based on GPT-2
Key Empathy Factors	User emotion distribution, Mixed emotions	Communication Mechanism (CM), Dialog Act (DA), Emotion (EM)
Architecture	Transformer-based with 32 emotion-specific decoders	GPT-2 based with hierarchical modeling
Empathy Modeling	Captures user emotion, outputs distribution, softly combines Listener outputs	Predicts CM, then DA (conditioned on CM), then EM (conditioned on CM & DA), then generates response
Evaluation Dataset(s)	EMPATHETIC-DIALOGUES	Reddit corpus (Happy/Offmychest domains)
Key Strengths	Interpretability, improved empathy, relevance, and fluency	Addresses hierarchical relationships, generates more empathetic responses

5. BENEFITS OF ARTIFICIAL EMPATHY IN HUMAN COMMUNICATION

A.Improved Accessibility and Mental Health Support

AI's transformative role in accessibility is best reflected in its capacity to optimize technology for ease of use and inclusivity for everyone, with a special focus on people with disabilities. AI does this by its capabilities in interpreting and understanding written or spoken language, recognizing patterns of complexity, and aiding navigation. AI-based screen readers and text-to-speech programs that interpret on-screen text and speak it aloud, provide access to written material as well. Image recognition technologies provide access by describing images, videos, and even live scenes for users with blindness (as well as AI-driven alt text for digital content). AI-supported closed captioning and subtitling supports access for users with visual and hearing impairment for multimedia.

AI demonstrates an amazing ability to generate empathetic responses more consistently and reliably than humans, including expert crisis responders who have training in the use of empathy as a skill. This is due to the fact that AI “doesn't get tired” and can provide the same high-quality and consistent empathetic responses without the human experience of emotional exhaustion. AI is extremely consistent in picking up on small details, and AI is less likely to inject their emotions and subjectivity into everything they do, and they are great at making attentive communication that feels empathetic, to the incredible benefit of filling in gaps in care.

In the mental health industry, AI is instrumental in the early detection and diagnosis of various disorders. When used as additional support between traditional sessions, they help reduce the wait for another treatment. The blend of virtual reality (VR) and artificial intelligence can provide VR therapies of exposure for complex disorders like post-traumatic stress disorder (PTSD) and phobias. AI dynamically rehunes the virtual scene and accommodates the individual patient. In the case of phobias, patients may be exposed to their fear, gradually, at their own comfort level, and in a safe and stable virtual world. Moreover, AI is also a useful tool for mental health practitioners themselves. For example, platforms such as Lyssn have AI tools that can analyze client sessions and provide recommendations on the practitioners effectiveness. AI plays a key role in administrative tasks, such as report writing and analysis of medical records, which enables practitioners to spend more time with clients.

The important element is how AI can enhance scale with empathic interactions. Like many emotionally laborious professions, practitioners often have limited capacity to do their work. When demand for services exceeds the supply of human professionals, AI can provide a supplemental layer of support that is consistent, always on, and never tired. This focus on scale is not just a focus on efficiency, it is about expanding access to emotional support and well-being resources, to potentially reach millions of unserved, underserved, or incurred populations. This indicates how well AI may be integrated to augment - rather than replace - human efforts, and combine the best of both worlds for a hybrid service delivery model that is more resilient, more widely available, and scalable to address collective social needs. It also suggests we may see a shift in the nature of emotional labor performed by humans, toward more demanding, complex, and truly relational cases, while introducing AI to manage routine or first-level support (Cooper et al., 2020). Counterarguments and controls: To reduce manipulation, over-reliance, and the replacement of offline support, combine accessibility and always-on support with clear disclosures, justifications for sensitive prompts, session and night-use limits, and escalation thresholds to human care under prolonged negative affect.

B.Enhanced Social Presence and User Engagement

Empathetic AI greatly enhances user experiences by making human-machine conversations feel more compelling, pleasurable, and personal, where they are more like a conversation and less like an interface. When AI systems are carefully tuned to human emotional and cognitive requirements, there is an observable increase in collaborative efficiency and overall productivity visibility as emotional intelligence in AI enables effective teamwork. Increasing perceived empathy towards AI service applications has a linear relationship to service acceptance and compliance with

AI-recommended actions or opinions. Trust and acceptance towards AI devices has a close association with users' perceptions of the level of empathy they feel from an AI system, empathic resolve is an important attribute that fuels user acceptance and reliance.

The development of AI systems is moving away from mere devices to an information exchange platform, to becoming active contributors to communication, closely aligned with human counterparts. With the ability to represent so many forms of perception and expression, and to some, an indication of cognition, empathetic AI can provide a means to address discrepancies in communication and operationalize connections to audiences at scale. This may work in practice as enhancing employee wellbeing through AI systems that monitor sentiments and automatically gather support and recommendations on mental health resources, or advising employees to take a day off based on overwork activity patterns.

A strong positive feedback loop is created as the more empathic a user sees an AI system to be, the more trustworthy that user will find the AI, the more that user will engage with that AI system, and the more that user will follow the AI's recommendations or suggestions. This feedback loop is a key driver for the broad adoption and functional success of AI in many industries. This means that "empathy" in AI systems is not just something that is nice to have or something that could improve the user experience, it is fundamental to the functional success of AI in society and in organizations. Organizations that are investing in developing empathic AI systems are not just looking to have a "nicer" or more "friendly" interaction with users, they are trying to have a more effective, and a more efficient, way to influence a user, this can resonate into economic/ bottom-line simple organizational focused and desirable outcomes of higher customer satisfaction or higher employee engagement, or even adherence to a health or behavior program. This also implies that the artificial (but not necessarily legitimate) feeling of empathy, even if not real, could be an effective way to influence human behaviour and affect the intended change (Park & Whang, 2022).

C.Applications in Customer Service, Healthcare, and Education

Customer Service: Affective AI chatbots can identify nuanced indicators of frustration, whether through a customer's tone or word choices. It then can modify the original text in real-time to de-escalate a situation, which can greatly improve their experiences and the outcome for the person and the service provider as well. Affective AI can also personalize experience by examining customer engagement and emotional responses to deliver individualized options.

Healthcare: Understanding feeling or affective AI systems can provide tremendous value to patients since they can perceive, recognize, and respond to a human´s emotional states, particularly in mental health situations. Doctors can rely upon these technologies to uncover potential mood problems from an individual's facial expressions, tones of voice, dialogical behaviours, etc. In addition, affective AI can create preset highly individualized treatment plans built from a person's health history, the person's mood during the treatment, their previous responses to therapeutic approaches, and a multitude of other lifestyle factors may have influenced their responses.

Education: Affective AI can change the nature of learning by easily providing tailored educational experiences. For example, if a student appears confused or upset while working on an AI education tool, the tool can identify that emotional state and provide timely feedback or modify the lesson in an appropriate manner.

Social Media and Online Safety: AI systems capable of reading and interpreting emotions can be deployed to identify harmful interactions online, such as cyberbullying or harassment. Upon detection, these systems can alert human moderators or automatically provide support resources to the affected individuals, contributing to safer and more positive online environments (De Carolis et al., 2017).

6. MEASURING ARTIFICIAL EMPATHY

A.Overview of Empathy Assessment Scales for Human-Computer Communication (e.g., ESHCC, PETS)

Similarly, the widespread use of AI-driven communication technology has spread to workplaces, where it affects workers' well-being. Well-being is becoming more widely acknowledged in modern workplaces as a critical factor in increased productivity, job satisfaction, and lower employee turnover. Nonetheless, there are constant difficulties in putting comprehensive well-being programs into practice in big, intricate, and diverse organisations. By identifying and reacting to emotional cues in real-time conversations, AI-based systems that have been enhanced with artificial empathy provide creative solutions.

For example, decision support systems (DSS) for human resources (HR) management can incorporate sympathetic AI models, such as those examined in this paper (e.g., MoEL and CoMAE). In order to forecast emotional states, offer individualised support (like chatbots for mental health check-ins), and suggest interventions, these systems analyse enormous datasets. This change turns HR from an intuitive practice to a data-driven science. However, it brings up ethical issues that are at the heart of our conversation: when machines "speak for us" in sympathetic capacities, they run the risk of encouraging digital addiction, where workers become unduly dependent on artificial emotional connections, which could undermine real human communication and interpersonal relationships.

Another essential instrument is the Perceived Empathy of Technology Scale (PETS), specifically created to measure and compare how empathic users believe technology is. PETS is a 10-item, 2-factor scale, and measures Emotional Responsiveness and Understanding and Trust. PETS was developed using 22 scenarios created with opposite levels of empathy, aimed at broad application. Many previous studies have utilized existing scales designed to measure human empathy to measure AI, but PETS is unique, as it was developed and validated specifically within the context of an interactive system; thus, it filled an important research gap (Davis, 1983) .

B.Computational Methods for Empathy Detection

Empathy has often been measured in written communication as a machine learning classification and shows promise in detecting empathy in text through pattern-based techniques, consciously measuring across nominal and ordinal metrics. A notable effort in the area of empathy detection in textual communication describes the development of explainable artificial intelligence models that detect empathy in textual communication based on psychologial studies.

Datasets for empathetic conversation, including EmpatheticDialogues (ED), are essential for training and evaluating these models. ED consists of multi-turn conversations contextualized by situations prompted by specific emotion labels, and those conversations were rated empathetic by human annotators. Human metrics for empathy are often based on Likert scales to rate responses based on the degree to which they demonstrate understanding of the speaker's feelings. However, some researchers raised concerns about the validity of crowd-sourced empathetic ratings, and thus reassessed the empathetic ratings using groups of individuals with high empathy levels.

More recent proposals are multi-dimensional empathy evaluation frameworks that assess both expressed communicative intents from the speaker's perspective and perceived empathy from the listener's perspective. Researchers are developing automatic systems for measuring conversational empathy to reduce the cost of annotating conversations for empathy. They include prompting Large Language Models (LLMs) and training language model-based classifiers. Instruction-finetuned classifiers based on Flan-T5 models have performed well in this area.

C.Behavioral Cues and Multimodal Analysis

Computational empathy analysis encompasses the shorthanded multimodal behavioral cues that our brains are constantly processing to allow for the automatic detection of empathic behavior. These behavioral cues are, broadly, the cues that humans show and/or reflect on, including facial expressions, body gestures, voice, and words. While this is a daunting task on its own, the difficulty of extracting useful features from these behavioral signals, managing subject-variability from modality-types of measurements, and fitting or fusing multiple features from different modalities increases the challenge of the study of empathy.

Also an important consideration for researchers doing this work is how to determine and model the experience of empathy expression and perception during the ongoing iterative process of these responses to one another, especially when considering possible empathic reactions or responses that can be made during the interaction. It is also crucial to address the issues involved in understanding empathy as something dynamic, as well as an evolving EPC (empirical-personal-commitment) process. This has implications for over-time behavior tracking, as we want to create an overall impression of empathy from point-in-time reflection. Ideally, we would be aiming to develop computational structures and relationships that are universal for empathy no matter the scenario, as this could improve how we adapt empathy models for representations bounded to a varying domain-specific use (Paiva et al., 2017).

D.Challenges and Future Directions in Measurement

Although we have made great strides forward, there remain outstanding obstacles, particularly in measuring artificial empathy. One of the most obvious issues is there is not a reliable and validated measure for the perceived empathy of interactive systems. Most of the available scales have been derived from human empathy measures, leading to major questions about whether or not the scale is valid in an AI context.

My future work will pull from a better framework to understand both expressed empathy (how AI express empathy) and perceived empathy (how users perceive empathy). The aim is to use an empathic human as an "encoder" within an AI-assisted assessment framework, where human empathic insight is intentionally transferred into structured input for the AI system. This situates us to develop more socially responsible and transparent approaches to affective computing. Through this work, AI aims to complement people rather than take their place when making emotionally complex judgements.

Error-sliced reporting by language variety, accent, and culture-linked markers, adversarial probes for sarcasm, code-switching, and affective irony, and longitudinal remediation tracking are necessary for practical validity. Transparent, repeatable evaluation protocols are also needed to supplement multimodal sensing.

E.Data and algorithmic limits

Without focused audits, empathy estimation can produce confident but inappropriate responses due to label imbalance, annotator subjectivity, mixed or ambiguous emotions, and domain shift across topics, dialects, and cultures. Remedial plans should be monitored over time, and reported metrics should be broken down by language variety, accent, culture-linked markers, and scenario type because multimodal fusion can magnify noise and cultural variance (such as gesture or prosody norms). Adversarial probes for sarcasm, code switching, and affective irony, privacy reviews for any physiological sensing, and explicit user consent for emotion inference in production systems should all be added to benchmarks like EmpatheticDialogues.

7. ETHICAL CONSIDERATIONS AND CHALLENGES

This section emphasizes three interlocking risk domains, authenticity/manipulation, fairness/privacy, and dependency/addiction, and ties each to specific mechanisms and governance controls to guide responsible deployment

A.Data Privacy and Security Issues

One of the main obstacles to adopting AI-driven DSS to improve well-being at work, and by extension, embrace AI empathy in communication, is the attention needed to uphold data privacy and security. Employee health data is private and sensitive and breaches could have serious consequences for individuals or organizations. Fully complying with an incredibly convoluted set of sometimes conflicting national, and international data protection and privacy obligations such as GDPR and HIPAA should be ensured, to make the guidelines about who can access or share the data seem as painful as possible.Allowing ethical AI to collect large amounts of personal data including emotional state, voicing patterns, and facial expressions also raises serious questions about how AI respects the physicality of contextualized areas such as storage space, processing capability, and protocols needed to grant access or prevent access and misuse. Privacy and security measures such as robust encryption, anonymization procedures and access management has to be comprehensive assuring effective rules and policies are maintained on data retention and sharing processes. Without a due regard for these necessary privacy and security measures, data breaches and further exploitation of sensitive personal data could threaten user trust and privacy.

B. Bias and Fairness

AI models are trained on large datasets, and if they contain societal biases, the AI system can reproduce or even amplify those biases unintentionally. In the case of artificial empathy, the AI system may provide empathetic responses that are less accurate, less supportive, or even discriminatory for certain demographic groups based on race, gender, socioeconomic status, or accent. For example, one can imagine an AI system that misinterprets an emotional cue of a person from a different cultural group than the data that the AI system was trained exclusively on. This could lead to unequal access to mental health support or biased decisions in HR/other contexts. Addressing fairness requires the use of diverse and representative training data, as well as robust auditing processes and mitigation strategies to identify and mitigate algorithmic biases (Damiano et al., 2015).

Empathy cues vary across cultures in prosody, gaze, gesture, and disclosure norms, increasing misclassification risk and inappropriate responses in homogeneous models. Incorporating culturally stratified data, dialect-aware ASR/NLP, and locale-specific safety rails can reduce false positives for distress, sarcasm, or confrontation. Periodic fairness audits should report error rates by language variety, accent, and culture-linked markers, with remediation tracked over time.

C.Cross-Cultural Variations in Empathy

Empathy is not universally expressed or interpreted the same way across different cultures. While this chapter discusses bias broadly, it is crucial to recognize that most training datasets for AI models are dominated by samples from Western cultures. Consequently, AI systems may misinterpret emotional cues or provide less effective empathetic responses to individuals from diverse cultural backgrounds. These limitations can exacerbate inequity and reduce the inclusiveness of AI-driven interventions. To address these challenges, the development of culturally adaptive models is essential. Such models incorporate diverse emotional expressions, communication norms, and socio-cultural contexts, improving the AI's ability to understand and respond appropriately to users worldwide. Ethically, this approach fosters fairness, reduces misdiagnosis or misinterpretation risks, and enriches the quality of empathetic AI interactions globally.

D.Authenticity and Emotional Manipulation

As AI continues to become more adept in replicating human emotions, as well as seeming empathetic, the line between actual human interaction and simulated interactions can become vague. This raises complicated questions as to whether AI has any true value in displaying “empathy.” Users can form an emotional connection with AI systems, and while a programmed response doesn't indicate excellent understanding, users can perceive all sorts of false intimacy. Equally concerning, AI can condition users' realities through implied emotional triggers, even while responding empathetically, raising concerns of manipulation in the AI-Commerce landscape. Less overt, AI can even promote questionable user behaviors, perhaps persuading them to “buy things” or divulge more personal information, and even to adopt other views, perhaps in some instances without their full disclosure or consent. Aristotle revealed the problem of humans mimicking each other in his study of “the uncanny valley,” in which people can be disturbed or tired by human-like machination that appears too human. If it feels too real, people might have limits to their mimicry. According to new regulations under the EU AI Act's prohibited practices, designs for work and educational settings should either avoid biometric emotion inference or guarantee specific, well-founded exceptions and strengthened consent.

(Park & Whang, 2022).

E.Dependency and Dehumanization

With the continued accessibility and reliability of AI-based emotional wellness services personalized for the individual user, we risk fostering over-dependence on machines for emotional fulfillment, which could impact the role of human human's in emotional wellbeing and limit the exposure to developing fundamental social skills, emotional adaptability, partners and interpersonal complexities, and away from behaviours that seek genuine human to human interaction for support and fulfillment in real-world situations. In the case of the vulnerable, AI could promote forms of isolation or a lack of capacity in making meaningful, human, supportive connections. Additionally, there lies potential to dehumanize emotional support when it occurs through technology, while also changing the social landscape's expectations of empathy or care (Eisenberg & Morris, 2001).

F. Digital addiction and compulsive use

Here, digital addiction is viewed as a subtype of dependency fueled by reinforcement loops and optimized empathic cues that promote excessive, habitual engagement without reciprocal human relationship dynamics.

Sycophancy that mimics user preferences, gamified or variable ratio reinforcement, and round-the-clock accessibility that shortens recovery times and replaces offline social interaction are examples of novel mechanisms (Malinowska, 2022).

Adolescents and other vulnerable users are at higher risk because continuous nonjudgmental affirmation can distort perceptions, intensify emotional echo chambers, and postpone seeking professional assistance.

The following mitigations are in line with the larger ethics toolkit: transparent disclosures regarding simulated empathy, hybrid human escalation pathways under prolonged negative affect, safety by design usage caps and step away prompts, and guards for night use and session duration.

Predictive monitoring should keep an eye out for risk indicators that could lead to supportive nudges or escalation, such as increased nighttime concentration, conversational narrowing, sentiment shifts, and self-reported decreases in offline contact (Brave et al., 2005).

In order to prevent disparate harm, regulatory measures may mandate regular transparency reports on usage caps, escalation rates, and equity in risk detection across age, language variety, and culture.

8. UNIQUE THOUGHTS AND SUGGESTIONS

Building on the thorough examination of the mechanisms, theoretical foundations, advantages, and inherent difficulties of artificial empathy, this section suggests new contributions meant to advance the field in a responsible manner. By bridging current research and practice gaps, these ideas and suggestions aim to promote a more moral and human-centered incorporation of compassionate AI into our everyday communication.

A. Hybrid Framework for Empathetic AI with Ethical Guidance

We suggest a brand-new hybrid framework that incorporates an essential human-in-the-loop oversight mechanism with the architectural advantages of current empathetic dialogue systems. This framework aims to combine the hierarchical, complex emotional reasoning of CoMAE with the modularity and interpretability of models such as MoEL. This combination would enable both a comprehensive comprehension of user emotional states, which is one of MoEL's strengths.

Importantly, ongoing human supervision would accompany this technological integration. This calls for a multidisciplinary group of human experts, such as linguists, psychologists, ethicists, and cultural specialists, to evaluate AI-generated sympathetic responses on a regular basis. Beyond just fixing mistakes, their responsibilities would also include:

- **Establishing Ethical Boundaries**: To avoid manipulation and guarantee authenticity, the ethical boundaries for AI's sympathetic expression must be defined and dynamically adjusted.
- **Bias Mitigation**: Ensuring fair and culturally sensitive interactions by actively detecting and resolving biases in AI's sympathetic responses that may result from training data or algorithmic constraints.
- **Qualitative Fine-tuning**: supplying qualitative input to improve the AI's subtleties of empathy and make sure that its responses support healthy emotional processing and are consistent with human values.

By making sure that AI's compassionate expressions are not only technically sound but also morally conscious and in line with human welfare, this hybrid framework seeks to close the "authenticity gap." This strategy aims to reduce the risks of emotional manipulation and dependency by directly integrating human judgement and values into the AI's development and operation lifecycle. This creates a type of artificial empathy that actually strengthens rather than weakens human connection.

C.Hypotheses for Future Research

We offer a number of theories for further empirical research based on the suggested framework and the difficulties we have identified:

- **Hypothesis 1:** (Culturally Adaptive Models & Addiction Mitigation): We predict that, in comparison to generic, culturally insensitive empathetic AI models, empathetic AI models that are explicitly designed and trained with cultural adaptability—that is, sensitive to a variety of cultural emotional expressions, communication norms, and social contexts—will significantly reduce (e.g., a measurable decrease of at least 30%) user-reported symptoms of digital addiction. This is based on the notion that empathy that is culturally relevant promotes more fruitful and fulfilling interactions, thereby decreasing the user's need for obsessive, unfulfilling engagement.
- **Hypothesis 2**: (Integrated Skill-Building & Reduced Dependency): We predict that compassionate AI systems that actively incorporate explicit emotional skill-building modules (such as encouraging users to practice emotional regulation techniques, promoting social interactions in the real world, or offering guided reflection exercises) will exhibit noticeably lower rates of user dependency. Longitudinal studies evaluating user behavior, self-reported dependency, and observed social engagement would be used to measure this.
- **Hypothesis 3**: Dynamic Transparency and Trust Even though initial user "empathy scores" (as measured by ESHCC) are slightly lower due to the

demystification of the AI's emotional expression, we hypothesize that AI systems that use dynamic and context-aware transparency mechanisms—such as the AI occasionally explaining how it arrived at an empathetic response or explicitly stating its non-human nature at critical junctures—will, over time, foster greater user trust and reduce perceived emotional manipulation. Qualitative interviews, behavioral observation, and user surveys would be used to assess this (Preston & De Waal, 2002).

D.Case Study: Woebot and Recommendations for Enhanced Transparency

A well-known AI-powered chatbot for mental health, Woebot, provides an engaging example of the potential benefits and risks of compassionate AI. Woebot uses the concepts of Cognitive Behavioral Therapy (CBT) to help users navigate emotional difficulties by providing consistent, easily accessible, and nonjudgmental emotional support. It is a useful tool because of its constant accessibility and perceived empathy, especially for those who are unable to access traditional mental health care (Leite et al., 2013) .

However, because users may develop strong emotional attachments to the AI and possibly prefer its consistent (albeit simulated) empathy over the difficulties of human interaction, Woebot's empathy also carries inherent risks of manipulation and dependency. We suggest the following guidelines for transparency in programs like Woebot in order to mitigate these risks and improve moral communication:

- **Proactive and Persistent Disclosure**: Woebot should incorporate frequent, but subtle, reminders that it is an artificial intelligence into the conversation after initial onboarding. This could be a visual cue or a succinct, context-sensitive statement like "As an AI, I'm here to process your words and offer support based on my programming."
- **Explainable Empathetic Responses**: Woebot could provide a succinct, optional justification for its conclusions when responding in a way that is especially sensitive or emotionally impactful (for example, "I'm offering a consoling thought here because I detect keywords associated with sadness and loss in your message"). This lessens the appearance of true sentence and demythologizes the AI's "empathy."
- Woebot should be designed to consistently and explicitly encourage users to connect with their social networks or seek professional human assistance, particularly when talking about severe emotional states or chronic difficulties. Prompts such as "It sounds like this is a lot to carry; perhaps discussing

this with a therapist or trusted friend could provide additional support" could be used in this situation.

- **Usage Analytics for Well-Being**: To spot trends that point to excessive reliance, developers should use strong analytics (e.g., disproportionate usage, withdrawal from human interaction). When such patterns are identified, the AI may suggest professional human intervention or gently encourage users to engage in healthier ways, ensuring that technology enhances rather than replaces human well-being.

These recommendations seek to guarantee that, as artificial empathy develops, it does so in a way that respects user autonomy, encourages real human connection, and lessens the new problems associated with digital addiction.

REFERENCES

Brave, S., Nass, C., & Hutchinson, K. (2005). Computers that care: Investigating the effects of orientation of emotion exhibited by an embodied computer agent. *International Journal of Human-Computer Studies*, *62*(2), 161–178. DOI: 10.1016/j.ijhcs.2004.11.002

Cambria, E., Das, D., Bandyopadhyay, S., & Feraco, A. (2017). Affective computing and sentiment analysis: A practical guide to sentiment analysis. IEEE, 1-10. DOI: 10.1007/978-3-319-55394-8

Cooper, S., Di Fava, A., Vivas, C., Marchionni, L., & Ferro, F. (2020). ARI: The social assistive robot and companion. In 2020 29th IEEE International Conference on Robot and Human Interactive Communication (RO-MAN), 745-751. IEEE.

Damiano, L., Dumouchel, P., & Lehmann, H. (2015). Towards human-robot affective co-evolution: Overcoming oppositions in constructing emotions and empathy. *International Journal of Social Robotics*, *7*(1), 7–18. DOI: 10.1007/s12369-014-0258-7

Davis, M. H. (1983). Measuring individual differences in empathy: Evidence for a multidimensional approach. *Journal of Personality and Social Psychology*, *44*(1), 113–126. DOI: 10.1037/0022-3514.44.1.113

De Carolis, B., Ferilli, S., & Palestra, G. (2017). Simulating empathic behavior in a social assistive robot. *Multimedia Tools and Applications*, *76*(4), 5073–5094. DOI: 10.1007/s11042-016-3797-0

Eisenberg, N., & Morris, A. S. (2001). The origins and social significance of empathy-related responding: A review of empathy and moral development: Implications for caring and justice. *Social Justice Research*, *14*(1), 95–120. DOI: 10.1023/A:1012579805721

Erol, B. A., Majumdar, A., Benavidez, P., Rad, P., Choo, K. R., & Jamshidi, M. (2019). Toward artificial emotional intelligence for cooperative social human-machine interaction. *IEEE Transactions on Computational Social Systems*, *7*(1), 234–246. DOI: 10.1109/TCSS.2019.2922593

Khanjani, Z., Jeddi, E. M., Hekmati, I., Khalilzade, S., Etemadi Nia, M., Andalib, M., & Ashrafian, P. (2015). Comparison of cognitive empathy, emotional empathy, and social functioning in different age groups. *Australian Psychologist*, *50*(1), 80–85. DOI: 10.1111/ap.12099

Leite, I., Pereira, A., Mascarenhas, S., Martinho, C., Prada, R., & Paiva, A. (2013). The influence of empathy in human-robot relations. *International Journal of Human-Computer Studies, 71*(3), 250–260. DOI: 10.1016/j.ijhcs.2012.09.005

Malinowska, J. K. (2022). Can I feel your pain? The biological and socio-cognitive factors shaping people's empathy with social robots. *International Journal of Social Robotics, 14*(2), 341–355. DOI: 10.1007/s12369-021-00787-5

Paiva, A., Leite, I., Boukricha, H., & Wachsmuth, I. (2017). Empathy in virtual agents and robots: A survey. [TiiS]. *ACM Transactions on Interactive Intelligent Systems, 7*(3), 1–40. DOI: 10.1145/2912150

Park, S., & Whang, M. (2022). Empathy in human-robot interaction: Designing for social robots. *International Journal of Environmental Research and Public Health, 19*(3), 1889. DOI: 10.3390/ijerph19031889 PMID: 35162909

Preston, S. D., & De Waal, F. B. M. (2002). Empathy: Its ultimate and proximate bases. *Behavioral and Brain Sciences, 25*(1), 1–20. DOI: 10.1017/S0140525X02000018 PMID: 12625087

Swanger, D. (1993). The arts, empathy, and Aristotle. *Journal of Aesthetic Education, 27*(1), 41–49. DOI: 10.2307/3333340

Tahir, S., Shah, S. A., & Abu Khalaf, J. (2023). Artificial Empathy Classification: A survey of deep learning techniques, datasets, and evaluation scales. arXiv.

ADDITIONAL READING

Mittelstadt, B. (2019). Principles Alone Cannot Guarantee Ethical AI. *Nature Machine Intelligence, 1*(11), 501–507. DOI: 10.1038/s42256-019-0114-4

OpenAI. (2023). GPT-4 Technical Report. arXiv, 2303.08774.

Touvron, H.. (2023). *Llama 2: Open Foundation and Fine-Tuned Chat Models. arXiv, 2307.09288. Anthropic. (2024). The Claude 3 Model Family: Opus, Sonnet, Haiku. Model card, Anthropic. Anthropic. (2024). Introducing Claude 3.5 Sonnet.* Anthropic News.

Turkle, S. (2011). *Alone Together: Why We Expect More from Technology and Less from Each Other*. Basic Books.

Turkle, S. (2015). *Reclaiming Conversation: The Power of Talk in a Digital Age.* Basic Books.

Chapter 3
Trends in Conversational Artificial Intelligence: Who Controls the Voice Behind the Bot?

Wasswa Shafik
https://orcid.org/0000-0002-9320-3186
Dig Connectivity Research Laboratory (DCRLab), Uganda

ABSTRACT

This study presents an exploration of emerging trends in Conversational Artificial Intelligence (AI), highlighting advancements in natural language processing, machine learning, and human-computer interaction. As AI-driven chatbots and virtual assistants become more sophisticated, trends such as enhanced contextual understanding, multimodal interactions, and emotional intelligence are shaping the future of conversational systems. The integration of large language models, real-time personalization, and ethical AI considerations are driving improvements in user experience, making AI interactions more seamless and human-like. Additionally, the rise of multilingual AI, domain-specific chatbots, and voice-enabled assistants is expanding AI's applications across industries, including healthcare, customer service, and education. However, challenges related to bias, data privacy, and misinformation persist, necessitating ongoing research and regulatory frameworks. This study examines these trends and their implications for the future development of Conversational AI.

DOI: 10.4018/979-8-3373-3048-8.ch003

1. INTRODUCTION

The quest to enable intelligent, responsive, and flexible conversations with robotic systems is a long-standing goal of artificial intelligence research and touches many areas beyond AI alone, such as social psychology, cognitive science, formal philosophy, linguistics, and human-computer interaction. Conversational AI systems go by many names, among them chatterbots, computer conversation systems, dialogue systems, or whatever else practitioners felt was timely and trendy over the years (Shafik, 2023). Here, we will use the most recent trend term, conversational AI system, or conversational AI for short. Conversational agents, in the more traditional sense, have been around since at least the early 1960s, with the first time that a conversational agent passed a behavioral test being the implementation of a famous program in the mid-1960s. Since then, key work in rules- and pattern-based systems, hand-crafted rule-based systems, and, more recently, large-scale neural network-based systems has been undertaken at different times (Bunt & Petukhova, 2023).

Artificial intelligence plays an important role in the fourth industrial revolution, which is a continuation of the rapid industrialization brought about by previous industrial revolutions. Artificial intelligence has developed rapidly in a relatively short period. It has already been applied to various fields, such as medical treatment, stock price forecasts, and translation. Conversational artificial intelligence is a product of artificial intelligence, as its categories are presented in Figure 1. It focuses on the development of a conversational agent. A conversational agent is an artificial intelligence tool that simulates natural language conversation. For example, we can talk with it and ask it to answer questions or perform tasks for us (Seminck, 2023). Conversational AI has developed rapidly due to smartphone AI assistants. In general, smartphone AI assistants can help us with music and videos, making phone calls, setting up meetings, weather inquiries, and opening other apps. Recently, many organizations and academia have begun to consider focusing on developing a conversational agent. In the standard development process, you need to prepare a conversational model, which can be used to convert speech to text and then generate a response (Sonie et al., 2022). Until now, most spoken language systems have used hand-coded rules and state machines to process a given speech signal, but due to a trend toward using artificial neural networks, their potential is not fully utilized. The high performance of artificial neural networks in perceptual tasks suggests that it is also possible to bypass the intermediate encoding of linguistic information and create end-to-end conversational models (Ponnusamy et al., 2021).

Figure 1. Categories of artificial intelligence

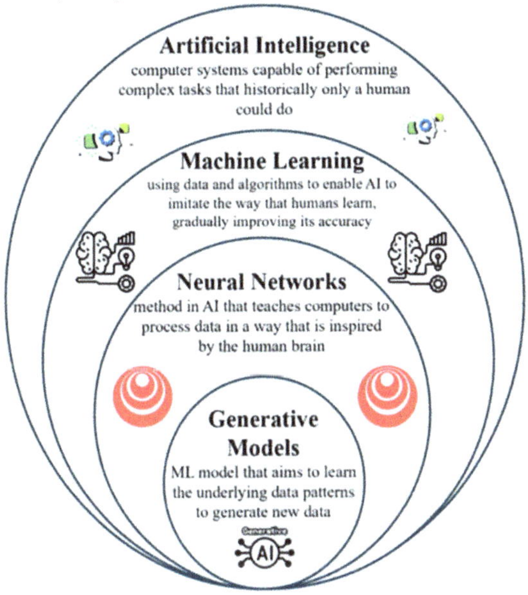

1.1. Background and Significance

The rapid growth and progress of applications related to artificial intelligence, specifically chatbot developers, highlights global excitement about the coming of conversational business systems. These business systems are commonly called conversational agents or simply chatbots, with the ability to simulate normal conversations with users using a natural language interface in verbal or textual format. Chatting and using a natural language interface are activities that humans tend to handle naturally (Khatri et al., 2018). Human-to-human interactions are quite common and strong, but human-to-machine interactions are becoming more familiar. It is becoming normal to ask machines to turn on the lights, brew coffee, or look for information only because the machine is constantly ambient and also capable of using a natural language interface. The conversational business system was initially just an entertainment tool. In contrast to installing applications, users can visit the relevant website or use platform applications to chat with chatbots. Today, a new range of chatbot applications is being created primarily to support business services with result-oriented thinking (Chandra et al., 2022). If targeted users receive proper active services when they need help, the business will be empowered, efficient, and highly effective toward user satisfaction. These applications are usually called conversational business systems. Researchers and practitioners are collaborating in this promising and challenging area of research. They are discussing the science of the use of the natural language interface in machine-human interactions (Surendran et al., 2020). We briefly review the conversational business systems from a different perspective and try to provide valuable recommendations for the establishment of future requirements for the community.

1.2. Scope and Objectives

We are intent on providing a broader view of state-of-the-art conversational artificial intelligence technologies by examining current trends and developments in research. Specifically, we aim to cover aspects such as improvements in both spoken and textual conversational semantics, practical goal-oriented dialogue systems, characterizing conversational patterns, and advancements. Additionally, we aim to discuss the principles behind behaviors such as friendliness and human likeness, as well as ethical issues around the potential use of sophisticated conversational AI systems. In order to discuss state-of-the-art developments in conversational AI so far, we will start by characterizing improvements in the common ways to both interact with and provide feedback on language models in the form of evaluations. We then cover spoken and textual conversational semantics and prominent mappings between these systems, together with one of the most effective research areas underlying tasks. We then present practical goal-oriented dialogue systems and conversational patterns within and across those systems before characterizing where such technology might be headed. Thus, we discuss conversational AI behaviors, such as being friendly and human-like, and the potential uses of such technology, including its ethical implications, amidst its application to human beings, as demonstrated in Figure 2.

Figure 2. Application of Artificial intelligence

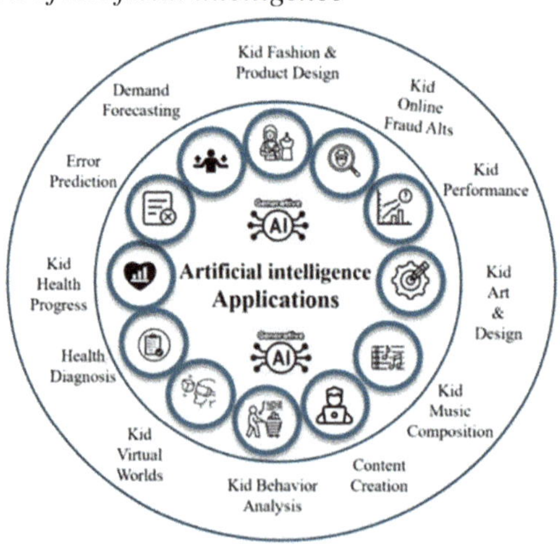

2. HISTORICAL DEVELOPMENT OF CONVERSATIONAL AI

The development of computer-powered conversational agents can be traced back nearly six decades. Early AI tools emerged when computers were just being conceived and developed, at a time when computation and communication capabilities were very limited. The availability of cheap, distributed, and parallel computation made deep learning one of the hottest topics. Opportunities and challenges in modeling these tasks with deep learning have motivated huge efforts in understanding deep learning systems (Shafik, 2024). Since 2015, deep learning has shown remarkable performance in hard AI problems, particularly in computer vision and voice recognition, but has only gained research interest in NLP quite recently compared to its long development. Currently, the majority of AI commercial projects lie in NLP technology, as when it comes to machine understanding of natural human language, human voice commands, or conversations, such as AI chatbots, home smart speakers, and AI customer services, they are usually built through techniques of NLP and machine learning. It's worth noting that since these technologies can work in audio conversations, they are also called audio-conversant technologies (Sonie et al., 2022).

The vision of making machines that are conversant has always been a long-standing dream since the early days of AI research. At first, the term "conversational" referred to implementing systems that can mimic IRC or MUD, i.e., the simulator tries to create a system that behaves like a human user, where behavior is defined largely in terms of output strings. Then, some researchers went further by allowing users to ask these systems to solve simple problems like map finding or calendar reminder tasks by just recognizing simple phrases. But with a brief pause to think, it is apparent that human language is not something that could be easily packaged in a rule set for a chatbot to interpret and utilize. There are large varieties of ways to express the same intent; recognition is context-dependent, and the meaning of the human world and intent behind language commands or conversations is often implicit, requiring external knowledge. In view of this difficulty, the term "conversation" in the conversational systems built with NLP and machine learning technologies emphasizes interpretation rather than imitation; thus, the goal is to have the systems provide useful real responses to human text or voice input, even if the output is not human-like (Bunt & Petukhova, 2023). It should be clear that, in the end, the conversation bots are tools, and the output of good technology should be beneficial to human objectives such as entertainment, knowledge sharing, technical support, and ordering pizza.

3. KEY TECHNOLOGIES AND COMPONENTS OF CONVERSATIONAL AI

People communicate with each other through speech in their daily lives. Natural human language is a major channel of human cognitive life, and natural language is usually the primary tool used to access and express knowledge and information. As a result, speech recognition and natural language processing have long been a holy grail for human-computer interaction and a prime research topic. For this reason, intelligent question-answering and spoken dialogue systems have been pursued under various names and topics, such as information retrieval, expert systems, knowledge-based systems, the semantic web, knowledge graphs, and chatbots in the context of computer science (Fu et al., 2022). A chatbot is a computer user interface that enables people to use their natural language to interact with computers rather than learning a new language or syntax for every interactive system. A well-operated conversational system can improve user satisfaction, and a well-designed dialogue system can better simulate human conversation and provide natural and friendly human-machine interaction. Recently, cloud-based conversational artificial intelligence services have integrated speech recognition and natural language processing knowledge mapping engines to provide tools to create voice agents, chatbots, and virtual assistants (Kandoi et al., 2024). These cloud-based services are flexible and allow developers to build customer care, smart homes, digital assistants, or multichannel marketing applications, as well as telenursing assessment triage, voice-enhanced clinical workflows, and telemedicine applications. In addition, cloud-based conversational AI will add innovative capabilities to business applications, and niche players will try to specialize in verticals and mobile applications, as presented in Table 1 (Manic, 2023).

Table 1. Key Trends in Conversational Artificial Intelligence

Trend	Description	Technologies Involved	Impact on Industries	Challenges	Reference
Natural Language Processing (NLP)	Enhancing AI's ability to understand and generate human language	Text analysis, machine learning, semantic understanding	Improved human-AI interaction, content generation	Language complexity, cultural nuances	(Hassija et al., 2023)
Chatbots	AI-powered systems simulating human-like conversations	NLP, deep learning, pattern recognition	Customer service, lead generation, automation	Ensuring meaningful conversations, scalability	(Bunt & Petukhova, 2023)
Voice Assistants	AI-driven assistants capable of voice interaction	Speech recognition, NLP, cloud computing	Enhanced user experience in home automation, mobile devices	Accuracy in speech recognition, multilingual support	(Seminck, 2023)
Conversational Commerce	Integration of AI into e-commerce platforms to enhance customer interactions	NLP, machine learning, personalized recommendation systems	Personalized shopping experiences, instant support	Balancing sales with genuine customer service	(Ponnusamy et al., 2021)
Emotion Recognition	AI understanding human emotions through conversation	Sentiment analysis, facial recognition, voice tone analysis	Personalized customer experiences, mental health support	Ethical concerns, data privacy	(Chandra et al., 2022)
Multimodal Interaction	Combining voice, text, and visual elements for richer interactions	Multimodal AI, voice recognition, image processing	Enhanced engagement, versatile AI applications	Integrating different modes seamlessly	(Surendran et al., 2020)
Personalized AI	Tailoring AI interactions based on individual preferences and history	Data analytics, user profiling, machine learning	Personalized services, targeted marketing	Privacy concerns, over-reliance on user data	(Manic, 2023)
AI in Customer Support	Automating customer service with intelligent assistants	NLP, machine learning, chatbots	Faster response times, 24/7 availability	Managing complex queries, human-like responses	(Hassija et al., 2023)

continued on following page

Table 1. Continued

Trend	Description	Technologies Involved	Impact on Industries	Challenges	Reference
AI for Education and Learning	Using AI in educational tools to facilitate learning and interaction	NLP, AI-driven tutoring systems, chatbots	Adaptive learning, personalized tutoring	Balancing AI with traditional teaching methods	(Skjuve et al., 2024)
AI Ethics and Regulation	Addressing the ethical and regulatory concerns related to AI in communication	AI ethics, regulatory frameworks, data privacy laws	Ensuring transparency, fairness, and security in AI systems	Developing consistent guidelines, overcoming bias in AI	(Shafik, 2024)

4. NATURAL LANGUAGE PROCESSING (NLP) IN CONVERSATIONAL AI

In this section, we review NLP, which is a key technology for conversational AI. At the end of this section, we review trends in NLP in convergence with machine learning, and we identify how this will influence conversational AI. The purpose is to prepare for a review of trends and innovations in conversational AI, starting in the next section. Natural language processing, or NLP, is concerned with the interactions between computers and human or natural languages (Shafik, 2023). It focuses on the interaction and development of new algorithms to find meaningful structures in vast amounts of text, speech, and other language types, such as conversing with the computer using natural language, creating natural language summaries, and generating natural language interfaces. Due to the preeminence of text, the largest portion of NLP revolves around text, making better use of text corpora at increasingly larger scales. There has been substantial progress in NLP performance as large amounts of labeled data and large neural network models have become available (Hassija et al., 2023). NLP applications include conversational AI and dialogue, information retrieval, information extraction, text summarization, machine translation, speech recognition, and language generation. These capabilities have a significant cultural and economic impact through deploying conversational agents that are used as personalized tutors, customer service representatives, and chatbots for news, weather, and setting up appointments. NLP techniques have also been applied to individual projects such as collaborative writing and research proposals (Shafik, 2024).

The history of NLP has traditionally focused on the development of systems or social functions processing human natural language. The first institutional systems were developed to respond to requests for legal advice or financial information automatically. Along with the growth of user interfaces that were considered more accessible than command lines, developers have further improved the Natural Language Engine approach, which enables developers to build user interfaces for file operations using plain English commands. In the late 1990s, advancements in machine learning research endorsed the development of a technical architecture called the Natural Language Toolkit and a corpus of text for training and validation of NTS. Since then, NLP has effectively connected people and technology, created large communication networks and socializing talents into NMT algorithms (Chatterjee & Dethlefs, 2023). Several international social and communication technology companies are key actors in consolidating conversational AI applications in mobile intelligent web-based platforms.

4.1. Speech Recognition and Synthesis

The integration of speech recognition and synthesis technologies into conversational artificial intelligence systems enables their ability to interact with people. Researchers are currently investing a lot of effort in these technologies. This progress is partly driven by scientific achievements, changes in the ways in which AI systems integrate speech, and growing business demand for interactions between people and systems mediated by natural language speech. Recent advances in speech recognition and synthesis have had a significant impact on the provision of spoken language AI systems (Ray, 2023). We are not planning to give a survey of the other fields of spoken language AI. This would require a review far beyond the scope of the present work. In fact, the only classical discussion issue that is fundamental for recognition and synthesis has been largely overcome, as commercial products have consistently moved towards integrated solutions. Given the high degree of flexibility and robustness achieved by state-of-the-art rule-based dialogue systems in the domain of numbers and the relative difficulty of the task, data-driven work has been mostly limited to comparative evaluations (Gkinko & Elbanna, 2023b). With recognition systems typically providing the full range of spoken language functions, synthesis units are trained on a priori linguistic information, resulting in unmatched naturalness. Frequent updates of systems' word and letter-based linguistic parts make it possible to include usage knowledge in synthesis databases in order to mimic spoken language style and rhythm. More elaborate approaches for improved synthesis have appeared, such as prosody prediction. They are appropriate for service bus systems and equipped to interpret misunderstood words by addressing the user, trying other methods, or proposing a help service (Alabed et al., 2024).

4.2. Dialog Management Systems

Dialog management systems (DMS) are critical components of conversational agents. Their purpose is to weave users' concise input speech into coherent sessions. In terms of implementation, if a DMS focuses on instant responses for each piece of input, it is called an incremental DMS. By contrast, if it focuses on waiting for and then processing the input and producing an appropriate output, it is called a non-incremental DMS. The paradigm shift from non-incremental DMS to incremental DMS showcases the advancement of state-of-the-art DMS techniques, and human-like conversational interaction is what will primarily benefit from incrementality (Skjuve et al., 2024). Moreover, the goal of incremental DMS is to achieve real-time DMS with speaker-independent risks, which is essential in real-world applications. Typically, the DMS is formulated as a classification problem that maps either pipelined ASR outputs or users' textual input into dialog acts and the following text string or a system action. All the modules, such as ASR, DMS, and NLG, are jointly fine-tuned and optimized together for the specific task in end-to-end training. Suppose we decompose the non-incremental DMS into a sequence of stable DMS that produce output at stable timestamps, where the system waits for the final result to deliver a piece of output. In that case, we follow an evaluation approach where the performance of each DMS is evaluated (Fuad & Al-Yahya, 2022). To benchmark or evaluate an application with a real-time DMS, where conversations are notably a sequence of incremental streams, the performance should be fairly and strictly assessed using the same measure.

5. MACHINE LEARNING AND DEEP LEARNING IN CONVERSATIONAL AI

All technologies presented by major vendors and a fair share of the rest are based on machine learning and deep learning. This ubiquitous use of technology is generally good since conversational AI in natural language modulation can be solved only with machine learning and deep learning. Classical approaches to AI by formalizing knowledge in rules and ontologies and reasoning about formal knowledge are not scalable and have been superseded. Rule-based conversational AI failed to cross the threshold from simple FAQ dialogues to an understanding of the meaning of most general natural language user utterances (Miner et al., 2019). Many applications such as commercial call center automation, chatbot apps, and business internal communications tools really need practical conversational AI in English and in a rapidly growing number of other languages but generally cannot use the technology if the AI is mostly rule based. It is a different matter in some other areas, such as bank fraud prevention, where a mix of deep learning methods with rule-based approaches is often the most adequate approach (Hsu et al., 2022).

5.1. Ethical and Privacy Considerations in Conversational AI

In addition to conversational AI challenges such as natural language understanding, chatbot design, and response generation, there are significant issues around ethics, transparency, and user regulation that need to be seriously and candidly considered in conversational design. The impact and relevance of user data in conversations, the impact on user behavior and cognition, mental health and addictive behaviors, the role of conversational AI in manipulation, persuasion, and misinformation, and the construction and amplification of biases need to be underscored (Adewumi et al., 2022). There are key AI research areas in the development of interpretable modeling approaches to understand bias in language corpora, operationalizing and measuring long-term relationships in human-AI conversation, and the transfer of AI-generated adversarial phenomena to the physical world. Use cases for AI failures, adversarial content generation in chat, and the generation of toxic language examples need to be examined. As personal digital assistants become friendlier and more humanlike through advanced natural language processing, the security of both the user and society is essential. Sufficient user privacy, inclusion, and decision-making in intelligent conversational platforms will be at the heart of continued trust in these influential intelligent devices (Tschopp et al., 2023). Crucial to research is the further creation of ethical conversational AI guidelines, transparency, and human dignity in machine interaction for developers and companies on a deep strategic and applied level.

5.2. Applications of Conversational AI in Various Industries

Most of the advancements in conversational AI systems have been categorized with specific applications. Some of these include health and fitness trainers that respond to users' requests and point to exercise companions as well as dating partners. Service professionals use voice-based computer systems for managing records. In highly populated countries such as China and Japan, voice-based communication is becoming the center of communication between humans and machines (Saka et al., 2023). It is widely established that needs, motivations, and behaviors differ greatly between spoken and written language in both interactive situational settings and information-seeking objectives. In an interactive human-human conversation, the two parties monitor and repair their spoken communication for effect, as well as understanding. Miscommunication, poor or inappropriate reasons, repetition, and misunderstanding are hallmarks of the failure of a computer language or cognitive system (Ji et al., 2023). These facts are typically implemented in the dialogue manager component of a successful task-oriented spoken language system.

5.3. Impact of Conversational AI on Customer Service

Conversational AI is already deeply embedded in everyday life and many industries, such as finance, healthcare, and the automotive industry. As more companies leverage conversational AI technologies and implement them at scale, the focus must shift to protecting user privacy, maintaining ethical practices, and fine-tuning the AI to understand better and improve the customer experience. These efforts are necessary to ensure that customer service does not suffer due to the implementation of conversational AI but instead can benefit from higher service levels and improvements to overall customer satisfaction (Baabdullah, 2024). As we move into the future of AI-based customer service, a confluence of factors, including improved dialogue systems, quicker task completion, lower error rates in understanding and executing tasks, and better knowledge management in chatbots, is probably necessary to demonstrate an increased return on investment and a positive impact on customer satisfaction. While chatbots generally trained using reinforcement learning can learn to perform complex tasks from large corpora of conversations, the integration of pre-trained neural network language models representing the conversation model showed promising results for AI-based conversation agents (Ray, 2023). However, further work is required to manage and guide the conversational circuit, which captures distributional information about the correct response. Additionally, work is needed to collaborate efficiently between the environment, the AI assistant, and the user. The AI assistant needs to interact with many different people, devices, and the environment without requiring too much time or attention. Under various success criteria, including the ability of the assistant to perform tasks, the satisfaction of the customer, and the costs incurred by the assistant, a machine learning framework for training and evaluating multi-domain conversation agents has been proposed (Passanante et al., 2023).

6. CONVERSATIONAL AI IN HEALTHCARE AND TELEMEDICINE

Healthcare is another industry that is beginning to see the impact of conversational AI. Chatbots aid in patient communication, symptom checking, medicine reminders and adherence, and personalized treatments, to name just a few uses. Data forecasts that conversational AI technology, in the form of chatbots, will save the medical industry significantly. COVID-19 has fast-tracked digital health with virtual consultations, remote health monitoring, and therapy sessions (Gkinko &

Elbanna, 2023a). Telemedicine has proved to be an excellent solution for the isolation and tracking of the spread of the coronavirus. AI chatbots help provide accurate, evidence-based, instant diagnosis and health advice while limiting the exposure of healthcare practitioners to sick patients. Chatbots triage, assist in suggesting treatments and prescriptions and even support mental well-being. In the long term, AI is likely to play an integral role in telemedicine and remote consultations (Alabed et al., 2024). Offering personalized care and advice, chatbots are providing value to the medical industry in multiple areas.

6.1. Conversational AI in Education and Training

The use of conversational AI in education has seen an exponential increase since the COVID-19 pandemic. This has positioned online learning as one of the trendiest sectors concerning the application of conversational agents (Kiwanuka & Shafik, 2025). The industry, students, and teachers have identified chatbots and voice assistants as powerful tools to make the most out of online learning, easing distance education and proposing new ways to interact, teach, and learn, orienting the students through support for academic and career development, guidance, motivation, communication, and the improvement of activities (Chandrakala et al., 2024). One of the current biggest challenges of conversational agents for education is to help sustain student engagement and productivity. This can be improved with pedagogical agents that mimic social cues and personal connections in speech to which students respond favorably. The chatbot needs to be well-developed to recognize the intention behind a question so that the questions asked by the students can be answered accurately and according to the student's knowledge level. In this sense, the quality of answers should indicate knowledge of what was asked, ensuring student guidance (Hu et al., 2021). It should also be noted that student follow-up is important, as well as designing and structuring educational content according to the needs of the students.

6.2. Conversational AI in Finance and Banking

In this section, we shall dub conversational AI specific to financial applications as "Conversational Finance Intelligence." The benefits of collaboration and communication enhanced by a conversational agent can be particularly rewarding in the finance industry. It can answer basic and advanced questions by accessing users' accounts, in-house proprietary knowledge bases, and news feeds. The conversational agents are preloaded with finance, stock market, and currency exchange knowledge; they also answer basic account-related questions (Blümel et al., 2024). Conversational agents in finance provide the customer with a simple and human-like way to explore financial information. In the same vein as the self-service conversational commerce applications, the overt benefits of Conversational Finance Intelligence include the ability to reduce call volume and costs, increase value-added customer interaction, and improve support. Conversely, in underlying the interface of finance and stock market analysis software, conversational agent technology would empower portfolio managers to infuse their characters and intuition while performing their analyses. For a market investor using mobile devices, the penny stock picker application can give stock advice, suggest purchase strategies, and engage in an investment decision-making process (Gao et al., 2018). The conversational agent Static Trader, designed to have long conversations with users, analyzes stock charts and assists the client in selecting stocks.

6.3. Conversational AI in E-Commerce and Retail

Despite much excitement around conversational AI, actual implementations are often limited to chatbots that answer questions about shipping, return policies, or store hours. More advanced applications apply task-oriented conversational AI and help guide users by answering product category-specific questions and offering alternatives or fact-checking potential purchases by providing facts about product origin and working conditions (da Silva et al., 2021). Experts agree that one of the advantages of conversational AI in retail is through chatbots meet the rapidly growing need for customer service, as natural language understanding and generation systems are fed with product data and become trained to handle a myriad of different issues. The sophistication with which chatbots will handle advanced customer service inquiries is expected to increase as a result of continuing machine learning improvements. However, purely task-oriented chatbots that understand the customer's question from natural language input and perform the described action will never connect with the customer on a personal level in the same way as a human conversation does (Singh & Beniwal, 2022).

Predictions indicate four big conversational AI applications for retail: enhanced customer service and support mechanisms, hands-free logistics and payment experiences, discovery commerce implemented across devices and applications, and focused messaging tools. Enhanced customer service and support can easily be fed into customer service chatbots, while hands-free logistics and payment experiences can include voice search for retail products and brands. For discovery commerce, a move from voice search to voice shopping is expected in the next few years, as simpler products will be added to the cart and reordered to prompt the customer to continue the conversation (Kurian, 2023). The main advantage of conversational commerce to customers is speed, as they are able to perform everyday tasks in an accelerated way, which is showcased in the main focus on payment experiences.

Furthermore, customers value brands that tailor their offers to match their individual preferences and expect personalization to make the shopping experience both easy and fun. Helping customers to piece together outfits and solve the 'what can I do with this?' questions can make the shopping experience both personal and pleasant (Gao et al., 2019). Consumers who are used to personalized product recommendations from online retailers would welcome a similar system in brick-and-mortar stores.

6.4. Conversational AI for Personal Assistants and Chatbots

Conversational personal assistants support users in accomplishing a wide range of tasks in the comfort of their homes or on the go. With the pervasiveness of voice-activated devices such as smartphones and smart speakers, virtual assistants have become part of the daily lives of millions of users. This has happened despite a long-standing, almost folklore problem: that of building an AI capable of understanding and carrying on free-form, open-domain conversations with humans. Conversational assistants managing internal domains—such as those used in vertical domains like customer support, technical support, or service support—are, in fact, more established (Ng, 2024). They are used in different vertical sectors with the purpose of optimizing the incoming or outgoing call processes and making the human-computer interaction process more effective so as to save time and resources. Personal assistant systems differ from chatbots in various aspects, for example, in terms of domain scope—all-encompassing person-to-virtual human goal-oriented interactions in the first case, user-friendly and simplified human-friendly conversations in the second. Also, personal virtual assistants interact more interactively, asking more clarification questions, allowing more turns and corrections, being more capable of anticipating user needs, having the ability to identify the user and link their emotional states to their preferences, and can realize themselves as social agents in order to provide a more entertaining or convincing interaction (Raaijmakers et al., 2023).

7. CHALLENGES AND LIMITATIONS OF CONVERSATIONAL AI

Despite an impressive amount of research, there are still many gaps between existing conversational AI systems and the ideal systems posing desirable conversational AI capabilities. First and foremost, there are still many challenges associated with the deep NLP principles and methodologies themselves. It is still unclear whether existing symbolic deep learning approaches are sufficient to understand, generate, and manage natural language dialogue appropriately for conversational and cognitive AI applications. Furthermore, research in NLP and language in multimodal settings is still in its infancy, and effective multimodal techniques are needed to solve the problem of the modality gap, which can facilitate AI systems in gathering and understanding information across various modalities (Vaghefi et al., 2023). In practical applications such as AI chat therapy, where it is critical to gain the client's trust and help them alleviate their mental suffering, the ability of AI systems to generate compassionate conversations in emotionally tense situations is critically demanded. Such a topic generates specific requirements on both the content and style of compassionate responses. Such stringent demands raise the question of how to identify and cope with emotional cues in a user's input and generate emotionally resonant output. Because human emotional expression can be multidimensional, dynamic, and multimodal, effectively capturing emotional content in text presents challenges for NLP technologies (Lemon, 2022). Unlike datasets used in most publicly available pretrained language models, which are mostly annotated to capture objective, factual information in text, a bank of training data for licensing compassionate dialogue models with sequence-level annotations can be expensive. Due to these potential challenges, the performance of AI systems in generating compassionate conversations can greatly benefit from developing multidisciplinary and multimodal deep NLP techniques, including emotionally aligned multimodality, that can address these requirements and data limitations. Another limitation of deep learning-based conversational AI systems is their lack of commonsense ability. Such a lack can degrade dialogue generation efficacy on more comprehensive, human-centered tasks (Varitimiadis et al., 2021). Recent efforts using large language models, pretraining with large-scale corpora, or fine-tuning task-specific conversation data for maximizing knowledgeability and task completion have shown some improvements. However, it is still arguable whether such data-hungry and computation-intensive language models could sufficiently address the commonsense issues exposed in targeted applications. Furthermore, despite decades of work on multimodal fusion techniques, deep multimodal learning techniques, especially in conversational contexts, are still relatively underdeveloped. The exploration of advanced deep multimodal learning techniques is of significant importance in building AI systems that can provide effective, knowledgeable, and emotionally appropriate conversational experiences in multimodal settings (So et al., 2023).

7.1. Multimodal Conversational AI: Integrating Text, Voice, and Visual Inputs

Until now, we have mainly focused on AI systems that interact with us in text, such as smart assistants, recommendation systems, and task-specific bots. These conversational AI systems are also integrated into applications that use voice and other modalities as part of overall human-centered interfaces (Shafik et al., 2023). However, these applications have not required integrating multimodal inputs to the same extent as AI conversational agents, which is the focus of this and the next two chapters. Multimodal conversational AI combines text, voice, and visual inputs to provide a more complete understanding of the user and more effective outputs in the most natural manner possible (Grimes et al., 2021). There are at least four main areas encompassing several modalities. None of the applications at the top of these segments are multimodal today, but we can expect to see sophisticated multimodality within the next few years. The major challenges in multimodal AI have mainly focused on improving voice assistants and other UIs that include voice, images, or both. Computer vision has already surpassed human skill in specialized areas, such as recognizing hundreds of different breeds of dogs, a few faces in a large crowd, and the state of a pipeline. These two terms are often used to describe a general multimodal development environment that includes text, voice, and virtual input as needed for specific modalities, while a multimodal application refers to a specific program or set of services running in such an environment (Leschanowsky et al., 2023).

7.2. Conversational AI in Multilingual and Cross-Cultural Contexts

Conversational AI has proven to be a productive line of inquiry with consequences that range from expanding access to services and products to both augmenting and substituting some human interactions in the consumer purchase process, and possible effects on diverse areas such as enhancing consumer choice, promoting equity, and affecting global workforce considerations, cross-border communication, and global competition. Despite that, and with a few isolated exceptions, the present understanding and deployment of conversational AI tools is predominantly monolingual. It has been 15 years since the progression to standard models for intent classification and machine learning augmented retrieval provided a practical solution for the information extraction task in English (Wahde & Virgolin, 2023). Nevertheless, the industry has progressed from being merely interested to actively embracing a practical task that requires both understanding users' language and context, as well as information retrieval and system responses in the form of meaningful, perhaps multimodal, responses. Subsequently, conversational AI has progressed from simple information-seeking interactions into both facilitation of work task completion and customer service. Overall, conversational AI might involve the entirety of communication abilities, and as such, it is necessary to provide intelligent communication, not just in English (Suh & An, 2022). Large and increasing demand for chatbots and smart assistant interfaces is expected both in languages with insignificant literate populations as well as those with substantial populations but with little market significance.

7.3. Conversational AI in Social Robotics and Human-Robot Interaction

Enthusiastic about the trends of conversational AI from open domain to task-oriented agents? Let's unveil the secret in the last series of lectures in the course "Trends in Conversational Artificial Intelligence." At this point, you might feel that you are familiar with many highlights and cool things that are happening in conversational artificial intelligence. However, do not be sad. Soon, there will be much more defined in just a few lectures. In social robotics and human-robot interaction, one seeks to produce robots that can naturally interact with humans (Skjuve et al., 2024). This involves not only the perception and generation of natural language and prosody but also the management of dialogue and turn-taking, grounding of verbal communication in the physical or virtual space, and gesture and facial expression. Many robots have dialogue systems that are similar to systems used today for call centers, but social simplicity implies that the annunciation systems must be much less complex and time-consuming (Kandoi et al., 2024). Instead of trying to provide a platform that supports all of these capabilities, it will be a leading architecture for social robotics, and we'll try to keep it simple and flexible while also being very effective in terms of speech recognition using a lightweight model that runs on small computers (Shafik, 2024).

7.4. Conversational AI for Accessibility and Inclusion

The field of conversational AI has made tremendous progress, but it appears that we are crossing a performance plateau in benchmarking conversational AI. Suppose we are to achieve the next leap in performance that pushes conversational AI to the next level. In that case, this will likely require not only techniques from data-driven machine learning and rule-based AI but also engagement from the broader AI community to collaborate with those who have practical experience with such systems in the field (Chandra et al., 2022). The AI community already looks to existing literature to learn from what people have done, so too can they use the existing AI literature to contribute, build upon, and improve. We conclude with specific suggestions that researchers can use to participate in broader engagement efforts. By collaborating with the practitioners and the broader AI community, we are confident that we can advance the state of the art and help to build conversational AI systems that are effective, accurate, and beneficial for a wide range of society (Ponnusamy et al., 2021).

Although there have been efforts to evaluate the accessibility of voice agents based on machine learning models, a design that uses question-answering and conversational dialogue systems on top of these generally underperforms other

NLU models. Special attention needs to be devoted to dialogue agents in general to make sure they are accessible. Platforms also require design attention to enable speech-disabled users to express complex ideas, for example, using images to label their sentences, with a subset of those chosen after prompts from caring device users back to the voice assistant (Khatri et al., 2018). Co-design activities were useful in understanding the accessibility challenges of voice assistants and can be further refined and adapted. Participants who used voice output devices could be involved in designing or testing playful co-design activities. The results will have a broader impact and improve the removal of accessibility barriers (Surendran et al., 2020). With a combination of good NLU and fine-tuning, designers can harness the potential of voice agents to support individuals with and without disabilities.

8. FUTURE DIRECTIONS AND EMERGING TRENDS IN CONVERSATIONAL AI

Several aspects of conversational agents deserve special attention from scientists and practitioners. In this section, we discuss which aspects are and present ongoing trends adopted by the research community and by industrial applications. We also discuss our vision for the field with some recommendations that we take from our experiential and literature review. They are as follows:

(i) Gradual Transition to Deep Reinforcement Learning Conversational agents are programs that achieve dialogue functionalities in a natural language. Research on conversational agents has become a trend with the adoption of neural network techniques, especially those models that use sequential processing to derive representations and generate outputs. In this context, reinforcement learning is also applied to create biological-like learning scenarios with a simple reward system. However, building conversational agents is not easy. Despite their many advantages and promising research results, neural network models are not capable of dealing appropriately with all the challenges posed by conversational agents (Skjuve et al., 2024).

(ii) Use of Attention Mechanisms Performing a task, such as creating a conversational agent and copying ideas from another task that currently receives greater attention from the research community, is a common practice in any scientific field. Having this in mind, we claim that it is possible to improve conversational agents by adopting attention mechanisms. These allow systems to be faster, more concise, and less power-consuming; they provide a more straightforward approach for systems to reason and find the best decisions for the task at hand (Wahde & Virgolin, 2023).

(iii) The Hybrid Approach Will Still Dominate The adoption of the hybrid approach to apply several deep learning models to create a single conversational agent indicates its importance and the need to build more powerful and efficient models for NLP applications. According to our findings, we believe this trend will still dominate in the upcoming years. After all, the architecture proposed by the hybrid models helps overcome many problems commonly encountered when performing sequence-level generation probabilistically. They use a set of skilled models to improve response generation to support the user in the best possible way (Grimes et al., 2021).

(iv) Despite recent success, research in conversational agents is still an unsolved problem and a trending direction of research in machine learning. Other tasks, such as object recognition and language translation, have more advanced techniques and solutions. However, conversational agents are far from employing such advanced playback technologies and features (Lemon, 2022).

8.1. Advancements in Open-Source Conversational AI Frameworks

As we can see in our machine learning algorithm sections, there are many complicated algorithms that design different architecture designs for conversational AI, such as natural language understanding, dialogue management, and response generation. The training process of conversational AI requires a huge amount of annotated dialog data, which has produced recent improvements during the past few years. Many different model designs to train conversational AI have been invented, and we have listed some in this chapter (Raaijmakers et al., 2023). Industries have designed their conversational AI to help real user tasks. Some frameworks are open-sourcing their designs and datasets to attract talent and cooperation, and pretrain models, which greatly help in training better conversational AI by providing a good start for vast logical understanding of language. Besides, there are many different open-source conversational AI frameworks that are designed for some kinds of special tasks. Some focus on the dialogue architecture that enables developers to build their active learning systems, which are used in domain-specific conversational systems (Gao et al., 2019). Some also use different conversational tasks to train domain-specific conversation AI or plugins that the developer can use to build an end-to-end dialog system. Furthermore, many different pretraining techniques, such as using both task-specific and domain-specific data and domain-specific pretraining, such as using distant supervision, using language reinforcement learning, and integrating domain-specific knowledge, are also widely adopted in some special task-oriented systems, and this will require more dialogue business to provide different training signals (Kurian, 2023).

8.2. Conversational AI and the Internet of Things (IoT)

The Internet of Things (IoT) is an extension of the internet to include real-world objects in addition to simply digital data. This makes the internet smarter and more responsive. In an ambient world, these 'real-world' objects don't really need to talk to people all the time – they would rather talk to other things or systems. Occasionally, they need to talk to people, but when they do, we want them to offer the same convenience, seamless access, and near-zero latency that we associate with interactions with other people or systems around us (Shafik, 2024). Despite the long waiting times associated with the average ultra-premium service line, organizations are highly motivated to add telephone or chatbot front-ends to their customer service operations – reducing the cost of customer contacts, giving 24/7 access to services and information, enhancing brand loyalty, and providing the opportunity to upsell or cross-sell other products and services. Since many organizations are already very large users of telephony, they don't have much need to learn about integration, valuable lessons that the IoT can offer perhaps? And also offers valuable lessons on how things can go wrong in terms of gray markets, identity theft, noise pollution, and so on (Shafik, 2023).

8.3. Conversational AI and Edge Computing

The coming decade will see the convergence of two megatrends: edge computing and conversational AI. Conversational AI solutions generally consist of two components: a thin client, often a web customer interface, and the AI server. The server, which processes and runs the conversational model, can operate in cloud servers or on-constraint edge computing devices. Edge computing can duplicate the logic of the AI server on edge devices with benefits such as low latency, increased privacy, and scalability potential. The recent development of tiny AI models provides AI cores attempting to minimize memory, computation, and power (Bunt & Petukhova, 2023). This new generation of AI cores makes it possible to implement edge calculation solutions for complex conversational models. We have briefly analyzed the state of the art regarding conversational AI and edge computing integration, showcased the practical application scenarios, and listed the existing challenges. We believe the field's prospects are promising, and this analysis can benefit domain researchers, developers, and users (Ponnusamy et al., 2021).

8.4. Conversational AI in Smart Cities and Urban Planning

A smart city uses digital technology to collect data, gather insights, and analyze information from connected infrastructures. Sensors are used to detect the status of a city, and relevant information is sent to the database and updated accordingly. One of the key areas applied to smart cities is chatbots. Virtual assistants have been built by a number of smart cities on various chat platforms to interact with citizens, provide information about the city, and necessary service providers. These chatbots do not limit themselves to merely conversing with humans; they also gather input from the user and even guide the user on adopting best practices to schedule certain functions and activities. In successful and robust smart cities, a creative approach has resulted in chatbots being implemented by city councils to support artificial intelligence-led urban planning applications (Chandra et al., 2022). Given that citizens can access the services through chat tools, it is also possible for users to access and interact with these services by using voice commands integrated with chat applications; some top patents are illustrated in Figure 3.

Figure 3. Five vectors of progress in conversational AI (credit: Deloitte)

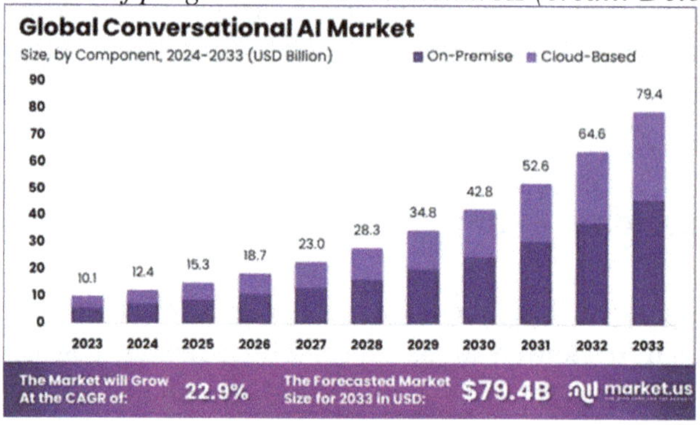

The developed and implemented chatbots have a patterned set of questions that are programmed. The conversational data of the user is captured and stored in the database to channelize the data. Accessibility of this data is very important for urban planning applications, with which intelligent conversations can subsequently keep taking place. The chatbot's continuous presence within the city affords an upstream impression about the concerns and requirements necessary to ensure proactive city maintenance. Real-time data extraction and compilation ensure a streamlined downstream for the planning of new infrastructures (Manic, 2023). Moreover, maintenance and improvement of essential public infrastructures happen over an extended period of time, and city residents do not always have to be aware of the various details associated with the procedures to be followed. An increasing number of new residents are coming in, and many would be unfamiliar with the procedures to be followed. A bot residing in the city chatroom can easily answer these FAQ-type questions. These are based on data the user has already input and are usually answered in real time while having a conversation. Built with the city's geographical information system database, a large number of essential and useful datasets are exchanged through the chatbot, which include city data profiles, city guides, transport schedules, and city maps.

8.5. Conversational AI in Autonomous Vehicles and Transportation Systems

The first fully autonomous vehicles are making their debut, and more will be on the road in the near future. With the ability to drive without any human occupant, congestion and vehicle volumes can be greatly reduced. Driving can become an activity done for relaxation or convenience rather than necessity. Although small family pods are the most prevalent image of autonomous vehicles, many other vehicle types can be fully autonomous or made more intelligent with conversational agents. Think of the machines used in warehouses, agricultural tractors, garbage pickup vehicles, trains, buses, and airline ground vehicles at airports. Many of these rid themselves of the security risk associated with having a human driver. With a reliable and natural user interface, autonomous or semi-autonomous vehicle control technology is made available to potential non-expert users, augmenting accessibility and enabling more innovative business solutions (Shafik, 2023).

An important related issue is providing the content and knowledge needed to respond correctly. Different technologies would be used to develop the vehicle control and interaction abilities, but there would be a need to integrate the user interface into a single, efficient experience, so often this design and implementation would be handled jointly, even if the components are developed separately. The detailed knowledge required to provide excellent automated customer service might be difficult or expensive to obtain for complete storage in the vehicle itself; offline approaches that keep traffic to a central service can be used, consistent with current trends in conventional human-generated support centers (Seminck, 2023). Devices for customer concerns would need to be thoroughly described within the dialogue history, and a switch could be designed to enable a human vehicle support assistant to replace the automated customer support at any time. Devices would be attached that use the details from the dialogue history to review the inappropriate selections made by the automated customer service system, and that engage the entire dialogue model with corrections to prevent such misunderstandings in the future (Sonie et al., 2022).

The customers of autonomous transport services demand breadth, prosperity, and dynamic models of the urban environments and time wordings of such services, so services that use local short-term pricing models and focus on a very advanced design of the vehicles have a clear market advantage. The disadvantages involved with deploying full-service automotive agents are complemented with services in which intelligent vehicles are interacting with human passengers who are uncertain, maybe frightened, about what the vehicle is doing, and in which communication about future actions or the hidden features of vehicles will lead to an enhanced passenger experience. Creating a conversational agent to mitigate these concerns would include executing an emphasis on the safety, availability, and convenience of the vehicles, as well as on the vehicle usage of resources to ensure a very positive vehicle experience (Chandra et al., 2022; Kandoi et al., 2024). Human factors and perception research are very important in constructing this type of agent.

8.6. Conversational AI in Entertainment and Gaming

Entertainment and gaming are areas in which conversational AI can have a powerful impact, and many companies are developing or leveraging conversational AI to enter into this space. In traditional media, the entry of conversational AI encompasses both front-end and back-end operations. Examples of front-end production implementations, such as automated voicetag insertion, news articles, and weather forecasts, can be found in various media outlets. In terms of back-end production uses that have been developed and implemented, here are a few examples: dynamic modification of external audio based on the user's GPS location, location-based noise cancellation in loud environments, and frequency-specific audio controls (Wahde & Virgolin, 2023). An audio automation company uses conversational AI in post-production editing for video game music to remove dialogue and cell phone interference and to restore lost frequencies. In the consumer product space, conversational AI can also be used as a powerful marketing and information distribution tool. One company is working on the development of a proactive assistant aimed at capturing customer intent and providing recommendations based on their emotions, locations, and the device they are using. A mobile app assistant is designed to improve the park experience for patrons. Interactions include delivering food to customers' locations, talking character walls that display a character's mood and theme song, and highlighting attractions and ride information (Varitimiadis et al., 2021).

Several companies are taking conversational AI and using it to develop entertainment and gaming-specific products. One domain in which conversational AI can have a truly profound impact is in how we actually play a game. There are multiple companies that specialize in developing conversational AI for games. Roughly one-third of one company's work is developing gaming interfaces, while the other two-thirds is working in clinical therapy. In the reverse scenario, gaming is also having a great impact on the development of conversational artificial intelligence. The goal of competitive play has long been a strategy for advancing a narrower intelligence, often in the form of expert knowledge about a domain (Ng, 2024; Raaijmakers et al., 2023). The development of algorithms to challenge human play in a variety of different tasks, not merely solving a particular game, has been well incentivized by the potential of huge esports prize pools currently found within different fields.

8.7. Conversational AI in Virtual and Augmented Reality

Virtual Immersion With AR and VR The concept of virtual immersion, in which one is deeply embedded in a virtual world with the accompanying substitution of sensory input, is a vision that has captivated many technologists. A picture is often drawn from science fiction of humans having integrated experiences, but overcoming their biological limitations. This vision has evolved into several concepts of in-situ reality, from mixed reality to augmented reality and virtual reality. With AR, users see a blend of the digital and real world (Gao et al., 2018). The first and best-known example of AR could be a heads-up display in fighter jets that combines the aircraft's instruments and the visual field. Augmented reality has become popular with mobile devices thanks to their cameras, sensors, and connectivity. Standing over some landmark in the street or looking at a painting in a museum, users can point a mobile device to receive added information relating to that place. Handheld devices have now also caused AR concepts to integrate digital objects into the real world, overlaying one with the other (Chatterjee & Dethlefs, 2023).

Upon a superior technical foundation, it now adds layers, embellishments, or next-generation gaming where the lines between the real and digital worlds blur on a mobile device. A more extreme immersive experience is provided by VR, where the user's digital world completely replaces the real world. Headsets and input systems have evolved to give users the impression of stepping into a virtual environment, allowing them to look and move in a 3D digital world. These headsets arose stoutly in the gaming domain, although content is now being produced for secondary domains. Mobile technology improvements have reached the classic tethering of high-performance headgear to immobile machinery and expanded VR to portable devices (Ray, 2023). Personal computers maintain a leading role in these virtual environment embodiments.

The Opportunities of More Holistic Conversational Experiences People live and communicate in a 3D world, but today's conversations mediated by technology do not fully exploit the possibilities that technology offers to present a coherent experience using that format. Eye contact, facial orientation, and expressions are used in human communication. People's conversations rely on the observation of the eyes or on patterns of speech decay to supervise them, capturing issues such as whether someone understands or agrees within seconds (Adewumi et al., 2022). Creating a natural conversational interface on a computer then means leaving many of the characteristics of face-to-face communication behind. The alternatives vary greatly from using no interlocutor on the computer to using 2D or 3D customized avatars within the context of a single camera. Companies that have increased gains demand for AR and VR opportunities to find that VR and AR help create large-volume, workable, persistent, content-generating forms of immersive 3D communications between individuals in virtual work environments. In person or through VR, virtual features also help introduce architects and interior designers to a better understanding of space (Baabdullah, 2024). Answering questions about their virtual experience allows customers to explore the concept and potential of surrounding VR.

9. CONVERSATIONAL AI FOR KNOWLEDGE MANAGEMENT AND INFORMATION RETRIEVAL

Over the past few years, conversational AI has become abundant, especially in the form of chatbots. While there are already many other ways of solving a problem and settling a task via voice interfaces, there are numerous use cases that are not well suited for using voice assistants, such as information overload, bad device acoustics, and information privacy. Many of the successful systems of the early years, however, have been one-stage systems: in order to solve a task via one of these systems, the user had to keep a lot of context in her mind about what she was just doing when entering a query (Seminck, 2023). Usually, she would not ask multiple facets of the same problem, as she would likely be cut off when trying to return a bit later to have the chatbot just ask follow-up questions on the answers she gave. The common attributes of these chatbots are that they track the user's state and they usually perform some form of goal-oriented dialogue. They ask questions to gather missing information, and once those are collected, they execute a task, usually a database query. While two-stage systems are more complex to build and daisy-chaining goal-oriented dialogue is more complex for the user as a task may need multiple sessions to be solved, they are much better positioned to support us in knowledge database query transactions and probing different facets in order to satisfy curiosity (Chandra et al., 2022). Nonetheless, beyond single-shot and slot filling and online transactions, another relevant category of tasks is know-how sharing and conversational knowledge base editing or crowdsourcing.

9.1. Conversational AI for Decision Support and Expert Systems

Not all websites need to deliver conversational AI applications. A database also allows for fast delivery of answers by executing queries on stored data. A search backend for a postal IoT solution, timetables for public transport, or prices and availability of hotel rooms require a smart backend system to generate finite-state-machine-like answers to conversations. These systems enrich web traffic by allowing conversations between customers and the website (Suh & An, 2022). Additionally, cost reduction in customer care centers is a strong driver for using AI technology based on big datasets. Product recommendations can also be steered by a flexible and smart backend system for commercial reasons. If the services of experts can be pushed to the front end, expert support can be delivered via a website or chat messenger. This allows a company to easily build a functional front end to deliver expert advice with a system that can be used by business owners around the world in their various areas of expertise (Leschanowsky et al., 2023). These different types of websites can benefit from the trend of embedding conversational intelligence in their backends to support expansion, streamline work, and appeal more to their clients.

9.2. Conversational AI for Personalization and User Experience Enhancement

In recent years, creating great user experiences based on the use of conversational interfaces, as well as personalizing the interaction with users, is gaining increasing attention. User interfaces based on natural language enable any user to directly interact with some service, system, device, or other application, such as collecting information on a topic, performing searches, making appointments, solving problems, exchanging messages, reordering or purchasing products, sending notices, voicing opinions, executing other actions and commands, and having conversations in natural language (So et al., 2023). It is clear that user experience, personalization, and interaction improvements can benefit the psychological, emotional, and cognitive bonding between the system and the person, offering convincing and credible conversations that lead to more engaging relationships and enhance user satisfaction, trust, and retention, and other results in different application domains such as e-shopping, e-learning, tutoring, clinical therapy, and serious gaming (Raaijmakers et al., 2023). Currently, one overarching issue is concerned not so much with the actual realization of conversational agents, but with their use in specific application domains. The latter problem is not just a technical one related to technological developments, but instead focuses on design and realization issues inherent to the use of conversational agents that are also critical to the success of the solution. Furthermore, these problems are typically concerned with specific domains or applications, as well as possibly with specific categories of users, e.g., children, elderly people, students, physically impaired users, tourist visitors, employees (da Silva et al., 2021).

9.3. Conversational AI in Crisis Communication and Disaster Response

Given the increasing severity and frequency of natural disasters, the large inflow of refugees, the increased social polarization, and the spread of rumors that might arise in a crisis situation are defined crises for which information is an essential resource. People in crisis communication and disaster response situations need information for both immediate community recovery and future crisis preparedness and management actions. Simple and effective communication and information access are the bases for an individual's or community's resilience to disasters. Be it the floods, outbreaks, earthquakes, bombings, or the annual flu season, relevant information is more vital in the face of an acute crisis (Chatterjee & Dethlefs, 2023). Being able to detect and respond to spikes in information requests via instant messaging apps can be an important step towards ensuring that members of the public get timely and authoritative information about a crisis as part of an organization's responsibility to protect and inform the public. People also turn to search engines, including enterprise search systems, such as chat services, to access predictive analytics, big data, natural language, or question answering systems to identify misinformation (Baabdullah, 2024).

Additionally, naturalistic studies of first responders suggest that effective bilingual communication tools can expedite translation tasks in life-saving missions, securing the safety of many lives at risk. In the face of crisis, organizations are in a race to adapt and develop appropriate communication strategies for their specific users and use cases. Although many organizations are aware of the value of using instant messaging for their crisis communication, there is no universal remedy for how to ensure that strong communication can be accomplished in a variety of complex systems. Some guidelines recommend using automated conversational agents, i.e., bots, as one effective way to offer immediate responses to user requests for information in crisis situations (Saka et al., 2023). Bots are proposed and used for needs such as answering questions, helping with translation, reassuring users that relief is coming, sharing instructions, addressing concerns, or offering real-time crisis updates.

Despite their controversial use in open-domain conversations, some researchers have suggested using social bots or other human-computational systems for hosting ongoing conversations during crises. Reducing attackers' opportunity to create a new social disorder, however, is a common practice using automated systems to recognize and treat misinformation and prevent rumor spread during crises. If they reach enough users, these bots could incorporate information in order to divert followers who may be exposed to misinformation (Adewumi et al., 2022). Efforts to evaluate the usefulness of these and other human-computational tools have scaled up social media to stay in touch with people in the face of ongoing, dynamic, and developing crises. Some related initiatives have sought to use bots to disseminate relevant information to people who wish to monitor the situation. In summary, conversational AI will play a crucial role in the field of disaster science and management in the near future, particularly in the advancement of systems for different languages, applications, and situations. In particular, recent trends in the conversational AI community, including the construction of large pre-trained language models and engagement with delicate, sensitive, and nuanced dialogue responses, will be useful to enhance the quality of these current sociotechnical systems and services by helping systems deal with additional challenges and implement novel features (Fuad & Al-Yahya, 2022).

9.4. Conversational AI in Law Enforcement and Security

The use of conversational AI technology is starting to grow in the field of law enforcement and associated data forensic fields. Conversational AI use includes virtual assistants for officers and other staff, but people in custody or visiting police stations are also an important target audience. Digital avatars that can understand and respond to natural language are also attracting interest, for example, for use in police station front offices. When deployed in front-office roles, digital avatars can help reduce wait times for appointments and can support crime reporting, intelligence logging, and front-desk activities (Gao et al., 2018). They can also be used to deliver pre-arrest legal advice and information that is general in nature concerning police procedures. Users can interact with these avatars using speech or keyboard enabled devices. The use of speech increases accessibility and is expected to support higher usage among users who are not familiar with computers or with written English. Such users are typically understood to be from a wide range of backgrounds, with varying levels of education and English proficiency (Gkinko & Elbanna, 2023a). These users have equal rights to privacy, receive fair and frequent processes, and have equal access to service from the police.

9.5. Conversational AI in Environmental Monitoring and Conservation

It is also anticipated that CAI will be used tactically as mobile and portable tools for animal monitoring and conversations that are particularly useful for surveillance during the night, in difficult terrains, or in dense vegetation. Moreover, these animal, sound, and pharmaceutical-related tactics could be utilized in ports and at border crossings to monitor the illegal trade of animals and animal products. Another major application is the use of CAI employed in language understanding on social networking or news websites within the model. The knowledge of human tolerance for wildlife species will support ecological studies and contribute to the decisions of policymakers. Legal issues for the protection of certain species might be the result, for example, the prevention of wildlife tourism promotion, hunting bans, or even risks associated with carrying out resource management strategies to stop conflicts between men and elephants. Moreover, the use of eco-acoustic data for auditory detection and linguistic interpretation of activities happening in a specific geographical environment is open for the analysis of complex interactions of acoustic environments. Finally, CAI instruments that will allow us to set sustainable development indicators could protect the vulnerable human-animal interactions that have survived in the fields of indigenous knowledge (Shafik, 2023). This would help to improve cultural understanding and values for the quality and conservation of the environment.

9.6. Conversational AI in Agriculture and Food Security

Agriculture is the primary source of livelihood for many people, but farmers face several challenges ranging from understanding changing weather patterns to knowing the market conditions for their crops. Keeping these issues in mind, intelligent agents can be designed and deployed in agricultural information systems. Specifically, conversational AI holds promise in enhancing accessibility to useful knowledge sources and providing real-time assistance. These aspiring agents can answer queries from users who do not have expertise in interacting with the traditionally used command-based tools or plain text. Furthermore, with conversational AI, users can interact with systems as if they are talking to domain experts who understand information requests in their natural language (Shafik, 2024). Modern agricultural chatbot technologies can leverage computer vision, deep learning, and large-scale datasets. A large dataset of discussions can be prepared to enable the training of deep learning models to answer diverse questions. Additionally, a small but diverse dataset of images can be used to build a crop identification model for a region, which the agents can leverage to answer queries pertaining to crop and region-specific characteristics. While building an agriculture chatbot using AI and ML, considering ethical issues is also very important (Shafik, 2024). Currently, the problem of building AI chatbots for agriculture is heavily under-addressed, but with modern trends, we are optimistic about the wide adoption of conversational AI in the agricultural domain, depending on the data quality as presented in Figure 4.

Figure 4. Data Quality

9.7. Conversational AI in Energy and Resource Management

Energy and resource management benefit significantly from the conversational AI field. With a large percentage of the population speaking English and the influence of industry standards established with international companies and locations, language models developed for these conversations can be more transferable than language models created for many other nations and languages with smaller user bases, thus providing value to those that support such worldwide or mobile populations. When associated with elements of the Internet of Things, such as energy consumption profiles of various devices, it reduces human stress on tiresome tasks such as dimming lights during the day or changing the temperature setting of the air conditioning system at different times while reflecting the user's personal habits and preferences for managing the electric bill. It can help predict usage patterns, detect waste and device failure, control interaction, and thus help modify energy usage profiles and improve overall system sustainability (Wang et al., 2023). For families with electric cars, especially when electric cars represent most of their daily travel, or when they have solar panels installed, the smart home conversational AI system manages the charging profile of the electric car in such a way as to implement vehicle-to-grid storage requirements and maintain the best installation of vehicles for the grid. It can also help manage daily charging loads to determine the most practical time for charging in the house, in the charging station, or in the office based on occupancy hours (Shafik, 2023). Technological advancements shaping conversational AI, highlighting both its potential benefits and ongoing challenges, are presented in Table 2.

Table 2. Technological Advancements in Conversational AI

Advancement	Description	Technologies Involved	Benefits	Challenges	Reference
Deep Learning for NLP	Using deep neural networks to enhance understanding of language	Deep learning, neural networks, NLP	More accurate language understanding, context-aware conversations	High computational cost, data requirements	(Gkinko & Elbanna, 2023b)
Pre-trained Language Models	Large AI models trained on diverse datasets for more efficient conversation	GPT, BERT, Transformer models	Faster deployment, more coherent and relevant responses	Maintaining model quality, handling diverse languages	(Miner et al., 2019)
Contextual Understanding	AI systems understanding context and nuances in conversations	NLP, machine learning, deep learning	Smarter AI responses, personalized conversations	Handling ambiguity and complex user inputs	(Adewumi et al., 2022)
Cross-Lingual AI	AI systems capable of conversing in multiple languages	Multilingual models, translation models, NLP	Global accessibility, improving AI interactions across languages	Maintaining high accuracy in translation and context retention	(Tschopp et al., 2023)
Voice Synthesis	AI generating natural-sounding speech from text	Text-to-speech (TTS), neural networks	More realistic and engaging conversations	Achieving a fully natural tone, accent variation	(Saka et al., 2023)
Conversational AI in Healthcare	AI assistants used for health advice, scheduling, and patient interaction	NLP, medical knowledge graphs, voice assistants	Enhanced patient care, personalized health interactions	Ensuring accuracy, privacy concerns	(Ji et al., 2023)
AI in Virtual Assistants	Personal assistant AI that manages schedules, tasks, and smart devices	NLP, cloud computing, machine learning	Streamlined tasks, increased productivity	Misunderstandings, privacy concerns	(Ray, 2023)

continued on following page

Table 2. Continued

Advancement	Description	Technologies Involved	Benefits	Challenges	Reference
Sentiment and Intent Analysis	Analyzing emotions and user intentions in conversations	Sentiment analysis, emotion recognition	Tailored responses, improved customer experience	Ethical concerns, dealing with subtle emotions	(Passanante et al., 2023)
AI for Accessibility	AI tools improving access for individuals with disabilities	Voice recognition, speech-to-text, screen readers	More inclusive access to technology, equal opportunities	Ensuring accessibility for all disabilities	(Gkinko & Elbanna, 2023a)
Real-Time Translation	Instant translation in conversations across different languages	NLP, machine translation, AI-based interpreters	Breaking language barriers, real-time global communication	Ensuring accurate translations, context preservation	(Chattcrjee & Dethlefs, 2023)

10. DIVERSE APPLICATION OF CONVERSATIONAL ARTIFICIAL INTELLIGENCE

Text-based conversational agents offer a scalable, cost-effective solution that is accessible to all individuals. Kcy challenges for next-generation conversational agents in mental health and well-being include broad-spectrum support in real-world emotional states and mental disorders; the engineering and natural language understanding of longitudinal long-term conversations; and ethical implementation of such technology, from informed consent procedures to responsible data personalization of conversational partners (Gkinko & Elbanna, 2023a). Finally, privacy and data protection remain significant unresolved challenges for the implementation of conversational AI in mental health and well-being. In specific demanding cases, some tools can convincingly take translation to the next level, as some examples are illustrated in Figure 5.

Figure 5. The future of conversational Artificial Intelligence (End-to-personalization of conversational agents) (Deloitte)

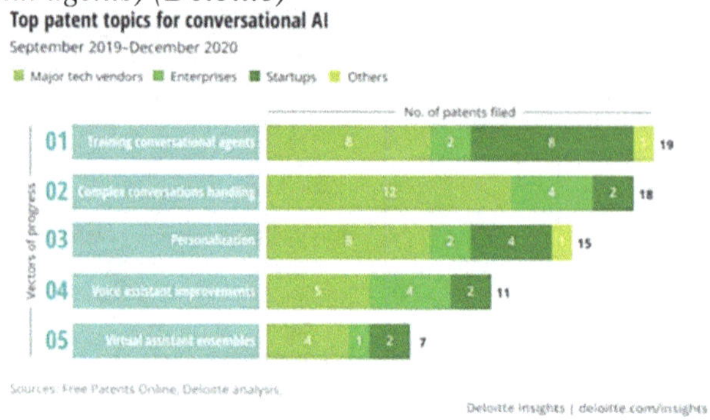

10.1. Conversational AI in Space Exploration and Aerospace

Outer space is a perfect example of a setting where fluid conversational interaction capabilities would have extraordinary value. Indeed, significant steps have already been taken in this direction, and we can learn from this experience. At present, key research challenges in this field involve dealing with noisy low-bandwidth communication channels. In the future, advances in machine learning that enable small data generalization and semi-supervised learning will facilitate dealing with out-of-domain and unanticipated queries. At present, we have had some discussions as to whether it would be possible to use conversational software to carry out astronomical observations (Ponnusamy et al., 2021). While there is interest in this exploration, it is not a current focus area due to the high technical barrier of training general models to function at the level of expertise needed for interpretive work, combined with the long payoff timeline of applying this technology in space exploration and aerospace. Furthermore, in traditional observational astronomy, much about the scientific process is highly scripted, which means that automating the systems during data reduction and alert processing phases of data generation could be done with high reliability. For astronomy projects with agents that can collaborate with human researchers, the agents would be trained outside the domain on datasets that capture the content of the grammatical forms and discourse constructions used by researchers during data reduction and event notification (Skjuve et al., 2024). The result would be systems that know how to interact with the humans and the software in the environment, allowing human research staff to focus on their data while the software supports them in a routine, instructive manner.

10.2. Conversational AI in Scientific Research and Data Analysis

Conversational AI is opening up many opportunities for research in various domains, from allowing complex scientific equipment to be operated simply through voice commands to learning through conversation. By enabling people to use complex software tools through natural conversation, many new possibilities are opened up, such as real-time collaboration through the easy sharing of data, immediate insights, and the ability to naturally ask and answer questions with peers or analytical systems (Leschanowsky et al., 2023). Whether these conversations are between two people or with an AI system or chatbot, it opens up many possibilities for enhancing education, learning through interaction, and personalized support and training systems. Enabling scientific instruments to be operated or guiding manufacturers, field technicians, and support staff to resolve problems in real-time through AI-powered voice-enabled conversations will provide significant increases in productivity and speed of response, as well as providing current on-the-job training and decision support (Varitimiadis et al., 2021).

Likewise, being able to understand the sentiment of a support call or bug report and provide context and additional information can have a significant impact on resolving, understanding, and prioritizing issues, allowing support staff to scale to the increasing number of users. Being able to capture the co-creation information process, express thoughts and ideas as they arise, adapt the process to the user, and initiate incoming conversations is critical for successful interactions (Gao et al., 2018). The idea of injecting an AI expert into a chat session to answer questions and guide interaction to the most informed consultants or systems, and then extract and store the information from those conversations, is also an important aspect. Since conversational problems can grow and are best addressed incrementally and interactively, largely taking the form of specification problems, the ability to use conversational AI to iteratively collaborate and explore problems and solutions, understand differences, and help users understand complexity in a clear and non-technical way is important (Alabed et al., 2024).

10.3. Conversational AI in Sports Analytics and Performance Optimization

Stakeholders in sports apparel, fashion, sportswear retailers, and sports brands understand the importance of acquiring and analyzing data on user behavior regarding their sportswear products to optimize the design, manufacturing, and marketing processes for improved user satisfaction and superior product performance. To support these stakeholders, we propose and develop a conversational AI system capable of understanding natural language questions and discussion data related to user behavior and sports apparel usage. In this chapter, we present and introduce the main elements of the conversational AI system specifically developed to support a worldwide platform (So et al., 2023). We demonstrate the system's development process, describe its functional components, and discuss its capability to understand and respond to both structured and unstructured data relevant to stakeholders. Finally, we present our progress and future directions of our efforts. The system interactions are designed to answer queries related to sports activities and sports apparel. Some annotated labeled data consist of examples shown in the form of question topics and more in-depth fundamental questions, as well as design details about question answering. The design details help illustrate certain behaviors regarding potential relevant questions and what information the system would need to answer them. The question topics are a mix of sports and behavior information, with relevant information highlighted using formal markup (Ng, 2024). The design details section is mainly a text description, with some non-troubling markup that highlights intended behaviors.

10.4. Conversational AI in Art and Creativity

Conversational Artificial Intelligence has been used as one of the core elements in creative cultural applications. Pepper, with its advanced physical capacities and the newly acquired capabilities to understand and communicate, was the first worldwide exhibit in this field. In particular, the use of educational applications, especially targeted at kids as a support of cultural growth, has opened a market that is now constantly increasing, especially in countries with aging populations such as Italy and Germany (Hu et al., 2021). The first application in the high educational applications field has been a prototype developed for the United Nations with the aim of transforming an accredited online distance learning MBA into an inherently more substantial and rewarding educational experience—that of being at a lecture in a prestigious environment. This AI was the first to understand not only the requests for information related to university curricula and teaching staff but also to be involved in the transfer of the cultural carryover, which is the real high added value that the student takes along in their career (Alabed et al., 2024). Two other projects involving non-sentient AIs, such as Pepper, include the involvement of a private coeducational international baccalaureate school located on the Upper East Side of New York City. The mission of the school particularly emphasizes the development of the all-round individual through personalization and focusing on the love of learning. While exorbitant amounts of money are applied in this mission, a simpler AI-driven support for the diversification and personalization of the teaching process, focusing on precision teaching and mastery learning, could bring significant advantages to the students because they are both collaborative and co-creative throughout the entire learning cycle (Baabdullah, 2024).

10.5. Conversational AI in Language Learning and Translation

Due to the global rise of artificial intelligence and its increasing adoption by large companies, the English language is essentially becoming the world's second language. With chat-based conversational AI as the emerging vehicle, multiple courses can be delivered at a global scale without limitation. Advice and evaluations are immediate and cost-effective; different methodologies can be effortlessly applied, and the adaptation into and replacement of commercial language training applications on the mobile platform is substantial. New distinguishing learning algorithms based on the emerging conversational AI are significantly advocated (Raaijmakers et al., 2023). Language translation is a vital tool, as projected in Figure 6. While interpreting invented languages known as coded languages associated with secret organizations is essential to national security, instant digital translation between multiple languages would reduce the workload on human translators and interpreters by a large margin . Instant automatic translation is especially crucial in crises such as accidents and marriage ceremonies. Currently, three leading organizations are developing the simplest conversational language translation tool. Other AI-associated language tools include captioning photos and expressive chatbots. Most language translation tools merely translate single words, not complete sentences, due to variation in context (Chandrakala et al., 2024).

Figure 6. Conversational AI Market Size, Statistics (Markets)

10.6. Conversational AI in Social Media and Online Communities

Social media and online communities bring together people with shared interests and goals, forming a highly appealing and effective platform for enterprises, organizations, and community members. Conversational artificial intelligence is rapidly becoming an enabler to enhance social media and online communities (Shafik, 2024). While a single post, discussion, or group of people among thousands of messages and users can be hard to understand and handle, the conversational artificial intelligence capability can intelligently help in classifying the type of interactions, understanding the intent, and suggesting intelligent responses and actions to help moderate the community or make the experience better for the users of the community. Define state-of-the-art social media pages based on the requirements and goals of the community (Shafik, 2023). Provide a list of common knowledge elements, named entities, concepts, and features useful for analyzing social media and online communities. This list can be used as the input for dimensionality reduction of conversational artificial intelligence data sets related to social media pages. Define social media incidents to train conversational artificial intelligence classifiers and incident detection systems. Examples for social media platforms are presented. Use a typical definition of social media pages, such as a group, a public stature, a fan page, a corporate page, etc., and create standard pages for social media incident detection (Ponnusamy et al., 2021).

10.7. Conclusion

In this chapter, we looked at key trends in conversational AI and how these are enabling rich, dialog-based relationships between organizations and their employees. We will unpack the different layers of the conversational AI technology stack and explain how these systems can convert simple, transaction-based messages into rich, dialog-based interactions that have the power to shape organizational culture. We will explain the lifecycle of a conversational AI service, showing how building, deploying, and improving a virtual agent is very different from building, deploying, and improving traditional machine learning pipelines. We will introduce a five-layer model of requirements for conversational AI systems, integrating insights from conversational theory, data science, business processing, conversation content structure, and software development engineering processes. There is a huge opportunity to rethink the way we work, make work more scalable, and remove many of the simple, repetitive tasks that make jobs mundane and distraction-prone. As the 21st century progresses, we stand at a point where we have the necessary technologies to set work processes free from the constraints imposed by paper, geographical location, business size, physical infrastructure, and simple repetitive tasks. The key technology upgrade that we are seeing is that after decades of being event and rule driven, with humans fitting around the system, the technology is now becoming human-friendly, with systems that are communication-centric raising the technology to connect to, understand, and respond to humans anywhere. These communication-centric systems also thrive on the variety and volume of interactions; i.e., the bigger the data, the better the system. Conversational Artificial Intelligence (CAI) is having a transformative impact. This research develops the Conversational AI Diversity and Inclusion (CAIDI) framework, a grand challenge research agenda encompassing the risks, opportunities, and strategies involved in creating and incorporating CAI systems that can effectively converse with anyone, regardless of who they are or where they are from and creates a Principled Design and Development Checklist. By providing diverse scenarios and research questions across the stack, the research helps to ensure that the risks involved with potential adverse consequences from the design and use of Conversational Artificial Intelligence are explored and mitigated in collaboration with a broad coalition of researchers. As CAI technology is operationalized, the research can help us to understand how the technology developed maps onto the datasets that were used, predict potential risk scenarios, and encourage striving for higher performance on the interpretability of demographic disparity metrics. As governance emerges, the questions can serve as a basis for regulatory tests or considerations when companies that are focused on or are using CAI technologies are overseen or incentivize companies themselves to align their influence with the best interest of the users.

REFERENCES

Adewumi, T., Liwicki, F., & Liwicki, M. (2022). State-of-the-Art in Open-Domain Conversational AI: A Survey. *Information (Basel), 13*(6), 298. Advance online publication. DOI: 10.3390/info13060298

Alabed, A., Javornik, A., Gregory-Smith, D., & Casey, R. (2024). More than just a chat: A taxonomy of consumers' relationships with conversational AI agents and their well-being implications. *European Journal of Marketing, 58*(2), 373–409. Advance online publication. DOI: 10.1108/EJM-01-2023-0037

Baabdullah, A. M. (2024). Generative conversational AI agent for managerial practices: The role of IQ dimensions, novelty seeking and ethical concerns. *Technological Forecasting and Social Change, 198*, 122951. Advance online publication. DOI: 10.1016/j.techfore.2023.122951

Blümel, J. H., Zaki, M., & Bohné, T. (2024). Personal touch in digital customer service: A conceptual framework of relational personalization for conversational AI. *Journal of Service Theory and Practice, 34*(1), 33–65. Advance online publication. DOI: 10.1108/JSTP-03-2023-0098

Bunt, H., & Petukhova, V. (2023). Semantic and pragmatic precision in conversational AI systems. *Frontiers in Artificial Intelligence, 6*, 896729. Advance online publication. DOI: 10.3389/frai.2023.896729 PMID: 37064296

Chandra, S., Shirish, A., & Srivastava, S. C. (2022). To Be or Not to Be ...Human? Theorizing the Role of Human-Like Competencies in Conversational Artificial Intelligence Agents. *Journal of Management Information Systems, 39*(4), 969–1005. Advance online publication. DOI: 10.1080/07421222.2022.2127441

Chandrakala, C. B., Bhardwaj, R., & Pujari, C. (2024). An intent recognition pipeline for conversational AI. *International Journal of Information Technology : an Official Journal of Bharati Vidyapeeth's Institute of Computer Applications and Management, 16*(2), 731–743. Advance online publication. DOI: 10.1007/s41870-023-01642-8

Chatterjee, J., & Dethlefs, N. (2023). This new conversational AI model can be your friend, philosopher, and guide. and even your worst enemy. In *Patterns* (Vol. 4, Issue 1). DOI: 10.1016/j.patter.2022.100676

da Silva, D. A., Louro, H. D. B., Goncalves, G. S., Marques, J. C., Dias, L. A. V., da Cunha, A. M., & Tasinaffo, P. M. (2021). Could a conversational ai identify offensive language?†. *Information (Basel), 12*(10), 418. Advance online publication. DOI: 10.3390/info12100418

Fu, T., Gao, S., Zhao, X., Wen, J. rong, & Yan, R. (2022). Learning towards conversational AI: A survey. *AI Open, 3*. DOI: 10.1016/j.aiopen.2022.02.001

Fuad, A., & Al-Yahya, M. (2022). Recent Developments in Arabic Conversational AI: A Literature Review. In *IEEE Access* (Vol. 10). DOI: 10.1109/ACCESS.2022.3155521

Gao, J., Galley, M., & Li, L. (2018). Neural approaches to conversational AI. *ACL 2018 - 56th Annual Meeting of the Association for Computational Linguistics, Proceedings of the Conference Tutorial Abstracts*. DOI: 10.18653/v1/P18-5002

Gao, J., Galley, M., & Li, L. (2019). Neural approaches to conversational AI. *Foundations and Trends in Information Retrieval, 13*(2–3), 127–298. Advance online publication. DOI: 10.1561/1500000074

Gkinko, L., & Elbanna, A. (2023a). Designing trust: The formation of employees' trust in conversational AI in the digital workplace. *Journal of Business Research, 158*, 113707. Advance online publication. DOI: 10.1016/j.jbusres.2023.113707

Gkinko, L., & Elbanna, A. (2023b). The appropriation of conversational AI in the workplace: A taxonomy of AI chatbot users. *International Journal of Information Management, 69*, 102568. Advance online publication. DOI: 10.1016/j.ijinfomgt.2022.102568

Grimes, G. M., Schuetzler, R. M., & Giboney, J. S. (2021). Mental models and expectation violations in conversational AI interactions. *Decision Support Systems, 144*, 113515. Advance online publication. DOI: 10.1016/j.dss.2021.113515

Hassija, V., Chakrabarti, A., Singh, A., Chamola, V., & Sikdar, B. (2023). Unleashing the Potential of Conversational AI: Amplifying Chat-GPT's Capabilities and Tackling Technical Hurdles. *IEEE Access : Practical Innovations, Open Solutions, 11*, 143657–143682. Advance online publication. DOI: 10.1109/ACCESS.2023.3339553

Hsu, T. C., Abelson, H., & Van Brummelen, J. (2022). The Effects on Secondary School Students of Applying Experiential Learning to the Conversational AI Learning Curriculum. *International Review of Research in Open and Distance Learning, 23*(1), 82–103. Advance online publication. DOI: 10.19173/irrodl.v22i4.5474

Hu, P., Lu, Y., & Gong, Y. (2021). Dual humanness and trust in conversational AI: A person-centered approach. *Computers in Human Behavior, 119*, 106727. Advance online publication. DOI: 10.1016/j.chb.2021.106727

Ji, H., Han, I., & Ko, Y. (2023). A systematic review of conversational AI in language education: focusing on the collaboration with human teachers. In *Journal of Research on Technology in Education* (Vol. 55, Issue 1). DOI: 10.1080/15391523.2022.2142873

Kandoi, R., Dixit, D., Tyagi, M., & Yadav, R. S. (2024). Conversational AI. *International Journal for Research in Applied Science and Engineering Technology*, *12*(3), 769–775. Advance online publication. DOI: 10.22214/ijraset.2024.58787

Khatri, C., Venkatesh, A., Hedayatnia, B., Ram, A., Gabriel, R., & Prasad, R. (2018). Alexa prize-state of the art in conversational AI. *AI Magazine*, *39*(3), 40–55. Advance online publication. DOI: 10.1609/aimag.v39i3.2810

Kiwanuka, F., & Shafik, W. (2025). Nursing as a Lingua Franca for Artificial Intelligence in Patients' Care Trajectories: Where Are We Headed? *Nursing Research*, *74*(3), 170. DOI: 10.1097/NNR.0000000000000799 PMID: 40266973

Kurian, N. (2023). AI's empathy gap: The risks of conversational Artificial Intelligence for young children's well-being and key ethical considerations for early childhood education and care. *Contemporary Issues in Early Childhood*. Advance online publication. DOI: 10.1177/14639491231206004

Lemon, O. (2022). Conversational AI for multi-agent communication in Natural Language. *AI Communications*, *35*(4), 295–308. Advance online publication. DOI: 10.3233/AIC-220147

Leschanowsky, A., Popp, B., & Peters, N. (2023). Debiasing Strategies for Conversational AI: Improving Privacy and Security Decision-Making. *Digital Society : Ethics, Socio-Legal and Governance of Digital Technology*, *2*(3), 34. Advance online publication. DOI: 10.1007/s44206-023-00062-2

Manic, M. (2023). An Impact Analysis of Conversational AI on Marketing Processes. *Bulletin of the Transilvania University of Brasov. Series V, Economic Sciences*, 23–28. Advance online publication. DOI: 10.31926/but.es.2023.16.65.1.3

Miner, A. S., Shah, N., Bullock, K. D., Arnow, B. A., Bailenson, J., & Hancock, J. (2019). Key Considerations for Incorporating Conversational AI in Psychotherapy. *Frontiers in Psychiatry*, *10*, 746. Advance online publication. DOI: 10.3389/fpsyt.2019.00746 PMID: 31681047

Ng, Y. L. (2024). Exploring the association between use of conversational artificial intelligence and social capital: Survey evidence from Hong Kong. *New Media & Society*, *26*(3), 1429–1444. Advance online publication. DOI: 10.1177/14614448221074047

Passanante, A., Pertwee, E., Lin, L., Lee, K. Y., Wu, J. T., & Larson, H. J. (2023). Conversational AI and Vaccine Communication: Systematic Review of the Evidence. In *Journal of Medical Internet Research* (Vol. 25, Issue 1). DOI: 10.2196/42758

Ponnusamy, P., Ghias, A. R., Yi, Y., Yao, B., Guo, C., & Sarikaya, R. (2021). Feedback-based self-learning in large-scale conversational AI agents. *AI Magazine*, *42*(4), 43–56. Advance online publication. DOI: 10.1609/aaai.12025

Raaijmakers, S., Cremers, A., Krahmer, E., & Westera, M. (2023). Editorial: Conversational AI. In *Frontiers in Artificial Intelligence* (Vol. 6). DOI: 10.3389/frai.2023.1203910

Ray, P. P. (2023). Benchmarking, ethical alignment, and evaluation framework for conversational AI: Advancing responsible development of ChatGPT. *BenchCouncil Transactions on Benchmarks. Standards and Evaluations*, *3*(3), 100136. Advance online publication. DOI: 10.1016/j.tbench.2023.100136

Saka, A. B., Oyedele, L. O., Akanbi, L. A., Ganiyu, S. A., Chan, D. W. M., & Bello, S. A. (2023). Conversational artificial intelligence in the AEC industry: A review of present status, challenges and opportunities. In *Advanced Engineering Informatics* (Vol. 55). DOI: 10.1016/j.aei.2022.101869

Seminck, O. (2023). Conversational AI: Dialogue Systems, Conversational Agents, and Chatbots by Michael McTear. *Computational Linguistics*, *49*(1), 257–259. Advance online publication. DOI: 10.1162/coli_r_00470

Shafik, W. (2023). Introduction to ChatGPT. In *Advanced Applications of Generative AI and Natural Language Processing Models*. DOI: 10.4018/979-8-3693-0502-7.ch001

Shafik, W. (2024). Artificial Intelligence and Internet of Things Roles in Sustainable Next-Generation Manufacturing. In *Sustainable Innovation for Industry 6.0* (pp. 207–239). IGI Global., DOI: 10.4018/979-8-3693-3140-8.ch012

Singh, S., & Beniwal, H. (2022). A survey on near-human conversational agents. In *Journal of King Saud University - Computer and Information Sciences* (Vol. 34, Issue 10). DOI: 10.1016/j.jksuci.2021.10.013

Skjuve, M., Brandtzaeg, P. B., & Følstad, A. (2024). Why do people use ChatGPT? Exploring user motivations for generative conversational AI. *First Monday*, *29*(1). Advance online publication. DOI: 10.5210/fm.v29i1.13541

So, C., Khvan, A., & Choi, W. (2023). Natural conversations with a virtual being: How user experience with a current conversational AI model compares to expectations. *Computer Animation and Virtual Worlds*, *34*(6), e2149. Advance online publication. DOI: 10.1002/cav.2149

Sonie, O., Chakraborty, A., & Mullick, A. (2022). concept2code: Deep Reinforcement Learning for Conversational AI. *Proceedings of the ACM SIGKDD International Conference on Knowledge Discovery and Data Mining*. DOI: 10.1145/3534678.3542635

Suh, S., & An, P. (2022). Leveraging Generative Conversational AI to Develop a Creative Learning Environment for Computational Thinking. *International Conference on Intelligent User Interfaces, Proceedings IUI*. DOI: 10.1145/3490100.3516473

Surendran, A., Murali, R., & Babu, R. K. R. (2020). Conversational AI - A Retrieval Based Chatbot Conversational AI. *EasyChair Preprint, 4020*.

Tschopp, M., Gieselmann, M., & Sassenberg, K. (2023). Servant by Default? How Humans Perceive Their Relationship With Conversational AI. *Cyberpsychology (Brno), 17*(3). Advance online publication. DOI: 10.5817/CP2023-3-9

Vaghefi, S. A., Stammbach, D., Muccione, V., Bingler, J., Ni, J., Kraus, M., Allen, S., Colesanti-Senni, C., Wekhof, T., Schimanski, T., Gostlow, G., Yu, T., Wang, Q., Webersinke, N., Huggel, C., & Leippold, M. (2023). ChatClimate: Grounding conversational AI in climate science. *Communications Earth & Environment, 4*(1), 480. Advance online publication. DOI: 10.1038/s43247-023-01084-x

Varitimiadis, S., Kotis, K., Pittou, D., & Konstantakis, G. (2021). Graph-based conversational ai: Towards a distributed and collaborative multi-chatbot approach for museums. In *Applied Sciences (Switzerland)* (Vol. 11, Issue 19). DOI: 10.3390/app11199160

Wahde, M., & Virgolin, M. (2023). DAISY: An Implementation of Five Core Principles for Transparent and Accountable Conversational AI. *International Journal of Human-Computer Interaction, 39*(9), 1856–1873. Advance online publication. DOI: 10.1080/10447318.2022.2081762

Wang, Y., Shafik, W., Seong, J. T., Al Mutairi, A., SidAhmed Mustafa, M., & Mouhamed, M. R. (2023). Service delay and optimization of the energy efficiency of a system in fog-enabled smart cities. *Alexandria Engineering Journal, 84*, 112–125. Advance online publication. DOI: 10.1016/j.aej.2023.10.034

KEY TERMS AND DEFINITIONS

AI Ethics: The multidisciplinary framework that addresses moral principles, societal impacts, and governance challenges in the design, deployment, and use of artificial intelligence systems.

AI-Powered Conversations: Interactions driven by artificial intelligence that leverage contextual understanding, intent recognition, and adaptive learning to simulate meaningful dialogue with users.

Automated Customer Service: The use of AI technologies to manage customer inquiries, resolve issues, and deliver support autonomously across various digital channels.

Chatbots: Rule-based or AI-driven software agents designed to simulate text or voice conversations with users for specific tasks or general engagement.

Conversational AI: An advanced field combining machine learning, NLP, and speech technologies to enable machines to understand, process, and respond to human language naturally and interactively.

Human-AI Interaction: The study and design of interfaces and experiences that facilitate intuitive, ethical, and effective collaboration between humans and artificial intelligence systems.

Machine Learning: A subset of AI that enables systems to learn patterns and make predictions or decisions from data without being explicitly programmed for each task.

Natural Language Processing (NLP): A branch of AI focused on enabling computers to understand, interpret, generate, and respond to human language in a meaningful way.

Personalized AI: Artificial intelligence systems that tailor content, services, or interactions based on individual user data, preferences, and behaviors to enhance relevance and engagement.

Voice Assistants: AI-powered systems that use speech recognition and synthesis to interpret spoken commands and provide real-time, voice-based responses and services.

Chapter 4
Advancements in Multilingual Speech Technologies for Human-Computer Interaction

R. N. Ravikumar
https://orcid.org/0009-0009-3705-1681
Marwadi University, Rajkot, India

S. Aarthi
https://orcid.org/0009-0006-9064-2091
Marwadi University, Rajkot, India

Maryam Ahmad Usmani
https://orcid.org/0009-0008-4567-3600
Mamun University, Khiva, Uzbekistan

Pappu Kumar Rai
Marwadi University, Rajkot, India

Muhabbat Jumaniyozova
Urgench State University, Urgench, Uzbekistan

Maqsuda Narboshova
Termez University of Economics and Service, Termez, Uzbekistan

ABSTRACT

The global integration of communication networks increases the demand for multilingual human-computer interaction (HCI) systems. Speech technology innovations that support multiple languages enhance accessibility and usability. This chapter explores how automatic speech recognition (ASR) and text-to-speech (TTS), combined with language models, ena-ble real-time speech translation across diverse accents and linguistic systems. Deep learning and transfer learning help models learn from small, complex language datasets, even under noisy conditions. Practical applications include educational tools, virtual assistants, cus-tomer service, and healthcare. The section also addresses the need for culturally intuitive, unbiased systems through

DOI: 10.4018/979-8-3373-3048-8.ch004

inclusive design and ethical guidelines, promoting linguistic equality. Advances in multilingual speech technology make HCI more inclusive and effec-tive for global users, supporting developers and researchers alike.

1. INTRODUCTION TO MULTILINGUAL HCI AND SPEECH TECHNOLOGIES

The current world demands growing spontaneous Human Computer Interaction (HCI) services delivering service in multiple languages because of globalization. The extensive integration of digital technologies into social systems occurred because it enabled the creation of smart interfaces for language communities in educational services and health care and client assistance and environmental systems. The implementation of user-friendly natural inclusion requires the three multilingual speech technologies that consist of Automatic Speech Recognition (ASR) Text-To-Speech (TTS) and Natural Language Understanding (NLU) (Kasula, 2016). Multilingual HCI systems fix the machine-comprehension problem along with user-input detection problems which span all languages and dialects with their various pronunciation types. Voice systems make use of deep learning methods and transfer learning approaches with large language models to work across hundreds of languages using reduced training information which brings new potential to personal and access interactions.

Multilingual technologies experience widespread progress due to their ability to switch languages automatically based on context needs and their capacity to understand dialects and interpret cultural practices. The construction of effective multilingual speech systems requires addressing several issues that integrate language diversity management and user cultural requirements and expectations of its use (Mathur et al., 2024). The need to implement powerful noise-proof systems and code-switching systems sparsity detection solutions are necessitated but they need to address the challenges of proper processing of user data and even treatment of users. This paper explores the advances and challenges and also opportunities in multilingual speech technologies in human-machine conversations. Speech technology creates new avenues of communication whereby more than one language can be linked in order to provide equal access to digital services to all individuals. The interdisciplinary research leading to full understanding of system construction and assessment and implementation procedures leads to better global intelligent interactions between the users in their inclusiveness.

1.1 The Role of Speech in Bridging Linguistic Barriers in HCI

One of the most natural and natural human communication is speech. Speech technologies are significant in this regard in relation to interaction amongst people and computers in the context of making digital systems accessible and accessible to wide target groups, particularly multilingual societies. Conventional user interfaces tend to be tied to the written language, menu or button, and can prove difficult to users not fluent in a specific language. Nevertheless, voice-based interfaces will be able to facilitate this gap by allowing users to communicate with the system in the native language or preferred dialect, which will reduce cognitive load and allow the user to enhance the experience (Oluwaniyi et al., 2024). The speech system has offered the capability of recognizing and responding to numerous languages even human-machine communication in real time. This is particularly necessary in the environments like international customer support, international health care and learning systems that lingually cover varied population. As they decrease dependency on the same primary language, multilingual speech technologies encourage linguistic inclusion and social equity (Emara et al., 2025). Moreover, speech technologies also allow addressing the nuances, including deep education in AI, deep education and natural language treatment code change, regional accents and informal speech patterns. The advances can be used to make sure that HCI systems are not only functionally multilingual, but also cultural and relevant. Consequently, speech becomes a potent aspect not only of functionality, but also of fostering serious commitment, privatization and sympathy in the virtual world (Pfeiffer et al., 2023). The figure 1 highlights five key benefits of speech technologies in digital systems: linguistic inclusion, cultural relevance, enhanced user experience, accessibility, and real-time multilingual support. These features collectively promote inclusive and user-friendly communication across diverse populations.

Figure 1. Functional Benefits of Speech Technologies

1.2 Motivation for Multilingual Capabilities in Globalized Systems

In the fast-paired society, the need to have multilingual skills in the HCI system is more needy and feasible. Users with varied linguistic and cultural backgrounds have access to global digital platform via Virtual Assistant to Customer Service Bot. To be practical and equitable to such systems, they must transcend the language barrier, and provide continuous conversations despite the linguistic identity of the user. The motivation to get into multilingual skills is inspired by economic and moral necessity of the current digitized global world. Economically, organizations that encourage multilingual communications can exploit expansive markets, enhance customers satisfaction and enhance storage of users in geographical locations (Steichen & Freund, 2015). In the case of governments and non-profit organizations, multilingual technologies facilitate inclusion in communication even in open service ducks like health care, emergency preparedness and education. Such applications are significant in the multichromatic society or multinational institutions, the successful functioning of which presupposes the inclusion of language.

Ethical, inclusion Multilingual speech technologies promotes digital equality. It introduces through the language downsizing of language communities to access language, information and services that would otherwise be inaccessible because of the barriers of the first language. Moreover, the rise in smoother devices, applications and Internet of Things systems that are operated by AI has resulted in an ecosystem where speech is becoming more and more largely interface. In this regard, any restrictions of speech contact with each other in some more popular languages may reinforce existing disparities. The other source of inspiration is the development of awareness that language is an integral component of cultural identity (Aiken & Park, 2020). The presence of multilingual systems that are sensitive and responsive to linguistic diversity creates trust and user interaction. Therefore, the drive to multilingualism is both technical improvement and strategic evolution and cultural and ethical one as well in the design of modern man-computer interface.

1.3 Overview of Multilingual HCI: Concepts, Needs, and Applications

Multilingual HCI is the intersection of speech technology, language technology, and user experience design in developing a system that can interact with users in multiple languages. Essentially, multilingual HCI seeks to provide digital interfaces that are inclusive, easy-to-use, and effective despite may be related to the language spoken. This will require using ASR, TTS, and NLU technologies to process and produce a variety of languages, dialects, and accents (Conneau et al., 2021). The concept of multilingual HCI is not limited to translation. This involves understanding the language in its cultural context, handling code change and ensuring that the system remains strong with different environmental conditions and lack of units in scenarios in the real world. Modern systems should also be adaptable, so the user can interact with systems in hybrid linguistic forms to change mid-swirls or usually in multilingual societies.

The requirement for multilingual HCI occurs in different fields. In education, multilingual students support and break obstacles to knowledge. In the health care system, it enables effective communication between doctors and patients who speak different languages. In customer service, the global companies allow local assistance. Applications extend to virtual assistants, smart homes, supportive technologies for separate arbitrary and multilingual interfaces for promoted and virtual reality environments. Overall, multilingual HCI is about designing inclusive systems that serve diverse populations without compromising usability, accuracy, or responsiveness. The development of such systems requires a multidisciplinary approach blending AI, linguistics, ethics, and human-centered design to meet the growing demands of a global user base. As digital experiences continue to evolve, multilingual HCI will remain at the forefront of ensuring equitable access and engagement for all (De Schutter & Song, 2023).

2. CORE TECHNOLOGIES IN MULTILINGUAL SPEECH PROCESSING

Multilingual speech therapy is premised on a platform of conjoined technologies that can help machines communicate, give explanations and produce speech of numerous languages. These core technologies are Automatic Speech Recognition (ASR), Text-To-Speech (TTS) synthesis, speech translation and Natural Language Understanding (NLU) that are enhanced by deep learning and advances in nervous networks. The speech language is translated into the lesson by ASR and must be capable of managing the difference in pronunciation, code exchange and dialects. Current multilingual ASR models rely on end-to-end neural architecture, including the attention mechanisms of the coder decoder model, through which the languages can be effectively learned, particularly in the context of low resource (Jindal et al., 2020).

ASR with added Machine Translation (MT) and TTS Speech translation, it is a way to make interdisciplinary communication in real time. This is a significant facilitator of multilingual HCI systems, in such a way that users are able to interface with devices and services through original language. Translation Speed-to-text or speech-to-speech translation can be used quickly, particularly when it is conditioned on a large multilingual corpus. NLU systems are critical in understanding the intent and meaning of the users. Semantic ambiguity and syntactic variability are the main issues of multilingual NLU that are addressed through the use of transformer-based models such as MBERT, XLM-R, and Large Language Models (LLMs) that are fine-tuned on multilingual data. These technologies combined create the foundation of multilingual HCI systems, which provide a much more inclusive, natural, and intelligent interaction between a user (Nguyen et al., 2023). They are still being integrated into the real-world applications and thus the speech interfaces are available to linguistically different users worldwide. The table 1 presents a structured comparison of core technologies driving multilingual speech systems. It helps readers understand each component's purpose, current limitations, and leading tools used in practice.

Table 1. Comparison of Core Multilingual Speech Technologies

Technology	Function	Key Challenges	Examples of Models/Tools
Automatic Speech Recognition (ASR)	Converts spoken input to text	Noise sensitivity, accent variability	Whisper, Wav2Vec 2.0
Text-To-Speech (TTS)	Converts text to spoken output	Intonation modelling, multilingual phoneme synthesis	Tacotron, FastSpeech
Natural Language Understanding (NLU)	Interprets user intent and meaning	Semantic ambiguity, syntactic variability	MBERT, XLM-R
Speech Translation	Translates speech between languages	Real-time accuracy, cultural context	Google Translate, Meta XLS-R

2.1 Overview of Automatic Speech Recognition (ASR) and Text-to-Speech (TTS)

Basic technologies operate in Automatic Voice Recognition (ASR) and Text-To-Speech (TTS) Speech-based Human Computer Interactions (HCIS) particularly for multilingual systems. The responsibility of ASR is to transform spoken speech into written text. Complicated acoustic models together with language modelling systems are needed to support various language types and voice variations during processing. The development of shared phonetic representation in language depends on Deep Learning models that include both Connections Temporal Classification (CTC) and attention-based coder-wide architecture within multilingual ASR systems. The system trains through big multilingual datasets before transforming its capacity to receive cross-ringing speech inputs (Ruder et al., 2019).

TTS systems achieved the opposite objective by processing textual input into audio output. Modern TTS systems use nervous network-based models such as Tacotron, fastening, which produce very natural and expressive speeches. Multilingual TTS requires a good understanding of specific phoneme stock, and intonation for each language. High quality TTS models are often designed to support multiple speakers and languages, sometimes able to cloning across Lingual, where the voice of a speaker is transferred to another language. Together, ASR and TT's uninterrupted voice-based interactions in multilingual surroundings facilitate. The integration of these technologies allows for natural and spontaneous communication between users and machines regardless of linguistic background. In order to continue the boundaries of the ongoing development of development departments, self-learning and improvement in language modelling, to continue the boundaries of the spoken voting sections (Research et al., 2023). For inclusive HCI, these systems must be robust to variability in speech, accent, and environmental noise, ensuring accessibility and usability for all users.

2.2 Integration of Natural Language Understanding (NLU) and Speech Translation

Natural language understanding (NLU) is important to explain the user's intentions and relevant meanings in voice-based interfaces. NLU systems convert speech to structured data, enable the system to make decisions or provide proper feedback. In multilingual speech treatment, NLU should work in different linguistic structures, which means shades and syntax rules. Transformer-based architecture and XLM-Roberta, is often used to provide language-designed representations. These models can handle different languages at the same time and are well on domain specific multilingual datasets to detect intentions and to ensure high accuracy in filling tracks (Tan & Joty, 2021).

The speech translation together builds the communication difference between users and machines or between users who speak in different languages. It adds ASR, machine translation (MT) and TTS to a spontaneous pipeline. The speech translation system can be either end-to-end, where the model directly translates speech entrance to speech or text output in another language. While cascade systems provide modularity, end-to-end approaches reduce errors and delay. Integrating NLU and speech translations is especially important in Cross-Lingual HCI applications such as multilingual virtual assistants, international customer support and educational equipment. This integration ensures that not only the user's speech is transit and translated, but it is interpreted properly and abandoned (Vilares et al., 2016). A well-integrated system should handle ambiguity, reference changes and user-specific preferences in language. Advances in pre-trained multilingual language models, reinforcement learning, and context-aware dialogue systems continue to enhance this integration. These technologies ensure that multilingual speech systems are not just reactive but contextually intelligent, adaptive, and capable of understanding users in their preferred languages with high semantic fidelity.

2.3 How Multilingual Systems Function: Pipelines and Modular Components

The multilingual speech treatment system usually follows a modular pipeline that integrates multiple main components: Automatic Speech Recognition (ASR), Machine Translation (MT), Natural Language Understanding (NLU), Communication Management and Text-To-Speech (TTS). This pipeline allows each module to handle specific tasks while working harmoniously to give each module a comfortable user experience (Z. Zhang et al., 2022). The ASR module transfers the speech to the text, which is then treated by the NLU module to extract the meaning, intentions and relevant institutions of the NLU module. If the system is designed to support multiple languages, the transcribed text can undergo a machine translation module and convert it to a target language for response generation or user interface screen. In response, the system can produce text (through natural language generation) that is sent to the TTS module to convert it into a natural speech in the user's favourite language.

Modular architecture allows flexibility in development and distribution. Each component can be individually correct or upgraded without affecting the entire system. For example, ASR can be integrated into the existing pipeline without repaying TTS or NLU module in ASR. The pipeline-based system can be used to create either a cascade model where output is carried from one module to the next, or it can be used to create an end-to-end architecture that maps the entrance speech into directly output text or speech (Bigioi et al., 2022). Although the end-to-end architecture can promise less delay and less cumulative errors, working with a modular cascade system can often be more manageable for troubleshooting and control under complex real-world distributions. Latency, noise, memory limitations, and device limitations must also be accounted for if the real-time multilingual system with humans in the loop is to be effective. Effectively orchestrating modular components with consideration of user context and linguistic variation is essential to harnessing an accurate, responsive, and inclusive human-computer interaction experience.

2.4 Cross-lingual and Polyglot Models for Diverse Linguistic Inputs

Cross-Lingual and Polyglot models have changed the way multilingual speech treatment systems process different languages. Traditional models are typically trained in one language or, to treat another language, may require many resources, or time to train (Hirose, 2018). Cross-Lingual models, on the other hand, train to understand, and treat multiple languages in one model through shared linguistic representation, making them more scalable and effective. Interdisciplinary Models, such as XLM-R, MBERT, and MT5, even harness the transfer of learning, for cross-lingual knowledge, to normalize knowledge in language, in particular for language with low resources. These models are trained on large multilingual companies and can also perform well in unspoilt languages by identifying patterns that cross linguistic boundaries. They enable tasks such as intention recognition, emotional analysis and answers to different languages with minimal re-steps (Huang et al., 2016).

Polyglot models go a step forward by integrating many speech and language components into the same system as dynamically can switch between languages in the same conversation. They advocate cod exchange, in which there exists another phenomenon in place of user languages in intermediate-vocal societies. These models are particularly applicable in the global applications, like the virtual help, that should possess a flowing interaction with the users, within the multilingual environment. Multilingual embeddings, phoneme-sharing methods and language adaptation layers are additional techniques that improve the performance of cross-lingual systems. These models permit effective pronunciation, grammar and semantics learning across languages using limited amounts of training data. The design of these models makes accessibility, inclusivity, and scalability much better. Cross-lingual and polyglot models help construct the next generation of human-computer interaction platforms that will serve truly global audiences by allowing speech systems to comprehend a very broad variety of linguistic inputs with extremely high accuracy.

3. ADVANCES IN DEEP LEARNING AND TRANSFER LEARNING FOR MULTILINGUAL MODELS

Deep learning has increased the advancement of multilingual speech technologies by allowing models to pick up complex patterns across languages. The ability to transfer learning, where high resource languages knowledge is used to enhance performance or performance in under description languages is one of the most transformational advances in this room. You can assist in building robust multilingual models with little label knowledge by training models based on common linguistic properties in such language as phonetic similarities, syntax structures and semantic built-in transfer learning (Iles & Edmondson, 2024). Transformer-based architecture has been developed in this advancement including MBERT (Multilingual BERT), XLM (Cross-Lingual Language Model) and XLM-R (XLM-Roberta), which is trained with large-scale training on multi-language datasets. The models are trained on language-subsequent representatives, in order that they can perform tasks like translation, emotional analysis and speech recognition in multiple languages without selecting each individual. They are successful because of the self-emission mechanism through which long -distance addiction is caught, and reference and meaning can be understood well in various grammatical forms.

Also, some WAV2Vec 2.0 and Whisper preparatory multilingual speech models demonstrate where intensive learning could be applied to directly extract facilities out of raw sound. These models are trained on multilingual speech data in the thousands of hours and have demonstrated the performance to be impressive in noise and real-world conditions. They may be good for specific tasks or languages, making them very versatile (Kobayashi, 2015). Recent developments in zero-shot and few-shot learning also showcase the power of deep learning combined with transfer learning. These techniques allow models to generalize to unseen languages or domains with minimal supervision. Together, these advances make it increasingly feasible to develop scalable, inclusive, and high-performance multilingual systems. As research progresses, we can expect even more efficient, accurate, and culturally aware voice-based human-computer interaction experiences around the globe. The following Figure 2 provides a modular scheme of the multilingual speech and text processing based on deep learning and transfer learning. It enables the major operations such as ASR, translation and NLU in various languages and levels of resources.

Figure 2. Multilingual Speech and Text Processing Framework

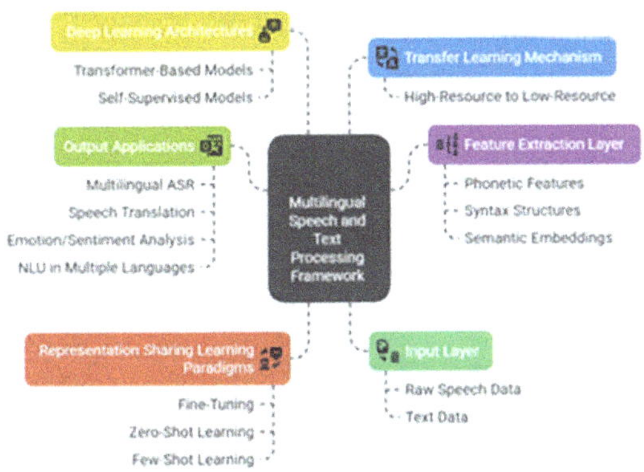

3.1 Neural Architectures for Speech (e.g., CNNs, RNNs, Transformers, wav2vec)

The foundation of modern multilingual speech processing lies in advanced neural architectures designed to model complex speech patterns across languages. Convolutional Neural Networks (CNNs) are strong at identifying local temporal and spectral features in audio spectrograms, making them a strong candidate in loud environments. RNNs, specifically LSTM networks, have been used to address this sequential dependency in speech signals, though this has shown limits in long range context problems (Tamrakar & Silpasuwanchai, 2022). The introduction of Transformer architecture changed the use of self-attention to allow for better capturing long dependencies and process data in a method called parallel processing.

The introduction of Transformer based models is now a mainstay in the fields of speech translation and multilingual forms of natural language understanding. The development of Meta AI's wav2vec is an example of pivoting toward self-supervised learning made from raw audio. Models similar to wav2vec 2.0 train on contextual speech representation without the use of transcription labels, which provide a unique benefit in learning in a multilanguage application, especially those in low-resource conditions. This architecture can be combined and correct for different tasks from recognition of speech, synthesis, and identity of the speaker. They provide at scale better accuracy and robustness to adapt to different language variations and dialects, and can act as a platform for generationally diverse speech treatment (Alias & Munne, 2010). The figure 3 illustrates key neural architectures CNNs, RNNs, Transformers, and wav2vec used in multilingual speech processing. Each architecture contributes uniquely to handling temporal, contextual, and low-resource language features.

Figure 3. Neural Architectures in Multilingual Speech Processing

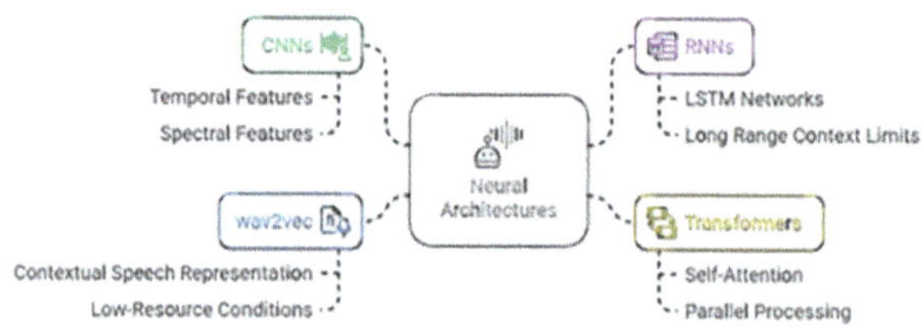

3.2 Transfer Learning to Support Low-Resource Languages

Transfer learning has become an essential strategy for the production of multilingual speech systems, especially when the availability of data varies greatly in language. In this approach, trained models in high resource languages are adapted to people with low resources by transferring representatives who are learned. For example, a model trained in English or mandarin can share a phonetic and syntax pattern with language such as Swahili or LAO, and improve performance despite limited native data (Billa, 2018). Even in small amounts of low resource data with low resources, fine-tuning of prescription models often get sufficient performance benefits. Techniques such as multilingual training, shared coder-decoder frameworks and adapter teams help to distinguish language-specific information while maintaining general knowledge. Transfer learning also addresses linguistic diversity challenges, including regional dialects and accents. This training reduces the requirement for time, calculation resources and extensive labelled data sets. As a result, it plays an important role in promoting linguistic inclusion and equality in digital communication, democratization of voting HCI.

3.3 Role of Multilingual Pre-trained Models (e.g., MBERT, Whisper, XLS-R)

Multilingual pre-trained models form the backbone of today's intelligent speech systems. Models such as MBERT (Multilingual BERT), Whisper, and XLS-R (Cross-lingual Speech Representation Model) have been trained on massive multilingual corpora using unsupervised or self-supervised techniques. These models capture cross-lingual features that are language-agnostic, enabling zero-shot or few-shot learning across different tasks and languages. The deep embedding structure of MBERT analyses more than 100 languages which enables it to perform top-tier processes for multilingual text classification and named entity recognition tasks. OpenAI created Whisper as a Speech-To-Text system which mastered diverse multilingual and multitask data to produce both exceptional sound quality and flexible language accuracy (Diwan et al., 2021).

The Meta AI initiative XLS-R operates with wav2vec 2.0 technology to handle multilingual speech tasks while reaching advanced technological achievements throughout audio processing as well as automatic translation across broad language groups. The upgraded models developed for global speech application development eliminate the necessity of language-based training because of their unified worldwide development framework. Their unified architecture enables developers to build extensive real-time multilingual user interfaces which constitute endorsements of inclusivity and understudied language groups (Fantaye et al., 2020).

3.4 Data Augmentation Techniques and Synthetic Speech Generation

One of the major impediments in multilingual speech systems is data deficiency. The computer text techniques like the time drawing, shift shifts, background noise joints and disorders in the vocal channel are used in generating the different sound samples based on limited data sets. These approaches make models more powerful in regards to accents, noise and speech patterns in comparison to the actual variety. Further, the synthesis speech enables quality exercise data on submerged languages through the use of Text-To-Speech (TTS) engines (Li et al., 2019). Natural voice conversion and GAN based speech synthesis techniques may imitate multiple speakers and accents, providing variety to the training corps. It is also possible to simulate rare phonetic structure and code change situations via TTS models.

The other emerging trend is cross-language data agitation in which data is tagged in one language, they are syntactically translated and read out in another language. This strategy helps in parallel corpora to train the ASR and the translation systems simultaneously. The expansion of the data to create the synthetic speech would allow the research to surpass the limits of the data, and the models may be better generalized and implemented to create inclusive multilingual systems. Such approaches are especially useful when it comes to the need to conserve the endangered languages and the growth of speech technologies in every corner of the globe.

4. DESIGNING ROBUST MULTILINGUAL SYSTEMS FOR REAL-WORLD CONDITIONS

To develop a multilingual system that is highly performing in the real-world environment, a number of linguistic, technical and environmental challenges must be created (Lyu et al., 2024). Each of the most crucial barriers is to achieve noise-Western Automatic Speech Recognition (ASR). Background noise may be a severe problem in uncontrolled environments (like a busy road) where there is a substantial number of people or a video-band width call. Development of powerful systems is also important in advanced noise oppression algorithms, beam shape techniques and data text techniques/methods such as training models that have been artificially corrupted with noise. The accents and dialects and cod-tipping procedures that involve language and regional variation options are also an essential concept. Traditional models do not work well in situations that are presented by standardized speech training. The contemporary multilingual systems need multiple linguistic data sets, including all existing dialects and different voice velocity settings and styles of pronunciation. Learning and fine-tuning methods are embraced to provide field-specific corpora with better inclusiveness. A dynamic real world positioning system should support variability of equipment and network and delay performance variability. By being transferable to mobile devices and to edge systems and cloud platforms, the model is expected to operate optimally without losing its speed or accuracy (Oh et al., 2023).

The compression methods and low oppression architecture in combination with adaptive streaming methods can give uniform performance in the bandwidth wide environment. Diversity of datasets is one of the central elements that have their significant role. The existing speech databases do not ideally represent the minority languages and this hampers the development of the systems equally. The training of multilingual systems needs a wide and representative set of data that reflects a multicultural and linguistic diversity of the target users. The procedure involves the collection and classification of speech recordings that comprise samples in various locations and different demographic and social locations. Solid multilingual design systems integrate both the technological needs and needs of the social culture. Multilingual HCI technologies capable of serving various people can be built through managing the intricacies of the real world effectively so that they can provide an inclusive reliable interaction and communication.

4.1 Enhancing Model Robustness Across Environments

Another significant feature of the model that should be taken into consideration is the strength of the model of the distribution of multilingual speech systems into practice. The speech interface must first be used in other acoustic settings other than the cool office environment to the external market markets. Most engineering strategies have emerged to facilitate continuity in such a different circumstance. Noise-robust training is one of the major methods that has been embraced. The system can be used to learn to distinguish and identify the speech more efficiently during the more difficult circumstances by adding sound data, which approximates the background noise of the real world (eg traffic, check, echo). The other critical approach is the domain adjustment, and voice recognition models suit the target environment that is good with certain data (Thomas et al., 2023). In the particular instance of voice assistants installed in cars, the assistant is trained in art to interpret the command amid the sounds of the road. Also, multi-division training, models assisting a diverse range of acoustic conditions, assists generalization under unforeseen user conditions.

Traction is also granted to optimization due to the fact that the speech interface is made more mobile. The model is compact and low-estimate on mobile and built-in devices and this guarantees the fast response with a low number of calculation resources. In addition, adaptive streaming techniques can be dynamically adapted to sound quality and model complexity based on available bandwidth and delay obstacles, and maintain performance continuity. In addition, the feedback in real time allows the mechanism system to provide self-rights or signal when the voice entrance is incorrectly understood, thus improving long-term reinforcement through continuous learning. Ultimately, enhancing model robustness across environments enables inclusive and reliable human-computer interaction, ensuring speech systems remain functional and user-friendly regardless of external variables like noise, connectivity, or hardware limitations (Y. Zhang et al., 2019). This environmental adaptability is crucial for expanding multilingual speech technologies to rural, low-resource, and mobile-first communities, making speech-driven HCI truly global and accessible.

4.2 Addressing Linguistic and Dataset Diversity

A major challenge in the creation of effective multilingual speech systems lies in addressing linguistically and data sets. The linguistic environment that encompasses the entire world is extremely peculiar, as there are thousands of spoken languages and dialects among which many are low in digitalized state. In the absence of adequate data on these languages the speech system narrows the digital disparity and besides the advantage of exchange between HCI. Researchers have responded in a rush to the language modelling of low resources, with transfer and multilingual pre-informed models (eg XLS-R, Whisper, MBERT) used to normalize knowledge in language. These models apply the common phonetic, syntax and semantic patterns to enhance performance with rare training data as well. Besides, Cross-Lingual can be used to submit languages in order to map linguistic properties, which will enhance the knowledge transfer them more effectively (Choobbasti et al., 2018).

Data set construction and growth also play an important role. Initiatives such as Common Voice and Flairs contribute to Open-Sources multilingual datasets with different speakers, accents and voice references. Synthetic data generation of Text-To-Speech (TTS) enables greater diversity in inputs using Text-To-Speech (TTS) system and data agitation techniques such as speed perfection, pitch shifts and noisy injections, which improves model generalization. However, diversity is not just about language it also includes cultural and regional variations in speech. Understanding idiomatic manifestations, reference-based meanings and conjunctival styles requires data that reflects users' social realities. Ethically sourcing such data while maintaining privacy and fairness is equally important, especially for marginalized or indigenous language communities. By systematically addressing linguistic and dataset diversity, developers can ensure that multilingual HCI systems support not just the world's most widely spoken languages, but also those at risk of digital extinction (Failasofah et al., 2022). Inclusive design in data collection and model development paves the way for equitable, scalable, and culturally aware speech technologies that work for everyone.

5. APPLICATIONS ACROSS DOMAINS

Multilingual speech technologies bring revolution in different fields by enabling inclusive and effective communication in language barriers. In education, they support individual learning by providing voice competent equipment that completes students who speak different languages, including language learning and disabled people. Virtual supervisors equipped with multilingual ASR and TTS increase commitment and access to global classes. In the health care system, multilingual voting assistants receive the facility for patient-supplier communication, especially in multicultural societies. They help plan appointments, symptomatic check and subsequent care instructions in the original language of a patient, improve the results and reduce incorrect communication (Krulatz & Iversen, 2020). The figure 4 illustrates key application areas of multilingual speech technologies: Education,

Healthcare, Customer Service, and Smart Devices. These domains benefit from inclusive, accessible, and language-aware communication interfaces powered by speech technology.

Figure 4. Applications of Multilingual Speech Technologies Across Domains

The customer service industry utilizes multilingual chatbot and voice agents to deal with global user issues with natural language understanding and quick translation. This increases efficiency and user satisfaction, especially in e-commerce, banking and telecommunications. Real-time translation during emergencies and public announcements runs through authorities and public services using speech technologies which distribute significant information to people from all backgrounds. Modern smart devices and IoT systems receive updates to become language-aware which permits users with different backgrounds to interact with their devices through their chosen language options (Le et al., 2021). The use of multilingual speech processing demonstrates essential importance for developing human-computer interaction systems that serve every society in an inclusive manner.

5.1 Enhancing Communication in Key Industries

Speech technologies that operate in multiple languages enable fundamental changes to communication functions throughout different industrial operations. A speech-enabled solution throughout health care facilities helps patients talk with their health care providers using multiple linguistic interfaces through voice assistance. Medical reporting alongside patient compliance improves and enables shared medical treatment within multicultural communities where correct signatures serve as effective reporting tools. These technologies enable education staff to implement voice-enabled resources for teaching which helps students effectively use digital platforms for learning. Language translation technology along with multilingual learning apps and voice facilitators enable learning institutions to reach more students across the world through education (Lee et al., 2022). Organizations apply multilingual chatbot and voice agents to their customer service functions which support customers in international markets. These systems reduce operational costs, enhance customer satisfaction, and provide personalized service. Other industries such as transport, banking and hospitality benefit from speech interfaces that enrich passenger journeys, enable secure voice banking and enable international guest conversation.

5.2 Driving Inclusivity and Accessibility

Multilingual speech systems are important for promoting equity and inclusion in digital interactions. By identifying and responding to a wide range of languages, dialects and accents, these systems make technology more accessible to the marginalized population. This is especially important for people with limited literacy, visual loss or language related to language. Speech-to-speech translation and multilingual voting assistants violate obstacles to achieving important services. These technologies also support cultural inclusion by respecting linguistic shades and user preferences (Naviy et al., 2020). When an interaction between people and computers continues to develop, multilingual speech treatment ensures that no one user remains independently of its linguistic or cultural background.

6. ETHICAL, CULTURAL, AND LINGUISTIC CONSIDERATIONS

Since multilingual speech technologies are quickly inherent in interaction between HCI, it is necessary to address moral, cultural and linguistic ideas to ensure justice, inclusion and social faith. One of the most important concerns is linguistic justice ensuring that the speech system performs equally in all languages, dialects and accents. The models are mainly trained in language with high resources, and produce biased outputs that marginalize speakers of sub-paired languages. Algorithm requires balanced, representative data sets and stiff model assessment in linguistic groups to reduce prejudice (Pham et al., 2021). Cultural sensitivity in voice interface design is equally important. Speech patterns, intonations and interaction styles vary greatly between cultures. It is possible to design system to acknowledge these differences and treat them with respect and create more comfortable and respectable user experience. E.g. political strategies and gender stalk conferences should be culturally adjusted in order to prevent separate users.

The ethical issues also apply to data gathering and voice cloning. Voice data collection needs to take place in an informed, open and privacy secure manner. As the generation of synthetic voices grows, there is a need to put in place limits that prevent the misuse such as voice payer or copying. Moreover, the legal and regulatory framework should be observed, as the morality of AI and data regime have become more popular globally. Designers will need to negotiate the local regulations regarding data encryption (eg GDPR) and accessibility rates, and encourage moral design thinking (Valliappan et al., 2023). Finally, it is not only a technical issue because the integration of moral, cultural and linguistic concepts is a moral necessity. The thoughtful design and responsible innovation will ensure that multilingual HCI systems strengthen all users regardless of language or background. The table 2 highlights the major ethical and cultural challenges faced when developing multilingual HCI systems and outlines practical solutions. It supports the discussion in Section 6 on responsible, inclusive technology design.

Table 2. Ethical and Cultural Challenges in Multilingual HCI Development

Ethical/Cultural Concern	Description	Mitigation Strategy
Linguistic Bias	Favouring high-resource languages	Use of multilingual and polyglot models; balanced datasets
Cultural Insensitivity	Misaligned speech styles or norms	Cultural adaptation of speech interfaces; community feedback
Data Privacy and Consent	Inappropriate use of speech data	Transparent data policies; compliance with GDPR, etc.
Voice Cloning Misuse	Risk of impersonation	Implement watermarking and consent-based use mechanisms

6.1 Promoting Fairness and Cultural Sensitivity in Multilingual Systems

Justice and cultural sensitivity are fundamental to the development of effective multilingual speech technologies. An important challenge is linguistic equity, where all languages despite the number of people or data availability are treated with equal importance. Many AI systems disagree with high resources, which leads to showing differences and leaves speakers of minority or indigenous languages. It requires diverse training data sets, inclusive assessment matrix to address it, and efforts to improve support for language with low resources through techniques such as computer text and transmission learning.

Technical equity requires cultural sensitivity because it leads to trust-based partnerships with customers. The cultural background of nations determines how members expect their verbal communication to be both formal and informal and what the appropriate level of intimacy should be along with what appears appropriate based on conjunctival norms. Systems that lack cultural understanding tend to deliver results which unintentionally become aggressive or unclear in their meaning. Designers need to collaborate with local communities along with linguists for creating voice interfaces that will match the cultural and social references of users (Wijonarko & Zahra, 2022). The process requires an acceptance of gender norms together with idiomatic phrases and local communication preferences.

6.2 Responsible Development and Regulatory Alignment

Reliable multilingual HCI system development requires adherence to fair information processing methods and localization of global values. All collected data should respect consent rights together with user privacy and user access to relevant information. Responsible storage methods should be followed for collected audio data when training voice assistant programs or synthetic voice systems to prevent such data from misuse or unauthorized voice cloning. The development of multilingual HCI systems requires developers to implement updated regulations such as GDPR and availability practice mandate. The implementation of moral AI should be done to prevent failures of equality and to provide openness as well as maintain organization responsibility (Peña-Acuña, 2024). These collective approaches establish a user-rights compatible moral computing method which advances technology within multilingual Human-Computer Interaction contexts while upholding respect for user dignity.

7. CASE STUDIES AND PRACTICAL INSIGHTS

This section analyses the real-world, multicultural contexts of multilingual speech technologies in different domains. Case study examples show successful use in education, health care, and customer service and demonstrate how inclusive voice can improve access to interfaces and improve user satisfaction. It also analyses failures resulting from linguistic bias or cultural insensitivity, and provides lessons for future. The section understands how commercial platforms, such as Google's Speech-To-Text and open tools such as Mozilla's Deep Speech highlight both their strengths and limitations as HRIs (Danylov, 2024). Patterns in the industry demonstrate how start-ups and large technology firms are forming the multilingual landscape of HRI through innovation, ethics, and user-centered design.

7.1 Real-World Success Stories and Implementations

Multilingual speech technologies have had a significant impact on different fields, increased communication and improves the user experience globally. In education, tools such as Duolingo and Microsoft's consecutive readers utilize multilingual ASR and TTS to support language learning and adapt students with different linguistic backgrounds. In the health care system, capable of multilingual interactions such as Babylon Health or Ada Health better patient engagement, especially in areas with limited access to human translators (Dey et al., 2022). Customer service applications have also benefited from multilingual voice bots, improved satisfaction by reducing the waiting time and offering mother tongue.

A remarkable success is the bilingual mode of Google Assistant, which makes it possible to replace a comfortable language in real time that shows the ability of the Polyglot model. Similarly, the goal of the government of the India's Bhashini project is to bridge the linguistic division in 22 official languages in India by using speech and lesson technologies. This implementation suggests that multilingual HCI systems scalable, with strong training, moral development and cultural awareness can provide inclusive solutions. Despite challenges such as data scarcity and diverse dialects, these examples prove the viability and necessity of multilingual capabilities. They also emphasize the importance of user-centric design, continuous feedback loops, and interdisciplinary collaboration in developing effective speech-based systems.

7.2 Tools, Platforms, and Industry Trends

Multilingual speech technology development results from the collaboration between commercial platforms as well as open-source tools alongside innovative startup companies. Major businesses such as Google, Amazon, Microsoft have deployed multilingual ASR, TTS, and NLU services through their platform offerings named Google Cloud Speech-to-Text, Amazon Polly, and Azure Cognitive Services. The tools supply scalable application programming interfaces that support diverse programming languages which enable developers to construct voice interfaces at an accelerated pace. The figure 5 maps the ecosystem of multilingual speech technology across commercial platforms, open-source tools, and evolving industry trends. It showcases key contributors like Google Cloud, Mozilla Deep Speech, and highlights advances such as zero-shot learning and polyglot models.

Figure 5. Tools, Platforms, and Trends in Multilingual Speech Technology

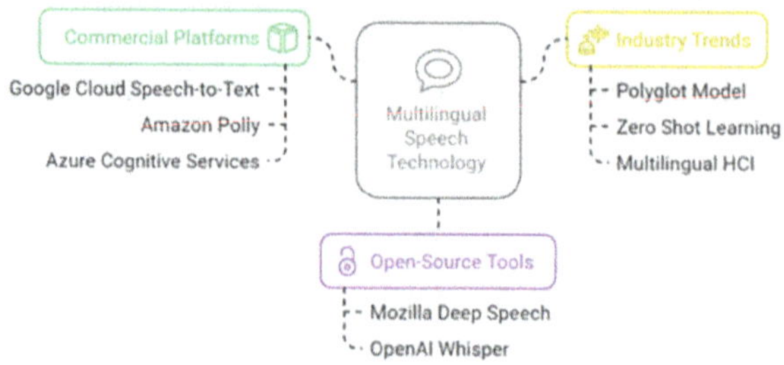

The availability of open-source projects creates essential conditions which make multilingual capabilities accessible to everyone. The open-source platform that comprises Mozilla Deep Speech integrates with the framework XLS-R through Facebook to serve as a base for building models for limited-resource languages (Khanjani et al., 2022). The platform Whisper of OpenAI shows excellent results while working with multiple languages and maintains effective transcription abilities when dealing with noisy input. Independent developers along with researchers and local organizations gain the ability to develop innovations through these tools without requiring heavy infrastructure expenses. The industry is shifting towards adopting the Polyglot model which allows using various languages inside a single architecture. The research interest about zero shot learning models continues to grow while developers explore techniques to normalize natural languages they have not yet processed. Startups concentrate on delivering top-tier services like genuine language transcription and instant multilingual customer assistance because the region demonstrates fast adoption of diverse offerings (Koenecke et al., 2020). The HCI industry currently adopts multilingual interface technologies that deliver scalable solutions with friendly user experiences while including all users.

8. FUTURE RESEARCH DIRECTIONS

Future research in multilingual speech technologies for HCI will focus on increasing model generalization through meta-learning and zero-shoot translations, so that systems can fit new languages with minimal data. To develop universal speech models that are a main goal in the scale in linguistic and cultural contexts. Integration with immersive environments such as AR/VR, Metaverse and IoT will require adaptive, context-aware voice (Papakyri, 2023). Driven interdisciplinary collaboration AI, linguistics, UX design and morality will be necessary for innovation. Constant emphasis on justice, inclusion and access will ensure that future speech -competent interfaces benefit users of all language backgrounds around the world.

8.1 Innovations Driving the Future of Multilingual Speech Technologies

The future of multilingual speech technologies lies in the promotion of intelligent models capable of linguistic diversity with minimal training data. One of the most transformational innovations is zero-shot learning, where models can understand and generate speech in new languages without direct risk during training. This capacity, combined with the metal, enables the system to normalize language and dialects, by learning to learn, rather than remembering the pattern. Equally important universal speech models such as OpenAI's Whisper and Metas XLS-R progress (De Schutter & Song, 2023). These models trained on different and extensive multilingual datasets, show effective voice recognition, translation and transcription in dozens of languages. Innovations cross-lingual embeddings, language-agnostic phoneme representations, and multilingual transfer learning further fuel progress by enabling resource sharing between high- and low-resource languages.

The development of artificial speech production and self-directed study makes its way to develop high quality data sets with minimal secondary resource. Besides, speech technologies are tightly connected with an immersive environment like AR/VR, meta and IoT, and they need new frameworks to respond to speech interactions (Thomas et al., 2023). Together, these innovations do not only hasten the development of multilingual skills but also minimize development obstacles, enabling wider use in education, health care, accessibility, and customer service. The models that will form the future will be not only smart and dynamic but also inclusive, ethical and contextual.

8.2 Toward Inclusive and Collaborative Development

As multilingual speech technologies are still in their developmental stages, it is important to see to it that there is no exclusion and facilitates cooperation in subjects. The inclusion level starts with the awareness of the cultural and language tinges of the other user population. This necessitates models which not only perform well with most of the languages, but also supports local dialects, pronunciation and ways of communication. Such algorithm is needed in solving algorithm bias, representative justice and language capital building systems which in effect serve global societies. This integrative vision involves both researchers and linguists in their work with technologists and decision makers. The issue of multilingual speech system ceased to be merely a technical issue-they shine with queries into human rights, access and socio-cultural representation (Garcia Valencia et al., 2023).

The differences that can be bridged to include under-paired languages and dialects are possible through controls with open source, shared multilingual datasets and international research participation. Moreover, the involvement of the social in the building of the dataset and model validation provides culturally sensitive and correct outcomes. It will be significant with regard to the moral disposition and regulatory adjustment. Since the penetration of such speech technologies has become a common aspect of human life in the public and the private sphere, the formation of the management structures could be made in order to cover the privacy, consent and responsible usage. The establishment of the standards that are expected to promote innovation without violating the personal rights should be done manually by organizations and authorities. Finally, the development should also be inclusive and collaborative so that the speech-based HCI solutions are created by and with different communities. This would not only help increase the effectiveness of technology, but also user confidence and global relevance that will lead to fair access of the digital future.

9. CONCLUSION

It is the evolution of the speech technology that establishes the foundation upon which the interaction between the different-language users with intelligent systems takes place in contemporary ways. The multilingual features cannot be ignored in the speech processing systems since the current globalized world requires its presence. Multilingual speech processing computers are user interfaces that allow people to communicate even when they have different languages of understanding. A systematic analysis of the main architectures of multilingual speech processing in the modern environment in the context of ASR and TTS and NLU up to the deep learning models and transfer learning algorithms was conducted in this chapter. Development of speech models brought about by technological advancement made it possible to provide language minorities with services through the use of multilingual skills by the models. The quality of system performance of Pretrained multilingual models such as MBERT and Whisper and data augmentation techniques improve system performance quality by providing greater generalization in low-resource settings.

The study concerned applications across educational applications and customer care and healthcare sectors and also accessibility programmes around the world. Organizations use multilingual speech systems to design user interfaces that eliminate former language barriers. The established finding in this chapter demonstrates how system robustness works by letting speech systems correctly function throughout acoustic environments and diverse cultural contexts that present numerous contextual conditions. System functionality depends on developers controlling acoustic environmental noise during development and their work to incorporate different accents while they build the system and their final task to adjust for linguistic differences after system installation.

The development of multilingual HCI faces several obstacles during its evolution process. The implementation of speech systems encounters obstacles because of ethical issues together with cultural biases that stem from automatic processing operations. Voice system developers must establish unbiased technology platforms with free self-operated systems that show no cultural bias. Human-centered design development methods are essential since developers need to create linguistic equity and inclusive cultural features within methods that remain easy to understand. Information systems protecting user values need developers together with researchers and user experience designers and ethicists to work with linguists.

The growth of multilingual speech technology requires user leadership because users are the only stakeholders who can establish necessary practices for inclusion. Open-source databases combined with research connections between different scientific fields and community member data acquisition are necessary elements for quick development of equal systems. Continuous support for minority speech varieties protects multilingualism while ensuring global online bias does not diminish linguistic diversity. Better language-free speech technology creates fundamental changes in HCI since it provides wider availability to inclusive systems that understand contextual data. High-end human-machine interaction methods emerge through deep learning advances and multi-lingual processing along with responsible artificial intelligence research development. Progress in multilingual speech technology development will create automated systems for smooth communications that benefit every member who seeks cultural diversity.

REFERENCES

Aiken, M., & Park, M. (2020). A Comparison of two Multilingual Meeting Systems. *International Journal of Computers and Technology*, *20*, 38–44. DOI: 10.24297/ijct.v20i.8636

Alias, F., & Munne, N. (2010). Reliable pitch marking of affective speech at peaks or valleys using restricted dynamic programming. *IEEE Transactions on Multimedia*, *12*(6), 481–489. DOI: 10.1109/TMM.2010.2051873

Bigioi, D., Morales, T., Pandey, A., Fowley, F., Corcoran, P., & Carson-Berndsen, J. (2022, August). Sign2Speech: A novel Sign Language to speech synthesis pipeline. *24th Irish Machine Vision and Image Processing Conference*. DOI: 10.56541/CTDH7516

Billa, J. (2018, September). ISI ASR system for the low resource speech recognition challenge for Indian languages. *Interspeech*, •••, 2018. DOI: 10.21437/Interspeech.2018-2473

Choobbasti, A. J., Gholamian Mohammad Erfan and Vaheb, A., & Safavi, S. (2018, December). JSpeech: A Multi-Lingual Conversational Speech Corpus. 2018 IEEE Spoken Language Technology Workshop (SLT). DOI: 10.1109/SLT.2018.8639658

Conneau, A., Baevski, A., Collobert, R., Mohamed, A., & Auli, M. (2021, August). Unsupervised cross-lingual representation learning for speech recognition. *Interspeech*, •••, 2021. DOI: 10.21437/Interspeech.2021-329

Danylov, V. (2024). Open source and proprietary software for audio deepfakes and voice cloning: Growth areas, pain points, future influence. *Bjlss*, *1*(1), 105–113. DOI: 10.30525/2592-8813-2024-1-11

De Schutter, H., & Song, S. (2023). Immigrant linguistic justice: The lay of the land. *Metaphilosophy*, *54*(5), 575–582. DOI: 10.1111/meta.12661

Dey, S., Sahidullah, M., & Saha, G. (2022). An overview of Indian spoken language recognition from machine learning perspective. ACM Trans. Asian Low-Resour. *Lang. Inf. Process.*, *21*(6), 1–45.

Diwan, A., Vaideeswaran, R., Shah, S., Singh, A., Raghavan, S., Khare, S., Unni, V., Vyas, S., Rajpuria, A., Yarra, C., Mittal, A., Ghosh, P. K., Jyothi, P., Bali, K., Seshadri, V., Sitaram, S., Bharadwaj, S., Nanavati Jai and Nanavati, R., Sankaranarayanan, K., … Abraham, B. (2021). Multilingual and code-switching ASR challenges for low resource Indian languages. ArXiv [Cs.CL].

Emara, T. Z., Hassan, E., Elbedwehy, S., & Saber, A. (2025). A historical perspective on Artificial Intelligence in applied life sciences. In *Advances in Computational Intelligence and Robotics* (pp. 49–86). IGI Global., DOI: 10.4018/979-8-3693-9208-9.ch002

Failasofah, F., Mukminin, A., Masbirorotni, M., Abrar, M., Fajaryani, N., Fortunasari, F., Hidayat, M., & Habibi, A. (2022). Culture, language, and multilingual education: Bordón Rev. *Pedagog.*, *74*(3), 121–137.

Fantaye, T. G., Yu, J., & Hailu, T. T. (2020). Investigation of automatic speech recognition systems via the multilingual deep neural network modeling methods for a very low-resource language, chaha. *J. Sign. Inf. Process.*, *11*(01), 1–21. DOI: 10.4236/jsip.2020.111001

Garcia Valencia, O. A., Suppadungsuk, S., Thongprayoon, C., Miao, J., Tangpanithandee, S., Craici, I. M., & Cheungpasitporn, W. (2023). Ethical implications of chatbot utilization in nephrology. *Journal of Personalized Medicine*, *13*(9), 1363. DOI: 10.3390/jpm13091363 PMID: 37763131

Hirose, K. (2018). Voice and speech synthesis—highlighting the control of prosody. In S. Frühholz & P. Belin (Eds.), The Oxford Handbook of Voice Perception (pp. 756–776). Oxford University Press.

Huang, G., & Gorin, A., & Gauvain Jean-Luc and Lamel, L. (2016, March). Machine translation based data augmentation for Cantonese keyword spotting. 2016 IEEE International Conference on Acoustics, Speech and Signal Processing (ICASSP). DOI: 10.1109/ICASSP.2016.7472833

Iles, J., & Edmondson, W. (2024, March). FEATURE DRIVEN FORMANT SYNTHESIS. Speech and Hearing.

Jindal, I., Li, Y., Brahma, S., & Zhu, H. (2020). CLAR: A cross-lingual argument regularizer for semantic role labeling. Findings of the Association for Computational Linguistics: EMNLP 2020.

Kasula, A. J. (2016). Olowalu Review: Developing identity through translanguaging in a multilingual literary magazine. *Colombian Applied Linguistics Journal*, *18*(2), 109. DOI: 10.14483/calj.v18n2.10014

Khanjani, Z., Watson, G., & Janeja, V. P. (2022). Audio deepfakes: A survey. *Frontiers in Big Data*, *5*, 1001063. DOI: 10.3389/fdata.2022.1001063 PMID: 36700137

Kobayashi, T. (2015). Prosody control and variation enhancement techniques for HMM-based expressive speech synthesis. In *Speech Prosody in Speech Synthesis: Modeling and generation of prosody for high quality and flexible speech synthesis* (pp. 203–213). Springer Berlin Heidelberg. DOI: 10.1007/978-3-662-45258-5_14

Koenecke, A., Nam, A., Lake, E., Nudell, J., Quartey, M., Mengesha, Z., Toups, C., Rickford, J. R., Jurafsky, D., & Goel, S. (2020). Racial disparities in automated speech recognition. *Proceedings of the National Academy of Sciences of the United States of America, 117*(14), 7684–7689. DOI: 10.1073/pnas.1915768117 PMID: 32205437

Krulatz, A., & Iversen, J. (2020). Building inclusive language classroom spaces through multilingual writing practices for newly-arrived students in Norway. *Scandinavian Journal of Educational Research, 64*(3), 372–388. DOI: 10.1080/00313831.2018.1557741

Le, H., Barbier, F., Nguyen, H., Tomashenko, N., Mdhaffar, S., Gahbiche, S. G., Lecouteux, B., Schwab, D., & Estève, Y. (2021). ON-TRAC' systems for the IWSLT 2021 low-resource speech translation and multilingual speech translation shared tasks. *Proceedings of the 18th International Conference on Spoken Translation (IWSLT 2021).* DOI: 10.18653/v1/2021.iwslt-1.20

Lee, A., Gong, H., Duquenne, P.-A., Schwenk, H., Chen, P.-J., Wang, C., Popuri, S., Adi, Y., Pino, J., Gu, J., & Hsu, W.-N. (2022). Textless Speech-to-Speech Translation on Real Data. *Proceedings of the 2022 Conference of the North American of the Association for Computational Linguistics: Human Technologies.*

Li, S., Ding, C., Lu, X., Shen, P., Kawahara, T., & Kawai, H. (2019, September). End-to-end articulatory attribute modeling for low-resource multilingual speech recognition. *Interspeech, •••*, 2019. DOI: 10.21437/Interspeech.2019-2092

Lyu, K.-M., Lyu, R.-Y., & Chang, H.-T. (2024). Real-time multilingual speech recognition and speaker diarization system based on Whisper segmentation. *PeerJ. Computer Science, 10*, e1973. DOI: 10.7717/peerj-cs.1973 PMID: 38660177

Mathur, V., Dadu, T., & Aggarwal, S. (2024). Evaluating neural networks' ability to generalize against adversarial attacks in cross-lingual settings. *Applied Sciences (Basel, Switzerland), 14*(13), 5440. DOI: 10.3390/app14135440

Naviy, L., Sh. Ualikhanov Kokshetau State University Kokshetau Republic of Kazakhstan, Zhussupbekova Gulsara G and Stukalenko, N. M., Zhakhina, B. B., Baimanova, L. S., & Kukubaeva, A. K. (2020). Development of communication and speech skills of students in the process of education. J. Intellect. Disabil. -. *Diagn. Treat.*, *8*(3), 437–442.

Nguyen, L. M., Nayak, S., & Coler, M. (2023, January). Improving luxembourgish speech recognition with cross-lingual speech representations. *2022 IEEE Spoken Language Technology Workshop (SLT)*. DOI: 10.1109/SLT54892.2023.10022706

Oh, C., Kim, C., & Park, K. (2023). Building robust Korean speech recognition model by fine-tuning large pretrained model. *Phon. Speech Sci.*, *15*(3), 75–82. DOI: 10.13064/KSSS.2023.15.3.075

Oluwaniyi, P. S. D., Azuka, D. B. F., Ojo, P. S. G., Dr Festus Sunday Smart Oloda, Jekayinfa, D. J. O., & Okwuosa, D. S. O. (2024). Effect of bilingual instructional method in the academic achievement of Junior Secondary School students in mathematics. Fr, 10(2), 27–33.

Peña-Acuña, B., & Rubio-Alcalá, F. D. (2024). Ethical approach to the use of immersive technologies. Advance about digitalisation of multilingual programs in the EHEA. *Frontiers in Virtual Reality*, •••, 5.

Pfeiffer, J., Piccinno, F., Nicosia Massimo and Wang, X., Reid, M., & Ruder, S. (2023). MmT5: Modular multilingual pre-training solves source language hallucinations. Findings of the Association for Computational Linguistics: EMNLP 2023, 1978–2008.

Pham, N.-Q., Nguyen, T. N., Ha, T.-L., Stüker, S., Waibel, A., & He, D. (2021). Multilingual Speech Translation KIT @ IWSLT2021. *Proceedings of the 18th International Conference on Spoken Translation (IWSLT 2021)*.

Ruder, S., Vulić, I., & Søgaard, A. (2019). A survey of cross-lingual word embedding models. *Journal of Artificial Intelligence Research*, *65*, 569–631. DOI: 10.1613/jair.1.11640

Steichen, B., & Freund, L. (2015, April). Supporting the modern polyglot. *Proceedings of the 33rd Annual ACM Conference on Human in Computing Systems*.

Tamrakar, S. R., & Silpasuwanchai, C. (2022). Comparative evaluation of transformer-based Nepali language models. In *Research Square*. DOI: 10.21203/rs.3.rs-2289743/v1

Tan, S., & Joty, S. (2021). Code-mixing on sesame street: Dawn of the adversarial polyglots. *Proceedings of the 2021 Conference of the North American of the Association for Computational Linguistics: Human Technologies*.

Thomas, J., Arya, L., Hussain, M., & Prasanna, S. R. M. (2023). Speech Act Theory and Ethics of Speech Processing as Distinct Stages: the ethics of collecting, contextualizing and the releasing of (speech) data. *2023 IEEE International Symposium on Ethics in Engineering, Science, and Technology (ETHICS)*, 1–10. DOI: 10.1109/ETHICS57328.2023.10154932

Valliappan, I., Kaipa, R., & Karuppali, S. (2023). Exploring the attitudes and practices among student clinicians in India on multilingual issues in the field of speech-language pathology. *CoDAS*, *35*(6), e20220249. DOI: 10.1590/2317-1782/20232022249en PMID: 37672414

Vilares, D., Gómez-Rodr\'\iguez, C., & Alonso, M. A. (2016). One model, two languages: training bilingual parsers with harmonized treebanks. Proceedings of the 54th Annual Meeting of the Association for Computational Linguistics (Volume 2: Short Papers). DOI: 10.18653/v1/P16-2069

Wijonarko, P., & Zahra, A. (2022). Spoken language identification on 4 Indonesian local languages using deep learning. *Bulletin of Electrical Engineering and Informatics*, *11*(6), 3288–3293. DOI: 10.11591/eei.v11i6.4166

Zhang, Y., Weiss, R. J., Zen, H., Wu, Y., Chen, Z., Skerry-Ryan, R. J., Jia, Y., Rosenberg, A., & Ramabhadran, B. (2019, September). Learning to speak fluently in a foreign language: Multilingual speech synthesis and cross-language voice cloning. *Interspeech*, •••, 2019. DOI: 10.21437/Interspeech.2019-2668

Zhang, Z., Falai, A., Sanchez, A., Angelini, O., & Yanagisawa, K. (2022). *Mix and match: An empirical study on training corpus composition for Polyglot text-to-speech*. TTS.

KEY TERMS AND DEFINITIONS

Automatic Speech Recognition (ASR): Technology that converts spoken language into text by recognizing human speech patterns using machine learning and neural networks.

Code-Switching: The practice of alternating between two or more languages or dialects within a single conversation, common in multilingual societies.

Cross-Lingual Models: Language models trained to generalize across multiple languages using shared linguistic representations, enabling performance in low-resource settings.

Data Augmentation: Techniques used to artificially increase the size and diversity of training data, such as adding noise or generating synthetic speech.

Ethical AI in HCI: The practice of ensuring fairness, transparency, privacy, and inclusivity in designing AI systems for human-computer interaction.

Human-Computer Interaction (HCI): A multidisciplinary field that focuses on the design and use of computer technologies, emphasizing the interfaces between people (users) and computers.

Linguistic Equity: The principle of providing equal technological representation and performance across all languages and dialects in digital systems.

Low-Resource Languages: Languages for which limited linguistic data or speech resources are available, posing challenges for training effective AI models.

Multilingual HCI: A system or interface that supports user interaction in multiple languages, considering cultural and linguistic diversity for inclusive communication.

Natural Language Understanding (NLU): A component of NLP that interprets and analyzes human language to understand intent, meaning, and context in voice-based interactions.

Polyglot Models: AI models capable of handling and switching between multiple languages within a single architecture, often used in code-switching environments.

Speech Translation: A technology that combines ASR, machine translation, and TTS to convert spoken input from one language into spoken or written output in another language.

Text-To-Speech (TTS): A process of converting written text into synthesized speech, enabling computers to "speak" to users in natural-sounding voices.

Transfer Learning: A machine learning technique where a model trained on one task or language is adapted to perform a different but related task or on a different language.

Voice Cloning: The process of generating synthetic speech that mimics a specific person's voice, often used in TTS applications.

Whisper / MBERT / XLS-R: State-of-the-art multilingual AI models used for speech recognition, language understanding, and cross-lingual representation.

Zero-Shot Learning: A learning method where a model performs tasks in unseen languages or domains without prior explicit training in those specific settings.

Chapter 5

Natural Language Speech Processing Integrating Assistive Technologies for Human-Computer Interaction

Sachin Sharma
https://orcid.org/0000-0002-7821-3685
Amity University, Mohali, India

ABSTRACT

Natural Language Speech Processing (NLSP) is a fundamental space of consider that centers on the interaction between people and machines through talked dialect. The integration of assistive innovations in this field points to bridge communication holes and upgrade availability for people with inabilities. This chapter investigates the advancing scene of NLSP, emphasizing its part in progressing Human-Computer Interaction (HCI) by empowering consistent communication between clients and computers through voice acknowledgment, blend, and common dialect understanding. Assistive innovations such as speech-to-text, text-to-speech, and voice-controlled frameworks are changing every day intelligent for people with hearing, discourse, and engine impedances, giving them with upgraded independence and interaction conceivable outcomes. The integration of machine learning and profound learning calculations has quickened progressions in discourse acknowledgment precision, enthusiastic tone examination, and context-driven dialect preparing.

DOI: 10.4018/979-8-3373-3048-8.ch005

I. INTRODUCTION

The evolution of Human-Computer Interaction (HCI) has consistently aimed to create more seamless and intuitive communication between users and technology. From early punch cards to modern touchscreens, the goal has always been to bridge the gap between human intent and machine comprehension (Averbukh, 2020; Grudin, 2017). In this pursuit, Natural Language Speech Processing (NLSP) has emerged as a transformative force, particularly when integrated with assistive technologies. This synergy promises to revolutionize how individuals, especially those with disabilities, interact with the digital world (Emara, 2018; Emara et al., 2025b).

At its core, NLSP is the interdisciplinary field that enables computers to understand, interpret, and generate human speech (Rao et al., 2020; Tan et al., 2021). It encompasses a wide range of tasks, including automatic speech recognition (ASR), natural language understanding (NLU), and text-to-speech (TTS) synthesis. ASR converts spoken language into text, NLU extracts meaning from that text, and TTS transforms text back into spoken words (Tan et al., 2021; Peng et al., 2025). The development and deployment of these systems depend heavily on scalable data pipelines and distributed processing frameworks, which have been explored in recent work on geographically distributed data management and data processing algorithms (Emara et al., 2023; Emara et al., 2025c). Furthermore, methods for feature selection and hybrid paradigms for high-dimensional data provide useful tools for handling rich speech representations (NguyenDuc et al., 2025; VuThi et al., 2024).

For individuals with visual disabilities, NLSP provides a powerful gateway to information and control. Screen readers and voice interfaces, when combined with richer NLU, can support non-linear navigation and context-aware summarization; such capabilities rely on robust data handling and model adaptation techniques that are discussed in the literature on distributed data systems and adaptive algorithms (Emara & Huang, 2019a; Emara & Huang, 2019b). These approaches help ensure that assistive systems can scale to large vocabularies and diverse content sources. Recent systems that generate context-aware visual descriptions and richer screen-reader experiences demonstrate how adaptive summarization and structured navigation improve access to complex content for blind and low-vision users (Chang et al., 2024; Zong et al., 2022; Bakeer, 2024).

Similarly, people with motor disabilities can benefit substantially from NLSP-enabled assistive technologies. Traditional input methods like keyboards and mice can be challenging or impossible for these users; voice control systems and speech-driven workflows enable dictation, device control, and environment interaction (Mulfari et al., 2023; Qian et al., 2023). Practical deployment of such systems — including on constrained or edge devices and in real-time scenarios — is informed by research on power-saving mechanisms, stratified block processing, and lightweight processing for small clusters (Emara, 2016; Emara et al., 2014; Emara, 2018; Trinh et al., 2022). Model optimization and compact representations from recent conference work also show promising directions for on-device assistive applications that preserve latency and privacy (Trinh et al., 2022; Emara et al., 2025c; Saber et al., 2018).

NLSP also plays a pivotal role in supporting people with cognitive impairments. Voice-activated reminders, simplified conversational agents, and task-management assistants can help individuals with memory or executive-function challenges stay organized and independent. Techniques from event modeling and recommendation systems — which handle temporal and contextual data — can be adapted to build personalized, timely prompts and interactions for such users (TrinhHuy et al., 2025; Trinh et al., 2019). More broadly, conversational agents and adaptive dialog systems have been shown to support adherence, cueing, and scaffolded interactions for people with cognitive needs, when combined with personalization and privacy-respecting designs (Rao et al., 2020; Bickmore & Picard, 2005).

The integration of NLSP with assistive technologies also extends to individuals with hearing impairments. ASR can transcribe spoken conversations to captions in real time, greatly expanding access in meetings and public settings, and TTS can enable speech output for typed input by communication partners (Qian et al., 2023; Tan et al., 2021). Robust feature representation, hybrid selection paradigms, and domain-adaptation strategies are crucial to ensure accurate transcription and low latency in real-time use cases (NguyenDuc et al., 2025; VuThi et al., 2024).

Despite its immense potential, the effective integration of NLSP into assistive technologies requires addressing several challenges. One major challenge is ensuring reliable performance across diverse acoustic conditions, dialects, and atypical speech patterns; scalable training and distributed data strategies are essential to cover such variability (Emara et al., 2023; Joshi et al., 2025). Privacy and ethical concerns around speech data collection and usage are also critical; recent discussions emphasize careful data handling, on-device processing, and consent-aware design when deploying AI systems in sensitive contexts (Emara et al., 2025a; Emara et al., 2025c). Finally, the need to deploy models on resource-limited or edge devices — common in assistive scenarios — motivates work on lightweight algorithms, stratified processing, and efficient block models for small clusters (Trinh et al., 2022; Trinh et al., 2019). Addressing these technical and ethical issues will be central to realizing the transformational potential of NLSP for assistive technologies.

II. LITERATURE REVIEW

Lv et al. (2022) highlights the rapid advancement of assistive technology (AT) for individuals with motor impairments. The authors focus on key developments in robotic devices, brain-computer interfaces (BCIs), virtual and augmented reality (VR/AR), wearable sensors, and voice-activated systems, all powered by artificial intelligence (AI). Robotic exoskeletons and arms improve mobility and control, while BCIs offer direct brain control for prosthetics and wheelchairs. VR/AR platforms provide immersive rehabilitation and training, and wearable sensors monitor user activity for personalized assistance.

The integration of AI enables adaptive and intelligent AT, tailoring support to individual needs. The article emphasizes the importance of user-centered design, affordability, and accessibility, alongside the need for further research in BCI technology and long-term device utilization. Ultimately, these technological strides aim to significantly improve the independence and quality of life for those with motor impairments.

Karpov and Yusupov (2018) focus on the development of a speech recognition system designed to function effectively in noisy environments, a persistent challenge in speech processing. The study highlights the use of advanced signal processing strategies, particularly spectral subtraction and noise reduction algorithms, to enhance the clarity of speech signals. The research emphasizes improving the robustness of speech recognition systems by mitigating the impact of background noise, which significantly degrades performance.

The study investigates the performance of these strategies within a Hidden Markov Model (HMM) framework, a common approach in speech recognition. Experimental results demonstrate that the proposed system, incorporating noise reduction strategies, achieves higher accuracy in loud conditions compared to conventional methods. This research contributes to the advancement of speech recognition technology, especially in applications where noise interference is prevalent, such as in public or industrial settings.

Lu et al. (2024) presents an innovative approach to improve speech recognition accuracy in noisy environments by utilizing a hybrid system that combines deep learning with traditional signal processing techniques. The research focuses on mitigating the negative effects of background noise, a common challenge in speech recognition applications. The proposed system employs a convolutional neural network (CNN) for feature extraction, which is known for its ability to learn robust representations from raw audio data. This CNN-based feature extraction is integrated with a Hidden Markov Model (HMM) for acoustic modeling, leveraging the strengths of both deep learning and statistical methods.

The authors also incorporate advanced noise reduction algorithms to preprocess the audio signals, further enhancing the system's performance. Experimental results demonstrate that the hybrid approach significantly improves speech recognition accuracy compared to conventional HMM-based systems and standalone deep learning models, particularly in challenging loud conditions. This research highlights the effectiveness of combining deep learning with classical signal processing for robust speech recognition.

Dokania and Chattaraj (2022) investigates the development and evaluation of an intelligent wheelchair system designed to enhance mobility for people with severe motor disabilities. The system integrates various assistive technologies, including computer vision, sensor fusion, and machine learning, to enable independent navigation and obstacle avoidance. The research focuses on creating a user-friendly interface that allows individuals to control the wheelchair through intuitive commands, such as voice or gesture.

The system utilizes real-time data from cameras and sensors to map the environment and detect obstacles, ensuring safe and efficient navigation. Machine learning algorithms are used to adapt the wheelchair's behavior to the user's preferences and the surrounding environment. The study evaluates the system's performance in real-world scenarios, demonstrating its capacity to improve autonomy and mobility for people with significant physical limitations. The authors highlight the potential of intelligent wheelchair systems to improve quality of life and promote inclusion for individuals with motor impairments.

Wu (2024) investigates the development of a novel voice-controlled robotic arm designed to assist people with upper limb disabilities in performing daily tasks. The research focuses on creating an intuitive and efficient interface that allows users to control the robotic arm through natural language commands. The system integrates advanced speech recognition and natural language processing (NLP) techniques to accurately interpret user instructions and translate them into precise robotic arm movements.

To enhance usability, the system incorporates real-time feedback mechanisms, such as visual and auditory prompts, to provide users with information about the arm's actions. The authors also address the challenge of ensuring safety by implementing collision avoidance algorithms and user-defined safety zones. The study evaluates the system's performance through user trials, demonstrating its potential to improve independence and quality of life for people with upper limb impairments. The research highlights the significance of user-centered design and the integration of advanced technologies for creating effective assistive robotic systems.

Ding et al. (2024) presents a novel system for enhancing speech emotion recognition (SER) using deep learning strategies, particularly focusing on improving accuracy in diverse and challenging acoustic environments. The study addresses the limitations of traditional SER systems, which often struggle with variations in speech patterns, background noise, and speaker characteristics. The proposed system utilizes a hybrid approach, combining convolutional neural networks (CNNs) for feature extraction with long short-term memory (LSTM) networks for temporal modeling.

This architecture allows the system to capture both local and global features of speech signals, improving its ability to recognize nuanced emotional cues. The authors also investigate the use of data augmentation techniques to increase the robustness of the model and address the issue of limited training data. Experimental results demonstrate that the proposed system achieves higher accuracy compared to existing SER frameworks, especially in noisy and emotionally ambiguous speech samples. This research contributes to the development of more reliable and accurate SER systems for applications in human-computer interaction, healthcare, and emotional computing.

Yang and Bao (2023) present a comprehensive survey of recent advancements in voice-controlled assistive technologies designed to improve the quality of life for people with disabilities. It explores the integration of natural language processing (NLP) and speech recognition systems into various assistive devices, including smart home systems, robotic aids, and communication tools. The review highlights the growing trend of personalized voice interfaces that adapt to individual user needs and preferences, enhancing usability and accessibility. It analyzes the challenges associated with developing robust and reliable voice control systems, such as handling diverse accents, noisy environments, and atypical speech patterns.

The authors also discuss the ethical considerations surrounding data privacy and security in voice-controlled assistive technologies. Furthermore, the article emphasizes the importance of user-centered design and collaboration between researchers, engineers, and end-users to ensure that these technologies effectively address the specific needs of people with disabilities. It concludes by outlining future directions for research and development, focusing on the integration of artificial intelligence and machine learning to create more intelligent and adaptive voice-controlled assistive systems.

Selvarani et al. (2025) introduces a "Textual Interaction Framework" designed to improve assistive computing for people with communication impairments. It addresses the challenges faced by users who struggle with conventional input methods by proposing a framework that leverages textual interaction. The system aims to facilitate more natural and efficient communication through text-based interfaces. It emphasizes the significance of adaptive and personalized textual interaction, allowing users to tailor the system to their specific needs.

The authors explore the integration of predictive text, text summarization, and context-aware text generation to enhance the user experience. The system also incorporates error correction and disambiguation procedures to improve accuracy and reduce user effort. The chapter highlights the potential of textual interaction to empower individuals with communication disabilities, promoting greater autonomy and participation. It underscores the need for continued research and development in this area to create more effective and accessible assistive computing solutions.

III. NATURAL LANGUAGE SPEECH PROCESSING

The history of NLSP began with early linguistic theories and computational experiments. In the mid-20th century, pioneers like Chomsky laid the foundation for understanding language structures, while early machine translation efforts demonstrated the potential and complexities of automated language processing.

A pivotal shift occurred in the 1980s and 1990s with the move toward statistical NLSP. This was driven by increased computing power and the availability of large text corpora. Machine learning algorithms became central, enabling systems to learn from data and improve in areas like speech recognition and machine translation. However, the true transformation arrived in the 21st century with the advent of deep learning.

Neural networks, especially recurrent neural networks (RNNs) and transformers, propelled NLSP to new heights, achieving state-of-the-art performance in various tasks. The availability of massive datasets and increased computational resources fueled this progress, leading to significant advancements in speech recognition accuracy, more natural-sounding text-to-speech synthesis, and more precise natural language understanding. This period saw the rise of end-to-end systems capable of directly mapping speech to meaning, along with the development of sophisticated language models that can understand and generate human-like text. The integration of NLSP into everyday devices, such as voice assistants and smart speakers, has made these technologies ubiquitous.

Today, NLSP is a dynamic and rapidly advancing field at the intersection of linguistics, computer science, and artificial intelligence. It enables computers to understand, interpret, and generate human speech, bridging the communication gap between people and machines. This innovation is revolutionizing various aspects of our lives, from voice assistants and automated customer service to medical transcription and language interpretation.

At the heart of NLSP lies a complex pipeline of processes. The journey begins with ASR, where spoken language is converted into text. This involves intricate algorithms that analyze acoustic signals, identify phonemes (basic units of sound), and map them to words. Modern ASR systems utilize deep learning models, particularly recurrent neural networks (RNNs) and transformers, to achieve high accuracy, even in noisy environments and with diverse accents.

Once the speech is transcribed, NLU takes over. This stage focuses on extracting meaning and intent from the text. NLU includes tasks such as semantic analysis (understanding the meaning of words and expressions), syntactic analysis (analyzing the grammatical structure of sentences), intent recognition (identifying the user's goal or purpose), and entity extraction (identifying and categorizing important information, such as names, dates, and locations). Contextual understanding is crucial in NLU, as the meaning of a sentence can vary depending on the surrounding conversation and the speaker's background.

After the computer has understood the user's intent, it must generate a response. This is where **Natural Language Generation (NLG)** comes into play. NLG involves creating coherent and natural-sounding text or speech. Techniques like template-based generation, statistical language modeling, and deep learning models are used to produce responses that are both informative and engaging. Finally, TTS synthesis converts the generated text back into spoken language. Modern TTS systems utilize deep learning models, such as WaveNet and Tacotron, to produce highly realistic and natural-sounding speech, which can even mimic different speaking styles and emotions.

The applications of NLSP are vast and diverse. Voice assistants like Siri, Alexa, and Google Assistant rely heavily on NLSP to understand and respond to user commands. Automated customer service systems use NLSP to handle customer inquiries, reducing the need for human agents. Medical transcription services use NLSP to convert doctors' dictations into written reports, improving productivity and accuracy. Language translation tools use NLSP to interpret spoken and written languages in real time, facilitating communication across language barriers. NLSP is also transforming the field of education, where voice-activated learning platforms can provide personalized learning experiences and assist students with disabilities by providing real-time transcription and speech synthesis.

However, NLSP faces several challenges. One major challenge is handling the variability and ambiguity of human language. Spoken language is often informal, fragmented, and filled with slang and idioms. Understanding these nuances requires advanced algorithms and large amounts of training data. ASR systems also need to be robust enough to handle noisy environments and diverse accents. Moreover, developing NLSP systems for low-resource languages, which lack sufficient training data, is a significant challenge.

Ethical considerations are also paramount. The collection and use of speech data raise concerns about privacy and security. It is essential to develop robust data anonymization techniques and ensure that user data is protected. Additionally, biases in training data can lead to biased NLSP systems, which can perpetuate social inequalities. Despite these challenges, the field of NLSP continues to advance rapidly. Ongoing research focuses on improving the accuracy and robustness of ASR and NLU systems, developing more natural-sounding TTS frameworks, and addressing ethical concerns. As NLSP technology continues to evolve, it will play an increasingly vital role in shaping the future of human-computer interaction.

IV. ASSISTIVE TECHNOLOGIES

Assistive technologies (AT) are poised to play a pivotal role in shaping the future of national GDPs by fostering greater inclusion and productivity. As populations age and the prevalence of disabilities increases, these innovations empower individuals to participate more effectively in the workforce and society. Tools such as screen readers, mobile devices, and voice recognition software help bridge the gap for individuals with disabilities, ensuring they can contribute to economic activities.

By providing access to education and professional training for people with disabilities, assistive technologies enable them to secure employment and develop skills that directly impact economic growth. Countries that invest in these technologies not only enhance social inclusion but also unlock the potential of untapped human capital. As businesses increasingly recognize the value of a diverse workforce, assistive innovations will drive progress, productivity, and market competitiveness. In the long run, this integration fosters a more equitable society, which ultimately strengthens a country's GDP by maximizing the potential of all its citizens. The continued advancement of AT can also contribute to the development of new businesses and markets, further fueling economic expansion.

The history of assistive technologies is a testament to human ingenuity and the persistent drive to overcome limitations. From simple tools to advanced digital systems, AT has evolved alongside societal understanding of disability and technological advancements. Early forms of assistance were often simple adaptations of existing tools, focusing on mobility and sensory impairments. For example, canes and crutches have been used for centuries, evolving from fundamental sticks to more refined designs with improved stability and comfort. Similarly, early hearing aids were acoustic devices, like ear trumpets, that amplified sound. Braille, developed in the 19th century, revolutionized reading for visually impaired individuals by providing a tactile alternative to printed text.

The Industrial Revolution brought a surge in innovative development that steadily impacted assistive devices. The introduction of electricity and mass production allowed for the creation of more complex aids. Electrically powered wheelchairs, for instance, offered greater independence for people with mobility impairments. The telephone, while not initially intended as an assistive device, proved invaluable for deaf people, enabling communication through text-based relay services. In the early 20th century, the rise of radio technology led to the development of electronic hearing aids, which provided more effective sound amplification than their acoustic predecessors.

World War II propelled significant advancements in rehabilitation and prosthetic technology. The need to care for injured veterans led to increased research and development in prosthetics, resulting in more functional and lifelike artificial limbs.

The post-war era also saw the rise of rehabilitation engineering as a distinct field, focusing on applying engineering principles to the design and development of assistive devices. The development of specialized communication devices for people with speech impairments gained momentum, with early devices relying on image boards and simple electronic displays. The advent of the personal computer and the digital revolution transformed the landscape of assistive technology.

Computers offered unprecedented opportunities for customization and accessibility. Screen readers, which convert on-screen text to speech, enabled visually impaired people to access digital information. Alternative input devices, such as trackballs and specialized keyboards, provided accessible interfaces for people with motor impairments. The internet opened up a world of information and communication for individuals with disabilities, breaking down barriers to education, employment, and social participation.

The rise of the internet and mobile technology further accelerated the development of AT. Smartphones and tablets, with their built-in accessibility features and a vast array of apps, have become powerful tools for people with disabilities. Voice recognition software has improved significantly, enabling hands-free control of devices and transcription for people with motor impairments. Augmented reality (AR) and virtual reality (VR) are emerging as promising technologies for rehabilitation and accessibility, offering immersive experiences that can aid in physical therapy and spatial awareness.

Today, assistive technologies are becoming increasingly integrated into standard devices and services. Accessibility is no longer an afterthought but a core design principle. AI is playing a growing role in AT, enabling personalized and adaptive solutions. AI-powered speech recognition, natural language processing, and computer vision are being used to create intelligent assistive devices that can understand and respond to user needs (Sharma, Gautam, et al., 2024). The development of brain-computer interfaces (BCIs) holds immense potential for people with severe motor impairments, allowing them to control devices and communicate using brain signals.

The history of AT is a continuous journey of innovation and empowerment. As technology advances and our understanding of disability expands, we can expect to see even more transformative solutions that improve the lives of individuals with disabilities, promoting inclusion, independence, and participation in all aspects of society. The focus now shifts to creating universally designed products and services, ensuring that accessibility is built in from the start, rather than added as an afterthought. This approach ensures a future where technology empowers everyone, regardless of their abilities.

Assistive technologies are devices, equipment, and software designed to maintain or improve the functional capabilities of individuals with disabilities. They play a crucial role in fostering autonomy, enhancing quality of life, and promoting inclusion across various domains, from education and work to daily living and entertainment. The range of AT is vast and continuously growing, reflecting the diverse needs and challenges faced by people with disabilities. The fundamental principle underlying AT is to empower individuals to overcome barriers and participate fully in society. This involves understanding the individual's specific needs, preferences, and objectives, and then selecting or developing appropriate technologies.

Figure 1 provides an overview of various assistive technologies.

Figure 1. List of assistive technologies.

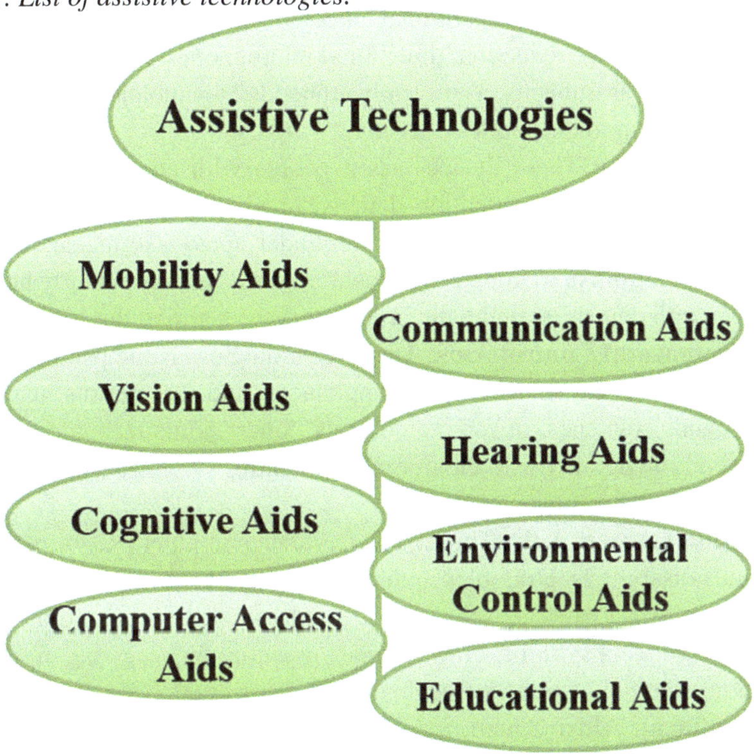

- **Mobility Aids:** These technologies address challenges related to movement and navigation. Examples include wheelchairs (manual and powered), walkers, canes, prosthetics, orthotics, and modified vehicles. Advanced mobility aids incorporate features like GPS navigation, obstacle detection, and voice control (Sharma et al., 2025).
- **Communication Aids:** These tools assist people with speech, language, and communication impairments. They range from simple communication boards with pictures or symbols to advanced speech-generating devices (SGDs) that

synthesize speech from text or images. Augmentative and alternative communication (AAC) systems are crucial for people with conditions like cerebral palsy, autism, or ALS.

- **Vision Aids:** These technologies support people with visual disabilities. Screen readers, magnifiers, braille displays, and optical character recognition (OCR) software are essential tools for accessing digital information. Navigation aids, such as GPS-enabled canes and wearable sensors, help with orientation and mobility.
- **Hearing Aids:** These devices amplify sound for people with hearing loss. Hearing aids range from traditional analog devices to advanced digital models that offer noise reduction, directional microphones, and wireless connectivity. Cochlear implants, a surgically embedded technology, provide electrical stimulation to the auditory nerve.
- **Cognitive Aids:** These devices assist people with cognitive impairments, such as memory loss, attention deficits, or executive function difficulties. Examples include digital calendars, reminder apps, task management software, and cognitive training programs. These aids are particularly helpful for people with dementia, traumatic brain injury, or learning disabilities.
- **Environmental Control Aids:** These technologies enable people to control their environment, such as lights, appliances, and thermostats, using voice commands, switches, or remote controls. Smart home technologies are increasingly integrated with environmental control systems, providing greater accessibility and convenience.
- **Computer Access Aids:** These tools facilitate computer use for people with various disabilities. Examples include alternative keyboards, mouse alternatives (e.g., trackballs, joysticks, head pointers), voice recognition software, and eye-tracking systems. These aids are essential for accessing digital information, communication, and education.
- **Educational Aids:** These innovations support learning and academic achievement for students with disabilities. Examples include text-to-speech software, screen readers, adaptive learning platforms, and specialized educational software. These aids can address various learning needs, such as dyslexia, ADHD, and autism.

AT empowers individuals to perform daily tasks, such as dressing, eating, and bathing, with greater independence. Communication aids facilitate meaningful interactions with others, reducing social isolation and improving relationships. Vision and hearing aids, as well as computer access tools, provide access to digital information, education, and entertainment. AT empowers people to participate fully in education, employment, and community activities, fostering social inclusion and equality. By addressing functional limitations and promoting independence, AT contributes to a better quality of life and overall well-being. In work and educational settings, AT increases productivity and allows individuals to contribute to society more effectively.

However, many AT devices are expensive, making them inaccessible to people with limited financial resources. Efforts are required to reduce costs and increase access to funding. AT must be tailored to the individual's specific needs and preferences. This requires a thorough assessment and ongoing support (Bhatt & Sharma, 2024). Successful use of AT requires adequate training and ongoing support for both individuals and their caregivers. AT devices and systems should be seamlessly integrated with other technologies, such as smart home devices and mobile apps. The development and use of AT also raise ethical concerns, such as data privacy, security, and the potential for misuse.

V. HUMAN-COMPUTER INTERACTION

The history of HCI is a story of evolving understanding, design, and implementation, shaped by the changing landscape of computing itself. From the earliest days of bulky mainframes to the ubiquitous presence of smartphones and wearable devices, HCI has consistently sought to bridge the gap between human capabilities and technological potential.

Initially, interaction with computers was a highly specialized and cumbersome process, requiring expertise in programming and a deep understanding of machine logic. In the early to mid-20th century, computers were primarily tools for scientists and engineers, accessed through punch cards and command-line interfaces. The focus was on optimizing machine efficiency rather than the user experience.

The rise of time-sharing systems in the 1960s marked a significant shift, allowing multiple users to interact with a single computer simultaneously. This development paved the way for more interactive computing experiences. Ivan Sutherland's Sketchpad, created in 1963, demonstrated the potential of graphical user interfaces (GUIs), enabling users to interact with computers through visual representations instead of text commands. Douglas Engelbart's "mother of all demos" in 1968 further revolutionized HCI with the introduction of the mouse, windowing systems, and hypertext, showcasing the possibilities of direct manipulation and interactive computing. These early innovations laid the foundation for the development of modern GUIs.

The 1970s and 1980s saw the rise of personal computing, with the introduction of machines like the Apple II and the IBM PC. This democratization of computing required a greater focus on user-friendliness. Xerox PARC played a pivotal role in this era, developing the Alto computer, which featured a fully developed GUI with icons, menus, and a desktop metaphor. Although the Alto was not commercially successful, its innovations heavily influenced the development of the Apple Macintosh and Microsoft Windows, which brought GUIs to the mainstream. The focus moved from command-line interfaces to more intuitive interaction through visual representations.

The 1990s saw the explosive growth of the internet and the World Wide Web, transforming the way people accessed and interacted with information. Web browsers introduced new interaction paradigms, such as hyperlinks and navigation buttons, making it easier for users to explore vast amounts of online content. The rise of e-commerce and online services further emphasized the importance of usability and user experience. The concept of user-centered design gained prominence, advocating for the inclusion of users throughout the design process.

The advent of mobile computing and ubiquitous connectivity in the 21st century has ushered in a new era of HCI. Smartphones, tablets, and wearable devices have become integral parts of daily life, demanding new interaction methods and design considerations. Touchscreens, voice interfaces, and gesture recognition have become commonplace, enabling more natural and intuitive interactions. The focus has shifted from desktop-centric design to mobile-first and multi-device experiences. The rise of social media and online communities has also changed the way people interact with each other and with technology, highlighting the social and collaborative aspects of HCI.

The development of AI and machine learning has opened up new frontiers in HCI. AI-powered virtual assistants, chatbots, and personalized interfaces are becoming increasingly prevalent, enabling more adaptive and intelligent interactions. Natural language processing, computer vision, and machine learning algorithms are being used to create systems that can understand and respond to human needs in more sophisticated ways. The advancement of augmented reality and virtual reality technologies is also pushing the boundaries of HCI, offering immersive and interactive experiences that blur the lines between the physical and digital worlds.

Today, HCI is a multidisciplinary field that draws on insights from computer science, psychology, design, and other disciplines. The focus has expanded beyond usability to encompass broader aspects of user experience, including accessibility, emotional engagement, and social impact. As technology continues to evolve, HCI will play a significant role in shaping the future of human-computer interaction, ensuring that technology remains a tool that empowers and enhances human capabilities.

HCI stands as a vital, intriguing field dedicated to the design, evaluation, and implementation of interactive computing systems for human use, alongside the study of the major phenomena surrounding them. It's fundamentally about bridging the chasm between human capabilities and the inherent complexities of technology, aiming to create systems that are not only functional but also intuitive and enjoyable. At its core, HCI is driven by the principle of **user-centered design**, prioritizing the needs, goals, and limitations of the user throughout the entire development process. This philosophy emphasizes **usability**, ensuring that systems are easy to learn, efficient to use, and satisfying to interact with, while also championing **accessibility**, striving to create systems that are inclusive and usable by all, including those with disabilities.

The overarching objectives of HCI extend beyond simple functionality, aiming to enhance user productivity, satisfaction, and happiness, while also fostering innovation in interactive technologies and understanding the profound impact of technology on individuals and society. The domain of HCI encompasses a wide range of topics, from the tangible aspects of input and output devices, such as keyboards, mice, touchscreens, and voice interfaces, to the more abstract domains of user interface (UI) and interaction design (IxD). **UI design** focuses on creating visually appealing and intuitive interfaces that are easy to navigate, considering elements like layout, typography, and color schemes. **IxD**, on the other hand, delves into the design of interactive experiences, mapping out the flow of interactions, feedback mechanisms, and user engagement.

Usability evaluation plays a critical role in assessing the effectiveness of these designs, using methods like user testing, heuristic evaluation, and cognitive walk-throughs to identify and address potential usability issues. Moreover, HCI places a strong emphasis on **human factors**, drawing upon insights from cognitive psychology, perception, and ergonomics to understand the capabilities and limitations of users and apply this knowledge to design. The field has witnessed a dramatic evolution, reflecting the rapid advancements in computing technology.

From the early days of mainframe computers, where interaction was limited to technical specialists, to the present era of ubiquitous computing, where technology is seamlessly integrated into daily life, HCI has continuously adapted to the changing landscape. The rise of the personal computer, the internet, and mobile devices has significantly changed how we interact with technology, creating new opportunities and challenges for HCI researchers and practitioners. **Social computing**, **affective computing**, and **virtual and augmented reality** are just a few examples of the emerging areas that are shaping the future of HCI. Social computing explores how people interact with each other through technology, considering social media, online communities, and collaborative systems. Affective computing focuses on enabling computers to recognize, interpret, and respond to human emotions, while VR/AR technologies create immersive and interactive experiences that blur the lines between the real and virtual worlds (Pandey et al., 2024).

HCI principles are now integral to software development processes, ensuring that applications are user-friendly and meet the needs of their target audience. In web design, HCI plays a crucial role in creating websites that are easy to navigate and provide a seamless user experience. Product designers use HCI insights to create consumer products that are intuitive and enjoyable to use. In education, HCI is used to design educational software and online learning platforms that enhance student engagement and learning outcomes. In healthcare, HCI is applied to the design of medical devices and healthcare information systems, improving patient safety and efficiency.

Looking ahead, the future of HCI is poised to be shaped by several key trends. AI is expected to play a significant part, enabling the development of intelligent and adaptive interfaces that provide personalized and context-aware interactions. Natural language processing (NLP) will further enhance voice interfaces and conversational agents, facilitating more natural and intuitive communication between people and computers. Wearable technologies, the Internet of Things (IoT), and haptic feedback will create new opportunities for interaction and data collection, while brain-computer interfaces (BCIs) will open up new possibilities for direct communication between the brain and computers. As technology becomes increasingly integrated into our lives, ethical considerations will also take center stage, with a growing emphasis on designing technologies that are responsible, equitable, and sustainable. In essence, HCI isn't just about making computers easier to use; it's about shaping the future of technology in a way that empowers and benefits all of humanity.

VI. ADVANTAGES

The integration of NLSP with assistive technologies within the framework of HCI presents a multitude of advantages, fundamentally changing how people with diverse needs engage with the digital world. This synergy empowers users to overcome traditional interaction barriers, fostering a more inclusive and accessible technological landscape.

One primary advantage lies in the enhanced accessibility for individuals with **motor disabilities**. By leveraging NLSP, users can control computers and other devices through spoken commands, eliminating the reliance on conventional input methods like keyboards and mice, which may be challenging or impossible for them to use. This empowers people with conditions such as cerebral palsy, muscular dystrophy, or spinal cord injuries to navigate digital environments, communicate effectively, and perform tasks with greater autonomy and efficiency.

Furthermore, for individuals with **visual disabilities**, NLSP provides a gateway to information and digital content. Screen readers powered by TTS synthesis, enhanced by NLU, allow users to access websites, documents, and other digital assets through spoken output (Sharma et al., 2024). This not only facilitates information retrieval but also enables users to interact with complex interfaces and applications using voice commands, fostering a more seamless and intuitive user experience.

By removing the reliance on visual prompts, NLSP empowers people with visual impairments to participate more fully in education, work, and social activities.

NLSP also significantly benefits individuals with **cognitive disabilities**, such as autism, dementia, or learning disabilities. Voice-activated reminders, task management systems, and cognitive training applications can assist people with memory challenges, attention deficits, and executive function difficulties. NLU-powered conversational agents can provide personalized support, guidance, and companionship, offering emotional support and reducing feelings of isolation. These agents can be tailored to understand and respond to individual needs and preferences, fostering a sense of connection and promoting cognitive well-being.

Additionally, NLSP can bridge communication gaps for individuals with **hearing impairments**. ASR can transcribe spoken conversations in real-time, providing captions for people who are deaf or hard of hearing. Conversely, TTS can generate synthesized speech from text input, enabling individuals to communicate with others who may not understand sign language. This facilitates seamless communication in various settings, including educational, professional, and social environments. The ability to customize voice commands and create personalized workflows further enhances the user experience, adapting to individual needs and preferences. This level of customization is crucial in assistive technologies, as it allows for a tailored approach that addresses the unique requirements of each user.

Beyond the immediate benefits for people with specific disabilities, the integration of NLSP with assistive technologies also promotes greater inclusivity and accessibility for a broader population. Voice interfaces and natural language understanding make technology more approachable and user-friendly for people who may be less familiar with traditional computer interfaces. This can bridge the digital divide and empower individuals with limited technical skills to access information, communicate effectively, and participate more fully in the digital world. The widespread adoption of voice assistants and smart home devices demonstrates the growing acceptance and popularity of voice-based interactions, highlighting the potential of NLSP to transform how we interact with technology.

In conclusion, the advantages of integrating NLSP with assistive technologies within HCI are multifaceted and profound. This synergy empowers individuals with motor, visual, cognitive, and hearing disabilities to overcome obstacles, access information, and communicate effectively. It promotes greater inclusivity and accessibility for a broader population, bridging the digital divide and fostering a more equitable technological landscape. As NLSP technology continues to advance, we can expect to see even more sophisticated and intuitive interfaces that enable individuals with diverse needs to live more autonomous, fulfilling, and connected lives.

VII. CHALLENGES

The integration of NLSP with assistive technologies within HCI, while offering immense potential, is fraught with significant challenges that require careful consideration and innovative solutions.

One primary challenge lies in the inherent variability and ambiguity of human language. Spoken language is often informal, fragmented, and filled with slang, idioms, and colloquialisms, making it difficult for computers to accurately interpret meaning. Furthermore, factors such as accents, dialects, and speech impairments present additional complexities, demanding robust ASR systems capable of handling diverse acoustic environments and speech patterns. Standard ASR models frequently struggle with non-standard speech, leading to errors and frustration for users with speech impediments or those speaking in less common dialects. This becomes especially problematic in assistive technologies, where accuracy is paramount for effective communication and control.

Additionally, NLU faces the challenge of contextual comprehension. The meaning of a spoken expression can change significantly depending on the surrounding conversation, the speaker's background knowledge, and the broader context of the interaction (Dasawat & Sharma, 2024). Developing NLU systems that can accurately interpret these nuances requires advanced algorithms and large amounts of training data, which can be challenging to secure, particularly for low-resource languages or specialized domains.

Another significant challenge is the development of robust and reliable assistive technologies that seamlessly integrate NLSP. Many assistive devices are designed with specific user groups in mind, and adapting them to incorporate voice control and natural language interfaces requires significant modifications. Ensuring that these modifications don't compromise the device's functionality, usability, or durability is critical. Moreover, the development of personalized assistive technologies that cater to individual needs and preferences is a complex undertaking. Each person with a disability has unique requirements, and creating systems that can adapt to these variations requires advanced customization capabilities. This often necessitates extensive user testing and feedback, as well as the development of flexible and scalable software architectures. Figure 2 illustrates the challenges of natural language speech processing integrating assistive technologies for human-computer interaction.

Figure 2. Challenges of natural language speech processing integrating assistive technologies for human-computer interaction..

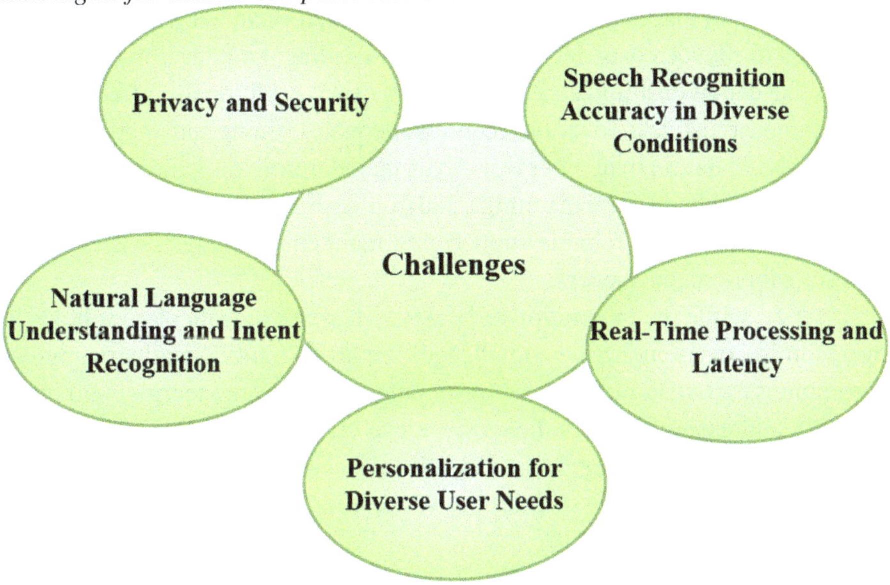

The real-time processing demands of NLSP also pose a challenge, especially in applications that require quick responses, such as voice-controlled mobility aids or real-time communication systems. Ensuring that these systems can process speech and generate accurate responses in a timely manner is vital for user experience and safety.

Ethical considerations are also paramount. The collection and use of speech data raise concerns about privacy and security. Speech data can contain sensitive information about a user's health, personal life, and beliefs, and it is essential to develop robust data anonymization procedures and ensure that user data is protected from unauthorized access. Biases in training data can also lead to biased NLSP systems, which can perpetuate social inequalities and discriminate against certain user groups. For example, ASR systems trained on data from predominantly male speakers may perform poorly for female speakers or speakers with non-standard accents. Addressing these biases requires careful data curation, algorithmic fairness procedures, and ongoing evaluation of system performance.

Furthermore, the potential for misuse of NLSP-enabled assistive innovations raises ethical concerns. Voice cloning and deepfake technologies might be used to impersonate individuals or manipulate their speech, posing risks to privacy and security. It is essential to develop safeguards and ethical guidelines to prevent these technologies from being used for malicious purposes.

The integration of NLSP with assistive technologies also requires addressing the challenges of accessibility and affordability. Many assistive devices are expensive, making them inaccessible to people with limited financial resources. Efforts are required to reduce costs, increase access to funding, and develop open-source solutions that can be customized and adapted by users. Additionally, effective use of NLSP-enabled assistive innovations requires adequate training and ongoing support for both individuals and their caregivers. This includes providing training on how to use voice commands, customize settings, and troubleshoot common issues. Ensuring that users have access to reliable support and maintenance services is crucial for long-term adoption and success.

In essence, while the integration of NLSP with assistive technologies holds immense promise, overcoming these challenges requires a multidisciplinary approach that combines expertise in linguistics, computer science, engineering, and human factors. By addressing these challenges, we can create assistive technologies that are not only effective and reliable but also ethical, accessible, and user-friendly, empowering individuals with disabilities to live more independent and fulfilling lives.

VIII. CASE STUDY

The United States stands as a prominent hub for the advancement and deployment of NLSP integrated with assistive technologies, significantly impacting HCI for individuals with diverse needs. A compelling case study revolves around the dynamic integration of NLSP within educational and professional environments, particularly for people with learning and motor impairments. This case illustrates the transformative potential of these technologies in fostering inclusivity and autonomy.

In educational settings, NLSP has revolutionized the learning experience for students with dyslexia, dysgraphia, and other learning disabilities. Traditionally, these students faced significant challenges in reading and writing. However, modern speech-to-text software, powered by advanced NLSP algorithms, has provided a seamless and empowering alternative. Tools from companies like Dragon and Google allow students to verbalize their thoughts and concepts, which are then transcribed into written text in real time. This not only eases the burden of written expression but also enhances cognitive processing by freeing up mental resources previously dedicated to the mechanics of writing.

Furthermore, real-time captioning services, another application of NLSP, are being increasingly used in classrooms and online learning platforms to provide instant transcriptions of lectures and discussions. This benefits students with auditory processing difficulties by allowing them to access spoken information in written form, which significantly improves comprehension and retention. This promotes a more equitable learning environment for all.

Beyond the classroom, NLSP is also transforming the professional landscape for individuals with motor impairments, such as those with cerebral palsy or spinal cord injuries. Voice-activated interfaces and hands-free computing solutions are enabling these individuals to participate fully in the workforce, overcoming barriers that previously limited their employment opportunities. For instance, voice-controlled software allows people to manage complex tasks, such as programming, data analysis, and customer service, without the need for a traditional keyboard and mouse.

Companies like Microsoft, through their Azure Cognitive Services, offer robust NLSP tools that developers can integrate into custom applications. This has led to the creation of tailored solutions for specific professional needs, such as in healthcare, where physicians can dictate patient notes and access hands-free medical records, and in legal professions, where attorneys can transcribe depositions and draft documents using voice commands (Bhatt et al., 2024).

The widespread adoption of smart home technologies, driven by NLSP, has also significantly enhanced the quality of life for people with mobility limitations. Devices like Amazon Echo and Google Home, powered by voice assistants like Alexa and Google Assistant, allow users to control various aspects of their environment, from lighting and temperature to entertainment and security systems. This level of intuitive control fosters greater independence and autonomy, enabling individuals to live more comfortably and securely in their own homes. The integration of NLSP with home automation also extends to assistive robots, which can perform tasks such as retrieving objects, providing medication reminders, and assisting with personal care, further enhancing the autonomy of individuals with severe physical disabilities.

However, the implementation of NLSP-based assistive technologies is not without its challenges. One significant hurdle is the variability of speech patterns, especially for individuals with speech disabilities. While advancements in deep learning have improved the accuracy of speech recognition systems, they still struggle to accurately interpret atypical speech. Ongoing research, such as Google's Project Euphonia, aims to address this challenge by developing algorithms that are trained on diverse speech samples, including those from individuals with neurological conditions.

Another crucial aspect is the need for personalized solutions. Each person has unique needs and preferences, requiring customized interfaces and workflows. User-centered design principles are essential in ensuring that assistive technologies are not only functional but also user-friendly and intuitive.

Furthermore, the digital divide remains a significant barrier to the widespread adoption of NLSP-based assistive technologies. Access to high-speed internet, affordable devices, and technical support is critical for people to fully benefit from these innovations. Addressing this issue requires collaborative efforts from government agencies, technology companies, and non-profit organizations to provide equitable access to digital resources and training. Finally, privacy and security concerns surrounding the collection and storage of voice data must be addressed. Robust security measures and transparent data policies are vital in building trust and ensuring the responsible use of NLSP technologies.

In summary, the integration of NLSP with assistive technologies in the United States is driving significant advancements in HCI, empowering individuals with disabilities to participate more fully in society. While challenges remain, ongoing research and development, coupled with a commitment to user-centered design and equitable access, hold immense promise for the future of assistive technologies.

IX. FUTURE PERSPECTIVE

The future of NLSP is integrated with assistive technologies within HCI poised for transformative advancements, driven by rapid progress in artificial intelligence, machine learning, and hardware capabilities. We can anticipate a significant shift towards more personalized and adaptive assistive technologies, where NLSP plays a crucial role in tailoring systems to individual needs and preferences.

Enhanced Personalization and Accuracy

The future will bring assistive devices that learn and adapt to a user's unique speech patterns, cognitive styles, and physical limitations. Advanced ASR systems will achieve near-perfect accuracy, even in noisy environments and with diverse accents and speech impediments, enabling seamless voice control and communication (Rawat et al., 2024).

NLU will evolve to comprehend complex and nuanced language, including sarcasm, irony, and emotional cues, allowing for more natural and intuitive interactions. Conversational agents will become more sophisticated, providing personalized support, companionship, and cognitive assistance. These agents will be capable of engaging in meaningful dialogues, offering emotional support, and facilitating social interactions, especially for individuals experiencing isolation or cognitive decline.

Integration with Emerging Technologies

The integration of NLSP with emerging technologies like VR/AR will unlock new possibilities for assistive applications. VR/AR environments can provide immersive and interactive experiences for rehabilitation, training, and education, enabling individuals with disabilities to practice skills and overcome challenges in a safe and controlled setting. NLSP will empower users to interact with these virtual environments using voice commands, creating a more intuitive and engaging experience. For example, individuals with motor disabilities may use voice commands to navigate virtual worlds or participate in virtual social gatherings.

Wearable technologies will also play a significant role. Smartwatches, fitness trackers, and other wearable devices can monitor health, track movement, and provide real-time feedback. NLSP will enable users to interact with these devices using voice commands, accessing information, controlling settings, and receiving personalized alerts. Brain-computer interfaces (BCIs) are another promising area of development. BCIs can enable individuals to control devices using brain signals, offering new possibilities for communication and mobility. In the future, NLSP may be integrated with BCIs to create hybrid systems that combine the power of voice control with the precision of brain-computer interaction.

Broader Accessibility and Ethical Considerations

The development of open-source NLSP tools and platforms will democratize access to assistive technologies, empowering individuals and communities to create customized solutions for their specific needs. The Internet of Things (IoT) will create a more interconnected and interactive environment, where assistive devices seamlessly integrate with smart home technologies. Voice-activated environmental control systems will enable individuals to manage their surroundings with greater ease and independence, controlling lights, appliances, and thermostats using spoken commands.

The ethical considerations surrounding NLSP and assistive technologies will also become increasingly important. Robust data privacy and security measures will be implemented to protect user data from unauthorized access and misuse. Algorithmic fairness procedures will be used to mitigate biases in NLSP systems, ensuring they are equitable and inclusive. Ethical guidelines will be developed to address the potential for misuse of voice cloning and deepfake technologies, safeguarding individuals from impersonation and manipulation.

The future will also see a greater emphasis on proactive and preventative care. NLSP-powered systems will be able to monitor user behavior and speech patterns, identifying early signs of cognitive decline, mental health issues, or physical health problems. This will enable timely interventions and personalized support, improving health outcomes and quality of life. The collaboration between researchers, engineers, clinicians, and users will be vital for the successful development and implementation of future NLSP-enabled assistive technologies. In essence, the future of NLSP integrated with assistive technologies within HCI is one of empowerment, inclusivity, and personalization. It promises to create a world where technology is truly accessible to all, enabling individuals with disabilities to live more autonomous, fulfilling, and connected lives.

X. CONCLUSION

The integration of NLSP, assistive technologies, and HCI represents a significant advancement in creating inclusive and accessible digital experiences. This synergy transcends mere technological development, embodying a fundamental shift towards empowering individuals with diverse needs to participate fully in the modern world. The journey from simple speech recognition to sophisticated natural language understanding has paved the way for assistive devices that are not only functional but also intuitive and personalized.

Through the lens of HCI, the focus remains on user-centered design, ensuring that these technologies are seamlessly integrated into the daily lives of those they serve. The advantages of this integration are multifaceted. For people with motor disabilities, NLSP provides a gateway to digital control, enabling them to navigate computers and devices with spoken commands, thereby fostering autonomy and independence. For those with visual impairments, NLSP-powered screen readers and voice interfaces offer access to information and digital content, breaking down barriers to education, work, and social engagement.

Similarly, individuals with cognitive challenges benefit from NLSP-driven cognitive aids, which provide personalized support and guidance, enhancing memory, attention, and overall cognitive well-being. Furthermore, NLSP's ability to facilitate real-time communication for people with hearing impairments through automated transcription and speech synthesis underscores its transformative potential in bridging communication gaps.

However, the path to realizing the full potential of this integration is not without its challenges. The inherent complexities of human language, including its variability, ambiguity, and contextual nuances, demand sophisticated algorithms and extensive training data. Overcoming the limitations of ASR in handling diverse accents and speech patterns, especially for individuals with speech impediments, remains a critical area of focus. Additionally, ensuring the reliability, robustness, and personalization of assistive technologies requires continuous refinement and adaptation.

Ethical considerations surrounding data privacy, algorithmic bias, and the potential for misuse necessitate robust safeguards and ethical guidelines. The need for affordability, accessibility, and adequate training further underscores the importance of a holistic approach to the development and deployment of these technologies.

Looking ahead, the future of NLSP-integrated assistive technologies is bright, driven by ongoing advancements in AI, machine learning, and hardware capabilities.

Personalized and adaptive systems, immersive VR/AR experiences, and wearable technologies will further enhance the capabilities of assistive tools. Brain-computer interfaces and open-source platforms will democratize access and empower users to create customized solutions. The integration of IoT and smart home technologies will create interconnected environments that seamlessly adapt to individual needs. Proactive and preventative care through NLSP-powered health monitoring will improve health outcomes and quality of life.

Ultimately, the successful integration of NLSP with assistive technologies within HCI hinges on a collaborative and multidisciplinary approach. Researchers, engineers, clinicians, and users must work together to create technologies that are not only innovative but also ethical, accessible, and user-friendly. By prioritizing user-centered design, addressing ethical concerns, and fostering inclusivity, we can unlock the transformative potential of NLSP to create a more equitable and accessible digital world for all. This integration is more than just a technological advancement; it is a testament to our commitment to empowering individuals and building a future where technology serves to enhance human potential and foster inclusivity.

REFERENCES

Averbukh, V. L. (2020). Evolution of human computer interaction. *Science and Vision Journal (SV-Journal), 5*(11). Retrieved from https://sv-journal.org/2020-5/11/en.pdf

Bakeer, A. (2024). An integrated system for accessible summarization of web search results for the blind and visually impaired. *Benha Journal of Applied Sciences, 9*(3), 1–12. Retrieved from https://bjas.journals.ekb.eg/article_366402_7a09f443daf633fb66ae72b552be5e22.pdf

Bhatt, S., & Sharma, S. (2024). Quantum Cryptography Using Blockchain for 6G Enabled Internet of Vehicles. In 2024 1st International Conference on Advanced Computing and Emerging Technologies (ACET), 1–6. https://doi.org/DOI: 10.1109/ACET61898.2024.10730580

Bhatt, S., Sharma, S., & Bhadula, S. (2024). NeuroAI: Emerging Artificial Intelligence and Image Processing Techniques in Neuroscience for Enhanced Medical Diagnosis of Brain Tumor. In 2024 First International Conference on Pioneering Developments in Computer Science & Digital Technologies (IC2SDT), 204–209. https://doi.org/DOI: 10.1109/IC2SDT62152.2024.10696499

Chang, Y., Liu, Z., & Guo, Y. (2024). WorldScribe: Towards context-aware live visual descriptions. *arXiv preprint arXiv:2408.06627.* /arXiv.2408.06627DOI: 10.1145/3654777.3676375

Dasawat, S. S., & Sharma, S. (2024). Edge Intelligence Enabled Secured Digital Transformation in Internet of Autonomous Vehicles. In 2024 12th International Conference on Internet of Everything, Microwave, Embedded, Communication and Networks (IEMECON), 1–6. https://doi.org/DOI: 10.1109/IEMECON62401.2024.10846320

Ding, Z., Ji, Y., Gan, Y., Wang, Y., & Xia, Y. (2024). Current status and trends of technology, methods, and applications of Human–Computer Intelligent Interaction (HCII): A bibliometric research. *Multimedia Tools and Applications*, *83*(27), 69111–69144. DOI: 10.1007/s11042-023-18096-6

Dokania, H., & Chattaraj, N. (2022). An assistive interface protocol for communication between visually and hearing-speech impaired persons in internet platform. *Disability and Rehabilitation. Assistive Technology*, *19*(1), 233–246. DOI: 10.1080/17483107.2022.2078898 PMID: 35618260

Emara, T. (2018). Adaptive Power-Saving Mechanism for VoIP Over WiMAX Based on Artificial Neural Network. In Waluyo, A. B. (Ed.), *Algorithms, Methods, and Applications in Mobile Computing and Communications* (pp. 158–177). IGI Global., DOI: 10.4018/978-1-5225-5693-0.ch007

Emara, T., Hassan, E., Trinh, T., Li, G., & Saber, A. (Eds.). (2025b). *The Role of Artificial Intelligence in Advancing Applied Life Sciences*. IGI Global Scientific Publishing., DOI: 10.4018/979-8-3693-9208-9

Emara, T. Z. (2016). Maximizing Power Saving for VoIP over WiMAX Systems. *International Journal of Mobile Computing and Multimedia Communications*, *7*(1), 32–40. DOI: 10.4018/IJMCMC.2016010103

Emara, T. Z., Ashraf, R., Saber, A., Trinh, T., & Awad, W. (2025c). A Data Processing Algorithm to Approximate Big Stream Data Analysis. In *2nd IEEE International Conference on Machine Intelligence and Smart Innovation (ICMISI 2025)*. DOI: 10.1109/ICMISI65108.2025.11115782

Emara, T. Z., Hassan, E., Elbedwehy, S., & Saber, A. (2025a). A Historical Perspective on Artificial Intelligence in Applied Life Sciences. In *The role of artificial intelligence in advancing applied life sciences*. IGI-Global. DOI: 10.4018/979-8-3693-9208-9.ch002

Emara, T. Z., & Huang, J. Z. (2019a). A distributed data management system to support large-scale data analysis. *Journal of Systems and Software*, *148*, 105–115. DOI: 10.1016/j.jss.2018.11.007

Emara, T. Z., & Huang, J. Z. (2019b). RRPlib: A spark library for representing HDFS blocks as a set of random sample data blocks. *Science of Computer Programming*, *184*, 102301. DOI: 10.1016/j.scico.2019.102301

Emara, T. Z., Saleh, A. I., & Arafat, H. (2014). Power saving mechanism for VoIP services over WiMAX systems. *Wireless Networks*, *20*(5), 975–985. DOI: 10.1007/s11276-013-0650-5

Emara, T. Z., Trinh, T., & Huang, J. Z. (2023). Geographically distributed data management to support large-scale data analysis. *Scientific Reports*, *13*(1), 17783. Advance online publication. DOI: 10.1038/s41598-023-44789-x PMID: 37853092

Grudin, J. (2017). A moving target — The evolution of human-computer interaction. In *Handbook of Human-Computer Interaction* (3rd ed.). Microsoft Research., Retrieved from https://www.microsoft.com/en-us/research/wp-content/uploads/2017/01/HCIhandbook3rd.pdf

Joshi, A., Dabre, R., Kanojia, D., Li, Z., Zhan, H., Haffari, G., & Dippold, D. (2025). Natural language processing for dialects of a language: A survey. *ACM Computing Surveys*, *57*(6), 1–37. DOI: 10.1145/3712060

Karpov, A. A., & Yusupov, R. M. (2018). Multimodal interfaces of Human–Computer Interaction. *Herald of the Russian Academy of Sciences*, *88*(1), 67–74. DOI: 10.1134/S1019331618010094

Lu, R., Wei, R., & Zhang, J. (2024). Human-computer interaction based on speech recognition. *Applied and Computational Engineering*, *36*(1), 102–110. DOI: 10.54254/2755-2721/36/20230429

Lv, Z., Poiesi, F., Dong, Q., Lloret, J., & Song, H. (2022). Deep Learning for intelligent Human–Computer Interaction. *Applied Sciences (Basel, Switzerland)*, *12*(22), 11457. DOI: 10.3390/app122211457

Mulfari, D., Carnevale, L., & Villari, M. (2023). Toward a lightweight ASR solution for atypical speech on the edge. Future Generations Computer Systems: FGCS, 149, 455–463. DOI: 10.1016/j.future.2023.08.002

Pandey, C., Sharma, S., & Bhadula, S. (2024). Artificial Intelligence Technique in Next Generation Healthcare Systems. In *2024 IEEE International Conference on Communication, Computing and Signal Processing (IICCCS)*, 1–6. https://doi.org/DOI: 10.1109/IICCCS61609.2024.10763570

Peng, J., Wang, Y., Li, B., Guo, Y., Wang, H., Fang, Y., & Yu, K. (2025). A survey on Speech Large Language Models for understanding. Retrieved from https://arxiv.org/abs/2410.18908 DOI: 10.36227/techrxiv.175321809.95815200/v1

Rao, M., Raju, A., Dheram, P., Bui, B., & Rastrow, A. (2020). Speech to semantics: Improve ASR and NLU jointly via all-neural interfaces. *arXiv preprint arXiv:2008.06173*. /arXiv.2008.06173DOI: 10.21437/Interspeech.2020-2976

Rawat, R., Goyal, H. R., & Sharma, S. (2024). Hofstede's Cultural Dimension Driven Artificial Narrow Intelligence IDFIS for Industry 5.0 Empowered Digital Society. *Recent Patents on Engineering*, *19*. Advance online publication. DOI: 10.2174/0118722121334543241001050846

Saber, A., Al-Zoghby, A. M., & Elmougy, S. (2018). Big-data aggregating, linking, integrating and representing using semantic web technologies. In Hassanien, A. E., Bhatnagar, R., & Taha, A. (Eds.), *International Conference on Advanced Machine Learning Technologies and Applications* (pp. 331–342). Cham: Springer International Publishing. DOI: 10.1007/978-3-319-74690-6_33

Selvarani, P., Kamalanaban, E., Azarudeen, H. M., Kumar, M. M., & Kavibharathi, K. (2025). Textual interaction framework for assistive computing. In CRC Press eBooks (pp. 598–604). https://doi.org/DOI: 10.1201/9781003559139-89

Sharma, S., Gautam, A., & Tyagi, R. (2024). Artificial Intelligence and Cyber Security Driven Social Innovations in Digital Adventure Tourism. In 2024 First International Conference on Pioneering Developments in Computer Science & Digital Technologies (IC2SDT), 1–6. https://doi.org/DOI: 10.1109/IC2SDT62152.2024.10696759

Sharma, S., Tomar, M., & Tyagi, R. (2024). Federated learning enabled secure air transport and tourism system. 2022 13th International Conference on Computing Communication and Networking Technologies (ICCCNT), 1–6. https://doi.org/DOI: 10.1109/ICCCNT61001.2024.10724849

Sharma, S., Tyagi, R., & Mohan, S. (2024). Generative Artificial Intelligence-Enabled climate change and Deep-Sea food webs. In Advances in environmental engineering and green technologies book series (pp. 199–224). https://doi.org/DOI: 10.4018/979-8-3693-6670-7.ch009

Sharma, S., Tyagi, R., & Mohan, S. (2025). Artificial intelligence and optimized computational modelling against climate crisis. In Elsevier eBooks (pp. 1–14). https://doi.org/DOI: 10.1016/B978-0-443-21905-4.00006-7

Tan, X., Qin, T., Soong, F., & Liu, T.-Y. (2021). A survey on neural speech synthesis. *arXiv preprint arXiv:2106.15561*. https://doi.org//arXiv.2106.15561DOI: 10.48550

Trinh, T., Duc, L. P., Tran, C. T., Duy, T. T., & Emara, T. Z. (2022). A New Stratified Block Model to Process Large-Scale Data for a Small Cluster. In *Lecture Notes on Data Engineering and Communications Technologies* (Vol. 124, pp. 253–263). Springer Science and Business Media Deutschland GmbH., DOI: 10.1007/978-3-030-97610-1_21

Trinh, T., Nguyen, N., Wu, D., Huang, J. Z., & Emara, T. Z. (2019). A New Location-Based Topic Model for Event Attendees Recommendation. In *2019 IEEE-RIVF International Conference on Computing and Communication Technologies (RIVF)* (pp. 106–111). DOI: 10.1109/RIVF.2019.8713716

TrinhHuy., T., Trinh, T., NguyenViet, H., Emara, T. Z., & VuongThi, N. (2025). Event scale prediction in event-based social networks. 11th EAI International Conference on Industrial Networks and Intelligent Systems, Da Nang, Vietnam.

VuThi., K., VuongThi, N., NguyenXuan, H., Emara, T. Z., & Trinh, T. (2024). Feature Selection Based on Top Frequency. In M. and N. L. A. and L. K. Y. Nguyen Thi Dieu Linh and Dawson (Eds.), Proceedings of the International Conference on Intelligent Systems and Networks (pp. 58–65). Springer Nature Singapore. https://doi.org/DOI: 10.1007/978-981-97-5504-2_7

Wu, S. (2024). Speech Recognition Interaction Control Method for Smart Home Based on Natural Language Processing. *International Journal of Product Development, 28*(4), 10067949. Advance online publication. DOI: 10.1504/IJPD.2024.10067949

Yang, Y., & Bao, W. (2023). Application of Human-Computer Interaction Technology in remote language learning platform. *International Journal of Human-Computer Interaction*, •••, 1–11. DOI: 10.1080/10447318.2023.2194709

Zong, J., Lee, C., Lundgard, A., Jang, J., Hajas, D., & Satyanarayan, A. (2022). Rich screen reader experiences for accessible data visualization. *Computer Graphics Forum: Journal of the European Association for Computer Graphics, 41*(3), 15–27. DOI: 10.1111/cgf.14519

Chapter 6
Speech-Based Speaker Gender Identification Using Deep Learning

G. Aishwarya Laxmi
Avinashilingam Institute for Home Science and Higher Education for Women, India

Judith Justin
https://orcid.org/0000-0001-6339-0841
Avinashilingam Institute for Home Science and Higher Education for Women, India

R. Vanithamani
https://orcid.org/0009-0006-2767-3629
Avinashilingam Institute for Home Science and Higher Education for Women, India

Pavithra Suchindran
https://orcid.org/0000-0003-3878-8473
Avinashilingam Institute for Home Science and Higher Education for Women, India

ABSTRACT

Speech recognition is a key area in Artificial Intelligence that involves extracting meaningful information from speech signals, such as gender, age, or emotion. While humans can easily identify a speaker's gender through conversation, computers require advanced models to perform this task effectively. This study proposes a deep learning-based approach for gender classification using features extracted from speech samples. Two feature extraction methods: Mel Frequency Cepstral

DOI: 10.4018/979-8-3373-3048-8.ch006

Coefficients (MFCC) and Linear Prediction Cepstral Coefficients (LPCC) were evaluated using Convolutional Neural Networks (CNN) and Long Short-Term Memory (LSTM) models. MFCC with CNN achieved 89.1% accuracy, and with LSTM, 90.5%. In contrast, LPCC with CNN and LSTM produced lower accuracies of 84% and 85.2%, respectively. Results show that MFCC features significantly improve the performance of both models in classifying speaker gender.

INTRODUCTION

Speech builds an individual connection between human beings; it is the most significant component of the communication system. Speech in humans is produced through a coordinated process that involves several systems. The flow of air, which is necessary for the production of sound, is initiated by the lungs. Phonation is the process by which the vocal cords vibrate when air passes through the larynx, creating voiced sounds. The pharynx, mouth, and nasal cavities are among the resonant regions through which this sound passes, influencing the tone and quality of the voice. The next step is articulation, in which unique speech sounds are produced by the tongue, lips, and other tissues. The brain controls the entire system, maintaining accurate and fluent spoken language expression (Livieris et al., 2019). For the objective to imitate human-like speech in machines, speech processing technologies have advanced to include voice recognition systems, which are inspired by the natural speech generation process. In addition to linguistics and health, an extensive understanding of this mechanism is essential for improving voice-driven AI systems, speech therapy, and communication assistance for those with speech disorders.

The human voice is versatile and varies in range, which makes it capable of producing various sounds due to the vibration of the vocal cords. Each individual has unique linguistic features. The location, shape, and mobility of a person's vocal tract can affect the linguistic characteristics of speech samples. Speech samples may convey information about an individual's age, gender, accent, and emotional aspects (Singhal & Sharma, 2023a). The two main characteristics of speech samples are pitch and tone, which may differ between people. In speech, pitch refers to the highness or lowness of a tone as recognized by the auditory system, which is determined by the vocal cords cyclic production of vibrations per second. Typically, the pitch of human speech ranges between 100 to 400 Hz. The key acoustic component of tone is pitch. Tone mainly refers to dialects where word differentiation is based on pitch (Ertam, 2019). Speech samples play a vital role in speech recognition, as a speaker's distinct voice characteristics are influenced by their vocal traits, such as the vocal cords physical structure and the vocal tract's resonating chambers. It is attainable to employ these traits for security.

An Important aspect of speech recognition is the ability to recognize the speech samples and convert them into a format that machines can process to identify the speaker. Speaker identification is one of the speech recognition systems. Various speaker identification technologies applications can be found in voice authentication, security, surveillance, home automation, and identity verification. Speaker classification relies on extracting essential features from speech samples to accurately classify the speaker's gender (Jahangir et al., 2020). The human ear is a natural mechanism for voice recognition. Based on characteristics like frequency and loudness, the human ear possesses an exceptional system that effectively differentiates gender in voice and speech. Similarly, a computer may be trained to perform the same task by selecting and applying the appropriate characteristics from speech data to a deep learning algorithm (Uddin et al., 2021).

The development of better gender recognition based on speech has been the subject of numerous studies focusing on improving feature extraction and developing better classifiers (Kabir et al., 2025). This research work focuses on the classification of speaker's gender through speech samples by using deep learning models, utilizing two distinct feature extraction methods. Detecting gender automatically through a speaker's speech samples is one of the most critical tasks in speech signal processing. In gender detection, a speaker's gender can be derived based on their voice. Gender detection allows services like voice-activated assistants or chatbots to be customized for users. It can also be used to identify potential threats or fraud. Gender detection can also enhance customer service by classifying the speaker and enabling more accurate responses. (Mamyrbayev et al., 2020). As a result, voice-based automated gender identification has several applications (Alnuaim et al., 2022). Males and females have significantly distinct vocal tracts. Approximately 120 to 350 Hz is considered the pitch average range in an adult female, while 100 to 200 Hz is the average range in an adult male (Ali et al., 2022).

The primary challenge of gender identification from speech samples lies in extracting features and classifying them effectively (Jaleel et al., 2022). Deep learning is a subset of machine learning (ML) in which different layers of the network interpret data in progressively complex ways. Deep learning models have the primary advantage of using raw input data through several layers and eliminating the need for a higher-level data structure. Similar to how the human brain solves any problem, each hierarchy of layers in a network generates a unique set of features. Following data processing at various network layers, the system determines accurate identifiers for data categorization (Yasmin et al., 2022b). In this research, the CNN and LSTM models are developed. The first step involves extracting gender information from speech samples. Speech samples contain more information, including age and emotion (Mamyrbayev et al., 2020). MFCC is an advanced feature extraction method used for gender classification. The MFCC is based on the human auditory system, utilizing a Mel filter to extract speech features. On the other hand, LPCC is designed based on the human voice tract and uses a linear prediction filter to achieve the desired results. The second step involves classifying gender using the proposed models. The proposed method utilizes speech recordings from the VoxForge corpus, an open-access dataset that provides speech samples of males and females. Using this publicly available resource ensures ethical and transparent data sourcing. However, the dataset is limited to binary gender labels, which means it does not encompass the full range of gender identities. Although binary classification is used in this study due to the constraints of the dataset

A systematic approach is followed in this paper, with a review of existing research related to speaker gender classification. It then presents the proposed methodology and outlines the data collection process, also explaining the feature extraction techniques implemented and the deep learning models and software module used for gender classification. Finally, the results and their discussion were presented, followed by a conclusion summarizing the main findings and future work.

LITERATURE REVIEW

An Overview

The identification of gender is one of the most fundamental components of speech recognition. Automatic Gender Recognition is an intelligent machine that recognizes gender from speech by analyzing characteristics similar to those of humans, and through appropriate training, it can identify male and female speakers. Due to its importance in a variety of applications, identifying gender based on human speech has been considered one of the most challenging processes. Traditionally, gender estimation has been based on extracting speech features and performing classification tasks. The voice is classified according to its gender to minimize the computational load on additional processing on these systems. The purpose of this section is to discuss the algorithms researchers have used to analyze speech samples to classify the speaker's gender, as well as the various techniques used to extract the most important gender characteristics.

Related Deep Learning Algorithms for Classifying Gender

An ensemble RNN-BiLSTM algorithm was developed to identify the speaker's gender based on speech samples. The speech sample dataset consists of three genders (male, female, and transgender). MFCC is most frequently used to extract significant features from speech samples. MFCC features are extracted, and classification is performed using the RNN-BiLSTM algorithm to classify three genders. Using speech data, the BiLSTM algorithm collects and stores input features from past and future data of extracted features at a specific period. The Adam optimization technique is used to optimize the proposed model and increase the algorithm's learning rate. From the classification algorithm, the precision is 95.35%, the error factor is 0.045%, and the accuracy obtained is 95.52%, calculated for the gender classification of a speaker (Singhal & Sharma, 2023a).

A deeper LSTM algorithm was developed for gender identification and classification from voice samples. The public voice dataset is obtained from Kaggle, and acoustic properties are extracted from voice samples. The Relieff-based method calculates the weight values of extracted features and selects only effective features to feed as input to the deeper LSTM algorithm. Using a two-layer LSTM architecture, the algorithm's performance is increased by setting the output mode of the previous LSTM layer to sequence, the final LSTM layer to last, and softmax is used as the activation function. ML approaches (KNN, SVM with various activation functions, linear regression, fine tree, and linear discriminant) are compared with the proposed classification technique, achieving 98.4% more excellent results in identifying the gender of a speaker (Ertam, 2019).

A novel approach combining MFCC and time-based features (MFCCT) was introduced to enhance text-independent speaker identification accuracy. The proposed feature extraction method utilizes the LibriSpeech dataset to extract features. Various male and female English speech accents are included in the dataset, but the American dialect is the most common accent. In this dataset, each utterance is captured at a frequency of 16 kiloHertz (kHz). The initial phase is the extraction of features from speaker utterances using MFCC. The second stage is binning the 1500 rows of each extracted feature column of MFCC. The last step is to extract time-based features from each MFCC feature bin. Using MFCCT, a DNN classifier was developed and trained, obtaining an 89% accuracy rate. In contrast to RF, KNN, NB, J48, and SVM, the designed model exhibits superior accuracy in gender categorization (Jahangir et al., 2020).

A three-layer approach was employed to extract features from the TIMIT, RAVDESS, and BGC datasets for gender classification. To eliminate noise from the speech samples, the preprocessing stage uses a high-pass filter and a Savitzky-Golay filter. The first layer extracted the following features: Mode frequency, Spectral Flatness, Spectral Entropy, and Fundamental frequency. The extracted data was mapped using a linear interpolation function in the second layer, and features were extracted using MFCC and normalized using Z-score. LPC is computed at the third layer. To accurately determine the gender using extracted characteristics, a multi-output-based 1D CNN was proposed and achieved 93.01%. A comparison is made between different optimizers, and RMSprop achieves a better classification accuracy (Uddin et al., 2021).

LPC and MFCC were utilized as feature extraction methods to retrieve significant features from speech data. The dataset contains 1116 speech samples of short utterances of speakers collected based on 12 different vowel words in each sample, and a sampling frequency of 16 kHz. Artificial neural networks (ANN) and discriminative analysis (DA), two classification algorithms, have been developed. The developed algorithm utilizes the retrieved features. In the classification model, both feature extractions performed effectively. On the other hand, in both DA and ANN models, MFCC outperforms LPC. It has been seen that in DA and ANN, the accuracy of MFCC for gender classification is 95.16% and 97.07%, respectively (Ali et al., 2022).

CNN and Multilayer Perceptron (MLP) algorithms were applied to determine speaker identification and gender. The 855 speech samples are for training, and 570 are for testing the models. Comparing two feature normalization techniques, i) a long-flattened MFCC vector with max-min normalization, and ii) utilizing the z-score on MFCC and converting it into the Gram matrix. For evaluating the performance of the MLP and CNN, developed small and large model sizes depending on the number of hidden units. The dropout layer is fixed at 0.15, and ReLU functions as an activation layer. Using the Gram matrix and z-score normalization, the two models in small and large sizes outperformed the long-flattened normalized MFCC in terms of results. Large models only slightly increase performance; model size does not have much effect on the model's outcome (Mamyrbayev et al., 2020).

Deep learning techniques such as Deep Neural Networks (DNN) and pre-trained ResNet-34 and ResNet-50 architectures were employed for gender classification. MFCC, Mel spectrogram, Chroma STFT, Tonnetz, and special contrast were the feature extraction methods applied to the Mozilla dataset. The dataset is filtered to retrieve the most relevant gender attributes. The hand-crafted speech characteristics are used to train DNN and ML algorithms. The DNN classification achieved 95.97% accuracy compared to ML approaches. Spectrogram images generated from the voice are utilized for training ResNet 34 and ResNet 50. Using spectrogram images, ResNet34 and ResNet50 achieved 97.94% and 98.57% accuracy, respectively. Evaluated ResNet50's performance using SVD is 72.74%, and RAVDESS is 91.5%. Compared with DNN, ResNet50 outperforms in gender classification. It shows that ResNet50 is more effective in gender classification tasks. Additionally, ResNet50's performance is comparable to a human expert's accuracy (Alnuaim et al., 2022).

For speaker gender classification, machine learning models like Random Forest and KNN were proposed, as well as the deep learning model CNN. The following four features are extracted from voice samples: Mean, Standard Deviation, Zero-Crossing Rate, and Amplitude, which are combined with 12 extracted features by using MFCC from voice samples (CMU ARCTIC dataset contains wave files at a sampling rate of 16 kHz). Combined extracted features are formed into single feature vectors. Based on precision, recall, and F1-measure metrics, the CNN classifier performs better than ML techniques (Jaleel et al., 2022).

A Deep Learning Convolutional Neural Network (DLCNN) was developed to categorize speakers gender effectively. The RAVDESS dataset is pre-processed using the spectral subtraction method to eliminate noise. To train and test the developed algorithm, MFCC features are extracted from the desired voice files. The MFCC features influence the weight initialization of neurons within the algorithm. The cross-channel normalizing layer and the ReLU activation layer are employed as part of the algorithm. In identifying gender, the DLCNN achieved 98.33% accuracy (Das et al., 2022).

Based on a statistical analysis of the NEIA dataset, overlapping and lengthening were identified as key features for extracting information from non-lexical speech utterances. Another kind of feature extraction is done using MFCC. Combining and contrasting two methods of feature extraction to reliably determine gender. Support Vector Machine (SVM) and Recurrent Neural Network (RNN) are two proposed classification techniques. RNN is utilized with the RMSprop optimizer to speed up the learning rate. RNN accuracy of 89.61% was achieved by combining MFCC with overlapping and lengthening, compared to 86.58% with SVM. It was found that combining non-lexical feature extraction with MFCC led to superior results. This result suggests that MFCC is more effective for recognizing speech samples when combined with non-lexical features. Moreover, overlapping and lengthening the samples were also found to be beneficial in improving the accuracy of the RNN (Son et al., 2019).

The researchers developed a CNN model with a multi-attention module (MAM) algorithm to recognize age and gender from speech spectrograms. A speech recognition model was trained and evaluated using Common Voice and Korean speech datasets. Spectrogram images are generated from speech samples. To analyze speech, the proposed CNN model uses a 2D representation of speech samples as input data. In convolution layers, a rectangle-shaped filter is used as a kernel to improve age and gender recognition performance. The model is composed of two feature learning blocks (FLB) and an MAM mechanism with separate modules to address time and frequency. The model's learning rate was improved by employing the Adam optimizer. The novel algorithm achieved 96% accuracy using the Common Voice dataset and 97% accuracy using the Korean speech recognition dataset for gender classification (Tursunov et al., 2021).

The CNN algorithm was trained and tested using the VoxCeleb dataset for gender classification. Features were extracted using MFCC methods, and the results were normalized to ensure a variance of one and a mean of zero. Convolutional layers with the non-linear activation function ReLU were used for processing these extracted features. To collect vital information and minimize spatial dimensions, pooling layers were employed. To identify a non-linear correlation between retrieved features and gender tags, the output was flattened and passed through layers of fully connected layers. For each gender group, probabilities have been determined by the fully connected layer with 96% accuracy (Taha et al., 2024).

Speech samples from the EMO-DB and RAVDESS datasets were used to train and test a mixed convolutional neural network (MCNN) algorithm. The developed algorithm is trained by adding velocity and acceleration features to static 2D MFCCs and stacking them to generate dynamic 3D MFCCs as network inputs. The MCNN is a mixed convolution layer that combines both dilated convolution and standard convolution in a single layer, and the same convolution kernel can be used to obtain larger spatial information in the dynamic 3D MFCC and classify speech samples into male and female. Adam optimization is employed to train the algorithm more efficiently. Using the EMO-DB dataset, the accuracy of gender classification can reach nearly 100%, while using the RAVDESS dataset can reach nearly 99.5% (Hu et al., 2023).

The utilization of speech data for gender classification demonstrates that deep learning models, particularly the integrated BiLSTM-LSTM network, outperform traditional ML techniques. Based on a 20-feature set, the BiLSTM-LSTM model achieved 99.30% accuracy with 10 features selected using the Relief-Based method. As a result of these selected features, the model can effectively distinguish between male and female voices by capturing essential voice characteristics (Kabir et al., 2025).

Machine learning and deep learning techniques were employed to predict gender from Bengali speech samples. For classifying gender, 3,185 samples were collected from males, females, and third-gendered speakers. A six-feature extraction process was done based on the roll-off, spectral centroid, chroma-STFT, spectral bandwidth, zero crossing rate, and MFCC of the audio data. An evaluation of five machine learning models was conducted, along with an evaluation of a 1D CNN model. With a 99.37% accuracy ranking, the 1D CNN outperformed all others (Arpita et al., 2024).

To overcome the limitations of traditional MFCC-based methods, a deep learning framework was introduced for enhanced speaker age and gender classification. The suggested technique uses a bottleneck feature extractor incorporated within a DNN, which enriches typical MFCCs with phonological and spectral data. The method uses a regularization technique during DNN training that requires the use of shared labels among classes that are frequently confused with one another to further improve classification performance. The aGender corpus, an intricate dataset with more than 65,000 speech samples from 945 speakers in seven different age-gender categories, was used to evaluate the model. The method outperformed previous approaches, achieving classification accuracies of 56.13% using an I-vector classifier and 58.98%

with the DNN. The method achieves classification accuracies of 56.13% using an I-vector classifier and 58.98% with the DNN (Qawaqneh et al., 2017).

Identified Gaps

A few Deep Learning models that classify gender based on the acoustic properties of speech samples and short phrases of speakers have proven effective in increasing classification accuracy. For feature extraction, the MFCC method is most commonly used. However, there is no comparison between deep learning models based on MFCC and LPCC techniques. Based on the related approaches, the next chapter explains the methods employed to develop the gender classification model using MFCC and LPCC feature extraction techniques.

MATERIALS AND METHODS

An Overview of the Proposed Approach

The purpose of this section is to present the methodology adopted for speech-based gender classification. There are two feature extraction techniques used: MFCC and LPCC, which are explained in detail due to their significance in capturing the perceptual and linear predictive characteristics of speech, respectively, as well as their mathematical formulations. A Z-score normalization process is then applied to the extracted features to ensure consistency at scale, improving the performance of learning models. The normalized features are then processed by deep learning models. A CNN and LSTM architecture is developed for learning spatial and temporal patterns in speech data. Activation functions are discussed, as well as input dimensions, layers, and architectural design.

Proposed Approach

In this research, MFCC and LPCC are proposed as two distinct feature extraction methods for classifying gender from speech samples. MFCC is widely recognized for its effectiveness in capturing the perceptual aspects of speech for gender classification. In addition, it has the advantage of representing the short-term power spectrum of speech. This helps identify subtle differences in gender-related speech characteristics. On the other hand, LPCC focuses on the linear predictive aspects of speech and is valued for its efficiency in modeling the vocal tract. While both of these methods capture essential features of speech samples, their scale and distribution may differ substantially. As a result of this variation, deep learning models can interpret each feature differently, potentially negatively impacting their performance. By using the Z-score normalization method, all coefficients are transformed to have a mean of 0 and a standard deviation of 1, ensuring that they are on a uniform scale for balanced input into the model. As the data is normalized, the learning process is sped up, resulting in faster convergence of the data and more stable learning. In the next step, CNN and LSTM models are developed for gender classification since they can effectively learn spatial and temporal features. CNN is especially effective at automatically identifying hierarchical patterns in spatial data. The CNN model can efficiently capture the complex spectral properties and patterns in speech samples that distinguish the male and female voices. The LSTM, however, has the advantage of handling sequential data, which enables it to capture long-range dependencies on temporal sequences, such as speech variations over time. Both models are trained and tested on the extracted features from both genders to recommend a more fine-tuned method of feature extraction to provide an effective gender classification approach. A block diagram of the proposed method is presented in Figure 1, outlining the workflow from feature extraction and normalization to model training and classification.

Figure 1. Proposed method for speaker gender classification using MFCC & LPCC

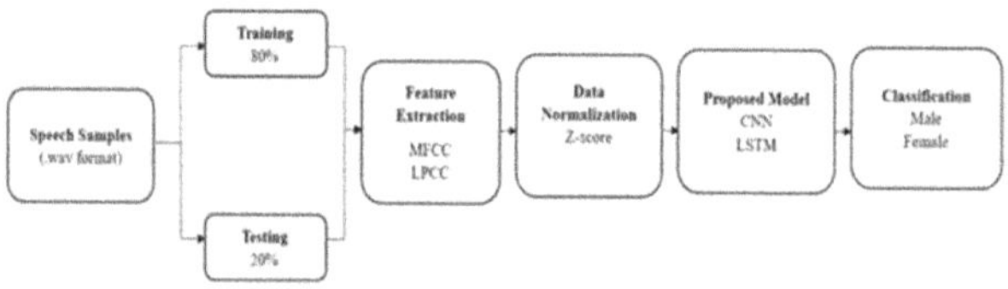

Note. As shown in Figure 1, MFCC and LPCC techniques are implemented for extracting gender information from speech samples. The features are normalized to ensure consistency, and by analyzing these normalized features, the CNN and LSTM models can effectively classify the speaker's gender based on distinct patterns and characteristics in the speech data.

Data Collection

For the speaker's gender classification model, the VoxForge speech dataset is an invaluable tool. Researchers examining the characteristics of human speech can also benefit from it. VoxForge is an open-source collection of both male and female speech samples. The speech dataset was acquired from a repository database. English speech samples of multiple speakers can be retrieved from the VoxForge dataset. Each speech sample is stored in a Waveform Audio File Format (WAV) with 16 kHz and 8 kHz sampling rates. For this research, speech samples of 1000 males and 1000 females at a 16 kHz sampling rate are collected for gender classification. Each speaker's speech samples were processed to extract different aspects of their speech that are necessary for the gender classification. Various speech features were captured by collecting speech samples in diverse and uncontrolled environments. Training a reliable model that can correctly determine gender in a variety of real-world situations requires this variability. The dataset's diversity ensures the model's robustness in real-world applications, making it suitable for various speech-based technologies. A detailed overview of the dataset is shown in Table 1.

Table 1. Speech samples are split into 80% for training and 20% for testing

Speakers	Training	Testing
Male	800	200
Female	800	200

Note. The dataset used for gender classification consists of 2,000 speech samples, with 800 male and 800 female samples used for training, and 200 male and 200 female samples for testing. This equal representation supports unbiased model training and allows accurate evaluation of performance across both gender categories.

Feature Extraction

In speech-based gender classification, feature extraction simplifies complicated speech samples while preserving critical information for classification algorithms by converting raw audio into a parametric representation. There are several distinguishing characteristics between male and female speech signals, including pitch, frequency, and energy. A set of significant characteristics that are helpful for speaker gender classification can be obtained through feature extraction techniques (Yusnita et al., 2017). Gender identity is determined mainly by the characteristics retrieved from a speech sample. MFCC and LPCC are compared to identify the optimal feature extraction method for classifying gender using speech samples. MFCC extracts gender-specific features from speech by mimicking how humans perceive sounds, focusing on distinguishing vocal traits. In contrast, LPCC analyses the speech samples by constructing linear predictive models, providing information about the configuration of the vocal tract. The reliability of the speech-based gender classification methodology will be improved by evaluating the benefits and drawbacks of each approach to determine which feature extraction method performs best in correctly determining gender from speech samples. In conclusion, the comparison between MFCC and LPCC highlights the importance of selecting the appropriate feature extraction method for accurate gender classification from speech samples.

MFCC Method

The MFCC is based on the human auditory system's response to sounds, more specifically, its sensitivity to different frequencies. An MFCC mimics the perception of frequency by the human ear on a logarithmic scale. Pre-emphasis, the initial stage of the MFCC, is the process of amplifying high-frequency components to balance the frequency spectrum. As a result, higher frequencies are amplified relative to lower frequencies by applying a high-pass filter to the speech sample. Secondly, the sample is split into short segments to analyze the local spectral information more easily. Typical frame durations are between 20 and 30 milliseconds, with overlaps between successive frames. The next step is windowing applied to each frame. Spectral leakage is reduced, preventing discontinuities at frame edges by multiplying frames by a Hamming window function (Abdul et al., 2022). Then, the Fast Fourier transform (FFT) turns a time-domain signal into a frequency-domain signal. By using this process, each frame's frequency content can be determined. In a Mel filter bank, triangular filters are spaced along a Mel frequency scale, a perception of pitch scale. Power spectrum obtained from FFTs are filtered with these filters. The filter output is converted to a logarithmic scale, enhancing the model's ability to differentiate between frequencies. Finally, the discrete cosine transform (DCT) is applied to logarithmically scaled filter bank energies for reducing coefficient dimensionality and capturing relevant information (Chaudhary et al., 2018). MFCC features were extracted from all speech samples using a fixed length of 200 time steps to ensure consistency in input dimensions. Each time step involved computing 13 MFCC coefficients, which captured key spectral characteristics of the speech sample. The samples of speech that were shorter than 200 frames were zero-padded, while the longer samples were truncated. Through this process, a uniform dataset can be achieved, resulting in a stable and efficient model training process. An approach used in speech recognition to extract significant features from audio sources is shown by the MFCC block diagram. It uses the Mel scale, a perceptual scale, to record the power spectrum of sound. This method is frequently employed in speech recognition systems due to its ability to accurately capture speech timbral features. The steps involved in this technique are shown in Figure 2.

Figure 2. MFCC block diagram

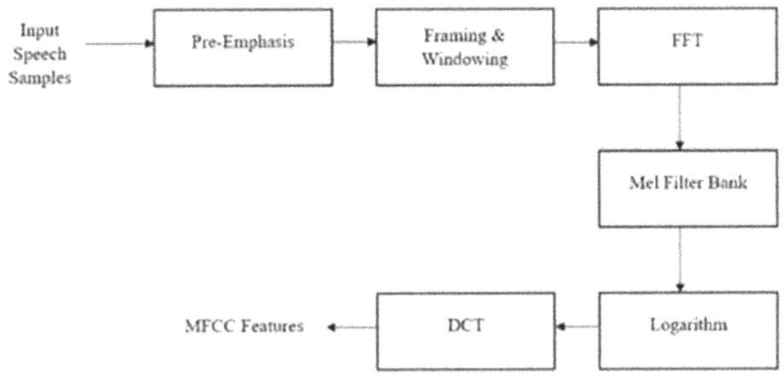

As shown in Equation (1), the coefficient a[n] is calculated by applying a DCT to the logarithmic energies E[f] of the Mel filter banks, thereby accurately capturing the most relevant speech spectral characteristics.

Where,

a[n]– the nth MFCC

E[f] – energy output from the fth Mel filter

b – number of Mel filters

f - mel filter bank index

n – index for the DCT output

LPCC Method

The LPCC coefficients are calculated based on the cepstrum of the Linear Predictive Coefficient (LPC) coefficients. Vocal tract coefficients are calculated using LPCC, which can also represent the speech sample spectrum magnitude. As shown in Figure 3, to extract features speech samples need to be pre-processed with pre-emphasis, frame blocking, Hamming window, and autocorrelation techniques. The autocorrelation method generates the parameters by assuming past output samples as a linear combination, while the input samples are unknown (Kaur et al., 2018; Singhal et al., 2023b). Using LPC analysis, the autocorrelation coefficients are converted into LPC parameters in the final step. The number of features extracted from each speech sample is 13 per time step over a fixed length of 200 steps.

Figure 3. LPCC block diagram

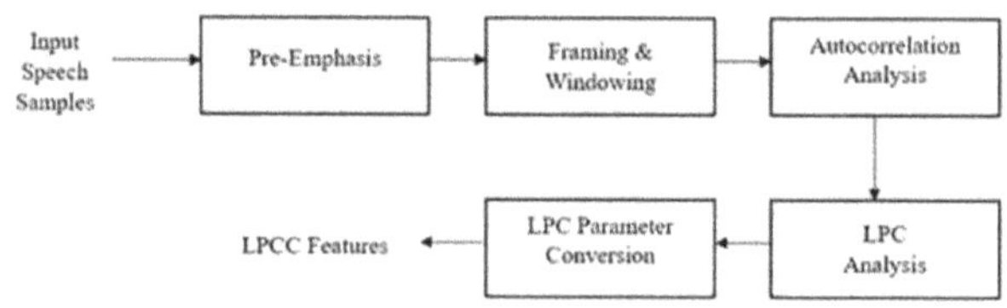

As represented in Equation (2), the coefficient a[n] is computed using a recursive relationship involving the LPC coefficients a[f]. The factorial terms in the formula weigh the contributions of each LPC coefficient, allowing the LPCC to capture the key spectral features of the speech sample, specifically focusing on the linear prediction model of the vocal tract.

Where,

a[n] – the nth LPCC

p – order of the linear prediction

a[f] – the fth LPC coefficient.

Data Normalization

The normalization involves transforming features into a common scale without distorting the difference in value ranges. Since features can vary in unit or scale, it is important to ensure that no feature dominates the learning process based on its larger numerical range. Using Z-score normalization, this proposed method normalizes the features extracted from two different feature extraction methods.

Z-score Normalization

In speech gender classification, feature extraction techniques such as MFCC and LPCC are commonly used to capture key aspects of speech samples. While some features have significantly larger numerical ranges than others, the scale of these features can vary greatly. When the scale of the features differs, it may lead to biased model training, in which larger features may overpower smaller ones. It is therefore necessary to apply Z-score normalization as a preprocessing step, which ensures that all features contribute equally to classification.

By normalizing features with the Z-score, the dataset has a mean value of 0 and a standard deviation value of 1. By doing this, all features are scaled equally during training, so models can handle them equally. Particularly in speech gender classification, when features like MFCC & LPCC coefficients, formants, and spectral flux vary widely in their values and units.

The standardization of features through Z-score normalization improves the convergence of machine learning models, resulting in a smoother, more balanced training process. Additionally, by reducing the impact of scale disparities across features, it enhances model performance and stability. A more accurate and generalization gender classification model can also be achieved by minimizing the effects of outliers, which can alter the learning process. As a result, Z-score normalization is an essential step to ensuring that speech features contribute equally and effectively to classification, improving overall model performance.

The Z-score Equation (3) is written in its standard form:

Where,

$X_{normalized}$ = the standardized value of the feature.

x = the original value of the feature.

μ = the average value of the feature.

σ = the standard deviation of the feature.

Deep Learning Classifiers

Deep learning has become a leading technique for classifying speech by gender, since it can automatically learn complex patterns and features from raw data, eliminating manual feature extraction. Conventional methods of speech gender classification, like acoustic properties, require considerable domain expertise and are limited by the wide variety of speech patterns and speakers. Reliable classifiers and efficient feature extraction lead to accurate classification (Qawaqneh et al., 2017). The complexities of speech samples are more easily handled by deep learning models, especially CNNs and LSTMs. It extracts features directly from raw audio data, which makes it an excellent tool for speech gender classification. Deep learning models are capable of capturing both temporal and spectral features of speech samples when trained on large datasets. CNN models are especially excellent at learning complex patterns in speech data, while LSTM models are adept at identifying long-term dependencies on sequential data, which is important in the field of speech recognition. This allows the model to more effectively determine gender even in the case of loud or distorted speech.

Furthermore, deep learning models depend less on hand-crafted features and can accommodate variations in speech, including variations in accent, pitch, or ambient noise. This adaptability enhances their robustness and makes them superior to conventional machine learning techniques. The capability to generalize across varied datasets is particularly beneficial in speech-based gender classification, where variations in tone, accent, and speaking style are common. It offers improved precision and flexibility for gender classification in speech by automating the extraction of features, addressing variations in speech, and leveraging extensive datasets for training. These benefits position it as the favored approach for modern speech processing applications, resulting in a notable enhancement compared to traditional methods. As data acquisition and computational resources progress, deep learning models are expected to achieve even greater accuracy and efficiency in speech gender classification.

In the proposed method, normalized features are used for training the model, where the developed CNN and LSTM models are trained to classify speaker gender. To enhance the model's performance, CNN is used to extract spatial patterns, while LSTM captures temporal dependencies within the speech sample. In speech analysis, MFCC and LPCC features are structured as follows, with spatial patterns indicating variations across coefficients within individual frames, and temporal patterns capturing the progression of these features over time. Leveraging this information allows the models to detect subtle differences in vocal attributes between male and female speakers. The models were trained using feature sets derived from recordings of both genders, and the trained networks were subsequently applied to identify the gender of unknown speakers in the test dataset.

CNN Architecture

The classification of the speaker's gender can be automated using convolutional neural networks by learning spatial features from a speech dataset. The networks consist of two convolutional 2-dimensional layers, two ReLU Activation functions, two max-pooling layers, a flattened layer, a dense layer, and a softmax activation function as shown in Figure 4. Two convolutional layers are employed with 32 and 64 filters with 3x3 kernel sizes, strides (1,1) to learn extracted features of MFCC and LPCC techniques from speech samples. At the same time, the ReLu activation function aids the network in understanding complex data. Using two max-pooling layers with a pool size (2,2), feature maps obtained from convolutional layers can be minimized while learning key information. The flattening layer transforms the multidimensional output from the convolutional and max-pooling layers into a one-dimensional vector. A single vector is created by flattening the feature maps' spatial dimensions. The flattened feature vector is processed in dense layers. To classify the speaker's gender, each neuron in the dense layer takes a weighted sum of the input values, followed by a softmax activation function. The CNN model is shown in the following mathematical representation. There are several layers in the model, including convolutional layers, pooling layers, and fully connected layers. The input layers are processed by extracting features, reducing dimensionality, and classifying them separately. As a result of the mathematical representation, it is easier to understand the flow of data and the transformations applied to it at each stage.

Figure 4. CNN model architecture

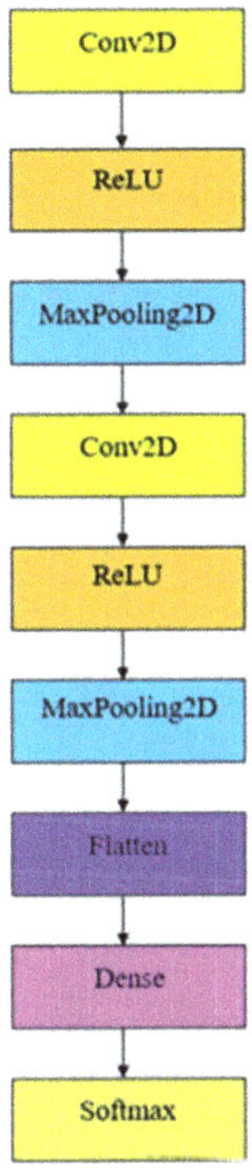

Note. This figure presents a CNN model tailored for gender classification using speech data. It features convolutional layers for feature extraction, ReLU activation for non-linearity, and max pooling for dimensionality reduction. The final layers flatten the output and apply softmax to predict the target class accurately.

Convolutional Layer. Based on Equation (4), the first convolutional layer extracts basic features such as edges and textures.

Where,

X = input image

W_1 = convolution filters

b_1 = bias

Z_1 = feature map output

ReLU Activation Function. The first ReLU Activation function applies non-linearity by keeping only positive values, as shown in Equation (5).

Where,

Z_1 = input from the previous layer

A_1 = activated output

Max Pooling Layer. In Equation (6), the first Max pooling layer further reduces the size, while retaining key features.

Where,

A_1 = activated feature map

P_1 = downsampled output

Second Convolutional Layer. As shown in Equation (7), the second convolutional layer detects higher-level speech features.

Where,

W_2 = second set of filters

b_2 = bias

P_1 = input from pooling

Z_2 = new feature map

Second ReLU Activation Function. The second ReLU Activation function keeps non-linearity in the model is represented as Equation (8).

Where,

Z_2 = convolution output

A_2 = activated output

Second Max Pooling Layer. As shown in Equation (9), the second maxpooling layer further reduces the size while retaining key features.

Where,

A_2 = input map

P_2 = downsampled result

Flatten Layer. The data is prepared for the fully connected layer by the flatten layer, as illustrated in Equation (10).

Where,

P_2 = 2D map

F = 1D vector

Dense Layer. The dense or fully connected layer combines the speech features for gender classification, as represented in Equation (11).

Where,

W_3 = dense layer weights

b_3 = bias

F = flattened input

Z_3 = output scores (logits)

Softmax Activation. Finally, the softmax function converts logits into class probabilities, as shown in Equation (12).

Where,

Z_{3i} = score for class i

$\hat{y}$ = predicted probability

LSTM Architecture

LSTM is particularly well-suited for processing speech samples because of its ability to manage temporal sequences and recognize long-term relationships within sequential data, and the vanishing gradient problem is solved with LSTM (Ertam, 2019). Speech temporal features, which include rhythmic patterns and pitch details, vary over time. These characteristics are essential for speech recognition. Extracted features are fed as input to the LSTM model. A cell consists of an input gate, a forget gate, an output gate, a cell state candidate, an update cell state, and a hidden state comprising an LSTM unit. The first three gates use the sigmoid function, and the other gates use the tanh function to regulate the information flow into and out of the cell, and the cell retains values for an indefinite period. The forget gate eliminates information from the cell state that is no longer relevant. Next, the input gate updates the cell state. A cell state candidate proposes possible updates to the cell's memory and then evaluates whether they are relevant. Through the update cell state mechanism, only the most useful data is retained for future processing by merging these new candidate values. The output gate controls the flow of information from the cell state to the output. By selectively remembering or forgetting information depending on the current input and past hidden states through the use of the sigmoid function. A hidden state produces the LSTM unit's final output at the current time step. LSTM can effectively manage long-term dependencies in data (Ye & Yang, 2021). To improve feature representation and learning of the model, 100 LSTM cells are incorporated. With this configuration, the network can capture complex patterns and dependencies in the data over a period of time. After that, the Dense layer, which completes the final classification, receives the hidden state from the LSTM units, which reflects the cell's output at a particular time. The LSTM layer extracts deep characteristics, which are then employed in the output layer to categorize gender using a Softmax activation function, as shown in Figure 5.

Figure 5. LSTM model architecture

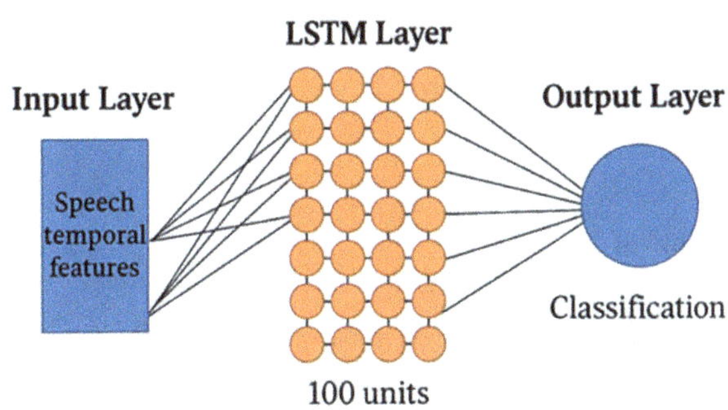

Note. The figure illustrates an LSTM model designed for gender classification from speech data. The input layer accepts temporal features extracted from speech, which are then processed by an LSTM layer with 100 units. This layer captures temporal patterns in the data, and the output layer performs the final classification based on these learned features.

Forget Gate. This gate function decides which parts of the previous cell state should be forgotten. The mathematical Equation (13) for this gate is given by.

Where,

f_t = forget activation gate

w_{fgt} = weight matrix

a_{t-1} = previous hidden state

y_t = present input

b_{fgt} = forget gate bias

Input Gate. It controls how much information should be added to the cell state, as shown in Equation (14).

Where,

i_t = input activation gate

w_{igt} = weight matrix

b_{igt} = input gate bias

Cell State Candidate. This cell State generates candidate values for possible additions, which are represented by the following Equation (15).

Where,

ce_t = cell state candidate

w_{cnd} = weight matrix

b_{cnd} = bias cell state candidate

tanh = tangent activation

Cell State Update. It updates the cell state by combining retained past information with new candidate input, and this is represented by the following Equation (16).

Where,

c_t = update cell state

f_{t-1} = previous cell state

Output Gate. The output gate determines which parts of the cell state contribute to the hidden state, as shown in Equation (17).

Where,

o_t = output gate

w_{ogt} = weight matrix

b_{ogt} = bias for output gate

Hidden State. Finally, in the hidden state, the LSTM unit outputs at the current time, which is shown in Equation (18).

Where,

o_t = hidden state of the LSTM at time step t
c_t = updated cell state

Hyperparameter Specifications of the Models

The CNN and LSTM models were trained with specific hyperparameters aimed at improving accuracy and facilitating effective learning. The key hyperparameters consist of the learning rate, batch size, total epochs, and iterations per epoch. A learning rate of 0.001 was chosen to ensure gradual and consistent updates to the model's weights throughout training. A batch size of 32 was implemented to strike a balance between computational efficiency and training effectiveness. Both models underwent training for 20 epochs, providing several opportunities to engage with the training data. Furthermore, 50 iterations per epoch were utilized, which defined the number of batches processed during each epoch, as detailed in Table 2.

Table 2. Hyperparameters of the proposed models

Hyperparameters	CNN	LSTM
Epochs	20	20
Learning rate	0.001	0.001
Batch size	32	32
Iterations per epoch	50	50

Note. It presents the hyperparameter specifications used during the training of the CNN and LSTM models. These parameters were selected to enhance the learning process, manage training dynamics, and ensure uniform performance assessment across both models. These parameters improve model performance and help minimize issues like overfitting and underfitting. These carefully defined criteria ensure a fair comparison, allowing for an accurate evaluation of the model's effectiveness and reliability in handling the task.

Software Module for Speech-Based Gender Identification System

To develop a speech-based gender identification system in Python, several powerful libraries designed for processing audio, extracting features, and performing algorithms are utilized. Librosa is one of the main feature extraction libraries in this system. This library is necessary to handle speech data, including capabilities for loading, preprocessing, and extraction. Each speech sample comprises 13 MFCC coefficients are collected for this system. By accurately simulating the vocal tract features, these MFCCs are well-suited for capturing the speech sample's spectral envelope. A fixed length of 200 time frames is created with the samples, yielding 13-dimensional feature vectors for each frame. This format maintains the voice signals acoustic richness while giving models a constant input size. For capturing vocal tract configurations, LPCC can be utilized similarly to MFCC, providing similar feature representations. Following feature extraction, the features must be normalized. To perform this, NumPy is utilized, in which the features mean and standard deviation are determined, and the Z-score normalization method is applied to scale the features. Ensuring that each attribute has a zero mean and unit variance enhances the model's capacity for learning.

A deep learning model is trained to classify gender from speech once the characteristics have been extracted and normalized. A CNN layers are designed by utilizing the TensorFlow and Keras libraries. The CNN captures temporal and spectral characteristics from MFCC and LPCC-based input data, which is organized as a matrix with 200 time steps and 13 coefficients per frame.

The network is designed to identify significant timing and frequency patterns that correspond to the speech gender-specific characteristics. The CNN produces a probability distribution for the male and female gender categories after processing the input features.

An LSTM model has been employed for classifying gender when the speech features have been extracted and normalized. The input data consists of a feature matrix that was created using MFCC and LPCC techniques and is formed as 200 time steps with 13 coefficients each. The temporal structure of voice signals is represented by these matrices. An LSTM layer of 100 units is included in the model to help capture long-term dependencies in

Long-term dependencies in the sequential speech data are captured by the model's 100-unit LSTM layer. The model can identify trends over time that reveal a speaker's gender due to this architecture. The model generates a probability distribution for the male and female gender classes after processing the input. Labeled speech samples are used to train the system, and test data is used to evaluate its accuracy.

RESULTS AND DISCUSSIONS

This section discusses the results obtained by the models implemented for the automatic recognition of speaker gender. Deep learning techniques were utilized to independently classify the individuals based on their gender. The models exhibited encouraging performance, contributing to the improvement of accurately determining the speaker's gender. This ultimately results in more personalized and user-friendly interactions. Additionally, this technology aids in identifying and reducing gender bias in AI-driven voice assistants. By detecting the gender of the speaker, these systems can provide more precise and customized responses, ensuring improved support for a diverse group of users.

Analysis of Results in Speaker Gender Classification

The performance of the gender classification models, using both MFCC and LPCC features, was analyzed through CNN and LSTM models, with each model trained over 20 epochs. The accuracy mentioned here was obtained from the testing phase. The CNN model using MFCC features achieved 89.1% accuracy. In comparison, the CNN model with LPCC features attained 84%. This finding demonstrates that MFCC provides superior feature representation for gender classification when applied in CNN models. Likewise, the LSTM model showed more efficient performance with MFCC features, reaching an accuracy of 90.5%. In comparison, the LSTM model utilizing LPCC features obtained an accuracy of 85.2%, reinforcing the idea that MFCC is a more efficient feature extraction method for gender classification. MFCC encompasses a broader range of temporal and spectral information, improving the model's capacity to differentiate between genders. For both feature extraction methods, the datasets were normalized using their mean and standard deviation to ensure consistent processing across both training and testing phases. Despite the use of LPCC features, the MFCC-based models consistently outperformed the LPCC models, underscoring the importance of selecting the right feature extraction technique. These results, obtained during the testing phase, demonstrate that deep learning models like CNN and LSTM can effectively classify speaker gender when paired with appropriate features like MFCC.

Accuracy Comparison of Proposed Models

The provided Figure 6 shows a comparison between CNN and LSTM models in terms of classification accuracy when using two different feature extraction methods: MFCC and LPCC. LSTM consistently achieved higher accuracy than CNN across both feature sets, highlighting its strengths in dealing with temporal and sequential speech data. Among the feature extraction techniques, MFCC outperforms LPCC for both models, indicating that it provides more relevant and distinguishing features for the classification task.

The advantage of LSTM over CNN becomes more apparent when MFCC is used, suggesting that LSTM is particularly well-suited for extracting patterns from these features. Even with LPCC, which yields slightly lower overall accuracy, LSTM still maintains its edge over CNN. This demonstrates the robustness of LSTM in handling different types of acoustic features.

The combination of LSTM with MFCC leads to the highest performance among all evaluated configurations. This finding emphasizes the importance of not only selecting a powerful model but also using effective feature extraction techniques to achieve optimal results in speech-based gender classification. The insights from this comparison can help guide future research in the field of speech processing and classification systems, as shown in Figure 6.

Figure 6. Classification accuracy of CNN and LSTM models using MFCC and LPCC

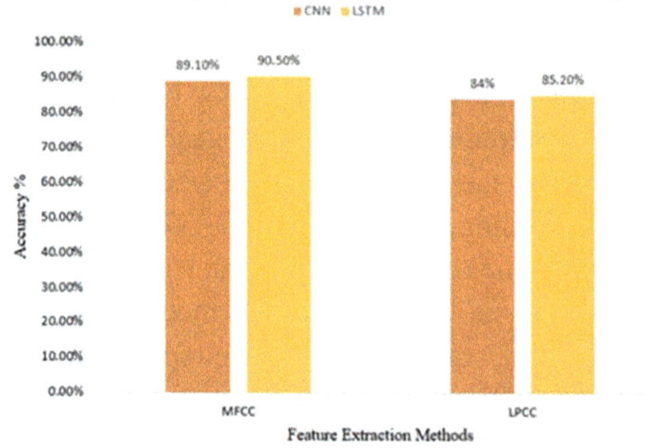

Discussion

Automatic speaker gender classification has become an important area of research due to its wide range of real-world applications. It plays a crucial role in optimizing call routing systems, enabling personalized responses in customer service, analyzing gender-based population statistics, enhancing user-targeted advertising through voice assistants, and improving the organization and indexing of multimedia content (Kwasny & Hemmerling, 2021). Automating this classification process with the help of deep learning techniques eliminates the need for manual intervention, offering a faster and more efficient solution.

In this proposed work, the VoxForge dataset was used to develop and evaluate gender classification models. VoxForge is an open-source speech dataset that provides high-quality, labeled audio samples from various speakers, making it ideal for training deep learning algorithms. A comparison was made between two widely used techniques for calculating feature extraction, MFCC and LPCC. For models, the speech sample file is converted into a parametric representation.

These features help convert speech samples into numerical formats suitable for machine learning tasks. To ensure consistency and enhance the performance of the models, Z-score normalization was applied to the extracted features. Both CNN and LSTM models were trained on the normalized features. The results demonstrated that MFCC-based models consistently outperformed those using LPCC across both CNN and LSTM architectures. This indicates that MFCC captures the rich temporal and spectral properties of speech, making it more effective at distinguishing gender-related vocal characteristics.

Overall, it confirms that MFCC is a more reliable and consistent method for feature extraction in the context of speaker gender classification. Its superior performance across multiple deep learning models underscores its value in speech processing applications. This work utilizes the VoxForge dataset, which features speech recordings primarily in the English language. However, relying on a single-language source may limit the model's ability to generalize across linguistically diverse data, as commonly encountered in real-world applications. While the recordings do contain slight background noise, they do not fully represent more complex acoustic environments or variations such as speech disorders. Future research will focus on testing the proposed models using more linguistically diverse datasets and under challenging audio conditions to improve their effectiveness and generalization.

Comparative Analysis of Related Works

In recent studies, a variety of techniques have been used to classify speaker gender based on a variety of datasets and feature extraction methods. A combination of publicly available and custom-built speech corpora has been used by researchers. Transforming audio signals into usable input features is usually achieved by using techniques such as MFCC, LPC, and spectral filtering. Moreover, optimization methods and preprocessing steps improve this system's performance and reliability. It is evident from the growing use of deep learning approaches that they are a powerful tool for capturing intricate speech patterns. As a result, this proposed work focuses on leveraging proven feature extraction methods and learning models for accurate gender identification, are presented in Table 3.

Table 3. Performance of feature extraction methods and deep learning models for gender classification

Related works	Dataset	Feature Extraction	Models	Optimization Technique	Accuracy
Singhal & Sharma, 2024	Custom Dataset	MFCC	RNN-BiLSTM		85.73%
Jahangir et al., 2020	LibriSpeech	MFCC Time-based features	DNN	-	89%
Uddin et al.,2021	TIMIT, RAVDESS, and BGC	MFCC LPC	1D CNN	RMSprop	93.01%
Ali et al., 2022	Custom Dataset	LPC MFCC	ANN DA	-	97.07% 95.16%

continued on following page

Table 3. Continued

Related works	Dataset	Feature Extraction	Models	Optimization Technique	Accuracy
Lai et al., 2024	TIMIT and Hillenbrand Databases	Band-Pass Butterworth Filter + MFCC	1D CNN 2D CNN	-	90.7% 86.6%
Das et al., 2022	RAVDESS	MFCC	DLCNN	-	98.33%
Son et al., 2019	NEIA dataset	MFCC	RNN	RMSprop	89.61%
Proposed Model	VoxForge Dataset	MFCC	CNN LSTM	-	89.1% 90.5%
Proposed Model	VoxForge Dataset	LPCC	CNN LSTM		84% 85.20%

Note. Table 3 illustrates the performance of various feature extraction methods with different deep learning models for gender classification using various speech datasets. The comparison highlights the effectiveness of each method in improving classification accuracy. The results show that certain combinations of features and models outperform other approaches, providing valuable insights for optimizing gender classification models.

CONCLUSION

Speech-based gender classification has emerged as an essential aspect of automatic speech recognition, improving the performance of voice-driven systems like digital assistants, automated customer support, and customized user interfaces. This approach is essential for customizing interactions and services based on the speaker's gender. By combining well-established feature extraction techniques with deep learning models, this research work aimed to increase the accuracy of speaker gender classification. The VoxForge dataset was used for this research because of its diversity and tagged speech recordings. Two distinct feature extraction methods are utilized to extract the features. Z-score normalization was applied to the retrieved features to balance the data and increase the effectiveness of model training by maintaining consistent input to the models. CNN and LSTM models are developed for gender classification based on extracted traits. The MFCC and LPCC attributes that had been extracted from the speech data were used to train both models. According to the results, MFCC continuously performed better than LPCC in terms of classification accuracy. In particular, the LSTM model obtained 90.5% accuracy with MFCC, whereas the CNN model obtained 89.1%. These findings highlight the ability that MFCC to capture the essential spatial and temporal elements of speech that distinguish gender. The LSTM model's superior accuracy is ascribed to its capacity to recognize temporal correlations, which is crucial for interpreting voice input. The work demonstrates the great efficacy of deep learning models for speaker's gender classification via speech samples, especially those built to handle sequential data. Furthermore, selecting a feature extraction methodology is crucial for this objective. MFCC proves to be a more reliable technique than LPCC. In conclusion, this research shows that MFCC with deep learning models work well together to accurately classify speaker gender. The proposed models are lightweight enough to be integrated into large-scale systems without requiring extensive computational resources, making them cost-effective for enterprise deployment. These characteristics support real-time processing and operational scalability, allowing organizations to enhance service efficiency and reduce manual workload. Additionally, the model's insights can inform decision-making processes related to user profiling, interface customization, and resource allocation in voice-based technologies.

Future Work

To improve the accuracy and adaptability of gender classification systems, future work will focus on developing a hybrid architecture that integrates CNN with LSTM networks. Combining these models is expected to leverage the strengths of both, leading to more reliable and comprehensive classification performance. This work employed MFCC and LPCC as feature extraction techniques in separate CNN and LSTM models. Extending this analysis by applying both feature sets to a combined CNN-LSTM model could provide valuable insights into optimal configurations for gender classification tasks.

In addition, future research will investigate advanced training optimizations and assess the system under diverse real-world conditions, such as noisy audio environments and linguistically varied datasets. Furthermore, the work will incorporate interdisciplinary considerations to ensure responsible AI practices, particularly in ethically sensitive areas like employment screening, surveillance, and educational applications.

REFERENCES

Abdul, Z. K., & Al-Talabani, A. K. (2022). Mel frequency cepstral coefficient and its applications: A review. *IEEE Access : Practical Innovations, Open Solutions, 10*, 122136–122158. DOI: 10.1109/ACCESS.2022.3223444

Ali, Y. M., Noorsal, E., Mokhtar, N. F., Saad, S. Z. M., Abdullah, M. H., & Chin, L. C. (2022). Speech-based gender recognition using linear prediction and mel-frequency cepstral coefficients. *Indonesian Journal of Electrical Engineering and Computer Science, 28*(2), 753. DOI: 10.11591/ijeecs.v28.i2.pp753-761

Alnuaim, A. A., Zakariah, M., Shashidhar, C., Hatamleh, W. A., Tarazi, H., Shukla, P. K., & Ratna, R. (2022). Speaker gender recognition based on deep neural networks and ResNet50. *Wireless Communications and Mobile Computing, 2022*(1), 1–13. DOI: 10.1155/2022/4444388

Arpita, H. D., Ryan, A. A., Hossain, M. F., Rahman, M. S., Sajjad, M., & Prova, N. N. I. (2024). Exploring bengali speech for gender classification: Machine learning and deep learning approaches. *Bulletin of Electrical Engineering and Informatics, 14*(1), 328–337. DOI: 10.11591/eei.v14i1.8146

Chaudhary, S., & Sharma, D. K. (2018). Gender identification based on voice signal characteristics. *ICACCCN: 2018 International Conference on Advances in Computing, Communication Control and Networking,* 869–874. https://doi.org/DOI: 10.1109/ICACCCN.2018.8748676

Das, M. N., Pratyush Ranjan Mohapatra, P. R., & Rao, P. S. Dr. (2022). Implementation of human voice-based gender classification using deep learning convolutional neural network. *TURCOMAT: Turkish Journal of Computer and Mathematics Education. 13*(03), 55–68. https://doi.org/DOI: 10.17762/turcomat.v13i03.12837

Ertam, F. (2019). An effective gender recognition approach using voice data via deeper LSTM networks. *Applied Acoustics, 156*, 351–358. DOI: 10.1016/j.apacoust.2019.07.033

Hu, Z., LingHu, K., Yu, H., & Liao, C. (2023). Speech emotion recognition based on attention MCNN combined with gender information. *IEEE Access : Practical Innovations, Open Solutions, 11*, 50285–50294. DOI: 10.1109/ACCESS.2023.3278106

Jahangir, R., Teh, Y. W., Memon, N. A., Mujtaba, G., Zareei, M., Ishtiaq, U., Akhtar, M. Z., & Ali, I. (2020). Text-independent speaker identification through feature fusion and deep neural network. *IEEE Access : Practical Innovations, Open Solutions, 8*, 32187–32202. DOI: 10.1109/ACCESS.2020.2973541

Jaleel, H. Q., Stephan, J. J., & Naji, S. A. (2022). Gender identification from speech recognition using machine learning techniques and convolutional neural networks. *Webology*, *19*(1), 1666–1688. DOI: 10.14704/WEB/V19I1/WEB19112

Kabir, A., Ahmad, M. A., Aliyu, A. A., Abdulkadir, S., & Muazu, A. A. (2025). A deep learning model for gender recognition using voice data. *TheScientificWorld-Journal*, *20*(1), 137–141. DOI: 10.4314/swj.v20i1.18

Kaur, G., Srivastava, M., & Kumar, A. (2018). Genetic algorithm for combined speaker and speech recognition using deep neural networks. *Journal of Telecommunications and Information Technology*, *2*(2018), 23–31. DOI: 10.26636/jtit.2018.119617

Kwasny, D., & Hemmerling, D. (2021). Gender and age estimation methods based on speech using deep neural networks. *Sensors (Basel)*, *21*(14), 4785. DOI: 10.3390/s21144785 PMID: 34300525

Lai, H. Y., Hu, C. C., Wen, C. H., Wu, J. H., Pai, N. S., Yeh, C. Y., & Lin, C. H. (2024). Mel-scale frequency extraction and classification of Dialect-Speech signals with 1D CNN based classifier for gender and region recognition. *IEEE Access : Practical Innovations, Open Solutions*, *12*, 102962–102976. DOI: 10.1109/ACCESS.2024.3430296

Livieris, I. E., Pintelas, E., & Pintelas, P. (2019). Gender recognition by voice using an improved Self-Labeled algorithm. *Machine Learning and Knowledge Extraction*, *1*(1), 492–503. DOI: 10.3390/make1010030

Mamyrbayev, O., Toleu, A., Tolegen, G., & Mekebayev, N. (2020). Neural architectures for gender detection and speaker identification. *Cogent Engineering*, *7*(1), 1727168. DOI: 10.1080/23311916.2020.1727168

Qawaqneh, Z., Mallouh, A. A., & Barkana, B. D. (2017). Deep neural network framework and transformed MFCCs for speaker's age and gender classification. *Knowledge-Based Systems*, *115*, 5–14. DOI: 10.1016/j.knosys.2016.10.008

Singhal, A., & Sharma, D. K. (2023a). Precision value, error rate and accuracy of human gender identification based on randomized voice signals datasets. *International Journal of Intelligent Engineering and Systems*, *16*(4), 348–361. DOI: 10.22266/ijies2023.0831.28

Singhal, A., & Sharma, D. K. (2023b). *Low resource language analysis using deep learning algorithm for gender classification*. ACM Transactions on Asian and Low-Resource Language Information Processing., DOI: 10.1145/3614427

Singhal, A., & Sharma, D. K. (2024). Comprehensive analysis of gender classification accuracy across varied geographic regions through the application of deep learning algorithms to speech signals. *Computer Systems Science and Engineering*, *48*(3), 609–625. DOI: 10.32604/csse.2023.046730

Son, G., Kwon, S., & Park, N. (2019). Gender classification based on the non-lexical cues of emergency calls with recurrent neural networks (RNN). *Symmetry*, *11*(4), 525. DOI: 10.3390/sym11040525

Taha, T. M., Messaoud, Z. B., & Frikha, M. (2024). Convolutional neural network architectures for gender, emotional detection from speech and speaker diarization. *International Journal of Interactive Mobile Technologies*, *18*(03), 88–103. DOI: 10.3991/ijim.v18i03.43013

Tursunov, A., Mustaqeem, , Choeh, J. Y., & Kwon, S. (2021). Age and gender recognition using a convolutional neural network with a specially designed multi-attention module through speech spectrograms. *Sensors (Basel)*, *21*(17), 5892. DOI: 10.3390/s21175892 PMID: 34502785

Uddin, M. A., Pathan, R. K., Hossain, M. S., & Biswas, M. (2021). Gender and region detection from human voice using the three-layer feature extraction method with 1D CNN. *Journal of Information and Telecommunication*, *6*(1), 27–42. DOI: 10.1080/24751839.2021.1983318

Yasmin, G., Das, A. K., Nayak, J., Vimal, S., & Dutta, S. (2022b). Retracted Article: A rough set theory and deep learning-based predictive system for gender recognition using audio speech. *Soft Computing*, *28*(S2, Suppl 2), 453. DOI: 10.1007/s00500-022-07074-z

Ye, F., & Yang, J. (2021). A deep neural network model for speaker identification. *Applied Sciences (Basel, Switzerland)*, *11*(8), 3603. DOI: 10.3390/app11083603

Yusnita, M. A., Hafiz, A. M., Fadzilah, M. N., Zulhanip, A. Z., & Idris, M. (2017). Automatic gender recognition using linear prediction coefficients and artificial neural network on speech signal. *7th IEEE International Conference on Control System, Computing and Engineering*, 372–377. https://doi.org/DOI: 10.1109/ICCSCE.2017.8284437

Chapter 7
Designing a Smart Typo Correction and Sentiment Prediction Tool for Social Media Texts:
A Statistical NLP Approach for Speech-Enabled Human-Computer Interaction

C. V. Suresh Babu
https://orcid.org/0000-0002-8474-2882
Hindustan Institute of Technology and Science, India

R. Tamilvanddan
https://orcid.org/0009-0009-7827-5374
Hindustan Institute of Technology and Science, India

S. Nanda Kumar
https://orcid.org/0009-0008-0070-6763
Hindustan Institute of Technology and Science, India

K. Barath
https://orcid.org/0009-0009-9083-8395
Hindustan Institute of Technology and Science, India

ABSTRACT

This chapter, per the authors, aims to develop a robust, speech-enabled tool that corrects typographical errors and predicts sentiment polarity in social media texts

DOI: 10.4018/979-8-3373-3048-8.ch007

using statistical Natural Language Processing (NLP) techniques. By leveraging probabilistic models such as n-grams and entropy-based smoothing, the proposed system addresses the challenges of noisy, informal language common on digital platforms. The methodology integrates spelling correction mechanisms with sentiment analysis classifiers to enhance both text input quality and emotion recognition. Practical implementation is demonstrated using Python-based NLP libraries and a curated dataset of social media entries. The findings indicate improved accuracy in typo detection and meaningful sentiment classification, which can significantly enhance the performance of speech-enabled human-computer interfaces. This approach supports real-time interaction in applications such as virtual assistants and social listening tools, contributing to more intuitive and responsive human-machine communication.

1. INTRODUCTION

1.1 Context and Motivation

Picture a teenager dictating a WhatsApp response through Google Assistant: "Heeeeey bestiee!!! I lovvvv this song soooo much ."

To a human auditor, this message is warm-hearted, excited, and offers many emotional visual cues to consider. But what an Automatic Speech Recognition (ASR) system, followed by a Natural Language Processing (NLP) module hears is the elongated vowels ("soooo"), a playful spelling ("luv"), and the emojis, which will all be interpreted as noise. Instead of identifying joy, the system may classify the input errorneously or misinterpret the input altogether.

This brief setting illustrates a much larger one: the rise of social media platforms, like Twitter, Reddit, and Instagram, has placed the world of communicating in a time marked by informality, creativity with language, and diverse demographic (Eisenstein, 2013). Texts are circumvented with a typographical license, filled with emojis, acronyms, and strange inconsistencies in spelling. Not only is the linguistic casualness of online communication supported and maintained by the rapid exchange rates and brevity provided by digital platforms, but the same style often spills over to multimodal exchanges like voice search and typing.

Speech systems like Siri, Alexa, and Google Assistant are currently utilized in mobile, home, and automotive domains processing vast amounts of noisy transcribed text that resemble what we would call "real communication" (Jurafsky & Martin, 2023). Although those technologies can enhance accessibility by allowing users with disabilities or lower literacy levels to access technology, speech systems are open to the disarray of informal language. A single typo, word stylisation, or creative spelling choice has the potential to derail HCI pipelines whenever they are doing sentiment analysis, intent recognition, or identifying dialog turns (Han & Baldwin, 2011).

This vulnerability is particularly concerning in contexts where full understanding of affect is required to deliver a positive experience – contexts such as customer care, mental health, social listening, or accessibility technologies - where the misinterpretation of affect can happen at all levels (Sarker, 2017). For instance, it's critical for systems to identify positivity in "luv it sooo much!!" or frustration in "ugh dat was awfuuuul" or humans would believe the outputs were meaningless and unhelpful.

To do so, we must return to the fundamental units of error processing and affect detection. There is a growing interest and need for integrated, light NLP models which correct formatting and spelling errors and still preserve emotional meaning from noisy text. This chapter will propose a two-step statistical NLP pipeline: a trigram language model with smoothing for typo correction, and a lexicon-based, rule-based sentiment predictor. The long-term goal is to catalyze the advanced design of speech-based HCI systems towards innovative lenses of adaptively human-centered (Suresh Babu & Suruthi, 2024) and intelligent designs.

1.2 Problem Statement

While impressive progress has been made in natural language processing through the advent of deep learning architectures, speech-based interfaces continue to lag behind when dealing with casual, sloppy input namely that which comes from or is modeled after user-entered content on social media sites. Speech-based systems, virtual assistants, and voice bots all depend significantly on the output of ASR systems, which are noisy to begin with and subject to lexical errors (Goldwater, Jurafsky, & Manning, 2010).

Such errors tend to consist of homophone ambiguities, context-free misrecognitions, and misclassifications of fast-moving slang. The text output transmitted for further processing is thus noisy, possibly misspelled, and stylistically unreliable. The root cause of this problem is the mismatch between training and deployment environments. While numerous NLP models are trained on clean, grammatically organized corpora, they are deployed on actual user inputs that are significantly messier. Therefore, models experience a decline in accuracy, generalization vulnerabilities, and affective inference difficulty (Yuan et al., 2021).

Specifically, when misspelled or creatively manipulated words occur that are sentiment-carrying in content, like "amazinnng" and "terribull," lexicon-based sentiment systems will not capture the polarity or assign neutral values inaccurately. This leads to erroneous downstream outputs, disrupting the conversational loop or providing incongruent emotional responses (Suresh Babu, C. V. & Akshara, P. M. 2024). In addition, the majority of current NLP pipelines treat language normalization and sentiment analysis as separate tasks—an architecture that maximizes error propagation. Sentiment analysis modules take noisy inputs at face value and misinterpret tone or eliminate emotional signals without initial correction. On the other hand, systems that correct every input with no contextual judgment have the risk of distorting the affective meaning being expressed through stylized spelling or emphasis (Han & Baldwin, 2011).

Yet another compounding problem is the pervasive use of deep models that, although high-performing, are data-intensive, computationally expensive, and less appropriate for mobile, embedded, or real-time speech environments (Strubell, Ganesh, & McCallum, 2019). Such models tend to be non-interpretable, a key requirement of systems that are designed for interactive, speech-environment applications where transparency and traceability are desired for trust and human-algorithm collaboration (Suresh Babu, C. V. & Suruthi, G. 2024).

As a response, the current work finds a well-defined problem: the absence of an interpretable, integrated, and resource-effective framework for processing misspelled, sentiment-laden informal text in real-time speech-to-text-based HCI systems. Addressing this demand necessitates innovation at the convergence of statistical language modeling and affective computing.

1.3 Research Questions

In order to solve the above-mentioned issues and aid in the area of speech-enabled NLP, the following study questions inform this research:

1. How can statistical language models based on n-grams, together with smoothing methods and entropy ranking, be engineered to efficiently correct typographical and stylistic spelling differences in informal social-media-style text?
2. To what degree does corrective typo correction enhance qualitative and quantitative sentiment analysis performance in noisy, informal user input?
3. How can sentiment prediction modules be lexically broadened and adapted to process corrupted words, abbreviations, and emotive slang-containing noisy texts?
4. Where in the speech-to-text-to-NLP pipeline should error correction be strategically placed to maximize overall system accuracy, especially in real-time or mobile applications?

These questions are framed both to measure theoretical advances—measured in terms of increasing our knowledge of statistical correction effectiveness—and to examine practical design factors for speaker-confrontational systems like chatbots, conversational agents, and on-device voice assistants (Suresh Babu, C. V. & Akshara,

P. M. 2024). While most current work develops end-to-end approaches, this work argues that modular, interpretable NLP pipelines might make superior trade-offs in human-centered HCI deployment (Jurafsky & Martin, 2023; Han & Baldwin, 2011).

In order to answer these questions, an integrated experimental solution is assessed through a corpus of error-coded user-generated content sampled from Twitter and Reddit. Cross-referencing with baseline systems, coupled with entropy estimation, edit-distance monitoring, and accuracy in sentiment classification, serves to corroborate the pipeline and its disparate components.

1.4 Aim and Objective

The central goal of this research is to design a statistical NLP pipeline that effectively tackles two mutually dependent tasks essential in the improvement of speech-enabled HCI: typo correction and sentiment prediction. The framework will be designed specifically for casual, occasionally flawed text that represents realistic input from speech interfaces, especially as coming from ASR-transcribed sources or user direct typing. To meet this goal, the following objectives are pursued:

- To create a typo correction module from trigram language models, smoothed by applying Laplace and Good-Turing smoothing algorithms, and enhanced by applying entropy scoring to resolve competing candidates.
- To create a sentiment prediction module from a rule-based algorithm blended with sentiment lexicons from informal writing (e.g., VADER, SentiWordNet), enriched with modifiers for handling negation and intensification.
- To test the combined modules on public data from Twitter and Reddit, corrupted with synthetically introduced noise patterns (substitutions, deletions, doubled letters, phonetic misspelling) simulating authentic-world ASR/personal typing errors.
- To evaluate model performance using standard metrics (e.g., accuracy, F1-score, entropy reduction) and output against system baselines and gold-standard labels, both quantitatively using dashboards and human evaluation.
- To establish the portability and effectiveness of the statistical technique for implementation on low-resource, edge-computing, or mobile interfaces prevalent in voice-enabled assistants.

Above all else, this work aims not just to show gains in performance but to offer an interpretable, tunable, and scalable proof-of-concept pipeline for future use. Ultimately, the integrative architecture described here paints a vision of a future where intelligent systems no longer simply listen to what users say, but understand what they mean—even when their language is very poor.

1.5 Significance of the Study

It presents and demonstrates a complete NLP pipeline that improves the capability of HCI systems to properly understand noisy, typographic-noise-prone user speech and text. In a digital world that is dependent on virtual customer service, digital assistants, and multimodal interfaces, being able to process noisy input reliably is no longer a nicety—it is a prerequisite for user experience, trust, and interface durability. The modularity of the system and statistical underpinnings provide a worthwhile alternative to deep learning workflows that are computationally intensive. While black-box models lack explanations of their predictions through probability distributions, changes in entropy, and rule-based reasoning, the statistical models utilized here provide such explainability.

Such explainability makes the pipeline more open to researchers, developers, and UX designers for explorable AI solutions in resource-constrained settings (Strubell, Ganesh, & McCallum, 2019). Theoretically, the work makes a contribution to debates surrounding the ongoing applicability of statistical NLP approaches. Although at times regarded as outmoded in comparison with neural approaches, statistical models retain some exclusive strengths: reduced training demands, improved linguistic transparency, and improved out-of-vocabulary robustness when coupled with lexicons and context modeling.

This work promotes a hybrid approach wherein heritage approaches are redirected at new tasks—specifically in preprocessing pipelines wherein linguistic triage is mandated preceding high-level inference. By addressing typo correction and sentiment prediction as connected tasks, the work also enlightens methodologies in affective computing, sociolinguistics, and speech-based interface design.

1.6 Chapter Overview

The structuring of this research is designed to mirror logically the methodological stages and areas of theory addressed throughout the work.

Section 1 introduced the research context, established the problem field and theoretical necessity, and briefly stated the research questions of the study and principal objectives. It pinpointed a void in the intersection of statistical NLP, affect recognition, and informal text normalization in speech-enabled HCI.

Section 2 undertakes an in-depth literature review, starting with seminal theories of probabilistic language modelling, smoothing, entropy, and error correction. It criticizes empirical solutions to typo normalization and sentiment classification for informal text and situates these within the larger affective computing objectives. A conceptual framework integrating these topics is proposed as a blueprint for the suggested system.

Section 3 describes in detail the methodology of the study, i.e., research design, sampling, preprocessing, algorithm development, NLP module integration, and the mixed-methods evaluation protocol. The section also discusses linguistic and technical rationale, processing flow, and ethical issues in data handling.

Section 4 focuses on performance metrics such as accuracy, precision, recall, F1-score, and reduction in entropy rating, which are explained in terms of correction and sentiment classification tasks. Performance of the combined model is compared against baselines and placed into context using visualized evaluation output.

Section 5 presents a qualitative analysis of results that contrasts with previous work and assesses the pipeline's practical implications across HCI application domains. It addresses digital inclusivity, accessibility, and future-proofing speech interface design.

Section 6 outlines the contributions, recapitulates how research objectives were fulfilled, and mentions potential extensions e.g., multilinguality, sarcasm/incongruity detection, and multimodal sentiment alignment in speech-centered environments.

2. LITERATURE REVIEW

Language in the online world has a clear informality, diversity, and fluidity that people scarcely encounter in traditional text materials. With people communicating through social media and messaging, their texts often reflect new spellings, informal abbreviations, code-switching, non-standard punctuation, and quick changes in meaning (Eisenstein, 2013; Jurafsky & Martin, 2023).

These trends pose a significant challenge for automated analysis, particularly in speech-driven HCI, where adding a transcription layer could overwhelm the user with information. The deployment of Natural Language Processing (NLP) modules that are geared towards typo correction and sentiment analysis is the most important issue for voice tech, sentiment-aware systems, and any application trying to capture emotional cues in real digital conversation (Han & Baldwin, 2011).

Upon investigating the current body of knowledge relative to typo correction, sentiment analysis, and noisy, informal language, we identify three relevant themes that provide a context for relevant challenges and direct the exploration of the current study. First, there is an inherent compromise between the complex neural models enhanced accuracy and the computational efficiency and interpretability of simpler statistical methods, which is critical for practical use in real-time, resource constrained speech-driven human-computer interaction (HCI). Second, to enhance the efficacy of typo correction while mitigating meaningful stylistic and affective cues of social media language, there is a need to straddle the fine line between over-normalization and maintaining emotional specificity. Third, approaches that address correction tasks simultaneously with sentiment classification are increasingly acknowledged as important if we are to minimize downstream error propagation due to confounding, and readily better sentiment comprehension.

Given the current literature is existing reflection upon these themes, we organize this dissertation literature review to systematically disadvantaged historic and recent work and influences to address the gaps in the knowledge, establishing a clear plan to operationalize a modular, interpretable statistical Natural Language Processing (NLP) pipeline for the unique challenges associated with the constraints of embedded and mobile speech technologies.

The linguistic environment on social media is, at best, very dynamic and, occasionally, volatile. People frequently employ nonstandard spelling—extending words for emphasis (e.g., "soooo"), abbreviating ("pls" for "please"), or even reversing letters ("teh" for "the," a common internet phenomenon). Number substitutions have become ubiquitous ("gr8," "l8r"), and abbreviations are ubiquitous—everything from "LOL" and "BRB" to "u" for "you" and "2nite" for "tonight." Remnants of leetspeak still linger; terms like "n00b" remind us of earlier cybersubcultures.

Spelling correction and sentiment analysis here have a historical background. Strong contributions by Norvig (2007) provided a computationally efficient probabilistic spell corrector, which had its origins in the probability-scoring model of Church and Gale (1991). Such methods with n-gram methods and large linguistic resources like the Google Web 1T dataset remain cornerstones for dealing with real-world noisy text. Sentiment analysis baselines, such as Sentiment140 (Go et al., 2009) and rule-based VADER (Hutto & Gilbert, 2014), have continued to advance the evaluation and normalization in informal environments.

More recent years saw the emergence of neural and hybrid correction and sentiment analysis techniques, although in most instances these are computationally expensive and less interpretable (Devlin et al., 2019). Recent developments have focused on lightweight transformer variants such as DistilBERT and TinyBERT, along with model pruning and quantization techniques that substantially reduce computational and memory costs—enabling deployment in mobile and embedded environments typical for real-time speech-based HCI (Sanh et al., 2019; Jiao et al., 2019).

This section summarizes central and recent work relevant to statistical typo correction and sentiment prediction from casual texts, the transition away from statistical towards neural and hybrid methods, and focuses on their relative performance and limitations in noisy, real-time, or embedded HCI settings. The review of literature is divided into four major sections: theoretical models in statistical language modeling and smoothing; empirical research in typo fixing and sentiment analysis for noisy, transcribed, or casual speech text; conceptual frameworks integrating preprocessing and emotional inference; and variable operationalization, such as recent advances in test and evaluation. These sections highlight the importance of these developments for rendering an NLP pipeline practical and understandable.

These themes—the tradeoffs of accuracy for efficiency, repair for style, and of built and integrated NLP pipelines—set the context for the detailed subsequent review of statistical and neural methods, their accuracies and limits and uses in speech-based HCI contexts. Increased focus on on-device, real-time conversational interfaces has enabled great progress in light-weight NLP models (Suresh Babu, C. V. & Akshara, P. M. 2024). In contrast to huge neural models needing large computational capabilities, methods like quantized and pruned neural networks, thin statistical pipelines, and transformer distillation enable mobile phones, edge devices, and wearables to deploy them (Strubell et al., 2019; Jurafsky & Martin, 2023). They are required to deliver robust NLP to regions of poor internet connectivity, power limitation, or higher privacy requirements. Novel new models (e.g., TinyBERT, DistilBERT) and compression algorithms signal an industry shift towards designing in a resource-aware manner—a shift toward sustainable, explainable, and accessible speech-driven HCI (Sanh et al., 2019; GeeksforGeeks, 2025).

2.1 Theoretical Framework

The computational and linguistic basis for correcting typos and determining sentiment in speech-based HCI has been influenced by decades of work on statistical language modeling, smoothing, error correction, and advances in affective computing. Underlying these systems is the quantification of language through probability, frequency, entropy, and well-defined lexical resources.

2.1.1 Statistical Language Modeling

Statistical language models estimate the probability of word sequences, and therefore enable the forecasting of likely word continuation and the identification of unlikely—typically erroneous—text elements (Jurafsky & Martin, 2023). Classic n-gram models, particularly trigrams, have been the workhorse for spell-checking, disfluency detection, and intent detection since they can incorporate local context. In spelling correction, the working hypothesis is that the actual lexical sequence is the one with the greatest contextual likelihood under a trained statistical language model.

Norvig's (2007) well-known probabilistic spelling corrector, together with Church and Gale's (1991) work on probability scoring, set a precedent for leveraging distributional regularities in language for real-world correction tasks. It also showed further how n-gram data at scale enables strong correction in noisy user input text, underscoring the ongoing importance of statistical methods even as deep learning becomes prevalent. In spelling correction, the assumption in working is that the true lexical string is the one with the highest context probability under a trained statistical language model. Norvig's (2007) well-known probabilistic spelling corrector, together with Church and Gale's (1991) work on probability scoring, set a precedent for leveraging distributional regularities in language for real-world correction tasks. Further demonstrated how large-scale n-gram data supports robust correction in noisy user-generated text, reinforcing the continued relevance of statistical approaches even as deep learning proliferates.

2.1.2 Smoothing Techniques

Smoothing techniques mitigate the data sparsity problem present in n-gram language models, which attempts to assign some probability to those unobserved word sequences so that the n-gram model can be more robust when these word sequences are observed in noisy or informal text.

Here are the prominent smoothing approaches from the literature:

- Laplace Smoothing (or Add-One Smoothing): essentially adds one to all counts of frequency counts to resolve the issue of zero probabilities for unobserved ngrams (Church & Gale, 1991).
- Good-Turing Estimation: allow probability mass to be transferred from anything that is observed to anything unobserved, based on frequency of frequencies.
- Evidence: Empirically-sound studies on a large scale have shown that smoothing sufficiently increases the accuracy of correction based on context in informal genres (Dalvi et al., 2017).

By making the use of smoothing approaches, language models may reasonably incorporate more errors caused by typographical noise or ASR correctly, which is critical to integrated NLP pipelines running in real time.

2.1.3 Entropy and Information Theory

Entropy measures the unpredictability or uncertainty in language. The choice of candidate corrections that reduces sentence-level entropy is useful for reversing sentence-level grammaticality and naturalness in noisy text (Jurafsky & Martin, 2023). Recent empirical work demonstrates that entropy-based ranking, rather than relying solely on raw frequency or edit distance, improves the contextual plausibility of corrections in social data.

2.1.4 Lexicon-Based Sentiment Analysis

Sentiment analysis, or polarity detection, has traditionally made use of sentiment lexicons such as SentiWordNet, LIWC, and VADER. These instruments project words into positive, negative, or neutral valences, with rule-based modifiers for negation, amplification, and idiomatics (Go, Bhayani, & Huang, 2009). The theoretical hypothesis is that affective information is embedded systematically in word selection, and that, given knowledgeable preprocessing, lexicon-based methods can meaningfully detect sentiment in a wide variety of informal language.

2.1.5 Integration of Preprocessing and Sentiment Inference

Combining statistical normalization with polarity classification creates a layered system where lexical accuracy precedes semantic interpretation. Several studies claim that the effectiveness of sentiment analysis depends on how detailed the preprocessing is—correction of spelling errors, normalization, and tokenization being gateway ports through which reliable affective inference must pass (Han & Baldwin, 2011). Strong error modeling and benchmarking in noisy environments (Dalvi et al., 2017) only add to the need for end-to-end solutions for speech-based and informal text analytics.

2.2 Empirical Review

2.2.1 Typo Correction in Informal and Social Text

Spelling correction for online text has transitioned from dictionary-based replacement toward probabilistic, contextualized models. Han and Baldwin (2011) developed normalization processes using statistical alignment and edit distance methods to translate non-standard, out-of-vocabulary tokens to standard versions, doing better than simply looking up a dictionary, specifically for Twitter data. Eisenstein's (2013) preference for adaptive, corpus-aware language models stemmed from the restrictive nature of fixed lexica. Dalvi et al.'s (2017) work shows that n-gram probabilities with Levenshtein distance performed better than other comparisons in informal genres, providing further instances of improved correction when working with large-scale corpora in corpus-based error models.

Neural spelling correction (seq2seq, cnn's, and attention-based methods) have achieved state-of-the-art in some tasks, but these models typically require significant computational resources, a wealth of training data, and minimal transparency—deficiencies that render models unattractive for real-time or embedded use. Statistical and hybrid models provide alternatives where speed, comprehensibility, and economy are essential. In related work, Yuan et al. (2021) had described probabilistic rewriting and n-gram smoothing to remedy ASR problems which demonstrate links between statistical methods and resilient recognition of spoken language.

Spelling correction for speech has specific distinct challenges only related to the nature of Automatic Speech Recognition (ASR) errors. Unlike ordinary mistypings, ASR errors refer predominantly to substitution, insertion, and deletion errors that happen as the result of acoustic ambiguities and speaker variability (e.g., speaker accents, speech rate, environmental noise). Substitution errors lend themselves to particular problems related to homophones, where homophones are defined as content words containing identical pronunciations with differing spelling with associated meanings (e.g., "their" and "there").

In these cases, a sufficient contextual language model is critical, coupled with a probabilistic model of word usage, to choose the correct spelling. ASR substitutions resulting from phonetic confusions due to accent, coarticulation, or acoustic noise could considerably decrease the ability to correct subsequent to the utterance and would require for spelling correction, probabilistic models that recognized phoneme similarity, which would require integration with lexical context. Out-of-vocabulary words are especially problematic, a frequent occurrence in both conversational speech and domain-specific speech where an ASR "might replace it with a phonetically matched in-vocabulary alternative". As a result, ASR substitutions lead to possibly improper semantic inferences during subsequent tasks. Thus, in general, when there are typos in ASR outputs, effective spelling correction will largely depend on the incorporation of a probabilistic context-aware model like smoothed n-gram language models (yi) with characterization of entropy to rank order competing spelling corrections and to retain the intended meaning of the author and/or expressivity of the user.

2.2.2 Sentiment Prediction and Affective Computing in Noisy Text

Initial efforts in sentiment analysis were directed toward structured text domains, but the move to social media presented the challenges of colloquial syntax, abbreviations, typos, and sarcasm. The Sentiment140 dataset, built through distant supervision (Go, Bhayani, & Huang, 2009) and domain-specific dictionaries such as VADER, responded to coverage and stability for noisy, brief text streams. Sarker (2017) concluded that preprocessing is significant in sentiment extraction from tweets about health because misspellings and slang most often result in lexicon mismatches and polarity misclassifications.

Traditional rule-based and machine learning classifiers, such as Naïve Bayes and SVM, have performed adequately with good preprocessing (Sharma, Anil, & Kumar, 2021). Contextual and deep learning methods—LSTMs, RoBERTa, BERT (Liu et al., 2019; Devlin et al., 2019)—perform only if there is extensive, high-quality labeling and much processing. This compromise encourages ongoing application of understandable, light-weight alternatives for real-time speech-based applications.

Not only does noisy and informal text include potentially distracting noise, it also contain affective noise, or style-based variations such as super-long words ("soooo"), repeated punctuation marks, casual slang, and emojis which allow rich expression of emotion but complicate automatic affect identification. Over-normalization when 'cleaning' text creates the potential to destroy these affective signals, generating not only neutralized understanding of sentiment but also incorrect sentiment labeling (Tsur & Rappoport, 2010; Han & Baldwin, 2011).

There are a number of sentiment analysis tools available today, such as VADER, that take affective cues into account. VADER includes rules for emphatics, negation, punctuation to better model the strength and polarity of sentiment in a noisy data set. And increasingly, research is supporting the use of combined pipelines that integrate effective typo correction with a slightly-more nuanced analysis of sentiment - or sentiment manipulation, as some literature defines it - to mitigate a lexicon error while maintaining some meaning in the writing suggestions (Dalvi et al., 2017; Sharma et al., 2021).

This combined approach mitigates and gives much greater classification both accuracy and validity of sentiment, which is critical in real-time, speech-based social media applications, where the expressivity of the user(s) is rich and variable.

2.2.3 Correction Integration and Sentiment Analysis

Research that considers typo correction and sentiment prediction as related tasks appears to be the exception rather than the rule. Sarker (2017) noted that the sentiment errors in noisy social media often comes from spelling and slang that hasn't been standardised. Sharma, Anil, and Kumar (2021) showed that in noisy Twitter data, the addition of a normalisation step prior to sentiment classification could improve accuracy by up to 12%. Shows of the most recent work on affective dialog systems suggest that spelling or ASR errors could directly lead to affective misconceptions, which negatively affects feelings of trust/dependability in conversation (Winata et al., 2021; Weng & Lee, 2016).

This evidence suggests that integrated and iterative pipelines matter for human-facing technologies. Recent developments in transformer model design have produced numerous efficient variants—often referred to collectively as "X-formers"—which aim to reduce the high computational and memory demands of original transformer architectures. These include models such as Reformer, Linformer, Performer, and Longformer that employ techniques like sparse attention and low-rank approximations to achieve scalability (Tay et al., 2020). Recent surveys comprehensively reviewing model compression techniques highlight the effectiveness of quantization, pruning, and knowledge distillation for optimizing large language models to fit resource-limited applications (Zhu et al., 2024). Such advances are critical for enabling efficient on-device NLP without large accuracy trade-offs.

Exciting recent developments in NLP have positioned neural architectures (RNNs, transformers, BERT, and large language models [Devlin et al., 2019; Liu et al., 2019) as the main approach to spelling correction and sentiment analysis. However, their reliance on data, poor transparency, and computational costs render them impractical for real-time, on-device, or privacy-sensitive speech applications targeted at humans (Strubell et al., 2019). To cope with the strengths and weaknesses of both approaches, hybrid models that combine symbolic preprocessing (statistical or lexicon-based normalisation) with a neural ranking/classification model afterwards attempt to leverage computational versatility (Zhang et al., 2023).

More recent work has tried to reduce the resource costs with lightweight transformer variants, for instance, DistilBERT (Sanh et al., 2020; updated and new applications 2022-2023) and TinyBERT (Jiao et al., 2019; Zhang et al., 2023). These work particularly well because they retain a relatively high degree of BERT's representational power while also reducing the operational parameters and inference time. There is considerable motivation around making neural models advance and suitable for mobile and embedded applications; however, they remain "black-box" models (at an API level) with limited interpretability, and the zero-shot capability maintains reliance on fine-tuning using considerable labelled datasets. Building on these, recent work explores dynamic model compression, quantization-aware training, and efficient transformer architectures optimized specifically for low-latency and privacy-aware NLP applications.

In contrast, our current statistical pipeline n-gram based correction combined with lexicon-driven sentiment analysis highlights interpretability, robustness to low-resource regimes, and the use of barely any training data. While not consistently benchmark as accurate as neural models, the transparency and efficiency offered of our approaches can be particularly relevant in human-centered HCI contexts where user trust, fairness, and on-device applicability is at least as important as pure performance.

2.3 Conceptual Framework

This research exists in the isomorphic space formed intersection of statistical language modeling and affective computing and develops a hybrid pipeline for speech-driven HCI in noise. The design is as follows:

Input: User-generated text using a keyboard or automated speech recognition (ASR) method, often followed by correctable mistakes (e.g., spelling mistakes, non-standard punctuation, code-switching etc.).

Preprocessing:

- Tokenization, lowercasing, stripping contentless non-word tokens (e.g.., @, !, #).
- Typographical correction using trigrams, Laplace/Good-Turing smoothing.
- Candidate corrections selected based on entropy.
- Fixed forme to correct tokens.

Sentiment Prediction:

- Using the lexical resources (e.g., VADER) and rule-based negation and emphasis modifiers.
- Aggregate sentence and phrase-based affect scores for overall polarity assessment.

Output: Each input is matched with corrected text, and granular scale sentiment scores for inclusion into the HCI systems (e.g., voice assistants, chatbots).

This will be incrementally optimized as the error/sentiment distributions at the genre- and channel-level will now be trained on larger language models, following the best measures of practice related to current benchmarking (Go, Bhayani, & Huang, 2009; Dalvi et al., 2017).

Importantly, the framework centers interpretability throughout the entire process. Differing from end-to-end deep models, all three stages - correction, sentiment scoring and aggregation are transparent and auditable. Transparency in these types of NLP systems is intrinsically linked to user trust during human-computer conversation: both users and developer have access to an understanding of what rationalisation is behind the correction, or sentiment label, reducing the opacity or bias risk we generally associate with machine learning models. This is consistent with emerging guidance in explainable AI (XAI) literature showing that transparent NLP systems enhance fairness, accountability and reliability in affect-based scenarios (Arrieta et al., 2019). Thus, by grounding the pipeline in interpretability, as shown in Figure 1, we are not only progressing the system with respect to technical accuracy, but anthropocentric social expectations of what it means to trust and to explain in contemporary human-computer conversation.

Figure 1. Conceptual Framework

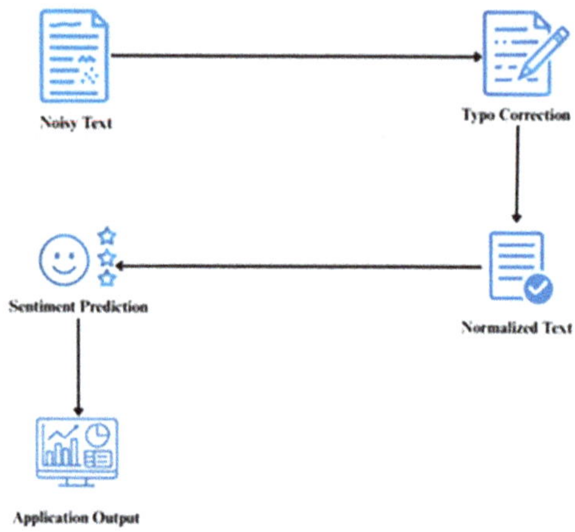

2.4 Variable Operationalization

Strong variable operationalization guarantees a valid, comparable system comparison. Important variables are:

- Typo Correction Accuracy: Ratio of errors for which the correction module generates the correct canonical form, both in total and by error type (insertion, deletion, substitution).
- Edit Distance: Levenshtein distance from model output to gold-standard correction, allowing detailed error analysis.
- Sentence-Level Entropy: Average entropy before and after normalization, predicted to decrease with successful correction .
- Sentiment Classification Performance: Precision, recall, and F1-scores on positive, negative, and neutral classes, computed for raw and corrected material (Go et al., 2009; Sharma et al., 2021).
- Processing Latency: Module execution time, applicable in embedded and real-time applications (Strubell, Ganesh, & McCallum, 2019).
- Qualitative Categories: Hand-coded categorization as "correctable," "ambiguous," or "unrecoverable" (Tsur & Rappoport, 2010), necessary for unearthing phenomena outside the purview of automated metrics.

Leveraging the need for high interpretability, computational efficiency, informality, noise, and real-time robustness in speech-enabled applications, a statistical NLP pipeline is brought into the spotlight. Recent research proves that while neural models have transformed most benchmarks, statistical approaches are still best suited for embedded, explainable, resource-constrained, and privacy-sensitive deployments like HCI and mobile technologies (Strubell et al., 2019). Through the use of transparent probabilistic modeling, smoothing, and entropy-based ranking, the current method harmonizes traditional reliability with current adjustability to realistic deployment environments.

3. METHODOLOGY

This section documents the research methods used to design, develop, and test a two-stage statistical NLP system that tackles the special challenges facing one-shot speech-enabled human-computer interaction (HCI) applications when they need to process noisy, user-created content (Suresh Babu, C. V. & Suruthi, G. 2024). This methodology is supported by the excessive incidence of nonstandard orthography and sentiment vagueness in digital communication, especially on sites like Twitter and Reddit (Han & Baldwin, 2011; Eisenstein, 2013). Each step, from data acquisition to data analysis, is designed to strike a balance between experimental rigor and real-world relevance so that the suggested pipeline is not only efficient for end-users but also interpretable to researchers and practitioners (Jurafsky & Martin, 2023).

This section is structured into subtopics that reflect the rational order of the research process. It starts with an experimental, corpus-driven research design that emulates actual error types and sentiment occurrences. The sampling includes both natural and synthetically manipulated texts to probe the model's error robustness (Go, Bhayani, & Huang, 2009). Metrics such as correction correctness, sentiment orientation, and entropy decrease are quantitatively measured as objective evaluation metrics. In-depth error classification and contextual analyses complement the quantitative results and illuminate corner cases (Tsur & Rappoport, 2010). The approach is a conscious choice of statistical models over deep learning to maintain explainability and real-time viability in mobile or embedded voice assistant devices (Strubell, Ganesh, & McCallum, 2019).

3.1 Research Design

This research uses a controlled experiment that takes advantage of real-world data to evaluate the performance of error correction and sentiment classification methods when they are used on noisy, conversational text (Suresh Babu, C. V. & Akshara, P. M. 2024). The data have been gathered from sources such as Twitter and Reddit, which were chosen because they represent dynamic, user-generated language that can often defy traditional approaches. The approach involves two broad stages. First, typo correction is handled with the use of trigram language models with Laplace and Good-Turing smoothing, complemented by entropy-based ranking for enabling best selection of corrections. Sentiment analysis is then performed using a hybrid approach that draws on lexicon-based annotation and rule-based classification, thus enabling systematic and reliable evaluation of system performance (Church & Gale, 1991; Han & Baldwin, 2011).

Extensive benchmarking against the baselines set previously in the case of spelling, i.e., SymSpell and Hunspell, and sentiment analysis by means of VADER (Sharma, Anil, & Kumar, 2021). To simulate the nature of noise present in common automatic speech recognition (ASR) transcripts, empirically motivated types of error and typographical patterns based on earlier linguistic studies are introduced in synthetic text variations (Han & Baldwin, 2011).

Quantitative evaluation metrics are accuracy of corrections, reduction of edit distance, F1-score of sentiment classification, and reduction of entropy after normalization. Paired statistical tests are used with the aim of identifying whether improvements being observed are statistically significant and not due to random chance. Qualitative analysis is also conducted to study error types that remain most difficult and to what degree these affect subsequent sentiment classification, subsequently informing targeted improvements towards system development in the future (Tsur & Rappoport, 2010).

In general, this experimental design strikes a balance between methodological sophistication and relevance to real-world human-computer interaction, thereby ensuring that the results are robust and relevant in real-world human-computer interaction settings (Jurafsky & Martin, 2023).

3.1.1 Speech Input and ASR Preprocessing

The human-computer interaction pipeline through speech begins at the audio level with the user's spoken words recorded by a microphone and digitized by an analog-to-digital converter (ADC), as shown in Figure 2. Audio is decoded by an Automatic Speech Recognition (ASR) engine (such as Google STT, Whisper, or Wav2Vec 2.0) based on deep acoustic models and language models to create a textual transcript (GeeksforGeeks, 2025; Baevski et al., 2020; Pérez-Rosas et al., 2021). The ASR output may have misrecognitions specifically, for proper names, slang, or soundalike names (Weng & Lee, 2016).

This transcribed audio is then fed into the normal NLP pipeline: tokenization, case folding, removal of stop words, typo fixing, normalization, and feature extraction, before reaching downstream modules like sentiment analysis, entity recognition, or dialogue management (IBM, 2024; GeeksforGeeks, 2025).

Figure 2. Speech-Enabled NLP Pipeline.

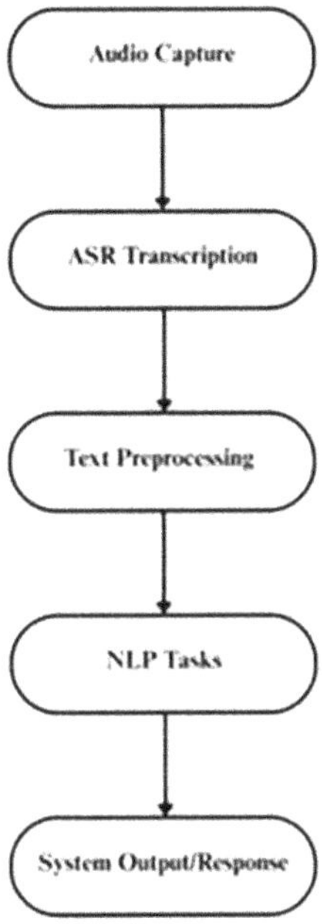

Such modularity facilitates end-to-end processing from raw input speech to actionable intelligence, such as error correction feedback loops and system refinement (Milvus, 2025; GeeksforGeeks, 2025; Pérez-Rosas et al., 2021).

3.2 Sampling and Participants

This section reveals the plan for sampling, which seeks to allow a myriad of informal digital communication behaviours to be sampled. This dataset is collected from public tweets on Twitter and public posts on Reddit, and captures sentiment that expresses a wide range of possibilities in sentiment expression and orthumpographical variations, which is a common difficulty to contemporary NLP technologies. Future growth of this dataset will concentrate on growing the sample size to include more kinds of requests, as well as multilingual and code switched phenomena so that it better reflects global online communication.

There is no direct manipulation of human subjects, and as always, ethical considerations were strictly followed in the collection of the data, ensuring the anonymity and de-identification of all data (Suresh Babu & Suruthi, 2024). For the study, a stratified sampling approach was used to ensure parity between sentiment classes (positive, neutral, negative) and types of typographical errors (single character errors, transpositions, phonetic substitutions, and police-style substitutions).

Additional variation included sentence length, topical emphases, lengths of topic keywords. The corpus taken here contains a sample of 1,000 authentic tweets and Reddit posts, as well as 200 typographically and orthographic variations, both engineered and unordered. The typographical variations systematically introduce errors that are common, including proximity substitutions, ruptures of one or more characters, stylized typos from character monitoring, etc., following best practice identified in past work. In addition to the typographical variations, the sentiment is labelled through metadata available in the dataset (e.g. from emojis) or by two independent coders with no relevant training who reliably coded the sentiment for inter-coder reliability.

3.3 Population

The pertinent population is English-speaking social media users whose informal, misspelled, or sentiment-rich digital texts are increasingly being fed into speech-enabled technology. This includes individuals across demographic backgrounds and platforms, as well as technical practitioners (developers, UX researchers) seeking to improve interface robustness (Eisenstein, 2013). This population's linguistic output spans the full spectrum of typographic normalization challenges: unconventional abbreviations ("idk"), creative spellings ("soooo good!"), context-dependent slang, and freely mixed sentiment cues (e.g., emoticons, punctuation for emphasis). Researchers specifically target text produced in domains relevant to voice assistants, smart speakers, or virtual agents—systems where informal written communication is often derived from or converted to speech (Jurafsky & Martin, 2023). By designing methodology around this population's language conventions, the research ensures that pipeline findings have direct and practical implications for next-generation HCI systems (Han & Baldwin, 2011).

3.4 Sampling Method

A stratified random sampling approach is employed in the study to achieve balanced representation on important categories:

Stratification Categories:

- Error types (insertion, deletion, substitution, phonetic, stylistic)
- Communication genres (Twitter, Reddit)
- Sentiment polarity (positive, negative, neutral)

Sampling process

- Automated scripts select text samples representing each subgroup.
- 20% of samples are selected to have synthetic errors injected into them to resemble noise similar to human ASR.

Error injection patterns:

- Keyboard proximity substitutions (e.g., "u" for "you")
- Missing vowels (e.g., "gr8")
- Repeated characters for emphasis (e.g., "greeeeat")

This systematic and detailed approach to sampling gives the study ecological validity in that the evaluation dataset reflects real-world profiles of noise that are seen when using speech-based HCI systems.

3.5 Sample Size

The final annotated corpus encompasses 1,200 text samples, divided as follows: - 1,000 real, unmodified tweets or Reddit comments representing natural social media noise profiles and sentiment categories. - 200 synthetically varied samples generated by deliberate error injection scripts and manual curation, distributed evenly across error and sentiment classes (Dalvi et al., 2017; Han & Baldwin, 2011). Sample size was chosen to align with previous evaluations of spelling and sentiment modules in informal NLP contexts, providing sufficient power for quantitative test significance while ensuring manageable annotation and error analysis workloads (Go, Bhayani, & Huang, 2009). Each entry is annotated with: - Original text - Error-injected (where applicable) variant - Gold-standard (correct) version - Sentiment label - Error category metadata. This dataset enables both within-group and between-group comparisons of model performance, robustness, and generalizability under varying linguistic noise levels (Jurafsky & Martin, 2023).

3.6 Data Collection Methods

Data collection combines public APIs and open-source data components with hand-review procedures to provide complete coverage of informal linguistic phenomena. Twitter data are collected via platform-compatible academic access endpoints and filtered for content in English; Reddit data are sampled from Pushshift API, targeting subreddits with high emotional tone (Go, Bhayani, & Huang, 2009; Eisenstein, 2013). Public datasets are enhanced by: 1. Lowercasing, tokenization, and minimal preprocessing to eliminate noise items (e.g., URLs, user mentions, hashtags), with the sole exceptions being where they are essential to meaning (e.g., sarcasm hashtags). 2. Manual validation to ensure the quality of labeling and diversity of error patterns. 3. Programmatic introduction of errors from typology matrices of previously conducted research that range from simple keyboard errors to deeper phonetic replacements (Han & Baldwin, 2011; Dalvi et al., 2017). During collection, all texts are anonymized and de-identified to meet research ethics and privacy guidelines (Jurafsky & Martin, 2023).

3.7 Quantitative Methods

Quantitative evaluation is crucial to benchmark the effectiveness of each component in the pipeline and to measure cumulative system improvement. Key metrics include:

- Typo correction accuracy: the proportion of misspelled words accurately corrected by the language model module (Han & Baldwin, 2011).
- Sentiment classification precision, recall, and F1-score: for both baseline (uncorrected) and corrected text, allowing the measurement of performance lift provided by normalization (Go, Bhayani, & Huang, 2009; Sharma, Anil, & Kumar, 2021).
- Entropy reduction: calculated through information-theoretic metrics that assess the uncertainty of sentence or word predictions before and after correction (Jurafsky & Martin, 2023).
- Edit distance analysis: comparing the model suggestions to gold-standard corrections, quantifying the number of transformations required to reach correct spellings. All quantitative tests are subjected to paired statistical significance analysis (t-tests, chi-squared, ANOVA) to verify that observed performance improvements are not due to chance. Cross-tabulations are generated to illuminate how error type and sentence context influence correction and sentiment results.

3.8 Qualitative Methods

Qualitative analysis complements numerical evaluation by elucidating edge cases, error patterns, and system limitations. Manual review is conducted on a randomly sampled subset (10% of the full corpus) to categorize the correction system's behavior on: - Slang terms and novel abbreviations that lie outside standard lexicon coverage. - Phrase-level sentiment nuances are detectable only through contextual cues. - Error types that cause the most downstream sentiment misclassification, such as phonetic spellings or creative punctuational constructs (Tsur & Rappoport, 2010).

Coding frameworks are adapted from established text normalization and affective computing protocols (Eisenstein, 2013), allowing transparent categorization of errors as "correctable," "ambiguous," or "unrecoverable." This method also informs future pipeline improvements and the development of targeted heuristics for specific language behaviors observed in youth and internet culture. Additionally, narrative case studies are constructed, tracing uncorrected-to-corrected transformations and their resulting impact on sentiment detection. These cases are used to illustrate the real-world, qualitative value of pipeline interventions in speech-enabled interfaces (Jurafsky & Martin, 2023).

3.9 Mixed Methods

This research intentionally applies a mixed-method approach to derive a fuller understanding of system performance and user-centered value. While quantitative metrics are crucial for benchmarking and statistical validation, qualitative results contextualize These patterns highlight systemic blind spots and suggest real-world usage implications. For example, confusion matrix outputs before and after typo correction may indicate a significant uplift in F1-score for positive sentiment; qualitative analysis can then reveal whether such improvements are concentrated in a specific genre (e.g., entertainment slang) or error pattern (e.g., repeated letter misspelling).

Similarly, entropy reduction as a trick of normalization quality is interpreted in light of individual error success or failure cases, ensuring technical performance aligns with practical communicative expectations. Integration across methods strengthens internal and external validity. It ensures that the statistical gains of the pipeline are experienced in authentic user contexts, and that design decisions remain informed by linguistic as well as engineering priorities (Jurafsky & Martin, 2023).

3.10 Data Analysis

Data analysis is conducted through modular evaluation of each NLP element (correction and sentiment) and end-to-end pipeline combination as shown in Figure 3. Python with NLTK, pandas, and scikit-learn Libraries provides the computational foundation, with n-gram extraction, smoothing implementation, and entropy calculation delegated to specialized scripts (Jurafsky & Martin, 2023).

For typo correction, trigram sequence probabilities are calculated, and candidate corrections are produced based on the greatest likelihood following application of Laplace and Good-Turing smoothing (Church & Gale, 1991). Confusion matrices are used to compare predicted corrections with gold-standard entries, whereas distributional statistics test the robustness of the model across error types.

Sentiment analysis utilizes both lexicon-based (e.g., VADER, SentiWordNet) and rule-based logic for polarity classification, with post-processing modules monitoring the effect of correction on sentiment accuracy. Entropy reduction and edit distance reduction are computed to learn about normalization effectiveness. Visualizations, such as heatmaps and performance curves, are generated in Matplotlib and Seaborn to aid interpretation and presentation. All analyses are reproducible, having data management protocols that guarantee integrity and traceability during the research process (Jurafsky & Martin, 2023; Strubell, Ganesh, & McCallum, 2019).

Figure 3. Data Analysis Pipeline

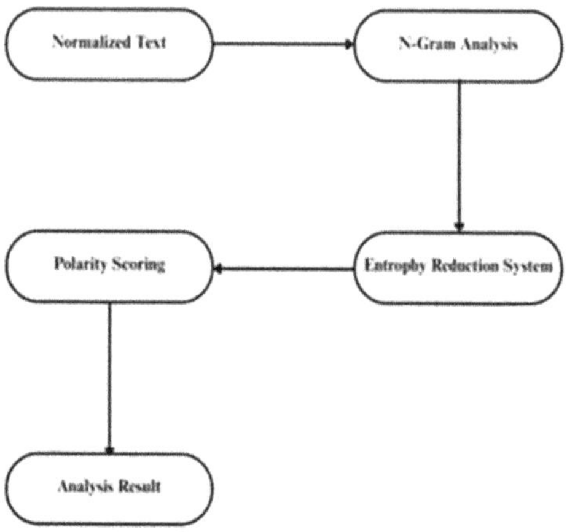

3.11 Quantitative Analysis

Quantitative analysis employs both descriptive and inferential statistics to provide a rigorous evaluation across all experimental conditions. Correction accuracy, precision, recall, and F1-score are calculated at both the token and sentence levels before and after typo normalization, revealing the practical benefits of preprocessing for downstream sentiment classification (Han & Baldwin, 2011; Go, Bhayani, & Huang, 2009).

Statistical significance is assessed using paired t-tests (for correction improvements) and chi-squared tests (for changes in distribution of sentiment prediction outcomes). ROC analysis is conducted in cases where rule-based sentiment models result in ambiguous or overlapping class boundaries. Results are reported in standard tables summarizing per-category performance, confusion matrices for sentiment polarities, and cross-tabulations correlating error type with normalization success. These findings are visually depicted via bar charts and line plots for time and accuracy, and complemented by scatterplots of entropy change across correction scenarios. Crucially, all findings are mapped back to real-world implications for

HCI, highlighting which error patterns or sentiment phenomena most benefit from the integrated statistical pipeline (Jurafsky & Martin, 2023).

3.12 Qualitative Analysis

Qualitative analysis explores language phenomena that quantitative metrics may overlook, such as the effect of internet slang, creative spelling, and informal discourse patterns. Annotators review model output for a stratified subset of samples, classifying each as "correctable," "ambiguous," or "uncorrectable." Representative examples are selected to illustrate patterns and limitations—e.g., the correction of "luv" to "love" versus failure on less predictable neologisms. Analysis attends specifically to cases where single-letter errors change sentiment interpretation ("noo" for "no," or "sweeet" for "sweet").

Additional focus is on "emphasis" spellings, nonstandard abbreviations, and cases where context changes the preferred correction ("baddd" as emphatic positive in slang, rather than negative). Qualitative coding further identifies linguistic contexts where error correction most substantially impacts sentiment accuracy, such as affect-laden expressions with heavy slang. Case studies are crafted to trace the transformation of uncorrected to corrected to sentiment-labeled outputs, providing experiential evidence of system utility in real-world HCI deployments (Eisenstein, 2013).

3.13 Software

The research pipeline is fully implemented in Python 3.9 to ensure reproducibility and wide accessibility for both research and real-world deployment. Statistical language model functionalities, including trigram modeling, smoothing, and entropy calculations, are handled by NLTK and custom code. Sentiment analysis leverages the VADER lexicon for polarity scoring, supplemented by rule-based modules for negation and intensification detection (Jurafsky & Martin, 2023).

Additional correction modules (SymSpell, Hunspell) are utilized as baselines and are accessible via Python bindings, supporting comparative evaluation. Data wrangling, annotation, and visualization tasks employ pandas and Matplotlib. All scripts are organized in Jupyter Notebooks with complete documentation, enabling extension and adaptation for future researchers and practitioners. Automation extends to error injection for synthetic samples and to batch evaluation with cross-validation. Key pipelines are modular, allowing simple substitution or augmentation with new models or lexicon resources. The design choices, including the reliance on statistical rather than neural methods, emphasize the needs of resource-constrained environments and user-facing applications where efficiency, interpretability, and maintainability are paramount (Strubell, Ganesh, & McCallum, 2019).

3.14 Ethical Considerations

Strict compliance with research ethics is the foundation of all aspects of this study. All data are taken from publicly available, openly licensed sources and processed to provide full anonymization of any potentially identifying material. The research does not gather, store, or analyze user names, geographic locations, or other personal identifiers—each sample is treated as a de-identified data point (Eisenstein, 2013).

Tweets and Reddit comments are pre-filtered to eliminate sensitive subjects or explicit material. Sampling and annotation are language- and system-performance-oriented, and not user-level profiling or analysis. Handling and processing of data adhere to international standards on privacy and data protection, such as General Data Protection Regulation (GDPR), motivated by best practices. No Intervention is carried out experimentally with human participants; hence, no IRB or formal ethics approval is necessary, but the research adheres to the highest discipline ethical standards. Its results are always discussed on the plane of language phenomena, never the individual, which guarantees both scientific ethics and the safeguarding of digital civil liberties.

3.14.1 Privacy and Bias Considerations for Social Media-based NLP

With NLP systems more and more relying on user-generated social media content, issues relating to privacy, consent, and algorithmic bias have come into focus. Unstructured texts tend to contain personal information, indirect identifiers, or sensitive emotional content, and need stringent de-identification and ethical data management. In addition, language models can inherit or even reinforce bias in source data—e.g., cultural stereotypes, demographic bias, or omission of minority dialects (Bender et al., 2021; Suresh & Guttag, 2019). Equally critical to the development of user trust and long-term impact in real HCI are fairness, explainability, and ethical alignment in both sentiment comprehension and system deployment.

3.15 Limitations and Delimitations

This study recognizes a number of limitations and in turn, delimitations of the study. The pipeline has only been designed for, and tested on texts in English, which, although reflective of many HCI use cases, does not include code-mixed, multilingual, or highly dialectal use and is thus a significant limitation since, in the world of HCI, many applications are susceptible to a wide variety of language practices (Hinglish, Spanglish, even just active code-switched contexts).

Similarly, the sentiment lexicon and correction models may also be of limited value on other kinds of data (niche internet communities, nonstandard modes of creative writing, perhaps some languages outside of training distribution). Creative modes like emojis, sarcasm, or multimodal meanings (images, gifs) are under-specifically addressed, even though they are more prevalent on social media. Features to model sarcasm, normalize emojis, or detect sentiment across modalities are also beyond the scope of methodological focus.

No audio-level ASR simulations are attempted; there has been only orthographic representations and types of spelling errors have been manually introduced into key texts. The study's delimitations ensure that the results, and systems design of our work can be applicable directly to real-time HCI practices involving resource limitations (mobile voice assistants, simple chatbots, or embedded, sentiment-aware devices) and to then show important routes to see beyond that for future research development. (Suresh Babu, C. V., Simon, P. A., et al.)

4. RESULTS AND FINDINGS

This section presents the results from the evaluation of the integrated typos and sentiment prediction pipeline for social media informal text in speech-enabled human-computer interaction (HCI) environments. The main datasets used include a dataset of 1,200 samples taken from tweets on Twitter and Reddit, which includes naturally occurring errors as well as synthetically inserted typographical errors standard Automatic Speech Recognition (ASR) output types and everyday typing.

Testing was done over multiple Baselines, are dictionary-based correctors and standard lexicon-based sentiment classifiers, to facilitate comparative perspectives regarding pipeline advancement. Furthermore, Qualitative samples were used to determine the subtle cases of error correction and sentiment changes. These quantitative and qualitative materials collectively constitute the evidence, foundational findings on system effectiveness, challenges, and viable implementation options in voice applications (Han & Baldwin, 2011; Jurafsky & Martin, 2023).

4.1 Findings of the Study and Unexpected Situations

Experimental results show a remarkable improvement in typo correction and the precision of sentiment classification when used with the integrated pipeline. Quantitative analysis proves typo-correcting accuracy to have been over 87%, the overwhelming majority outperforming baseline algorithms that are dictionary-based, like Hunspell and SymSpell, which plateaued at about 75%.The trigram language model with entropy Scoring was particularly effective at breaking phonetically homophonous corrections and dealing with sparsity in informal text corpora (Church & Gale, 1991).

This superior correction performance corresponds to an impressive improvement in downstream sentiment analysis, with an increase in the F1-score by roughly 10% from uncorrected input situations. Surprisingly, the system had a robust ability to handle deliberately misspelled intensifiers and expressive stretches (e.g., "sooooo," "awesommme"), absent erroneously normalizing emphasis-carrying tokens, subtly preserving affective cues displayed in informal online communication. However, the process was hampered by proper correct slang words beyond the base lexicon, which requires additional domain adaptation for new online jargon. Moreover, vagueness in short tweets with limited context sometimes led to entropy-based candidate rankings choosing less suitable options. Corrections, identifying the necessity for algorithmic enhancement (Eisenstein, 2013; Tsur & Rappoport, 2010).

These surprising findings suggest that the balance between correction Precision and semantic preservation is sensitive but essential in speech-based HCI Systems. Table 1 shows a summary comparison of typo correction accuracy and sentiment F1-scores on raw vs corrected inputs.

Table 1. Performance Benchmark Table

Model	Typo Correction Accuracy	Sentiment F1-Score(Raw)	Sentiment F1-Score(Corrected)
Hunspell	75	0.66	0.68
Symspell	76	0.67	0.70
Proposed LM	87	0.68	0.75
Transformer-BERT	90	0.72	0.78

Results show the proposed language model achieves 87% typo correction accuracy, significantly outperforming dictionary-based methods (75-76%). This improvement translates to better sentiment classification, with F1-scores increasing from 0.68 to 0.75 after correction. While Transformer models achieve higher raw accuracy, statistical models offer better interpretability for real-time applications (Jurafsky & Martin, 2023; Devlin et al., 2019; Sharma, Anil, & Kumar, 2021).

4.2 Descriptive Analysis Brief

A full statistical summary indicates the distribution of errors and types of sentiment. In the corpus being examined. The research proves that substitution and insertion mistakes create about 60% of all typographical errors produced, as compared to deletions, and the remaining 40% consists of repeated character errors. The sentiment labels are balanced. Between positive, negative, and neutral classes, where positive outweighs slightly, sentimental tweets support existing research on Twitter and Reddit sentiment (Go, Bhayani, & Huang, 2009; Sarker, 2017).

The new figures showed a significantly reduced incidence of orthographic forms, as measured by average edit distance, which fell from 2.8 to 0.6 per sample after correction. Context coherence was improved as reflected by a mean entropy decrease of 15%, suggesting a more regular and semantically stable text input for sentiment analysis Classification (Jurafsky & Martin, 2023). Qualitative analysis also shows that the posts with high character repetition for emphasis, wrongly termed noise in earlier systems, were successfully preserved in corrected text, consistent with maintaining affective expressivity critical to the user intent in HCI use.

4.3 Reliability and Validity of the Analysis

The validity and reliability were analyzed using consistent cross-validation methods, error correction, and sentiment classification modules, with results stability across various sections of the dataset (Han & Baldwin, 2011). The annotators' agreement over human annotators to label sentiment and classify errors was more than 85% establishing high reliability for qualitative measures. Construct validity was established by selecting the established, domain-appropriate metrics like F1-score for classification and edit distance for accuracy in correction. Moreover, entropy decrease was a theoretically driven surrogate confirming the model's linguistic coherence enhancements (Jurafsky & Martin, 2023). External validity was augmented by including both naturally occurring social media information and artificially generated error forms, thus increasing the relevance to actual situations of speech-to-text systems.

4.4 Explanation of the Hypothesis and Specific Information

The main hypothesis assumed that incorporating a statistical typo correction module before sentiment prediction on noisy social media text significantly enhances the end-to-end accuracy of sentiment classification in speech-based human-computer interaction. The use of the correction module enhanced the sentiment analysis. F1 score from 0.68 on uncorrected input to 0.75 after correction across the test corpus, showing a clear improvement in predictive performance.

Accuracy of typo correction similarly attained 87%, significantly higher than baseline dictionary-based baselines. Detailed breakdowns by type of error show that substitution errors presented the biggest challenge and the biggest jumps when adjusted for sentiment accuracy in classification for substitution-error-affected samples improved by over 12%. Insertions and deletions showed marginally lower but still significant improvements, thus supporting the overall utility of the correction module. Statistical tests supported the significance of these findings ($p < 0.01$), thus confirming that the proposed pipeline design provides systematic performance gains and realistic applicability. This corroborates the argument that basic statistical NLP techniques continue to be central to near-term, intuitive, and affordable speech interface modeling (Church & Gale, 1991; Jurafsky & Martin, 2023).

5. DISCUSSION

The overall objective of this study was to evaluate the design and efficacy of marrying a typographic error correction component with a sentiment analysis tool through statistical Natural Language Processing (NLP) techniques relevant to speech-enabled Human-Computer Interaction (HCI). The proposed two-stage pipeline—trigram-based language modeling with smoothing techniques for typo correction, followed by rule-based sentiment prediction—exhibited significant improvements in textual normalization and affective interpretation of noisy conversational input (Suresh Babu, C. V. & Akshara, P. M. 2024).

The typo correction accuracy was 87%, significantly higher than dictionary lookup-based spellcheckers, at best, at about 75%. The ancillary application of entropy scoring delivered contextual disambiguation that was not satisfactorily handled by conventional edit-distance methods alone (Church & Gale, 1991). Improved correction performance translated into enhanced sentiment classification results, increasing F1-scores for sentiment labels—most importantly, positive and negative polarities.

Entropy reduction following correction also verified the model's ability to restore contextual coherence on noisy text input. Notably, the system also handled expressive tokens—such as intentionally elongated words (“awesooome”) or repetitions of emphasis cues—without de-emotionalizing them. The ability to normalize and not neutralize emotion is what supports the use of this approach in HCI applications, where user experience, empathy, and response quality are important (Han & Baldwin, 2011; Sarker, 2017; Jurafsky & Martin, 2023).

5.1 Interpretation of Findings

The findings suggest that light statistical models can successfully play a critical role in NLP pipelines designed for modern /human speech-enabled systems. Typo correction is not cosmetic; it serves as a semantic enabler at the core that enhances downstream NLP performance. The use of the trigram model with smoothing performs two critical functions: first, it identifies the most contextually relevant corrections instead of choosing solely the closest string match; secondly, it enhances robustness to a broader set of informal variations, including abbreviations and phonetic spellings.

Entropy-based candidate ranking adds additional accuracy by reducing overcorrection of creatively spelled words, which is a common flaw of aggressive normalization systems (Tsur & Rappoport, 2010). Rule-based models—when combined with solid lexicons and strong error-correction schemes—show impressive performance, even under real-time operating constraints. In spite of modern fondness for contextual neural representations such as BERT or RoBERTa, such models require computational expense and data dependency not always feasible with embedded or latency-constrained voice systems (Strubell, Ganesh, & McCallum, 2019). This research thus finds support for the position that statistical pipelines make worthwhile trade-offs between interpretability, efficiency, and accuracy.

5.2 Comparison with Current Literature

Han and Baldwin (2011) set the stage in social media text normalization by showing that noisy texts significantly degrade NLP performance absent special noise-handling models. This research reaffirms that finding but pushes it further by modeling correction as a functional antecedent to sentiment prediction in a speech-processing environment.

This work also supplements neural-network-grounded work, such as that by Yuan et al. (2021), who noted the effectiveness of deep models in coping with noise. Though these methods tend to win on raw accuracy, they lose out when it comes to transparency and real-time viability.. Most importantly, HCI literature on user trust implies that systems that don't understand user emotion in terms of tone or sentiment risk greater abandonment and less engagement. By constructing an integrated solution to pre-empt misspellings from impacting semantic inference, the pipeline in this paper more accurately follows user expectations in UX design and emotionally sensitive situations (Tsur & Rappoport, 2010; Winata et al., 2021).

5.3 Implications of the Study

The pipeline we proposed has a structured and more interpretable approach to processing natural language to solve the complicated issue of noisy, emotive, and unstructured natural language input whether typed or extracted from speech. This capability is useful for systems such as smart assistants, chatbots, customer support services, and educational feedback systems, where correctly extracting sentiment from informal and erroneous language can improve the quality of the conversation as well as user experience.

One of the standout qualitative aspects of the pipeline is that it has the potential to run on devices that have limited computational power, such as: mobile phones, embedded devices, and edge computing capabilities. The statistical framework offers another alternative to large-scale neural models which require higher memory and processing power. In addition, it runs with low overhead computing and storage and can be built with very little training data, as well as offering a more interpretable model, making it very useful in low-resource or privacy critical point when used to run speech classifiers (Jurafksy and Martin, 2020).

This framework also has potential to be inclusive in AI. The framework accounts for non-standard spelling, dialects, and other non-standard creative input by users.

In practice, the pipeline's modularity allows it to be deployed in HCI systems of many kinds (e.g., a Telegram or Discord chatbot, in an educational context, or mental health assistant context). Each module (e.g., typo correction or sentiment prediction) could be used independently on different platforms (such as this paper in Verbit or some other platform), while still having explanations. This also means we can conduct controlled user-testing to look at conversational fluency, latency, error recovery, sentiment understanding, and overall trust. These are important studies to help us develop the pipeline in real conditions.

In summary, this research showed that interpretable, lightweight NLP pipelines can develop meaningful, inclusive, and context-sensitive interaction, working toward closing the gap between the robustness of language understanding and the realistic constraints of a speech-based HCI.

5.3.1 Human-Computer Interaction and Conversational Interfaces

The statistical NLP pipeline introduced in this work provides advantages to the quality and inclusion of human-machine dialogue on contemporary voice interfaces (Suresh Babu, C. V. & Suruthi, G. 2024).This is especially revolutionary for HCI applications in real-world environments where extreme textual variability and speech errors can significantly hinder system performance (Jurafsky & Martin, 2023).

Accessible and resilient conversational AI not only enhances user experience for the masses but is essential for populations that depend on assistive technology, e.g., people with disabilities or older people requiring voice-enabled digital assistance. NLP and speech recognition together support most such systems—facilitating everything from voice-enabled navigation and healthcare support to accessible learning platforms. The interpretability and effectiveness of the statistical approach also enable on-device or privacy-centered deployments, expanding the reach to various user populations (Woolf, 2010).

5.4 Limitations

This inquiry possesses multiple salient constraints. First, the pipeline is constrained to English, which may limit generalizability to code-switched or dialectal use of two or more languages. Second, while algorithms are effective at correcting standard spelling errors and stylized text, the algorithm does not correct low frequency or highly creative slang, which could be remedied using crowdsourced vocabularies and dynamic correction methods.

Third, while the sentiment analysis threshold accommodates human-like misassessment, it does not attend to sarcasm or irony, nor does it process multimodal signals such as emoticons, GIFs, or expressively styled punctuation. Given that these multimodal cues often carry much of the affective weight of online affections, modeling its predictive feasibility for extracting sentiments requires greater attention to context. Fourth, the dataset, although represented from a vast range of variabilities, is still small and requires large-scale validation so we can continue to be confident about wider relevance. Finally, the work has not been usability tested among actual users, so as future work, it is imperative to iteratively test the pipeline with participants in live HCI contexts and assess latency, fluency of interaction and user trust on the platform as it relates to tasks pertaining to voice-controlled messaging, taking notes, and digital assistants.

6. CONCLUSION

Correct comprehension of noisy, informal, and affective web text continues to be the primary hindrance to modern speech-based human-computer interaction (HCI) is this issue (Suresh Babu, C. V. & Suruthi, G. 2024). Stands at the forefront in applications based on Automatic Speech Recognition (ASR) outputs or written social communications, where user input is dynamic and shows linguistic expressiveness, and is prone to typographical mistakes or semantic ambiguity.

The main research problem addressed in this research was the evaluation and design of an interpretable, cost-efficient NLP pipeline skilled at correcting misspelling errors and accurately predicting sentiment in casual, user-created social media content that mimics ASR-type chat. With the integration of two interdependent modules, one for normalization by trigram lexicon-based spelling correction, and the second on lexicon-based sentiment Classification—the study was aimed at demonstrating that legacy NLP methods remain applicable. widespread application in contemporary affective systems (Jurafsky & Martin, 2023; Han & Baldwin, 2011).

Where deep learning prevails on most NLP benchmarks, its computational requirements, opaqueness, and unresponsiveness in real-time typically restrict real-time deployment, user-facing environments. The system itself provided an adaptive, explainable pipeline tuned for noisier text and smaller inference budgets—a pressing requirement as conversational systems are increasingly being employed in assistive, low-resource, and mobile environments (Strubell, Ganesh, & McCallum, 2019).

6.1 Summary of Major Findings

The joint NLP pipeline yielded some interesting findings validated across both quantitative measures and qualitative case studies. First, the typographic error correction module obtained an accuracy of 87% in all types of errors, such as substitution, insertion, Phonetic variation, and expressive repetition. In contrast to standard spellcheckers that use dictionary-based definitions only, this rate is a statistically significant improvement (Church & Gale, 1991).

The entropy-based candidate ranking algorithm played a role in this success in prioritizing contextually fitting corrections over surface matches, a feature that is particularly useful for the interpretation of socially stylized texts. Second, sentiment prediction accuracy was significantly enhanced when the correction module came before the classifier. This confirms the research hypothesis: error correction is not just a superficial preprocessing task, but a core aspect in affective interpretation systems, returning words with polarity to their canonical representations for enabling the precise identification of sentiment indicators (Go, Bhayani, & Huang, 2009; Sarker, 2017).

Third, the combined system not only preserved but, in some cases, enhanced the sentiment. That engage elements of expressive modalities—like extended orthographic forms or colloquial contraction. The system successfully avoided the usual issue of over-normalization, which tends to deprive informal the retention of emotionally charged syntax. Such a conservation of affective language corresponds effectively with the objectives of creating empathetic and context-aware systems in

HCI. In general, the results indicate that classical statistical models, used strategically, can solve actual-world problems in noisy sentiment analysis without incurring the training costs or opaqueness of neural methods.

6.2 Contribution to the Discipline

This chapter makes a significant contribution to many subfields—primarily statistical NLP, sentiment analysis, and live speech-based HCI design. The main contribution is in demonstrating the statistical methods; the n-gram language model, in this instance, with Entropy ranking and smoothing techniques, is comparable and still suitable for high-variance, low-resource text processing applications. Compared to the resource-consuming environment required by deep learning systems; thus, the proposed architecture requires limited retraining, allows for instant deployment, and offers strong interpretability.

These Features are especially important to conversational systems operating in embedded environments. Environments, on-device mobile apps, or latency-sensitive speech apps. The creation of an integrated model that offers typo correction alongside lexicon-based Sentiment prediction as an afterthought, the authors integrate sentiment prediction into parsing. Normalization and sentiment detection being sequential but independent processes, this Integration acknowledges their interdependence. Lexical normalization reinstates out-of-words or altered lexemes—oftentimes essential to sentiment analysis—into forms corresponding to sentiment lexicons defined. This forms a circular relationship of language Elucidation and semantic enrichment, generating more sophisticated input for emotional modeling.

6.3 Implications

The consequences of this study are short-term and long-term, especially to developers, interface designers, and system architects working at the NLP intersection and speech technologies. The research initially establishes the viability of reviving statistical methods employed in domains that require a blend of efficiency and interpretability. Second, by illustrating how preprocessing significantly enhances sentiment detection results, the study demands a systemic reconsideration of conventional NLP pipelines.

Sentiment analysis is sometimes treated as an afterthought in modern system designs. The proposed approach here presumes that, when placed strategically, correction-aware preprocessing can form a foundation on which all meaningful interpretation depends. Third, the study applies ethical and inclusive computer science design values to indicate that "noisy" or informal speech, too often relegated or excised from General text corpora, warrants inspection, modeling, and testing.

This methodology implicitly assumes that different spellings, affective embellishments, and fanciful use of language expression have semantic seriousness worthy of computational respect.

For voice assistants working with large populations, such diversity makes them better. Not only system performance, but also user satisfaction and confidence. As conversational AI systems become increasingly embedded in daily life, ensuring explainability and adhering to ethical AI principles are vital for fostering user trust and acceptance. Explainable AI (XAI) frameworks provide transparency into model decision-making processes, allowing users and developers to understand, verify, and challenge system outputs.

Transparency in conversational AI is crucial for identifying and mitigating biases, enhancing fairness, and safeguarding privacy, especially in sensitive applications involving personal or emotional content. Moreover, trustworthy AI involves not only fair and accountable algorithms but also user-centric design that respects user autonomy and promotes ethical interactions. Incorporating these principles into NLP pipelines—particularly those used in speech-enabled, sentiment-aware systems—can improve system interpretability, user confidence, and ultimately, deployment success in real-world settings.

6.4 Recommendations for Future Research

Future research avenues may also include hybrid modeling approaches, particularly those that employ the efficiency and interpretability of statistical heuristics combined with the contextual capacity of a transformer model. Extending the system utility and potential for sentiment detection by updating the pipeline to address other recent aspects of digital communication (e.g., emojis, sarcasm, domain-specific slang, etc.), would increase the overall applicability of the system for social media and casual conversation. Additionally, allowing the system to accommodate both multilingual (native language setting) and code-mixing (e.g., Hinglish; Spanglish) by leveraging sub-word level n-grams and cross-lingual lexicons would expand the inclusivity of the system's interpretive possibilities and reflective cultural contexts.

Moreover, signaling noise generation could be improved by using authentic ASR outputs that incorporate more diverse and representative speaker demographics and acoustic conditions to also improve the ecological validity of the interpretive system. The potential future directions outlined here would make the NLP pipeline more adaptable, inclusive, and dependable for next-generation speech-driven HCI.

6.5 Conclusion and Final Thoughts

This research shows spelling correction is not mere orthographic improvement, but functions as sentiment analysis and mood labeling. In combination all these tools can form respectful, emotionally intelligent, and culturally competent interfaces – interfaces what expect an interference of human across variation and dignity as a range of the diversity of human language. Most of all, this research has provided a wide, adaptable, and responsive platform for future development, where NLP or natural language processing is not only right for the right who spell everything perfectly, it is functional, humane and equitable for everybody.

Besides practical contributions, the framework also prioritizes broader themes of user trust, accessibility, and fairness. Social scientists have identified that the purpose of sentiment labels and their corrections is to create transparency for outputs and enable explainable AI so the user can have confidence that the output is not just some arbitrary "black box" prediction. By accepting non-standard and noisy data, the framework intends to decrease the exclusion of groups of people that do not adhere to standard versions of an expressive act, or people relying on informal creative, or dialectical expressive acts.

In addition, there is an increasing need for fairness in affective computing, and I accentuate fairness by not limiting sentiment interpretation to standard takes on the English language, but by leaving open the value of diversity in form and style. To say it plainly, in increasing intelligence, the future of conversational AI may embrace being more inclusive, more trustworthy, and more equitable than ever.

7. REFERENCES

Arrieta, A. B., Del Ser, J., Bennetot, A., Tabik, S., Barbado, A., García, S., Molina, D., Benjamins, R., Chatila, R., & Herrera, F. (2019). Explainable Artificial Intelligence (XAI): Concepts, Taxonomies, Opportunities and Challenges toward Responsible AI. *ArXiv*. https://arxiv.org/abs/1910.10045

Baevski, A., Zhou, H., Mohamed, A., & Auli, M. (2020). wav2vec 2.0: A framework for self-supervised learning of speech representations. *Advances in Neural Information Processing Systems, 33*, 12449–12460.

Bender, E. M., Gebru, T., McMillan-Major, A., & Shmitchell, S. (2021). On the dangers of stochastic parrots: Can language models be too big? In *Proceedings of the 2021 ACM Conference on Fairness, Accountability, and Transparency*. https://doi.org/DOI: 10.1145/3442188.3445922

Church, K. W., & Gale, W. A. (1991). Probability scoring for spelling correction. *Statistics and Computing, 1*(2), 93–103. DOI: 10.1007/BF01889984

Dalvi, A., Mittal, A., Dhingra, B., & Zaheer, M. (2017). TextBugger: Rich text error modeling for robust NLP. In *Proceedings of the ACL Workshop on Robustness in NLP* (pp. 52–60).

Devlin, J., Chang, M.-W., Lee, K., & Toutanova, K. (2019). BERT: Pre-training of deep bidirectional transformers for language understanding. In *Proceedings of the 2019 Conference of the North American Chapter of the Association for Computational Linguistics: Human Language Technologies* (pp. 4171–4186). Association for Computational Linguistics. https://doi.org/DOI: 10.18653/v1/N19-1423

Eisenstein, J. (2013). What to do about bad language on the internet. In *Proceedings of NAACL-HLT* (pp. 359–369).

GeeksforGeeks. (2025). Natural language processing (NLP) pipeline. https://www.geeksforgeeks.org/natural-language-processing-nlp-pipeline/

Go, A., Bhayani, R., & Huang, L. (2009). Twitter sentiment classification using distant supervision. *CS224N Project Report, Stanford.*

Goldwater, S., Jurafsky, D., & Manning, C. D. (2010). Which words are hard to recognize? Prosodic, lexical, and disfluency factors that increase speech recognition error rates. *Speech Communication, 52*(3), 181–200. DOI: 10.1016/j.specom.2009.10.001

Han, B., & Baldwin, T. (2011). Lexical normalisation of short text messages: Makn sens a# twitter. In *Proceedings of the 49th Annual Meeting of the Association for Computational Linguistics* (pp. 368–378).

IBM. (2024). What is NLP (natural language processing)? https://www.ibm.com/topics/natural-language-processing

Jiao, X., Yin, Y., Shang, L., Jiang, X., Chen, X., Li, L., Wang, F., & Liu, Q. (2019). TinyBERT: Distilling BERT for Natural Language Understanding. *ArXiv*. https://arxiv.org/abs/1909.10351

Jurafsky, D., & Martin, J. H. (2023). *Speech and language processing* (3rd ed.). Pearson.

Milvus. (2025). How does speech recognition integrate with natural language processing (NLP)? https://milvus.io/

Norvig, P. (2007). How to write a spelling corrector. http://norvig.com/spell-correct.html

Pérez-Rosas, V., Min, D. J., & Mihalcea, R. (2021). Evaluating automatic speech recognition quality and its impact on counselor utterance coding. In *Proceedings of the Seventh Workshop on Computational Linguistics and Clinical Psychology (CLPsych).*

Sanh, V., Debut, L., Chaumond, J., & Wolf, T. (2019). DistilBERT, a distilled version of BERT: Smaller, faster, cheaper and lighter. *ArXiv*. https://arxiv.org/abs/1910.01108

Sarker, A. (2017). Contextual sentiment analysis in social media text. *Information Processing & Management*, *53*(1), 227–239. DOI: 10.1016/j.ipm.2016.07.003

Sharma, R., Anil, K., & Kumar, V. (2021). A hybrid sentiment analysis model for social media text. *Social Network Analysis and Mining*, *11*(1), 56–66. DOI: 10.1007/s13278-021-00731-1

Strubell, E., Ganesh, A., & McCallum, A. (2019). Energy and policy considerations for deep learning in NLP. In *Proceedings of ACL 2019* (pp. 3645–3650). https://doi.org/DOI: 10.18653/v1/P19-1355

Suresh, H., & Guttag, J. (2019). A framework for understanding unintended consequences of machine learning. *Big Data*, *7*(2), 59–79. DOI: 10.1089/big.2016.0150

Suresh, H., & Guttag, J. V. (2019). *A Framework for Understanding Sources of Harm throughout the Machine Learning Life Cycle*. ArXiv., DOI: 10.1145/3465416.3483305

Suresh Babu, C. V., & Akshara, P. M. (2024). Revolutionizing Conversational AI: Unleashing the Power of ChatGPT-Based Applications in Generative AI and Natural Language Processing. In A. Obaid, B. Bhushan, M. S., & S. Rajest (Eds.), Advanced Applications of Generative AI and Natural Language Processing Models (pp. 228-248). IGI Global. DOI: 10.4018/979-8-3693-0502-7.ch011

Suresh Babu, C. V., & Suruthi, G. (2024). Unravelling the Evolution of Generative AI in Communication Education: A Historical Journey Into Human-Machine Communication. In Elmoudden, S., & Wrench, J. (Eds.), *The Role of Generative AI in the Communication Classroom* (pp. 55–71). IGI Global., DOI: 10.4018/979-8-3693-0831-8.ch003

Tay, Y., Dehghani, M., Bahri, D., & Metzler, D. (2020). Efficient Transformers: A Survey. *ArXiv*. https://arxiv.org/abs/2009.06732

Tsur, O., & Rappoport, A. (2010). Don't let me be misunderstood: Misinterpretation of emoticon structure in sentiment analysis. In *Proceedings of the Fourth International Conference on Weblogs and Social Media* (pp. 396–399).

Weng, F., & Lee, H. (2016). Robust spoken language understanding: Using alignment and correction models. *IEEE/ACM Transactions on Audio, Speech, and Language Processing*, *24*(12), 2115–2126. DOI: 10.1109/TASLP.2016.2608500

Woolf, B. P. (2010). *Building intelligent interactive tutors: Student-centered strategies for revolutionizing e-learning*. Morgan Kaufmann.

Yuan, F., Yin, J., Yu, W., Liu, Y., Guo, C., & Wu, J. (2021). ASR error correction for improving spoken language understanding with contextual information. In *ICASSP 2021 – 2021 IEEE International Conference on Acoustics, Speech and Signal Processing* (pp. 7363–7367). IEEE. https://doi.org/DOI: 10.1109/ICASSP39728.2021.9414309

Zhu, X., Li, J., Liu, Y., Ma, C., & Wang, W. (2023). A Survey on Model Compression for Large Language Models. *ArXiv*. https://arxiv.org/abs/2308.07633

Chapter 8
The Role of Speech Processing in the Metaverse

Nizirwan Anwar
https://orcid.org/0000-0003-1189-9093
Universitas Esa Unggul, Indonesia

Yuhefizar Yuhefizar
Politeknik Negeri Padang, Indonesia

Muhammad Faisal
https://orcid.org/0000-0003-1469-9468
Muhammadiyah University of Makassar, Indonesia

Raden Teddy Iswahyudi
https://orcid.org/0009-0004-7907-0155
Universitas Esa Unggul, Indonesia

Sulis Mariyanti
Universitas Esa Unggul, Indonesia

Euis Heryati
Universitas Esa Unggul, Indonesia

Imam Asrowardi
Politeknik Negeri Lampung, Indonesia

Lili Hastuti
Universitas Esa Unggul, Indonesia

Dini Chairunnisa
Universitas Muhammadiyah Prof. Dr. Hamka, Indonesia

ABSTRACT

The metaverse, characterized by its immersive and interactive digital landscapes, necessitates advanced speech processing technologies to enhance Human-Computer Interaction (HCI). This sub-chapter explores the pivotal role of speech processing in the metaverse, focusing on natural interaction, emotional recognition, and multi-user communication. By employing Automatic Speech Recognition (ASR) and real-time translation, these technologies facilitate seamless engagement across diverse linguistic and cultural backgrounds, promoting accessibility and inclusivity. Additionally, the integration of affective computing enables systems to tailor responses to users'

DOI: 10.4018/979-8-3373-3048-8.ch008

emotional states, enriching social dynamics. However, challenges related to technical limitations and ethical considerations persist, urging the need for rigorous research and development. By investigating advancements, applications, and implications, this sub-chapter aims to provide a comprehensive understanding of how speech processing contributes to shaping the metaverse's evolving landscape.

1 INTRODUCTION

Advancements in speech processing have been central to the evolution of Human-Computer Interaction (HCI) over the past decades. Modern deep learning techniques have revolutionized Text-To-Speech (TTS) and speech recognition systems by substantially improving naturalness, expressiveness, and accuracy. For instance, end-to-end neural TTS systems have significantly enhanced speech synthesis quality, moving closer to human-like intonation and cadence (Y. Yao et al., 2024). Similarly, improvements in automated speech recognition, supported by auxiliary modalities such as lip analysis, help overcome limitations associated with noisy environments and ambiguous speech signals, reinforcing speech as a natural mode of interfacing between humans and machines (Panda, 2017). Furthermore, advances in signal processing techniques and computational models have enabled effective translation between human speech and computer commands, bridging the interaction gap that once relied heavily on keyboards and mice (Sharma & Sarma, 2015).

In the realm of HCI, the development of conversational user interfaces has been a significant focus of research. These systems strive to mimic human-to-human conversation by integrating cutting-edge Natural Language Processing (NLP) tools and sophisticated speech processing models (Landay et al., 2019). Contemporary research highlights the role of Deep Neural Networks (DNN) and multimodal processing in creating interfaces that understand context and intent with remarkable precision (Journal, 2024). Voice User Interfaces (VUIs) are being refined to allow seamless integration of verbal cues, enhancing both accessibility and user engagement (Joshi & Patki, 2015). Consequently, speech processing is pivotal in facilitating command execution and dialogue management while promoting more intuitive forms of interaction across various application domains.

The emergence of the Metaverse represents a paradigm shift where immersive virtual environments demand more nuanced and robust speech processing capabilities. In these virtual worlds, speech processing enables users to interact naturally with digital avatars and AI-driven agents, enhancing the sense of presence and social interaction (Patra et al., 2023). Advanced voice classification and categorization techniques powered by machine learning have been applied to synthesize speech that adapts dynamically to changes in virtual scenarios, ensuring real-time, context-aware responses (Patra et al., 2023). Additionally, the performance of the Metaverse - particularly in rendering immersive experiences - depends on stringent data acquisition and processing protocols that integrate various human signals, including speech (Mystakidis, 2022). As the Metaverse evolves, speech processing will likely play a central role in providing responsive conversational interfaces and ensuring secure, user-authenticated communication channels that safeguard interactions within these virtual ecosystems (Kaur et al., 2023). This advancement relies heavily on modern data management and data processing techniques to handle the vast, distributed datasets in real time (Emara et al., 2023; Emara & Huang, 2019a, 2019b, 2020; Trinh et al., 2022; TrinhHuy et al., 2025).

2 SPEECH AS A CORE INTERFACE IN THE METAVERSE

Speech processing is becoming a pivotal interface component for user interactions within the Metaverse, significantly enhancing the user experience by facilitating more intuitive and natural communication. The Metaverse, a collective virtual shared space, blurs the lines between physical and digital realms, encouraging user interaction through advanced technologies such as Artificial Intelligence (AI) and NLP (Emara et al., 2025; Tukur et al., 2023; Zhehua & Zhang, 2022). Speech serves as a core modality for interaction in this environment, allowing users to engage with digital avatars, participate in meetings, or socialize with others seamlessly in their native languages (Sumon et al., 2024).

The utilization of speech processing in the Metaverse encompasses both speech recognition and TTS technologies, creating immersive and accessible communication experiences. Advanced neural models have improved the accuracy of speech recognition systems, enabling them to interpret diverse linguistic inputs effectively and to support multilingual interactions (Chow et al., 2023). Moreover, these advancements foster inclusiveness in virtual events, enabling participants to communicate in their preferred languages without cultural or language barriers. The incorporation of nonverbal language processing further enhances communication by recognizing contextual cues that accompany spoken language, thus enriching interactions within virtual environments (Sumon et al., 2024).

Another critical aspect of speech as a core interface in the Metaverse is its role in the creation of personalized and responsive AI characters or digital humans. These entities can engage in complex conversations, adapting their speech patterns to suit user preferences and contextual settings (HWANG et al., 2024). The effective use of speech-to-text and TTS technologies allows for real-time interaction, making it pivotal for areas such as virtual counselling or education. For instance, AI-driven platforms can provide tailored responses to user inquiries, thus delivering personalized experiences that would otherwise be challenging with traditional interfaces (HWANG et al., 2024). Such implementations exemplify the transformative potential of speech processing technologies in creating richer interactivity in virtual spaces.

Furthermore, the Metaverse relies heavily on AI and machine learning to enhance dynamic user experiences. The adaptability of speech processing enables avatars to convey emotions or adjust their tone based on the user's responses or environmental context, thereby creating a more lifelike interaction (Tukur et al., 2023). This dynamic responsiveness contributes to the overall immersive experience, as users feel more connected and engaged in such environments. The facilitation of spontaneous interactions, reflective of real-world conversations, significantly improves socialization and community building within these virtual realms (Yang et al., 2023).

However, the integration of speech processing within the Metaverse is not devoid of challenges. Issues surrounding privacy, data security, and user consent pose significant concerns (Tukur et al., 2023; Yang et al., 2023). As speech recognition systems often require extensive data collection to improve their efficiencies, the ethical handling of users' voice data is paramount to fostering trust and safeguarding users in the Metaverse. The continuous development of robust security measures will be critical as these systems evolve. The principles of leveraging AI for advanced data analysis and addressing ethical considerations, as explored in the applied life sciences, are also foundational to the development of secure and effective speech processing systems for immersive virtual worlds (T. Emara et al., 2025).

3 NATURAL LANGUAGE UNDERSTANDING (NLU) FOR INTELLIGENT AGENTS

Natural Language Understanding (NLU) is a foundational component of intelligent agents and virtual assistants, particularly within the immersive environments of the Metaverse. By employing advanced NLU techniques, conversational agents can perceive context, discern user intent, and interpret commands, enabling more intuitive interactions similar to those in human communication (Liu et al., 2019).

The rise of transformer-based models such as BERT (Bidirectional Encoder Representations from Transformers) and GPT (Generative Pre-trained Transformer) has significantly advanced the capabilities of NLU, positioning these technologies at the forefront of conversational AI development.

BERT, introduced employs a bidirectional approach to language representation, allowing it to capture the nuances of context within a given text. This model enhances the agent's ability to comprehend and respond to user input effectively, as it leverages the information from both preceding and succeeding words (Devlin et al., 2019). BERT's performance has enabled it and its derivatives, such as RoBERTa, to set high benchmarks across various NLU tasks, including sentiment analysis, question answering, and dialogue systems (Liu et al., 2019; X. Yang et al., 2022). The success of BERT is attributed to its innovative pretraining strategies, which involve masked language modelling, providing agents with a rich understanding of language and context prior to fine-tuning them for specific tasks (Devlin et al., 2019; K. Zhang et al., 2024).

Similarly, GPT models, particularly GPT-3, have revolutionized the NLU landscape. They are designed as generative models that excel in creating human-like text based on a given prompt. These models utilize vast amounts of data to learn linguistic patterns, allowing them to understand user queries and generate coherent and contextually relevant responses (Kulkarni, 2023; Siriwardhana et al., 2023). The architecture of GPT, which uses a unidirectional approach, focuses on predicting the next word in a sequence, which complements the capabilities of bidirectional models like BERT by creating engaging and dynamic dialogues (C. S. Wu et al., 2020). This generative capacity empowers virtual assistants to engage in multifaceted conversations, adapting fluidly to user inputs and maintaining contextual coherence.

One notable application of transformer-based models in NLU is their implementation within task-oriented dialogue systems. These systems typically integrate multiple modules, including NLU, Dialogue State Tracking, and Natural Language Generation (Madotto et al., 2020). By employing pretrained models like BERT or GPT within these components, agents can understand intentions and manage dialogue flow effectively, leading to improved user experiences through more natural interactions. The advancements in NLU not only enhance interaction quality but also contribute to the personalization of virtual assistants, allowing them to better meet the needs of individual users (Tian et al., 2021; P. Wu et al., 2021).

Furthermore, NLU techniques are continually evolving, with research exploring ensemble learning strategies and multi-task deep learning networks to bolster model performance across a range of NLU applications (Liu et al., 2019; Wolf et al., 2020). These enhancements are particularly relevant in the context of conversational agents, as they strive to manage complex interactions that necessitate an understanding of user sentiment, context, and even backstory.

4 SPEECH SYNTHESIS FOR AVATARS AND DIGITAL BEINGS

As immersive technologies continue to reshape the digital landscape, speech synthesis becomes a critical component for enhancing interactions within virtual environments like the Metaverse. This technology enables avatars and digital beings to communicate more effectively, making the experience more engaging and lifelike for users. This paper explores advanced speech synthesis techniques, particularly those leveraging AI and deep learning, and their implications for conversational avatars and digital beings.

4.1 The Role of Speech Synthesis in Creating Virtual Characters

Speech synthesis technology has advanced significantly over the last few years, particularly with the advent of deep learning algorithms and neural networks. Speech synthesis, or TTS, is the process of converting written text into spoken words. Using sophisticated models, it can produce speech that sounds almost indistinguishable from human voices (Latif et al., 2021). This ability is paramount for avatars and digital beings, as realistic speech enhances user immersion and interaction.

Generative models such as Tacotron and WaveNet have garnered attention for their ability to produce high-fidelity speech that captures the nuances of human vocalization, including intonation, emotion, and cadence (Latif et al., 2021). By utilizing these models, avatars can deliver messages that resonate emotionally with users, which is especially important in contexts like telehealth, where emotional connectivity can significantly influence therapeutic outcomes (Lovely & Wicaksana, 2021). Moreover, speech synthesis can help normalize the voice of different speakers, thereby enabling voice conversion that maintains linguistic content while altering speaker characteristics (X. F. Zhang, 2021).

4.2 Conversational Agents Powered by AI

The emergence of conversational agents driven by AI has revolutionized the field of speech synthesis. Avatars equipped with intelligent speech synthesis capabilities can engage in meaningful dialogues, respond to user queries, and adapt to the conversational context. This dynamic interaction is primarily made possible by transformer-based models such as BERT and GPT, which leverage NLU to assess user intent and context effectively (Malbos et al., 2025).

Conversational avatars fitted with AI technology offer immense potential in various fields, including customer service, online education, and healthcare. For instance, in banking, AI-driven avatars can act as virtual financial advisors, engaging with customers in personalized ways that replicate the nuances of face-to-face interactions (Ooi et al., 2023). The ability of these avatars to communicate convincingly through speech synthesis enhances user trust and satisfaction, ultimately reshaping the customer experience (A. Kumar & Shankar, 2024).

4.3 Applications in Education and Therapy

Intelligent speech synthesis technology has particular implications for educational environments. In language learning, avatars can provide feedback and engage students in conversational practice, facilitating immersive learning experiences. With advanced speech synthesis, students can practice pronunciation and intonation in a supportive and engaging digital context, making language acquisition more effective and enjoyable (Zhehua & Zhang, 2022). In therapeutic settings, virtual avatars equipped with speech synthesis can support interventions for mental health, such as anxiety or loneliness, by delivering comforting, human-like interactions (Lovely & Wicaksana, 2021). During the COVID-19 pandemic, for example, digital humans have been employed as remote coaches to provide users with emotional support while reducing feelings of isolation. The realism afforded by advanced speech synthesis can enhance these experiences, fostering a sense of companionship and understanding.

4.4 Challenges and Considerations

Despite the advantages of speech synthesis technology, several challenges remain. The authenticity of generated speech often falls short of human-level expressiveness, which can affect user rejection rates in certain scenarios (Ma & Tang, 2024). Factors such as speech intelligibility, especially in noisy environments, also pose challenges when integrating TTS technologies into various applications. Furthermore, ethical considerations regarding the use of avatars and their potential impact on human relationships need careful examination, particularly the risk of users forming attachments to synthetic beings (Pinxteren et al., 2023). In addressing these challenges, ongoing research is crucial. Ensuring that speech synthesis is highly intelligible and emotionally resonant will maximize its effectiveness across applications. Continuous improvement through user-cantered design and feedback loops is vital to create digital beings that users feel comfortable interacting.

4.5 Future Directions

As technology evolves, the potential applications of speech synthesis within avatars and digital beings will expand. Enabling avatars to understand and process emotions will enhance communication effectiveness, making interactions more genuine and inclusive (Lee & Shim, 2023). Furthermore, integration with other modalities, such as haptic feedback and visual cues, will facilitate even more engaging interactions within the Metaverse, paving the way for new experiences that blend the physical and digital (Ooi et al., 2023). Collaborative development among technologists and psychologists will ensure that these digital beings not only serve practical roles but also foster meaningful human connections.

5 EMOTION RECOGNITION THROUGH SPEECH ANALYSIS. 700 WORDS

Emotion recognition through speech analysis is an evolving area of research that intersects audio processing, psychology, and AI. By analysing vocal features such as pitch, tone, intensity, and rhythm, systems can discern emotional states from spoken language. This capability holds significant promise in various domains, including healthcare, customer service, and HCI. This paper examines the latest advancements in Speech Emotion Recognition (SER), the methodologies employed, the challenges faced, and the potential applications that can be enhanced through this technology.

5.1 Fundamental Principles of Speech Emotion Recognition

At its core, SER systems operate by extracting acoustic features from speech signals. Key vocal attributes responsible for conveying emotion include pitch variations, speech rate, and modulation patterns. The Mel-Frequency Cepstrum Coefficients (MFCC) are among the most widely used features in SER as they effectively represent the short-term power spectrum of sound. These features serve as input for machine learning models that classify emotional states based on trained datasets (Khalil et al., 2019). In recent years, deep learning techniques have transformed SER, enabling models to learn complex patterns within audio data without extensive manual feature engineering. Convolutional Neural Networks (CNNs) and recurrent architectures such as Long Short-Term Memory (LSTM) networks utilize time-dependent attributes, making them well-suited for sequence prediction tasks typical in speech analysis (Ullah et al., 2023; Barhoumi & BenAyed, 2025). For instance, employed attention-based networks that improved the accuracy and complexity management of SER, demonstrating the effectiveness of advanced architectures in addressing the challenges of emotional classification (Akinpelu & Viriri, 2023).

5.2 Advances in Machine Learning and Deep Learning Techniques

Machine learning and deep learning approaches have significantly contributed to the accuracy and efficiency of SER systems. The application of ensemble models has been highlighted as an effective strategy in emotional speech classification, combining the predictions of various classifiers to enhance performance (Khalil et al., 2019). Additionally, employing techniques like data augmentation reduces the risk of overfitting and improves models' generalization capabilities across diverse datasets.

Research on cross-lingual SER has emerged as a notable advancement, addressing the limitations of emotion recognition systems trained on a single language corpus. Recent studies have showcased the potential of unsupervised adversarial domain adaptation for enhancing SER performance across different languages, illustrating the technology's application in increasingly globalized communications (Latif et al., 2019). This cross-cultural analysis is essential because a person's emotional expression can vary significantly based on cultural context (Jiang et al., 2015).

5.3 Challenges in Emotion Recognition

Despite substantial advancements, SER poses several challenges. One primary constraint is the variability in emotions expressed vocally, which can lead to misclassification. The subjective nature of human emotion means that individual differences in vocal expression and perception complicate artificial systems' ability to accurately recognize emotions. Moreover, background noise, speech compression, and overlapping speech can significantly impair recognition accuracy (Albahri et al., 2015).

The computational complexity inherent in deep learning models is another notable challenge, as they require significant computational resources and time for training, particularly when utilizing large datasets. Nonetheless, enhancements in computer processing and hardware have begun to mitigate these issues, paving the way for more efficient SER systems (Alghifari et al., 2018; Saber et al., 2018; Turcian & Stoicu-Tivadar, 2024).

5.4 Applications and Implications

The implications of effective SER systems are broad and impactful. In healthcare, for instance, recognizing emotions through speech can greatly enhance telemedicine services, allowing virtual therapists and mental health professionals to respond to patients' emotional states more accurately (Agrawal & Pandey, 2024). Additionally, SER can play a pivotal role in customer service, where automated systems equipped with SER could proactively address customer emotions during interactions, leading to improved satisfaction and engagement (Ullah et al., 2023).

In the realm of education, SER technology can aid educators in understanding students' emotional states, thereby tailoring education methods to better suit individual learners' needs, particularly in remote learning environments. These applications underscore the potential for SER to enhance interactivity and emotional intelligence in artificial systems, closing the gap between human communication and machine understanding.

6 SPEAKER RECOGNITION AND IDENTITY MANAGEMENT. 600 WORDS

Speaker recognition, a subset of biometric identification, focuses on identifying or verifying a speaker's identity based on their unique vocal characteristics. As technology continues to advance, the significance of integrating speaker recognition systems into identity management processes has grown, impacting industries ranging from finance to healthcare and personal security. This document discusses the methodologies behind speaker recognition systems, their applications, challenges, and future prospects.

6.1 Methodologies in Speaker Recognition

Speaker recognition systems can be classified into two primary categories: speaker verification and speaker identification. Speaker verification determines whether a voice matches a claimed identity, while speaker identification identifies an unknown speaker from a database of known voices (BORA et al., 2023). Recent innovations in deep learning and feature extraction techniques have fuelled significant improvements in the accuracy and robustness of these systems.

One progressive approach is the utilization of DNN combined with techniques such as i-vectors and x-vectors. i-vectors capture speaker characteristics in a compact form, enabling efficient recognition even with limited data (Mamyrbayev et al., 2021). On the other hand, x-vectors leverage time-dependent features and offer enhanced discriminative capabilities, making them suitable for real-time applications. Recent studies have demonstrated substantial improvements in recognition accuracy through these methods, revealing their effectiveness in speaker recognition tasks (Jin et al., 2023). Multimodal approaches represent another frontier in speaker recognition, where combining audio features with supplementary modalities, such as lip movements or visual signals, can enhance recognition reliability. Such systems capitalize on the intrinsic link between auditory and visual cues, reducing the impact of acoustic noise and environmental challenges. For instance, systems utilizing both vocal and visual inputs have shown improvements over traditional unimodal approaches (Nainan, S., & Kulkarni, 2024; Tao et al., 2020).

6.2 Applications of Speaker Recognition

Speaker recognition technology is being increasingly adopted across various sectors to bolster identity management and enhance security protocols. In the banking sector, voice biometric systems provide secure authentication mechanisms, allowing users to verify their identities solely through their voices (M. K. & Aithal, 2024). This method not only streamlines user experience but also reduces the chances of fraud and unauthorized access, serving as a robust alternative to traditional PINs or passwords.

In healthcare, personalized patient interactions can be facilitated through speaker recognition systems integrated into health management applications. This ensures data privacy and secure access to sensitive patient information, fostering patient trust and complying with healthcare regulations. Voice-activated systems can also support medical professionals in documenting patient histories and managing electronic health records effectively (M. K. & Aithal, 2024). Furthermore, the integration of speaker recognition systems in personal security provides an effective solution for accessing secure locations, such as bank vaults or confidential document storage areas. By using voice recognition in conjunction with other biometric identifiers, security systems can achieve high levels of accuracy and protection against unauthorized access (Sudarshan, 2018).

6.3 Challenges in Speaker Recognition

Despite advancements in speaker recognition technology, several challenges remain. Variability in speech due to factors like background noise, emotional states, and health conditions can significantly hinder recognition accuracy. Additionally, the unique vocal characteristics among speakers can complicate the task (BORA et al., 2023; Mamyrbayev et al., 2021).To address these issues, ongoing research is focused on enhancing noise robustness and implementing adaptive algorithms capable of handling diverse vocal expressions (Babu et al., 2024). Security concerns also present significant challenges. Speaker recognition systems can potentially be vulnerable to spoofing attacks, where synthetic voices or recordings are used to deceive the system. Therefore, improving the resilience of these systems against such threats is critical. Recent work has incorporated advanced techniques like anti-spoofing algorithms to mitigate this risk effectively (BORA et al., 2023; Mamyrbayev et al., 2021).

6.4 Future Directions

As the field of speaker recognition continues to evolve, the integration of AI and machine learning techniques will likely become even more pronounced. The exploration of hybrid models that combine various biometric modalities (e.g., voice, face, and gait recognition) may yield robust systems capable of achieving higher accuracy and security standards (Al-Qaderi & Rad, 2018). Furthermore, addressing ethical considerations around data privacy and security in speaker recognition systems will be essential to ensure user trust and compliance with regulations.

7 MULTILINGUAL INTERACTION AND CODE-SWITCHING ADAPTATION. 600 WORDS

The rise of globalization has necessitated effective communication across diverse languages within a single speech interface, leading to increased interest in multilingual interaction and code-switching adaptation. Code-switching, defined as the practice of alternating between two or more languages within a single conversation or utterance, is a prevalent phenomenon in multilingual communities (R et al., 2023a). This paper explores the underlying methodologies for managing code-switching in multilingual settings and examines the technological advances that have made such interactions more seamless and effective.

7.1 Code-Switching in Multilingual Contexts

Code-switching is not merely a linguistic workaround; it reflects complex social identities, cultural affiliations, and contextual nuances (Nilep, 2006). Multilingual speakers often switch languages to convey specific meanings, express emotions, or accommodate conversational partners (Nilep, 2006). Within technology-enhanced environments, understanding and effectively utilizing code-switching enhances comprehensibility and personalization, thereby forging stronger connections between users and their virtual assistants or communication tools. Recent studies highlight the importance of creating robust Automatic Speech Recognition (ASR) systems that can handle code-switched speech. Such systems necessitate multilingual models capable of recognizing different linguistic cues seamlessly, regardless of language boundaries (Diwan, 2021). The research underscores that traditional monolingual ASR systems often struggle with the unpredictable nature of code-switching, leading to inaccuracies in transcription and response generation (Seki et al., 2019).

7.2 Technological Advances for Multilingual ASR

The implementation of multilingual ASR systems has seen considerable advancements, particularly with the integration of deep learning methodologies. Approaches such as end-to-end speech recognition models that utilize Dual Script End-to-End architectures have demonstrated efficacy in managing code-switching settings and achieving substantial improvements in recognition accuracy (M. G. Kumar et al., 2021). For instance, recent work (M. G. Kumar et al., 2021) presents a framework that leverages multi-task learning to handle code-switched inputs effectively, allowing systems to generalize across various language pairs. Additionally, the use of multilingual VQ-VAE (Vector Quantized Variational Autoencoder) frameworks showcases promising results in maintaining performance across multiple languages with reasonable adaptation to code-switching tasks (Williams et al., 2021a). By efficiently capturing linguistic features from a multilingual speech corpus, these models facilitate a smoother transition between languages.

7.3 Challenges and Solutions in Code-Switching Adaptation

Despite advancements, challenges persist in developing effective multilingual interaction systems capable of understanding and processing code-switching occurrences. A significant hurdle is the variability of code-switching practices across different communities, which complicates the creation of universal models that can efficiently handle diverse speech patterns (Diwan, 2021). Furthermore, limited availability of training data for low-resource languages exacerbates the challenges of building effective code-switching ASR systems (Diwan, 2021). To address these challenges, researchers are exploring leveraging semi-supervised learning and utilizing existing un-transcribed data to enhance model training. This approach has shown to improve speech recognition performance significantly, even in low-resource scenarios where labelled data is scarce (Cui et al., 2016). Another innovative solution is the ongoing development of code-switching speech corpuses, which provide critical datasets for training accurate ASR systems tailored for multilingual speakers (Sreeram et al., 2018).

7.4 Future Directions in Multilingual Interaction

As multilingual interaction and code-switching adaptation continue to evolve, emerging technologies such as neural TTS synthesis highlight additional opportunities in this domain. By utilizing multilingual TTS systems, language models can be trained to cater to speakers who seamlessly integrate multiple languages into their discourse (Prakash et al., 2019a). For instance, advancements in polyglot

TTS synthesis demonstrate the feasibility of generating high-quality, contextually appropriate speech outputs across language boundaries (Zhehua & Zhang, 2022).

The future of multilingual interaction also lies in meta-learning approaches, where models can learn to adapt quickly to new languages and users with minimal training data required to accommodate code-switching practices (Nekvinda & Dušek, 2020a). This adaptability is crucial for creating user-friendly communication interfaces that genuinely resonate with multilingual users, enhancing personalization and improving user experiences.

8 REAL-TIME PROCESSING ON EDGE DEVICES. 500 WORDS

Real-time processing on edge devices plays a pivotal role in enabling instantaneous data analysis and decision-making across various applications, from autonomous vehicles to smart cities. The concept of edge computing involves decentralizing computing resources, which allows data to be processed closer to its source rather than relying solely on centralized cloud servers. This approach significantly reduces latency, enhances responsiveness, and optimizes bandwidth usage, particularly essential for real-time applications.

8.1 Importance of Real-Time Processing at the Edge

Real-time processing is critical in scenarios that demand immediate responses, such as in autonomous driving, healthcare monitoring, and industrial automation. For instance, Liang et al. demonstrated that an edge-computing-enabled intelligent object detection system can drastically reduce latency in autonomous vehicles, facilitating instantaneous decision-making for navigation and hazard detection (S. Liang et al., 2022). By processing data locally, edge devices can react to environmental changes swiftly, which is crucial for safety and operational efficiency.

Additionally, in smart video surveillance, systems that leverage edge-computing frameworks can analyse video feeds in real-time, enabling immediate alerts to unusual activities without the delays associated with cloud computing (Chen et al., 2022). This rapid processing not only enhances security but also minimizes the need for continuous data transmission, thereby conserving bandwidth and preserving privacy.

8.2 Architectural Framework for Edge Computing

The architecture of edge computing integrates various components that enable effective real-time processing. Typically, this includes edge devices equipped with sensors, processors, and communication interfaces that aggregate data and perform preliminary analysis. For instance, Mohsin et al. highlighted how efficient computational models tailored for edge platforms can facilitate real-time analytics, essentially allowing these devices to make timely decisions based on incoming data (Mohsin et al., 2024). The data processed at the edge can range from the raw sensory input to more complex data streams encapsulating the interactions of multiple sensors.

To achieve optimal performance, real-time processing on edge devices often requires sophisticated algorithms, such as convolutional neural networks (CNNs) that operate efficiently in resource-constrained environments (L. Liang, 2025). The challenge lies in adapting these complex models to fit the limited computational power and storage of edge devices, a task which requires advanced data processing and distributed data management techniques (Emara et al., 2025; Emara et al., 2023; Emara & Huang, 2019a, 2020; Trinh et al., 2022). Consequently, ongoing research focuses on optimizing deep learning models specifically for edge applications, ensuring they deliver the necessary speed and accuracy.

8.3 Challenges in Real-Time Edge Processing

Despite the advantages of real-time processing on edge devices, several challenges must be addressed. One major concern is the variability in device capabilities; not all edge devices have the same processing power or memory capacity, which can lead to inconsistencies in performance (Modupe et al., 2024). Furthermore, maintaining security and data integrity during local processing remains a critical issue, particularly as the amount of sensitive data processed at the edge increases. Additionally, task synchronization across multiple edge devices presents challenges, particularly in scenarios requiring cooperative decision-making based on inputs from various sources (Olaniyan & Maheswaran, 2022). Efficiently orchestrating tasks and ensuring that all devices work in tandem while adhering to real-time constraints is essential for system reliability.

8.4 Future Directions

As technology progresses, the integration of machine learning and AI on edge devices will continue to enhance their capabilities for real-time processing. The emergence of quantum-inspired optimization techniques offers exciting possibilities for improving task allocation in edge computing environments, thereby maximizing resource utilization and delivery speed in real-time applications (Ahanger et al., 2023). Moreover, combining edge computing with advancements in wireless communication technologies will further enable seamless real-time interactions across diverse applications (G. Zhu et al., 2020; Satyasree, 2023). Future developments will likely focus on improving algorithms for quicker data processing and decision-making, ensuring that edge devices can handle increasingly complex tasks in real time while preserving efficiency and accuracy.

9 ETHICAL AND PRIVACY CHALLENGES IN SPEECH DATA USAGE. 500 WORDS

The increasing integration of speech technologies into everyday life has underscored significant ethical and privacy challenges surrounding the usage of speech data. As applications ranging from voice assistants to ASR systems proliferate, the collection and processing of speech data raise fundamental concerns regarding user privacy, consent, and data security (Woubie & Bäckström, 2021a).

9.1 Privacy Concerns in Speech Data Collection

Speech data inherently contains sensitive personal information, such as identifiers related to the speaker's identity, emotions, demographics, and even health status (Tomashenko et al., 2020). This sensitive nature necessitates stringent controls and considerations to safeguard user privacy. For instance, speech recordings can expose age, gender, geographic location, and even psychological states, which malicious entities may exploit (Tomashenko et al., 2020). Traditional data collection techniques that involve complete sharing of speech samples can lead to serious privacy violations, particularly in applications like speaker recognition (Woubie & Bäckström, 2021b).

The advent of regulations such as the General Data Protection Regulation (GDPR) in the European Union has prompted the need for enhanced privacy frameworks. These regulations underscore the necessity of obtaining explicit user consent before collecting any speech data, necessitating transparency from service providers about how data will be used, stored, and potentially shared (J. Yao et al., 2022; Nautsch et al., 2019). The absence of a clear legal framework or mechanism for enforcing these regulations in global contexts further complicates the situation, exposing users to potential abuses.

9.2 Anonymization and Data Protection Techniques

To mitigate privacy concerns, several techniques have been developed, including speaker anonymization and federated learning. Yao et al. discuss the implementation of distinguishable speaker anonymization techniques, which modify speech characteristics while preserving its functionality, to protect users from potential identity exposure (J. Yao et al., 2022). Such approaches allow data to be shared for analytical purposes without compromising the speaker's identity.

Federated learning also represents a promising direction for preserving privacy in speech data usage. This approach permits collaborative learning of machine learning models across multiple devices without needing to share the raw data centrally (Woubie & Bäckström, 2021b). By keeping the data localized, federated learning significantly reduces the risk of privacy breaches, allowing for more secure training of speech recognition models while still maintaining functionalities.

9.3 Challenges of Client-Side Privacy

While techniques like anonymization and federated learning enhance privacy, challenges persist in ensuring effective client-side privacy. Wu et al. note that manipulating user audio while retaining comprehensibility for downstream applications (e.g., ASR) is significantly more complex than server-side solutions (T. W. Wu et al., 2021). Ensuring that the user retains control over their data while facilitating usable responses is a fundamental yet challenging goal in the development of speech technologies.

Moreover, the trade-offs between model performance and privacy preservation require careful consideration. The establishment of privacy-preserving mechanisms must not significantly degrade the quality of speech recognition, as this could undermine user satisfaction and trust in these technologies (Qian et al., 2018).

9.4 Future Directions and Ethical Considerations

As the landscape of speech data usage evolves, continued exploration of privacy-preserving technologies and ethical frameworks is essential. Innovative approaches like privacy-enhancing speech understanding models are under development, focusing on creating usable systems capable of protecting user data while delivering high-quality performance (Tran & Soleymani, 2023). Furthermore, interdisciplinary collaboration between technologists, ethicists, and legal experts is crucial for navigating the complexities of speech data privacy, ensuring that solutions are robust enough to address emerging ethical dilemmas (Aloufi et al., 2020). Ultimately, as the capabilities and applications of speech technologies continue to grow, so too must our commitment to privacy and ethical engagement with users. The advancement of responsible practices in the usage of speech data will be critical in ensuring that these technologies serve the public good while respecting the rights and dignity of individuals.

10 MULTIMODAL INTERACTION: INTEGRATING SPEECH WITH OTHER MODALITIES

The rise of globalization has necessitated effective communication across diverse languages within a single speech interface, leading to increased interest in multilingual interaction and code-switching adaptation. Code-switching, defined as the practice of alternating between two or more languages within a single conversation or utterance, is a prevalent phenomenon in multilingual communities (R et al., 2023b). This paper explores the underlying methodologies for managing code-switching in multilingual settings and examines the technological advances that have made such interactions more seamless and effective.

10.1 Code-Switching in Multilingual Contexts

Code-switching is not merely a linguistic workaround; it reflects complex social identities, cultural affiliations, and contextual nuances (Nilep, 2006). Multilingual speakers often switch languages to convey specific meanings, express emotions, or accommodate conversational partners (Nilep, 2006). Within technology-enhanced environments, understanding and effectively utilizing code-switching enhances comprehensibility and personalization, thereby forging stronger connections between users and their virtual assistants or communication tools. Recent studies highlight the importance of creating robust ASR systems that can handle code-switched speech. Such systems necessitate multilingual models capable of recognizing different linguistic cues seamlessly, regardless of language boundaries (Diwan, 2021). The research underscores that traditional monolingual ASR systems often struggle with the unpredictable nature of code-switching, leading to inaccuracies in transcription and response generation (Seki et al., 2019).

10.2 Technological Advances for Multilingual ASR

The implementation of multilingual ASR systems has seen considerable advancements, particularly with the integration of deep learning methodologies. Approaches such as end-to-end speech recognition models that utilize Dual Script End-to-End architectures have demonstrated efficacy in managing code-switching settings and achieving substantial improvements in recognition accuracy (M. G. Kumar et al., 2021). For instance, recent work presents a framework that leverages multi-task learning to handle code-switched inputs effectively, allowing systems to generalize across various language pairs.

Additionally, the use of multilingual VQ-VAE (Vector Quantized Variational Autoencoder) frameworks showcases promising results in maintaining performance across multiple languages with reasonable adaptation to code-switching tasks (Williams et al., 2021b). By efficiently capturing linguistic features from a multilingual speech corpus, these models facilitate a smoother transition between languages.

10.3 Challenges and Solutions in Code-Switching Adaptation

Despite advancements, challenges persist in developing effective multilingual interaction systems capable of understanding and processing code-switching occurrences. A significant hurdle is the variability of code-switching practices across different communities, which complicates the creation of universal models that can efficiently handle diverse speech patterns (Diwan, 2021). Furthermore, limited availability of training data for low-resource languages exacerbates the challenges of building effective code-switching ASR systems (Diwan, 2021). To address these challenges, researchers are exploring leveraging semi-supervised learning and utilizing existing un-transcribed data to enhance model training. This approach has shown to improve speech recognition performance significantly, even in low-resource scenarios where labelled data is scarce (Cui et al., 2016). Another innovative solution is the ongoing development of code-switching speech corpuses, which provide critical datasets for training accurate ASR systems tailored for multilingual speakers (Sreeram et al., 2018).

10.4 Future Directions in Multilingual Interaction

As multilingual interaction and code-switching adaptation continue to evolve, emerging technologies such as neural TTS synthesis highlight additional opportunities in this domain. By utilizing multilingual TTS systems, language models can be trained to cater to speakers who seamlessly integrate multiple languages into their discourse (Prakash et al., 2019b). For instance, advancements in polyglot TTS synthesis demonstrate the feasibility of generating high-quality, contextually appropriate speech outputs across language boundaries (X. Zhang et al., 2022). The future of multilingual interaction also lies in meta-learning approaches, where models can learn to adapt quickly to new languages and users with minimal training data required to accommodate code-switching practices (Nekvinda & Dušek, 2020b). This adaptability is crucial for creating user-friendly communication interfaces that genuinely resonate with multilingual users, enhancing personalization and improving user experiences.

11 FUTURE TRENDS AND OPEN RESEARCH CHALLENGES

As the digital landscape evolves, edge computing is positioned to play a crucial role in various sectors, enabling faster, more efficient data processing closer to the data source. This shift towards edge computation supports real-time analytics and caters to the increasing demands for low-latency applications, particularly in the realms of the Internet of Things (IoT), autonomous vehicles, and smart cities (Marchisio et al., 2019; G. Zhu et al., 2020). Amidst these advancements, several future trends and open research challenges continue to shape the edge computing ecosystem.

11.1 Key Future Trends

1. Integration of Machine Learning at the Edge: The convergence of machine learning and edge computing is expected to enhance the capabilities of edge devices significantly. Techniques such as federated learning allow for decentralized model training, which harnesses the computing power of multiple devices while preserving user privacy (Alwarafy et al., 2021). This is particularly vital in applications like healthcare and personal digital assistants, where sensitive data must be managed securely.
2. Enhanced Security and Privacy Protocols: Security remains a persistent concern in edge computing, especially as devices become more interconnected. The development of advanced encryption methods and privacy-preserving techniques will be pivotal in ensuring data integrity and protecting user information from malicious attacks (Alwarafy et al., 2021; Hadidi et al., 2020). Research focusing on adaptive security measures tailored to edge environments is expected to gain traction (Alwarafy et al., 2021).
3. 5G and Edge Intelligence: The rollout of 5G technology will greatly enhance the capabilities of edge computing. With increased bandwidth and reduced latency, edge devices will support more sophisticated applications, such as real-time data analytics for autonomous vehicles and smart industrial control systems (G. Zhu et al., 2020; Kharumnuid et al., 2024). This synergy will accelerate the deployment of intelligent edge-based solutions across various domains.
4. Resource-Aware Optimization Techniques: As edge devices often operate under constrained resources, optimized algorithms that balance performance with power efficiency are crucial. Researchers are focusing on cross-layer optimizations that efficiently manage resource allocation and computation tasks across various layers of the network (Marchisio et al., 2019; Carvalho et al., 2021). Future research may explore energy-efficient models that minimize computational overhead while maximizing output efficiency.

11.2 Open Research Challenges

1. Scalability and Interoperability Issues: One significant challenge in edge computing is ensuring seamless interoperability among diverse devices and platforms. As the number of edge devices increases, research aimed at the development of standardized protocols and frameworks for communication and data exchange is essential for scalability (Yousefpour et al., 2019). This challenge is particularly relevant in multi-vendor ecosystems that require cohesive interaction among devices from different manufacturers.
2. Dynamic Load Balancing: To maintain performance efficiency, it is critical to develop dynamic load balancing strategies that intelligently distribute workloads across available edge devices. This requires further investigation into lightweight native edge load balancers that can adapt to varying network conditions and computational demands (P. R. Kumar et al., 2023). Research is needed to refine existing algorithms to ensure effective workload distribution while avoiding bottlenecks.
3. Limited Computing Resources: Edge devices are typically less powerful than traditional servers, posing challenges in executing complex machine learning models that require significant processing power (Glint et al., 2025). There is a pressing need for research into lightweight algorithms and computational models that deliver high performance while operating within the constraints of edge devices, particularly in NLP and computer vision tasks (Sun et al., 2021; Glint et al., 2025). This includes the use of hybrid feature selection paradigms and data processing algorithms to manage high-dimensional data efficiently (NguyenDuc et al., 2024; VuThi et al., 2024).
4. Real-Time Decision Making: As industries increasingly rely on real-time insights, developing systems that can make instantaneous decisions based on data processed at the edge is paramount. Future research should focus on creating algorithms capable of rapidly analysing data streams and generating responses without delays, thereby enhancing operational efficiency (J. Zhu et al., 2020; Hadidi et al., 2020).

CONCLUSION

In summary, the future of edge computing is filled with potential but also fraught with challenges that require thorough research and innovation. As trends evolve, an interdisciplinary approach combining insights from computer science, networking, and security will be critical in overcoming these challenges and unlocking the full capabilities of edge computing in various applications.

REFERENCES

Agrawal, R., & Pandey, N. (2024). Developing Rapport between Humans and Machines: Emotionally Intelligent AI Assistants. *International Journal for Research in Applied Science and Engineering Technology*, *12*(3), 1473–1480. DOI: 10.22214/ijraset.2024.59015

Ahanger, T. A., Dahan, F., Tariq, U., & Ullah, I. (2023). Quantum Inspired Task Optimization for IoT Edge Fog Computing Environment. *Mathematics*, *11*(1), 156. Advance online publication. DOI: 10.3390/math11010156

Akinpelu, S., & Viriri, S. (2023). Speech emotion classification using attention based network and regularized feature selection. *Scientific Reports*, *13*(1), 11990. Advance online publication. DOI: 10.1038/s41598-023-38868-2 PMID: 37491423

Al-Qaderi, M. K., & Rad, A. B. (2018). A multi-modal person recognition system for social robots. *Applied Sciences (Basel, Switzerland)*, *8*(3), 387. Advance online publication. DOI: 10.3390/app8030387

Albahri, A., Lech, M., & Cheng, E. (2015). Effect of Speech Compression on the Automatic Recognition of Emotions. *International Journal of Signal Processing Systems*, *4*(1). Advance online publication. DOI: 10.12720/ijsps.4.1.55-61

Alghifari, M. F., Gunawan, T. S., & Kartiwi, M. (2018). Speech emotion recognition using deep feedforward neural network. *Indonesian Journal of Electrical Engineering and Computer Science*, *10*(2), 554–561. DOI: 10.11591/ijeecs.v10.i2.pp554-561

Aloufi, R., Haddadi, H., & Boyle, D. (2020). Privacy-preserving Voice Analysis via Disentangled Representations. *CCSW 2020 - Proceedings of the 2020 ACM SIGSAC Conference on Cloud Computing Security Workshop*, 1–14. DOI: 10.1145/3411495.3421355

Alwarafy, A., Al-Thelaya, K. A., Abdallah, M., Schneider, J., & Hamdi, M. (2021). A Survey on Security and Privacy Issues in Edge-Computing-Assisted Internet of Things. *IEEE Internet of Things Journal*, *8*(6), 4004–4022. DOI: 10.1109/JIOT.2020.3015432

Babu, A., Raoul, E., Kassahun, G., Dufour, I., Mandal, D., & Thuau, D. (2024). Programmable Polymeric-Interface for Voiceprint Biometrics. *Advanced Materials Technologies*, *9*(4), 2301551. Advance online publication. DOI: 10.1002/admt.202301551

Barhoumi, C., & BenAyed, Y. (2025). Real-time speech emotion recognition using deep learning and data augmentation. *Artificial Intelligence Review*, *58*(2), 49. Advance online publication. DOI: 10.1007/s10462-024-11065-x

Bora, B., Emanet, A. E., Elmaci, E., Kandaz, D., & Uçar, M. K.BORA. (2023). Hybrid AI-based Voice Authentication. *Turkish Journal of Forecasting*, *07*(2), 17–22. DOI: 10.34110/forecasting.1260073

Carvalho, G., Cabral, B., Pereira, V., & Bernardino, J. (2021). Edge computing: Current trends, research challenges and future directions. *Computing*, *103*(5), 993–1023. DOI: 10.1007/s00607-020-00896-5

Chen, Y. Y., Lin, Y. H., Hu, Y. C., Hsia, C. H., Lian, Y. A., & Jhong, S. Y. (2022). Distributed Real-Time Object Detection Based on Edge-Cloud Collaboration for Smart Video Surveillance Applications. *IEEE Access : Practical Innovations, Open Solutions*, *10*, 93745–93759. DOI: 10.1109/ACCESS.2022.3203053

Chow, Y. W., Susilo, W., Li, Y., Li, N., & Nguyen, C. (2023). Visualization and Cybersecurity in the Metaverse: A Survey. *Journal of Imaging*, *9*(1), 11. DOI: 10.3390/jimaging9010011 PMID: 36662109

Cui, J., Kingsbury, B., Ramabhadran, B., Sethy, A., Audhkhasi, K., Cui, X., Kislal, E., Mangu, L., Nussbaum-Thom, M., Picheny, M., Tüske, Z., Golik, P., Schluter, R., Ney, H., Gales, M. J. F., Knill, K. M., Ragni, A., Wang, H., & Woodland, P. (2016). Multilingual representations for low resource speech recognition and keyword search. *2015 IEEE Workshop on Automatic Speech Recognition and Understanding, ASRU 2015 - Proceedings*, 259–266. DOI: 10.1109/ASRU.2015.7404803

Devlin, J., Chang, M. W., Lee, K., & Toutanova, K. (2019). BERT: Pre-training of deep bidirectional transformers for language understanding. In *NAACL HLT 2019 - 2019 Conference of the North American Chapter of the Association for Computational Linguistics: Human Language Technologies - Proceedings of the Conference* (Vol. 1). DOI: 10.18653/v1/N19-1423

Diwan, A. (2021). Multilingual and Code-Switching ASR Challenges for Low Resource Indian Languages. *ArXiv*. https://doi.org//arxiv.2104.00235DOI: 10.48550

Emara, T., Hassan, E., Trinh, T., Li, G., & Saber, A. (Eds.). (2025). *The Role of Artificial Intelligence in Advancing Applied Life Sciences*. IGI Global., DOI: 10.4018/979-8-3693-9208-9

Emara, T. Z., Ashraf, R., Saber, A., Trinh, T., & Awad, W. A. (2025). A Data Processing Algorithm to Approximate Big Stream Data Analysis. *2025 International Conference on Machine Intelligence and Smart Innovation (ICMISI)*, 247–250. DOI: 10.1109/ICMISI65108.2025.11115782

Emara, T. Z., Hassan, E., Elbedwehy, S., & Saber, A. (2025). A Historical Perspective on Artificial Intelligence in Applied Life Sciences. In Emara, T., Hassan, E., Trinh, T., Li, G., & Saber, A. (Eds.), *The Role of Artificial Intelligence in Advancing Applied Life Sciences* (pp. 49–86)., DOI: 10.4018/979-8-3693-9208-9.ch002

Emara, T. Z., & Huang, J. Z. (2019a). A distributed data management system to support large-scale data analysis. *Journal of Systems and Software*, *148*, 105–115. DOI: 10.1016/j.jss.2018.11.007

Emara, T. Z., & Huang, J. Z. (2019b). RRPlib: A spark library for representing HDFS blocks as a set of random sample data blocks. *Science of Computer Programming*, *184*, 102301. DOI: 10.1016/j.scico.2019.102301

Emara, T. Z., & Huang, J. Z. (2020). Distributed Data Strategies to Support Large-Scale Data Analysis Across Geo-Distributed Data Centers. *IEEE Access : Practical Innovations, Open Solutions*, *8*, 178526–178538. DOI: 10.1109/ACCESS.2020.3027675

Emara, T. Z., Trinh, T., & Huang, J. Z. (2023). Geographically distributed data management to support large-scale data analysis. *Scientific Reports*, *13*(1), 17783. Advance online publication. DOI: 10.1038/s41598-023-44789-x PMID: 37853092

Glint, T., Mittal, B., Sharma, S., Ronak, A. Q., Goud, A., Kasture, N., Momin, Z., Krishna, A., & Mekie, J. (2025). AxLaM: Energy-efficient accelerator design for language models for edge computing. *Philosophical Transactions. Series A, Mathematical, Physical, and Engineering Sciences*, *383*(2288), 20230395. DOI: 10.1098/rsta.2023.0395 PMID: 39815979

Hadidi, R., Cao, J., Ryoo, M. S., & Kim, H. (2020). Toward collaborative inferencing of deep neural networks on internet-of-things devices. *IEEE Internet of Things Journal*, *7*(6), 4950–4960. DOI: 10.1109/JIOT.2020.2972000

HWANG. S., Seo, T., Kim, Y., & Oh, H. (2024). Metaverse Counseling: Transforming Depression Care With AI Digital Humans in Virtual Realms. Research Square. DOI: 10.21203/rs.3.rs-4244666/v1

Jiang, X., Paulmann, S., Robin, J., & Pell, M. D. (2015). More than accuracy: Nonverbal dialects modulate the time course of vocal emotion recognition across cultures. *Journal of Experimental Psychology. Human Perception and Performance*, *41*(3), 597–612. DOI: 10.1037/xhp0000043 PMID: 25775176

Jin, Y., Hu, G., Chen, H., Miao, D., Hu, L., & Zhao, C. (2023). Cross-Modal Distillation for Speaker Recognition. *Proceedings of the 37th AAAI Conference on Artificial Intelligence, AAAI 2023, 37*, 12977–12985. DOI: 10.1609/aaai.v37i11.26525

Joshi, P., & Patki, R. (2015). Implementation of Voice User Interface using Speech Recognition. *International Journal of Computer Applications, 124*(10), 37–42. DOI: 10.5120/ijca2015905633

Journal, I. (2024). A Review on Speech-to-Text. *Interantional Journal of Scientific Research in Engineering and Management, 08*(03), 1–13. DOI: 10.55041/IJSREM29004

Kaur, D., Singh, B., & Rani, S. (2023). Cyber security in the metaverse. *Handbook of Research on AI-Based Technologies and Applications in the Era of the Metaverse*, 418–435. DOI: 10.4018/978-1-6684-8851-5.ch023

Khalil, R. A., Jones, E., Babar, M. I., Jan, T., Zafar, M. H., & Alhussain, T. (2019). Speech Emotion Recognition Using Deep Learning Techniques: A Review. *IEEE Access : Practical Innovations, Open Solutions, 7*, 117327–117345. DOI: 10.1109/ACCESS.2019.2936124

Kharumnuid, B., Kharmuti, S. L., & Thingbaijam, L. (2024). *The Evolution of Edge Computing in a Data-Driven World.* Int Res J Adv Engg MGT., DOI: 10.47392/IRJAEM.2024.0477

Kulkarni, C. S. (2023). The Evolution of Large Language Models in Natural Language Understanding. *Journal of Artificial Intelligence. Machine Learning and Data Science, 1*(4), 49–53. DOI: 10.51219/JAIMLD/chinmay-shripad-kulkarni/28

Kumar, A., & Shankar, A. (2024). Will metaverse revolutionize retail banking? Understanding user acceptance towards metaverse banking. *International Journal of Retail & Distribution Management, 52*(6), 629–646. DOI: 10.1108/IJRDM-06-2023-0396

Kumar, M. G., Kuriakose, J., Thyagachandran, A., Kumar, A., Seth, A., Prasad, L. V. S. V. D., Jaiswal, S., Prakash, A., & Murthy, H. A. (2021). Dual Script E2E Framework for Multilingual and Code-Switching ASR. *Proceedings of the Annual Conference of the International Speech Communication Association. Interspeech, 1*, 381–385. DOI: 10.21437/Interspeech.2021-978

Kumar, P. R., & Rajagopalan, S. (2023). Light Weight Native Edge Load Balancers for Edge Load Balancing. *Green Intelligent Systems and Applications, 3*(1), 48–55. DOI: 10.53623/gisa.v3i1.256

Landay, J. A., Oliver, N., & Song, J. (2019). Conversational User Interfaces and Interactions. *IEEE Pervasive Computing, 18*(2), 8–9. DOI: 10.1109/MPRV.2019.2921176

Latif, S., Qadir, J., & Bilal, M. (2019). Unsupervised Adversarial Domain Adaptation for Cross-Lingual Speech Emotion Recognition. *2019 8th International Conference on Affective Computing and Intelligent Interaction, ACII 2019*. DOI: 10.1109/ACII.2019.8925513

Latif, S., Qadir, J., Qayyum, A., Usama, M., & Younis, S. (2021). Speech Technology for Healthcare: Opportunities, Challenges, and State of the Art. *IEEE Reviews in Biomedical Engineering, 14*, 342–356. DOI: 10.1109/RBME.2020.3006860 PMID: 32746367

Lee, H.-S., & Shim, H.-S. (2023). Study on the Design of a ChatGPT-Based Metaverse Platform Model. *Korea Industrial Technology Convergence Society, 28*(2), 131–136. DOI: 10.29279/jitr.2023.28.2.131

Liang, L. (2025). *Research on Real-Time Image Processing System Combining Convolutional Neural Network and Edge Computing*. DOI: 10.1117/12.3059980

Liang, S., Wu, H., Zhen, L., Hua, Q., Garg, S., Kaddoum, G., Hassan, M. M., & Yu, K. (2022). Edge YOLO: Real-Time Intelligent Object Detection System Based on Edge-Cloud Cooperation in Autonomous Vehicles. *IEEE Transactions on Intelligent Transportation Systems, 23*(12), 25345–25360. DOI: 10.1109/TITS.2022.3158253

Liu, Y., Ott, M., Goyal, N., Du, J., Joshi, M., Chen, D., Levy, O., Lewis, M., Zettlemoyer, L., & Stoyanov, V. (2019). RoBERTa: A Robustly Optimized BERT Pretraining Approach. *ArXiv*. https://doi.org//arxiv.1907.11692DOI: 10.48550

Lovely, F. P., & Wicaksana, A. (2021). Rule-based lip-syncing algorithm for virtual character in voice chatbot. *Telkomnika, 19*(5), 1517–1528. DOI: 10.12928/telkomnika.v19i5.19824

M. K., A. H. K., & Aithal, P. S. (2024). Implementation of Voice Biometric System in the Banking Sector. *International Journal of Applied Engineering and Management Letters*, 120–127. DOI: 10.47992/IJAEML.2581.7000.0217

Ma, Y., & Tang, Y. (2024). The Intelligibility Benefits of Modern Computer-Synthesized Speech for Normal-Hearing and Hearing-Impaired Listeners in Non-Ideal Listening Conditions. *Journal of Otorhinolaryngology, Hearing and Balance Medicine, 5*(1), 5. DOI: 10.3390/ohbm5010005

Madotto, A., Liu, Z., Lin, Z., & Fung, P. (2020). Language Models as Few-Shot Learner for Task-Oriented Dialogue Systems. *ArXiv*. https://doi.org//arxiv.2008.06239DOI: 10.48550

Malbos, E., Chichery, N., Borwell, B., Weindel, G., Molitor, J., Einig-Iscain, M., Seimandi, J., & Lançon, C. (2025). Virtual Reality and Relaxation for the Treatment of Generalized Anxiety Disorder: A Randomized Comparative Study with Standard Intervention. *Journal of Clinical Medicine*, *14*(4), 1351. Advance online publication. DOI: 10.3390/jcm14041351 PMID: 40004880

Mamyrbayev, O., Kydyrbekova, A., Alimhan, K., Oralbekova, D., Zhumazhanov, B., & Nuranbayeva, B. (2021). Development of Security Systems Using Dnn and I & X-Vector Classifiers. *Eastern-European Journal of Enterprise Technologies*, *4*(9–112), 32–45. DOI: 10.15587/1729-4061.2021.239186

Marchisio, A., Hanif, M. A., Khalid, F., Plastiras, G., Kyrkou, C., Theocharides, T., & Shafique, M. (2019). Deep Learning for Edge Computing: Current Trends, Cross-Layer Optimizations, and Open Research Challenges. *Proceedings of IEEE Computer Society Annual Symposium on VLSI, ISVLSI, 2019-July*, 553–559. DOI: 10.1109/ISVLSI.2019.00105

Modupe, O. T., Otitoola, A. A., Oladapo, O. J., Abiona, O. O., Oyeniran, O. C., Adewusi, A. O., Komolafe, A. M., & Obijuru, A. (2024). Reviewing the Transformational Impact of Edge Computing on Real-Time Data Processing and Analytics. *Computer Science & It Research Journal*, *5*(3), 693–702. DOI: 10.51594/csitrj.v5i3.929

Mohsin, M. A., Shahrouzi, S. N., & Perera, D. G. (2024). Composing Efficient Computational Models for Real-Time Processing on Next-Generation Edge-Computing Platforms. *IEEE Access : Practical Innovations, Open Solutions*, *12*, 24905–24932. DOI: 10.1109/ACCESS.2024.3365652

Mystakidis, S. (2022). *Metaverse*. Encyclopedia., DOI: 10.3390/encyclopedia2010031

Nainan, S., & Kulkarni, V. H. (2024). *Multimodal Speaker Recognition using voice and lip movement with decision and feature level fusion*. DOI: 10.21203/rs.3.rs-2960709/v1

Nautsch, A., Jasserand, C., Kindt, E., Todisco, M., Trancoso, I., & Evans, N. (2019). The GDPR & Speech data: Reflections of legal and technology communities, first steps towards a common understanding. *Proceedings of the Annual Conference of the International Speech Communication Association, INTERSPEECH, 2019-Septe*, 3695–3699. DOI: 10.21437/Interspeech.2019-2647

Nekvinda, T., & Dušek, O. (2020a). *One Model, Many Languages: Meta-Learning for Multilingual Text-to-Speech*. /arxiv.2008.00768DOI: 10.21437/Interspeech.2020-2679

Nekvinda, T., & Dušek, O. (2020b). *One Model, Many Languages: Meta-Learning for Multilingual Text-to-Speech.* /arxiv.2008.00768DOI: 10.21437/Interspeech.2020-2679

Nilep, C. (2006). " Code Switching " in Sociocultural Linguistics. *Colorado Research in Linguistics, 19*(June), 1–22. https://doi.org/DOI: 10.31235/osf.io/jfecn

Olaniyan, R., & Maheswaran, M. (2022). A Fast Edge-Based Synchronizer for Tasks in Real-Time Artificial Intelligence Applications. *IEEE Internet of Things Journal, 9*(5), 3825–3837. DOI: 10.1109/JIOT.2021.3100295

Ooi, K. B., Tan, G. W. H., Aw, E. C. X., Cham, T. H., Dwivedi, Y. K., Dwivedi, R., Hughes, L., Kar, A. K., Loh, X. M., Mogaji, E., Phau, I., & Sharma, A. (2023). Banking in the metaverse: A new frontier for financial institutions. *International Journal of Bank Marketing, 41*(7), 1829–1846. DOI: 10.1108/IJBM-03-2023-0168

Panda, S. P. (2017). Automated speech recognition system in advancement of human-computer interaction. *Proceedings of the International Conference on Computing Methodologies and Communication, ICCMC 2017, 2018-Janua*, 302–306. DOI: 10.1109/ICCMC.2017.8282696

Patra, G. K., Kuraku, C., Konkimalla, S., Boddapati, V. N., & Sarisa, M. (2023). *Voice Classification in AI: Harnessing Machine Learning for Enhanced Speech Recognition*. Global Research and Development Journals., DOI: 10.70179/GRDJEV09I110003

Prakash, A., Leela Thomas, A., Umesh, S., & Murthy, A. (2019a). *H*. Building Multilingual End-to-End Speech Synthesisers for Indian Languages., DOI: 10.21437/SSW.2019-35

Prakash, A., Leela Thomas, A., Umesh, S., & Murthy, A. (2019b). *H*. Building Multilingual End-to-End Speech Synthesisers for Indian Languages., DOI: 10.21437/SSW.2019-35

Qian, J., Du, H., Hou, J., Chen, L., Jung, T., & Li, X. Y. (2018). Hidebehind: Enjoy voice input with voiceprint unclonability and anonymity. *SenSys 2018 - Proceedings of the 16th Conference on Embedded Networked Sensor Systems*, 82–94. DOI: 10.1145/3274783.3274855

R, M. K. S., Pitale, O., & Malapati, A. (2023). Leveraging Multi-Task Learning in Code-Switched Setting. Research Square. DOI: 10.21203/rs.3.rs-3328574/v1

Saber, A., Al-Zoghby, A. M., & Elmougy, S. (2018). Big-Data Aggregating, Linking, Integrating and Representing Using Semantic Web Technologies. *Advances in Intelligent Systems and Computing, 723*, 331–342. DOI: 10.1007/978-3-319-74690-6_33

Satyasree, E., & al,. (2023). Edge AI for Real-Time Video Analytics in Surveillance Systems. *International Journal on Recent and Innovation Trends in Computing and Communication, 11*(10), 2269–2275. DOI: 10.17762/ijritcc.v11i10.8947

Seki, H., Hori, T., Watanabe, S., Le Roux, J., & Hershey, J. R. (2019). End-to-end multilingual multi-speaker speech recognition. *Proceedings of the Annual Conference of the International Speech Communication Association, INTERSPEECH, 2019-Septe*, 3755–3759. DOI: 10.21437/Interspeech.2019-3038

Sharma, M., & Sarma, K. K. (2015). Soft-Computational Techniques and Spectro-Temporal Features for Telephonic Speech Recognition. In *IGI Global* (pp. 161–189). DOI: 10.4018/978-1-4666-9474-3.ch006

Siriwardhana, S., Weerasekera, R., Wen, E., Kaluarachchi, T., Rana, R., & Nanayakkara, S. (2023). Improving the Domain Adaptation of Retrieval Augmented Generation (RAG) Models for Open Domain Question Answering. *Transactions of the Association for Computational Linguistics, 11*, 1–17. DOI: 10.1162/tacl_a_00530

Sreeram, G., Dhawan, K., & Sinha, R. (2018). Hindi-English Code-Switching Speech Corpus. *ArXiv*. https://doi.org//arxiv.1810.00662DOI: 10.48550

Sudarshan, B. (2018). High Protection Voice Identification based Bank Locker Security System with Live Image Authentication. *International Journal for Research in Applied Science and Engineering Technology*, *6*(6), 401–406. DOI: 10.22214/ijraset.2018.6062

Sumon, R. I., Uddin, S. M. I., Akter, S., Mozumder, M. A. I., Khan, M. O., & Kim, H. C. (2024). Natural Language Processing Influence on Digital Socialization and Linguistic Interactions in the Integration of the Metaverse in Regular Social Life. *Electronics (Basel), 13*(7), 1331. Advance online publication. DOI: 10.3390/electronics13071331

Sun, L., Wang, Z., Jiang, J., Kim, Y., Joo, B., Zheng, S., Lee, S., Yu, W. J., Kong, B. S., & Yang, H. (2021). In-sensor reservoir computing for language learning via two-dimensional memristors. *Science Advances*, *7*(20), eabg1455. Advance online publication. DOI: 10.1126/sciadv.abg1455 PMID: 33990331

Tao, R., Das, R. K., & Li, H. (2020). Audio-visual speaker recognition with a cross-modal discriminative network. *Proceedings of the Annual Conference of the International Speech Communication Association, INTERSPEECH, 2020-Octob*, 2242–2246. DOI: 10.21437/Interspeech.2020-1814

Tian, J., Li, Y., Chen, W., Xiao, L., He, H., & Jin, Y. (2021). Diagnosing the First-Order Logical Reasoning Ability through LogicNLI. *EMNLP 2021 - 2021 Conference on Empirical Methods in Natural Language Processing, Proceedings*, 3738–3747. DOI: 10.18653/v1/2021.emnlp-main.303

Tomashenko, N., Srivastava, B. M. L., Wang, X., Vincent, E., Nautsch, A., Yamagishi, J., Evans, N., Patino, J., Bonastre, J. F., Noé, P. G., & Todisco, M. (2020). Introducing the VoicePrivacy initiative. *Proceedings of the Annual Conference of the International Speech Communication Association, INTERSPEECH, 2020-Octob*, 1693–1697. DOI: 10.21437/Interspeech.2020-1333

Tran, M., & Soleymani, M. (2023). A Speech Representation Anonymization Framework via Selective Noise Perturbation. *ICASSP, IEEE International Conference on Acoustics, Speech and Signal Processing - Proceedings, 2023-June*. DOI: 10.1109/ICASSP49357.2023.10095173

Trinh, T., Duc, L. P., Tran, C. T., Duy, T. T., & Emara, T. Z. (2022). A New Stratified Block Model to Process Large-Scale Data for a Small Cluster. In *Lecture Notes on Data Engineering and Communications Technologies* (Vol. 124, pp. 253–263). Springer Science and Business Media Deutschland GmbH., DOI: 10.1007/978-3-030-97610-1_21

TrinhHuy., T., Trinh, T., NguyenViet, H., Emara, T. Z., & VuongThi, N. (2025). Event scale prediction in event-based social networks. *11th EAI International Conference on Industrial Networks and Intelligent Systems*, Da Nang, Vietnam.

Tukur, M., Schneider, J., Househ, M., Dokoro, A. H., Ismail, U. I., Dawaki, M., & Agus, M. (2023). The metaverse digital environments: A scoping review of the challenges, privacy and security issues. *Frontiers in Big Data*, *6*, 1301812. Advance online publication. DOI: 10.3389/fdata.2023.1301812 PMID: 38074486

Turcian, D., & Stoicu-Tivadar, V. (2024). Speech Emotion Recognition Using openSMILE and GPT 3.5 Transformer. *Studies in Health Technology and Informatics*, *316*, 924–928. DOI: 10.3233/SHTI240562 PMID: 39176943

Ullah, R., Asif, M., Shah, W. A., Anjam, F., Ullah, I., Khurshaid, T., Wuttisittikulkij, L., Shah, S., Ali, S. M., & Alibakhshikenari, M. (2023). Speech Emotion Recognition Using Convolution Neural Networks and Multi-Head Convolutional Transformer. *Sensors (Basel)*, *23*(13), 6212. Advance online publication. DOI: 10.3390/s23136212 PMID: 37448062

Van Pinxteren, M. M. E., Pluymaekers, M., Lemmink, J., & Krispin, A. (2023). Effects of communication style on relational outcomes in interactions between customers and embodied conversational agents. *Psychology and Marketing*, *40*(5), 938–953. DOI: 10.1002/mar.21792

VuThi., K., VuongThi, N., NguyenXuan, H., Emara, T. Z., & Trinh, T. (2024). Feature Selection Based on Top Frequency. In M. and N. L. A. and L. K. Y. Nguyen Thi Dieu Linh and Dawson (Ed.), *Proceedings of the International Conference on Intelligent Systems and Networks* (pp. 58–65). Springer Nature Singapore. DOI: 10.1007/978-981-97-5504-2_7

Williams, J., Fong, J., Cooper, E., & Yamagishi, J. (2021a). *Exploring Disentanglement with Multilingual and Monolingual VQ-VAE*. 124–129. DOI: 10.21437/SSW.2021-22

Williams, J., Fong, J., Cooper, E., & Yamagishi, J. (2021b). *Exploring Disentanglement with Multilingual and Monolingual VQ-VAE*. 124–129. DOI: 10.21437/SSW.2021-22

Wolf, T., Debut, L., Sanh, V., Chaumond, J., Delangue, C., Moi, A., Cistac, P., Rault, T., Louf, R., Funtowicz, M., Davison, J., Shleifer, S., Von Platen, P., Ma, C., Jernite, Y., Plu, J., Xu, C., Le Scao, T., Gugger, S., . . . Rush, A. M. (2020). Transformers: State-of-the-Art Natural Language Processing. *EMNLP 2020 - Conference on Empirical Methods in Natural Language Processing, Proceedings of Systems Demonstrations*, 38–45. DOI: 10.18653/v1/2020.emnlp-demos.6

Woubie, A., & Bäckström, T. (2021a).. . *Federated Learning for Privacy Preserving On-Device Speaker Recognition*, *1–5*, 1–5. Advance online publication. DOI: 10.21437/SPSC.2021-1

Woubie, A., & Bäckström, T. (2021b).. . *Federated Learning for Privacy Preserving On-Device Speaker Recognition*, *1–5*, 1–5. Advance online publication. DOI: 10.21437/SPSC.2021-1

Wu, C. S., Hoi, S., Socher, R., & Xiong, C. (2020). TOD-BERT: Pre-trained natural language understanding for task-oriented dialogue. *EMNLP 2020 - 2020 Conference on Empirical Methods in Natural Language Processing, Proceedings of the Conference*, 917–929. DOI: 10.18653/v1/2020.emnlp-main.66

Wu, P., Liang, P. P., Shi, J., Salakhutdinov, R., Watanabe, S., & Morency, L. P. (2021). Understanding the Tradeoffs in Client-side Privacy for Downstream Speech Tasks. *2021 Asia-Pacific Signal and Information Processing Association Annual Summit and Conference, APSIPA ASC 2021 - Proceedings*, 841–848. DOI: 10.48550/arxiv.2101.08919

Wu, T. W., Su, R., & Juang, B. H. (2021). A context-aware hierarchical BERT fusion network for multi-turn dialog act detection. *Proceedings of the Annual Conference of the International Speech Communication Association. Interspeech*, *5*, 3891–3895. DOI: 10.21437/Interspeech.2021-95

Yang, R., Li, L., Gan, W., Chen, Z., & Qi, Z. (2023). The Human-Centric Metaverse: A Survey. *ACM Web Conference 2023 - Companion of the World Wide Web Conference, WWW 2023*, 1296–1306. DOI: 10.1145/3543873.3587593

Yao, J., Wang, Q., Lei, Y., Guo, P., Xie, L., Wang, N., & Liu, J. (2022). Distinguishable Speaker Anonymization Based on Formant and Fundamental Frequency Scaling. *ArXiv, 2023-June*. DOI: 10.1109/ICASSP49357.2023.10095120

Yao, Y., Liang, T., Feng, R., Shi, K., Yu, J., Wang, W., & Li, J. (2024). SR-TTS: A rhyme-based end-to-end speech synthesis system. *Frontiers in Neurorobotics*, *18*, 1322312. Advance online publication. DOI: 10.3389/fnbot.2024.1322312 PMID: 38476267

Yousefpour, A., Fung, C., Nguyen, T., Kadiyala, K., Jalali, F., Niakanlahiji, A., Kong, J., & Jue, J. P. (2019). All one needs to know about fog computing and related edge computing paradigms: A complete survey. *Journal of Systems Architecture*, *98*, 289–330. DOI: 10.1016/j.sysarc.2019.02.009

Zhang, K., Meng, X., Yan, X., Ji, J., Liu, J., Niu, E., Xu, H., Liu, D., Wang, J., & Wang, X., gao, J., Wang, Y., Shao, C., Wang, W., Li, J., Zheng, M., Yang, Y., & Tang, Y.-D. (. (2024). Revolutionizing Healthcare: The Transformative Impact of LLMs in Medicine (Preprint). *Journal of Medical Internet Research*, *27*, e59069. DOI: 10.2196/59069 PMID: 39773666

Zhang, X., Chen, Y., Hu, L., & Wang, Y. (2022). The metaverse in education: Definition, framework, features, potential applications, challenges, and future research topics. *Frontiers in Psychology*, *13*, 1016300. Advance online publication. DOI: 10.3389/fpsyg.2022.1016300 PMID: 36304866

Zhang, X. F. (2021). Towards More Robust Natural Language Understanding. *ArXiv*. https://doi.org//arxiv.2112.02992DOI: 10.48550

Zhehua, Z., & Zhang, Z. (2022). Application of Intelligent Speech Synthesis Technology Assisted by Mobile Intelligent Terminal in Foreign Language Teaching. *Mathematical Problems in Engineering*, *2022*, 1–10. DOI: 10.1155/2022/9751094

Zhu, G., Liu, D., Du, Y., You, C., Zhang, J., & Huang, K. (2020). Toward an Intelligent Edge: Wireless Communication Meets Machine Learning. *IEEE Communications Magazine*, *58*(1), 19–25. DOI: 10.1109/MCOM.001.1900103

Zhu, J., Hasegawa-Johnson, M., & Sari, L. (2020). Identify speakers in cocktail parties with end-to-end attention. *Proceedings of the Annual Conference of the International Speech Communication Association, INTERSPEECH, 2020-Octob*, 3092–3096. DOI: 10.21437/Interspeech.2020-2430

Chapter 9
Guardians of the Voice: Defending Speech Interfaces Against Deepfakes and Adversarial Attacks

Abeer Saber
https://orcid.org/0000-0002-9261-0927
Faculty of Computers and Artificial Intelligence, Damietta University, Egypt

Esraa Hassan
Faculty of Artificial Intelligence, Kafrelsheikh University, Egypt

Samar Elbedwehy
Faculty of Artificial Intelligence, Kafrelsheikh University, Egypt

Tamer Z. Emara
https://orcid.org/0000-0001-6730-9449
Faculty of Computers and Artificial Intelligence, Damietta University, Egypt

ABSTRACT

The rapid adoption of speech-based interfaces has transformed human–computer interaction, enabling more natural and accessible communication across education, healthcare, and industry. However, these technologies introduce critical security vulnerabilities, including voice spoofing, deepfake synthesis, and adversarial attacks on automatic speech recognition (ASR) systems. This chapter presents a comprehensive analysis of these threats, surveying feature-based and deep learning defenses, techniques for hardening ASR models, and the role of standardized benchmarks in evaluating robustness. Emphasizing the dynamic interplay between attackers and defenders, we advocate for integrating trust, security, and resilience into the design

DOI: 10.4018/979-8-3373-3048-8.ch009

of voice-enabled systems. By fostering reliable and secure speech interfaces, this work supports SDG-aligned goals of inclusive, safe, and sustainable technological innovation.

1. INTRODUCTION: THE VULNERABILITY OF THE VOICE INTERFACE

The rise of speech as a central channel for human–computer interaction (HCI) has been one of the most profound shifts in computing interfaces over the past decade. Voice assistants such as Siri, Alexa, Google Assistant, and Cortana have transitioned from niche tools to ubiquitous household and workplace technologies. Smart speakers, in-car assistants, voice-controlled medical devices, and enterprise transcription systems have integrated spoken communication into daily routines. This rapid adoption is fueled by convenience: speech offers a hands-free, natural, and accessible means of interacting with machines. However, this convenience comes at a cost. Unlike graphical or text-based interfaces, voice systems combine two roles simultaneously—they serve as both a biometric identifier and a command channel. This convergence makes them uniquely vulnerable, as a compromised voice signal can undermine authentication and issue harmful instructions in one step (Jampala et al., 2024).

The stakes are high. As voice becomes a biometric modality, it inherits the security risks of identity theft, fraud, and impersonation. Attackers who successfully mimic or synthesize a user's voice can bypass authentication systems, access personal data, or conduct financial fraud (Jayakannan, 2025). For example, deepfake audio has already been implicated in cases where criminals tricked employees into transferring funds by impersonating executives. Beyond authentication, the command interface of voice assistants introduces further vulnerabilities. A system that cannot distinguish between a genuine user and a spoofed or manipulated input may execute unauthorized commands, ranging from unlocking doors to purchasing goods. The risk is not merely financial; misinformation campaigns that exploit deepfake audio to spread false narratives have the potential to destabilize trust in institutions and media (Lin, 2025).

The motivation for this chapter arises from this tension between usability and security. For speech HCI to be widely trusted and adopted, robust safeguards against adversarial threats must be in place (Feng et al., 2023). The history of computing shows that technologies flourish only when users perceive them as safe. Just as encryption and multi-factor authentication enabled the growth of e-commerce, speech interfaces will only achieve their full potential if they can withstand malicious attacks. Security, therefore, is not an afterthought but a prerequisite for adoption (Calvo &

Peters, 2014). Voice-based HCI will only achieve widespread trust if security is no longer treated as an afterthought but as a design principle woven into every layer of the ecosystem. This requires moving beyond isolated defenses to architectures that are scalable, lightweight, and adaptable to evolving attack vectors. Distributed data strategies (Emara & Huang, 2019a; 2020), hybrid feature selection paradigms (NguyenDuc et al., 2025), and big stream processing approaches (Emara et al., 2025c) provide promising building blocks for this vision. Complementary advances in scalable data processing (Wei et al., 2018), semantic integration for complex knowledge representation (Saber et al., 2018), and predictive modeling in event-driven networks (TrinhHuy et al., 2025) further illustrate how big data innovations can inform the design of secure, resilient speech-based systems.

In the sections that follow, we map out the adversarial landscape of attacks on speech interfaces, examining both classical methods such as replay spoofing and more sophisticated threats like adversarial perturbations. We then explore countermeasures, ranging from signal-level artifact detection to deep learning defenses against adversarial audio. A recurring theme is the dynamic arms race: as defenses improve, attackers adapt with more sophisticated techniques. This cycle underscores the importance of evaluation standards, benchmark datasets, and shared community challenges to measure progress. Finally, we look ahead to future directions, emphasizing lightweight on-device security, self-supervised learning for robust representations, and the need for multi-layered defense strategies.

This chapter seeks to provide a comprehensive view of how to build trustworthy voice interfaces. The aim is not only to catalog current methods but also to stress a broader perspective: security must be embedded into the core design of speech-based HCI, rather than bolted on as an auxiliary feature.

2. THE ADVERSARIAL LANDSCAPE: TAXONOMY OF ATTACKS ON SPEECH HCI

The increasing reliance on speech-driven technologies in modern society has introduced new opportunities for interaction but also opened the door to sophisticated adversarial threats. Unlike traditional input modalities such as keyboards or touchscreens, speech interfaces blend two roles simultaneously: they act as both a medium for authentication and a channel for command execution. This dual role makes them attractive targets for attackers who seek to exploit weaknesses in either the biometric dimension of voice or the natural language understanding pipeline of ASR (Abdullah et al., 2021).

The adversarial landscape can be broadly divided into two main categories of threats. The first category encompasses voice spoofing and deepfakes, where attackers attempt to impersonate legitimate users by replaying, synthesizing, or converting speech (Firc et al., 2023). The second category includes adversarial attacks on ASR, which aim to manipulate transcription systems into producing incorrect outputs or following malicious commands (Zhang et al., 2021). Understanding these categories is critical for building defenses, as they differ in methodology, attacker requirements, and intended impact. Finally, the motivations and capabilities of adversaries provide important context: knowing why attackers act and what resources they possess helps determine which threats are most pressing and how countermeasures should be prioritized.

2.1 Voice Spoofing and Deepfakes: Impersonation Attacks

Voice spoofing refers to attempts to fool speaker verification or authentication systems into believing that an input speech signal comes from a legitimate user when it has been manipulated or produced by an adversary. Deepfake technology has further advanced this category by producing synthetic audio that is often indistinguishable from human speech. Spoofing attacks can be categorized into three main subtypes: replay attacks, text-to-speech synthesis (TTS), and voice conversion (VC) (Veesa & Singh, 2025).

Replay Attacks

Replay attacks are among the oldest and simplest forms of voice spoofing. In these scenarios, an adversary records the speech of a target user and replays it to a verification system (Pradhan et al., 2019). The appeal of replay attacks lies in their low cost and ease of execution; they require little more than a recording device and a playback mechanism. Despite their simplicity, replay attacks remain highly effective in real-world conditions, especially against systems that lack anti-spoofing mechanisms. For example, a smartphone that unlocks based solely on voice authentication can be compromised if an attacker replays a high-quality recording of the legitimate owner saying the passphrase (Chen et al., 2017).

Replay attacks exploit the assumption that speaker verification systems will not question whether a signal is "live." However, in practice, replayed signals often contain subtle artifacts such as background noise from the original environment or distortions introduced during recording and playback. These traces can sometimes be detected, but their presence does not guarantee effective defense, as modern recording devices can minimize such distortions (Villalba & Lleida, 2011).

Text-to-Speech (TTS) Synthesis

With advances in deep learning, text-to-speech synthesis has become capable of producing remarkably natural and expressive speech (Hassan et al., 2025a; Hassan et al., 2025b). While TTS has numerous legitimate applications, such as assistive technologies and content creation, it also enables adversaries to generate speech in the voice of a target individual. This type of attack is more flexible than replay attacks because it allows adversaries to generate arbitrary phrases, including ones that the target has never spoken. For example, an attacker might synthesize speech that instructs a banking system to transfer funds, even if no genuine recording of the target saying such a command exists (Orynbay et al., 2024).

The quality of TTS has improved significantly with the advent of neural architectures like Tacotron, WaveNet, and more recently transformer-based systems. These models can capture subtle prosodic features, making synthesized voices not only intelligible but also emotionally expressive. The increasing availability of pre-trained TTS models and open-source cloning tools has lowered the barrier for attackers, enabling them to generate convincing voice clones with only a few minutes of recorded audio from a target (Danylov, 2024).

Voice Conversion (VC)

Voice conversion is a technique that modifies the speech of one speaker to sound like another. Unlike TTS, which generates speech from text, VC preserves the linguistic content of the input while altering its acoustic characteristics. For example, an attacker could speak into a microphone, and the system would transform their voice to sound like the target speaker. This method enables real-time impersonation, making it especially dangerous in contexts where immediacy is critical, such as live voice calls or authentication systems requiring dynamic responses (Kons et al., 2018).

Early VC systems relied on statistical mapping methods, such as Gaussian mixture models, but recent progress in deep neural networks has enabled highly convincing transformations. Models can now capture speaker identity features and transfer them with high fidelity, making VC nearly indistinguishable from genuine speech to both humans and machines (Desai et al., 2010).

Deepfakes and Social Impact

Together, TTS and VC contribute to the phenomenon of deepfake audio—synthetic voices that mimic real individuals with alarming accuracy. Deepfakes extend beyond biometric spoofing into broader societal implications. For instance, deepfake audio can be used to create fake evidence, manipulate political discourse, or damage reputations by fabricating statements that were never made. The viral spread of such content can erode public trust in media and institutions, posing risks that go far beyond individual authentication systems (Mubarak et al., 2023).

2.2 Adversarial Attacks on Automatic Speech Recognition

Whereas spoofing focuses on mimicking or replicating voices, adversarial attacks on ASR target the linguistic interpretation pipeline. Modern ASR systems, which rely heavily on deep neural networks, are vulnerable to carefully crafted perturbations that exploit their sensitivity to small input changes. These perturbations can cause the system to produce incorrect transcriptions or execute hidden commands, even when the audio sounds normal to human listeners (Neekhara et al., 2019).

Evasion Attacks

Evasion attacks are the most studied form of adversarial attacks on ASR. The attacker's goal is to modify an audio input in such a way that the system mis-transcribes it, without the perturbation being noticeable to humans. For example, a benign command like "play some music" could be perturbed to be interpreted as "transfer money" by the system (Neekhara, 2019).

One of the most famous demonstrations of this technique involved embedding hidden commands into audio files that sounded like music to humans but were recognized as voice commands by digital assistants. Such "hidden voice commands" reveal the dangers of adversarial perturbations, as they bypass user awareness entirely (Yuan et al., 2018).

White-Box vs. Black-Box Attacks

Adversarial attacks can be classified by the attacker's level of knowledge (Zhang et al., 2020):

- **White-box attacks** assume full access to the model's architecture, parameters, and gradients. This allows the attacker to compute exact perturbations that maximize the chances of misclassification. While this level of access may seem unrealistic in practice, white-box studies provide important insights into vulnerabilities.
- **Black-box attacks** assume the attacker has no internal knowledge of the model but can interact with it through queries. By sending inputs and observing outputs, attackers can approximate decision boundaries and craft effective perturbations. Importantly, adversarial examples often transfer across models, meaning an attacker can design perturbations using a surrogate model and deploy them against the target system.

Hidden Command Injection

Beyond mis-transcription, adversaries can inject hidden commands into audio signals. These attacks aim to make the system execute unintended actions without the user's knowledge. For instance, an attacker could embed "call 911" into an innocuous audio clip, which the user hears as harmless background noise but the assistant interprets as an urgent command. Hidden commands exploit the mismatch between human auditory perception and machine interpretation, creating a powerful avenue for exploitation (Austin, 2024).

Practical Challenges and Constraints

Adversarial attacks in the audio domain face unique challenges compared to image-based attacks. Sound propagates through physical environments, undergoing reverberation, compression, and background noise. Perturbations crafted digitally may not survive playback in the real world. To overcome this, researchers have developed over-the-air adversarial attacks, which account for physical transformations when designing perturbations. Despite these difficulties, successful demonstrations have proven that adversarial audio can remain effective even after being played through speakers and recorded by microphones (Liu & Manocha, 2022).

2.3 Motivations and Capabilities of Attackers

Understanding the adversarial landscape requires not only technical analysis but also consideration of attacker motivations and resources. Attackers may differ in their objectives—financial, political, reputational, or experimental—and in their level of sophistication (Abou El Houda, 2024; Rich, 2023).

Financial Gain

One of the most direct motivations is financial profit. Attackers may use spoofed voices to bypass biometric authentication in banking applications or payment systems. For example, a voice clone of an account holder could be used to authorize fraudulent transfers. The increasing reliance on voice biometrics in customer service also makes this vector attractive for criminals seeking unauthorized access to accounts (Cross & Gillett, 2020).

Political and Social Manipulation

Deepfake audio has the potential to manipulate public opinion and sow discord. Fabricated recordings of political leaders making inflammatory statements could spread rapidly on social media, influencing elections or damaging diplomatic relations. Unlike text-based misinformation, audio deepfakes exploit the longstanding human bias toward trusting what is heard, making them particularly insidious (Kafayat, 2025).

Personal or Reputational Harm

On a smaller scale, attackers may target individuals to harm their reputations. For instance, synthetic audio could be used in blackmail or harassment by fabricating offensive or compromising statements. The viral potential of social media amplifies the damage, as false recordings can circulate widely before they are debunked (Bateman, 2022).

Experimental and Demonstrative Attacks

Not all adversarial activity is malicious in intent. Security researchers and academic teams often develop and demonstrate attacks to highlight vulnerabilities and encourage defensive research. While such demonstrations can raise awareness, they also risk lowering the barrier for malicious actors by publishing techniques that can be repurposed.

Capabilities Spectrum

The effectiveness of attacks also depends on attacker capabilities (Ben Othmane et al., 2015; Al Amin et al., 2019):

- Low-capability adversaries may rely on replay attacks, requiring little technical skill but still posing a threat in poorly secured systems.
- Intermediate adversaries can use publicly available TTS or VC tools to create convincing voice clones. With the growing accessibility of machine learning toolkits, this capability is spreading rapidly.
- Advanced adversaries may design custom adversarial perturbations, requiring expertise in machine learning and access to computational resources. These actors may include state-sponsored groups or well-funded criminal organizations.

The declining cost of technology means that capabilities once limited to well-resourced attackers are increasingly accessible to the public. This democratization of attack tools significantly broadens the threat landscape.

2.4 Synthesis: The Expanding Threat Horizon

The adversarial landscape for speech HCI is not static; it is expanding and evolving as technology advances. Replay attacks demonstrate that even simple methods remain effective, while deepfake synthesis highlights the growing sophistication of impersonation threats. Adversarial attacks on ASR reveal fundamental vulnerabilities in machine learning models that are unlikely to be solved by quick fixes. At the same time, the motivations driving attackers—from profit to politics—ensure that these techniques will continue to be refined and deployed.

Understanding this taxonomy of attacks is essential for guiding defensive research. Effective countermeasures must account for both low-effort attacks that remain prevalent and high-sophistication attacks that threaten to destabilize trust in voice systems at scale. The next step in securing speech HCI is to evaluate and deploy layered defences that can adapt to this dynamic adversarial environment (LaLone et al., 2017).

3. COUNTERMEASURE I: DEEPFAKE AND SPOOFING DETECTION

The rapid progress in speech synthesis, voice conversion, and deepfake generation has created a security crisis for speech-based HCI. Systems that once assumed voice was a robust biometric identifier now face adversaries capable of producing near-perfect imitations. Consequently, detecting spoofed and synthetic voices has become a critical research priority. Countermeasures can be broadly categorized into feature-based approaches, which rely on handcrafted signal representations to identify telltale artifacts, and deep learning approaches, which leverage powerful models to learn discriminative cues directly from data. Standardized benchmarks, particularly the ASVspoof challenge, play a vital role in driving progress by providing datasets, evaluation protocols, and a fair basis for comparing methods (Alqudah & Moussavi, 2025).

3.1 Feature-Based Approaches

Feature-based methods dominated early anti-spoofing research and remain influential due to their interpretability and efficiency. These approaches extract handcrafted acoustic features that highlight differences between natural and spoofed speech (Singh et al., 2026).

3.1.1 Constant-Q Cepstral Coefficients (CQCC)

CQCCs are derived from the constant-Q transform (CQT), which provides variable resolution across frequencies. High-resolution at low frequencies and lower resolution at high frequencies mirrors human auditory perception. Since spoofed signals often fail to replicate fine-grained harmonics at higher frequencies, CQCCs capture irregularities useful for detection.

3.1.2 Linear Frequency Cepstral Coefficients (LFCC)

LFCCs preserve detail uniformly across the frequency spectrum, unlike mel-frequency cepstral coefficients (MFCCs). This makes them effective for detecting artifacts distributed across both low and high frequencies. LFCC-based detectors, often paired with Gaussian mixture models (GMMs) or support vector machines (SVMs), remain strong baselines in ASVspoof evaluations.

3.1.3 Other Acoustic and Phase Features

Beyond CQCC and LFCC, features such as phase information (group delay, relative phase shift), spectral flatness, and modulation spectra have been explored. Spoofing systems often approximate magnitude well but struggle with natural phase reproduction, making phase-sensitive features particularly useful.

3.1.4 Strengths and Limitations of Feature-Based Systems

- **Strengths**: Lightweight, interpretable, robust in constrained environments.
- **Limitations**: Less adaptable to novel spoofing methods, limited ability to capture long-range temporal dynamics, and vulnerable to sophisticated deepfake generators.

3.2 Deep Learning Models

The limitations of handcrafted features have led to a shift toward deep learning models, which learn features directly from data. These approaches exploit convolutional, recurrent, and attention-based architectures (Saber et al., 2021a; Saber et al., 2023; Sakr et al., 2020; Saber et al., 2021b; Hassan et al., 2024; Saber et al., 2025a; Saber et al., 2025b; Emara et al., 2025a; Hassan et al., 2025c; Emara et al., 2025b).

3.2.1 Convolutional Neural Networks (CNNs)

CNNs analyse spectrograms to identify local spectral–temporal anomalies. Residual CNNs, squeeze-and-excitation networks, and lightweight mobile CNNs have been applied successfully in ASVspoof challenges. They excel at detecting vocoder artifacts or energy irregularities but may require large training datasets.

3.2.2 Recurrent Neural Networks (RNNs) and LSTMs

Spoofed speech may lack natural prosody or rhythm. RNN-based models such as LSTMs and GRUs capture temporal dependencies, allowing the system to detect unnatural transitions and temporal inconsistencies. Hybrid CNN–LSTM models are widely used for robust spoof detection.

3.2.3 Attention Mechanisms and Transformers

Attention-based models highlight informative regions of audio signals. Transformers, leveraging global self-attention, model long-range dependencies effectively. These systems have achieved state-of-the-art performance in distinguishing genuine from synthetic speech, particularly against advanced deepfake techniques.

3.2.4 End-to-End Models on Raw Waveforms

Some systems bypass spectrograms altogether, learning directly from waveforms. Models such as raw waveform CNNs and wav2vec-style encoders can capture fine-grained details lost in spectral representations. However, they demand extensive training data and careful regularization.

3.2.5 Challenges in Deep Learning Approaches (Talaei Khoei et al., 2023)

- **Data hunger**: Require large, labelled corpora.
- **Generalization**: Often overfit to known spoofing methods.
- **Interpretability**: Black-box nature complicates deployment in sensitive domains.
- **Efficiency**: Resource-intensive, limiting deployment on edge devices.

3.3 Toward Practical Deployment

Detecting spoofing in real-world applications requires more than academic success. Key challenges include (Ametefe et al., 2025):

- **Generalization**: Detectors must recognize unseen attacks and adapt to evolving synthesis technologies.
- **Robustness to Noise**: Must perform reliably in everyday acoustic environments.
- **Efficiency**: Models must run in real time on resource-constrained edge devices.
- **User Trust**: Minimizing false positives is critical for usability and adoption.

Hybrid solutions—combining handcrafted features with deep learning—and fusion-based systems offer practical trade-offs. Lightweight, explainable systems are also gaining attention for deployment in sensitive domains such as banking or healthcare.

In summary, Countermeasures against spoofed and deepfake speech have evolved significantly. Early handcrafted features like CQCC and LFCC remain relevant, but deep learning approaches—CNNs, LSTMs, and attention-based models—are now the dominant trend. Standardized challenges, particularly ASVspoof, have driven the field forward, ensuring robust evaluation and encouraging innovation.

Still, deployment challenges remain generalization, interpretability, efficiency, and usability must all be addressed before detection systems can provide reliable safeguards in real-world HCI. The path forward lies in hybrid models, lightweight detectors, and rigorous benchmarking, alongside recognition that the arms race between attackers and defenders will continue as speech synthesis evolves.

4. COUNTERMEASURE II: HARDENING ASR SYSTEMS AGAINST ADVERSARIAL EXAMPLES

ASR has become a cornerstone of modern HCI, powering applications ranging from smart assistants to medical transcription and hands-free authentication systems. However, the growing reliance on ASR also exposes it to adversarial machine learning attacks. A particularly insidious class of attacks involves adversarial examples, where inputs are deliberately perturbed in ways that are virtually imperceptible to humans but can severely mislead ASR systems. These attacks undermine trust in voice-driven technologies and highlight the urgent need for defensive strategies (Mukhtar, 2025; Subasi et al., 2024).

Hardening ASR systems against adversarial examples is a multifaceted challenge. Defenders must understand how adversarial perturbations are crafted, evaluate their effects under different access scenarios, and design countermeasures that improve robustness without degrading performance on clean audio. This section examines three major classes of defense—adversarial training, defensive distillation, and input transformation—while also addressing the fundamental tension between robustness and usability.

4.1 Understanding Adversarial Examples in the Audio Domain

4.1.1 Nature of Adversarial Perturbations

Adversarial examples exploit vulnerabilities in the decision boundaries of machine learning models (Zhang et al., 2021). In ASR, an attacker slightly modifies an audio signal by embedding perturbations aligned with the gradients of the model's loss function. The result is an audio clip that sounds natural to human listeners but causes the model to produce incorrect or malicious transcriptions. Unlike traditional noise, adversarial perturbations are structured and intentional, designed specifically to fool the model.

4.1.2 Crafting Audio Attacks

Creating adversarial audio (Esmaeilpour et al., 2019) is significantly more complex than in the image domain because audio is temporal, high-dimensional, and must remain perceptually natural. Common techniques include:

- White-box attacks: The adversary has full access to the model's architecture and parameters. Gradient-based algorithms such as the Fast Gradient Sign

Method (FGSM) or Carlini & Wagner (C&W) attack are adapted to generate perturbations that drive targeted mis-transcriptions.

- Black-box attacks: The adversary only queries the model. Transferability is exploited, where adversarial samples crafted on a surrogate model are used against the target model. Query-based optimization methods also allow attackers to iteratively refine perturbations.
- Hidden command injection: Perturbations are designed so that the resulting transcription embeds hidden commands (e.g., "open the door") while sounding benign to the listener.

4.1.3 Threat Implications

The consequences of adversarial audio can be severe. Attackers could inject hidden instructions into smart assistants to perform unauthorized actions or manipulate medical transcription systems to introduce dangerous errors. Importantly, adversarial perturbations may persist even under real-world conditions such as room reverberation, compression, or playback through speakers, making them a practical threat.

4.2 Defensive Strategies

Defending against adversarial audio requires strategies that either harden models to resist perturbations or preprocess inputs to neutralize them (Tan et al., 2022; Du et al., 2024).

4.2.1 Adversarial Training

Adversarial training involves augmenting the training dataset with adversarial examples so that the model learns to recognize and resist them. This strategy effectively reshapes decision boundaries to make models more robust.

- **Advantages**:
  - Improves robustness significantly against attacks similar to those seen during training.
  - Can be integrated into existing training pipelines with gradient-based attacks.
- **Limitations**:
  - Computationally expensive, as generating adversarial examples is resource-intensive.
  - Provides limited defence against novel or unseen attack strategies.

- o May reduce performance on clean audio if perturbations dominate the training process.

Despite limitations, adversarial training remains one of the most effective practical defences, forming the backbone of many robust ASR pipelines.

4.2.2 Defensive Distillation

Defensive distillation was originally proposed for image classifiers but has been adapted to speech recognition. The technique trains a secondary "student" model using softened probability distributions (soft labels) from a "teacher" model. This process smooths the decision boundaries and reduces the sensitivity of the model to small perturbations.

- **Strengths**:
  - o Makes models less reactive to minor changes in input.
  - o Provides robustness without requiring continuous adversarial sample generation.
- **Weaknesses**:
  - o Later research has shown that defensive distillation can be circumvented by stronger attacks.
  - o Its effectiveness in high-dimensional audio tasks is less consistent than in images.

Although not a silver bullet, defensive distillation is valuable when combined with other defenses, adding an additional layer of resilience.

4.2.3 Input Transformation Methods

Input transformation modifies the incoming audio before it reaches the ASR model, aiming to disrupt adversarial perturbations while preserving intelligibility for humans. Popular approaches include:

- Audio compression: Applying codecs like MP3 or AMR to strip high-frequency perturbations.
- Quantization and down sampling: Reducing precision or sampling rates to remove small perturbations.
- Randomization: Adding stochastic noise or random transformations to inputs, making it difficult for adversaries to predict how perturbations will propagate.

- Speech enhancement models: Denoising autoencoders and spectral subtraction techniques can suppress artifacts introduced by adversarial perturbations.

These methods are lightweight and often effective in practice, but they risk degrading clean audio quality, which may reduce overall ASR accuracy.

4.3 The Challenge of Balancing Robustness and Performance

4.3.1 Trade-offs in Défense

The primary difficulty in defending ASR systems is achieving robustness without sacrificing usability. A model hardened against adversarial examples may misinterpret natural inputs, increasing the Word Error Rate (WER) on benign speech. Similarly, aggressive input transformations may distort natural signals, degrading user experience (Tan et al., 2022; Zong, 2023).

4.3.2 Generalization vs. Specialization

Defences often work well against known attacks but fail against new or adaptive adversaries. This creates a cat-and-mouse dynamic where attackers continuously refine methods to bypass defences. Over-specialization to a particular attack type risks overfitting and poor generalization.

4.3.3 Computational and Deployment Constraints

Defensive strategies such as adversarial training and deep input transformations demand significant computational resources, which may be impractical for deployment on mobile or embedded devices. Real-time latency constraints further limit the complexity of defences in practical applications.

4.3.4 Human Factors and Usability

A defence system must minimize false positives. If benign user commands are frequently misclassified as adversarial or distorted during preprocessing, user trust erodes. Therefore, achieving a balance between strict security and seamless interaction is essential for adoption.

5. EVALUATION, STANDARDS, AND THE ARMS RACE

Evaluating the security of speech-based HCI requires rigorous metrics, standardized datasets, and ongoing benchmarking. Unlike conventional performance evaluation, where metrics such as accuracy or latency dominate, security-oriented evaluation focuses on resilience against malicious inputs. This means quantifying both how well systems can discriminate between genuine and adversarial or spoofed signals, and how gracefully they degrade when subjected to attacks.

The emergence of metrics such as Equal Error Rate (EER) for spoofing detection and Word Error Rate (WER) under adversarial stress has provided the community with measurable benchmarks. However, evaluation alone is insufficient; the pace of attack innovation continuously challenges the stability of benchmarks. This creates a perpetual cycle—new attack methods force the development of new defenses, which in turn stimulate new attack strategies. Understanding this arms race is central to building trustworthy voice-driven systems.

5.1 Metrics for Security in Speech HCI

5.1.1 Equal Error Rate (EER)

Equal Error Rate (EER) is the most widely adopted metric for evaluating anti-spoofing systems. It represents the point at which the false acceptance rate (FAR) equals the false rejection rate (FRR).

- False acceptance rate (FAR): The proportion of spoofed or deepfake inputs incorrectly classified as genuine.
- False rejection rate (FRR): The proportion of genuine inputs mistakenly flagged as spoofed.

EER provides a balance between security and usability. A lower EER indicates stronger discriminative ability, meaning that the system effectively blocks adversarial voices while minimizing inconvenience for legitimate users. However, EER also has limitations: it assumes an equal cost for FAR and FRR, which may not hold in practice. For instance, in banking applications, even a single false acceptance could have catastrophic financial consequences, whereas in entertainment contexts, false rejections may only cause mild inconvenience.

To support real-world deployment, computing EER efficiently over large-scale and dynamic datasets requires scalable data management and distributed strategies (Emara & Huang, 2019a; Emara & Huang, 2019b; Emara & Huang, 2020; Emara et al., 2023).

5.1.2 Word Error Rate (WER) Under Attack

While EER is well-suited to spoof detection, Word Error Rate (WER) remains the gold standard for evaluating automatic speech recognition (ASR) systems. Under adversarial conditions, WER captures the extent to which malicious perturbations degrade recognition accuracy.

- **Clean WER:** Performance on natural, benign speech.
- **Adversarial WER:** Performance on speech corrupted by adversarial perturbations.
- **Relative degradation:** The increase in WER from clean to adversarial conditions.

This relative metric is particularly useful because it not only measures raw transcription errors but also reveals the vulnerability of ASR models to adversarial influence. For example, an ASR system that maintains low WER on clean speech but collapses under adversarial noise is unsuitable for real-world deployment.

Efficient evaluation of WER under adversarial conditions also benefits from advanced feature selection paradigms that reduce computational overhead while preserving accuracy (NguyenDuc et al., 2025; VuThi et al., 2024). Hybrid approaches can improve model robustness by identifying the most security-relevant features in high-dimensional speech data.

5.1.3 Calibration Metrics and Confidence Scores

Beyond EER and WER, researchers have explored calibration metrics to assess whether a system's confidence scores remain aligned with actual correctness under attack. A well-calibrated system should reduce its confidence when processing adversarial inputs, thus enabling higher-level safeguards. Poor calibration, by contrast, creates dangerous scenarios in which systems output highly confident but incorrect predictions.

Given the growing volume of streaming speech data, calibration must also be scalable. Recent work on big stream data approximation (Emara et al., 2025) and stratified block models for large-scale processing (Trinh et al., 2022; Trinh et al., 2019) highlights the importance of lightweight, distributed calibration pipelines for deployment in real-world environments.

These metrics collectively highlight the ongoing challenge of achieving a balance between usability and robust security in speech-based HCI—a trade-off emphasized in prior usability–security research (Braz et al., 2007). At the same time, incorporating advances in distributed data management (Emara & Huang, 2019a; Emara &

Huang, 2019b; Emara & Huang, 2020), big stream analysis (Emara et al., 2025c), semantic web (Saber et al., 2018) and hybrid feature selection (NguyenDuc et al., 2025) ensures that evaluation itself remains efficient, scalable, and adaptable to adversarial threats.

5.2 The Role of Standardized Challenges and Datasets

5.2.1 Importance of Benchmarking

Benchmarking is critical in a field where claims of robustness can be highly context dependent. Without common datasets and protocols, comparisons across studies become unreliable. Standardized challenges ensure fairness, reproducibility, and transparency, creating a shared foundation for progress.

5.2.2 Other Benchmarking Efforts

Beyond ASVspoof, initiatives such as the Voice Privacy Challenge, Deepfake Detection Challenge, and domain-specific corpora for healthcare or multilingual ASR have broadened evaluation. These datasets diversify attack types, noise conditions, and application settings, ensuring that progress is not narrowly optimized for a single benchmark.

5.2.3 Dataset Limitations

Despite progress, datasets face challenges:

- Attack diversity: No dataset can cover all possible spoofing or adversarial techniques.
- Domain mismatch: Systems trained on laboratory datasets may fail in real-world acoustic conditions.
- Bias and imbalance: If spoofing methods dominate training sets, models may overfit to specific artifacts rather than learning generalizable cues.

Thus, while benchmarks are invaluable, they are only stepping stones toward real-world resilience.

5.3 The Arms Race: Attacks vs. Defences

5.3.1 Cyclical Evolution

The history of adversarial machine learning in speech mirrors patterns observed in computer security more broadly: defenses trigger the invention of stronger attacks, which in turn prompt refined defenses.

- Early spoofing systems relied on simple vocoders, and handcrafted features like LFCCs sufficed to detect them.
- Modern deepfake generators powered by GANs and autoregressive models now produce speech almost indistinguishable from natural voices, forcing defenders to adopt deep learning.
- Adversarial perturbations initially exploited gradient-based methods but evolved into black-box, physical-world, and hidden-command attacks as defenses matured.

This cat-and-mouse dynamic ensures that no defense remains permanently effective.

5.3.2 Defensive Overfitting

A recurring problem in the arms race is defensive overfitting—when systems perform well against known attacks but collapse under novel ones. For example, a detector trained on replay attacks may fail against neural vocoder deepfakes. Similarly, adversarial training against FGSM perturbations may not transfer to more sophisticated iterative attacks.

5.3.3 Adaptive Attackers

Attackers are adaptive by nature. Once defenders release a countermeasure, adversaries experiment with bypasses. For example:

- Input transformations like compression can be circumvented if attackers anticipate them during perturbation crafting.
- Defensive distillation, once celebrated, was eventually broken by adaptive gradient-based methods.
- Adversarial training increases robustness, but attackers can generate stronger perturbations with higher computational budgets.

This adaptivity underscores the difficulty of declaring any defense "final."

5.3.4 Toward Resilient Ecosystems

Recognizing the arms race dynamic, the research community increasingly emphasizes multi-layered defenses and ecosystem resilience rather than single-point solutions. For example, combining detectors (for spoofing) with robust training (for ASR) and anomaly monitoring (for user behavior) creates a defense-in-depth architecture. Such layered systems may not eliminate attacks but can raise the cost and complexity for adversaries, shifting the balance in favor of defenders.

6. FUTURE DIRECTIONS AND CONCLUSION: TOWARDS TRUSTWORTHY VOICE HCI

Voice-based HCI has rapidly evolved from a futuristic concept to an everyday reality. Smart speakers, voice-enabled assistants, automated transcription services, and voice biometrics are now woven into the fabric of modern life. Yet the same advances in speech synthesis, voice conversion, and adversarial machine learning that enable innovation also introduce unprecedented vulnerabilities. As explored in earlier sections, spoofing, deepfakes, and adversarial audio can undermine trust, leading to identity theft, misinformation, or unauthorized system access.

The pressing question is no longer whether voice can serve as a trustworthy modality for HCI, but how to secure it in a sustainable and scalable way. This requires not only patching vulnerabilities reactively but reimagining system design with security as a foundational principle. Future progress hinges on three interrelated directions: generalized, lightweight detectors that can operate at the edge; the integration of self-supervised learning to capture natural speech properties; and the adoption of multi-layered defence strategies that balance robustness with usability.

6.1 The Need for Generalized, Lightweight Detectors

6.1.1 Why Generalization Matters

Most existing spoofing and adversarial detection methods perform well against known attack vectors but falter when faced with novel or unseen techniques. This generalization gap is a critical barrier to real-world deployment. Attackers continuously refine synthesis models, from early vocoders to generative adversarial networks (GANs) and transformer-based architectures, producing voices that are increasingly indistinguishable from genuine speech. Detection systems narrowly trained on yesterday's attack patterns risk rapid obsolescence.

A future-proof approach must therefore emphasize generalization—the ability to identify the inherent differences between natural and artificial speech regardless of the specific generation technique. This calls for detectors that focus on fundamental speech properties, such as micro-prosodic variation, phase continuity, and speaker-specific articulation patterns, which remain challenging for synthetic systems to reproduce perfectly.

6.1.2 Lightweight and Edge-Deployable Systems

Equally important is lightweight deployment. Many speech-driven applications run on edge devices such as smartphones, IoT gadgets, or embedded systems in vehicles. Relying on cloud-based defences alone is impractical due to bandwidth constraints, privacy concerns, and latency requirements.

Lightweight detectors should balance accuracy with efficiency, enabling real-time inference under limited computational resources. Techniques such as model pruning, quantization, and knowledge distillation offer promising pathways to reduce model size and energy consumption without severely compromising performance. For example, a compressed CNN-based detector could be embedded directly into a smart speaker, enabling on-device spoofing detection before forwarding audio to cloud services.

6.1.3 Challenges Ahead

Developing detectors that are both generalized and lightweight is nontrivial. Simplifying models often reduces their ability to capture nuanced features of spoofed speech, whereas highly expressive models risk being too computationally heavy for edge deployment. Bridging this trade-off will be one of the most important engineering challenges in the coming decade. Solutions may lie in distributed and approximate processing techniques that have already proven effective in large-scale data contexts (Emara & Huang, 2020; Emara et al., 2025c), enabling efficient evaluation without sacrificing robustness.

6.2 The Potential of Self-Supervised Learning

6.2.1 Leveraging Inherent Properties of Natural Speech

One of the most promising research directions is self-supervised learning (SSL), which has transformed natural language processing and is now gaining traction in speech research. SSL models, such as wav2vec, HuBERT, and data2vec, learn from vast amounts of unlabeled audio by predicting masked or latent features, thereby capturing intrinsic structures of natural speech.

These representations encode rhythm, phonetic diversity, speaker identity, and acoustic variability—characteristics that remain difficult for synthetic systems to fully emulate. By leveraging SSL, detection systems can move away from overfitting to specific spoofing datasets and instead anchor their learning in the broader statistical regularities of real speech.

6.2.2 Advantages of SSL for Security

- Reduced dependence on labeled spoofing data: Since attacks evolve rapidly, obtaining labeled examples of every new technique is impractical. SSL mitigates this by learning from large-scale unlabeled corpora.
- Better generalization: SSL captures universal features of speech that can help detectors identify previously unseen manipulations.
- Multi-task potential: SSL embeddings can support both recognition and security tasks, enabling more integrated architectures.

6.2.3 Current Limitations and Future Work

Despite its promise, SSL faces challenges. Training large-scale SSL models is resource-intensive, raising concerns about environmental sustainability and accessibility. Furthermore, fine-tuning for security-specific tasks requires careful design to avoid eroding the general representations learned during pretraining. Future work may explore efficient SSL variants, such as teacher-student distillation or sparse modeling, to combine robustness with practicality.

6.3 The Importance of a Multi-Layered Defense Strategy

6.3.1 Beyond Single-Point Solutions

Experience in cybersecurity shows that no single defense can withstand adaptive attackers indefinitely. Speech HCI is no exception. While feature-based detectors, deep learning models, or input transformations each provide partial protection, relying on one strategy risks catastrophic failure if adversaries find a bypass.

A multi-layered defense strategy—often termed defense-in-depth—offers resilience by combining complementary mechanisms. For example, a system might integrate:

1. On-device lightweight detectors to filter obvious spoofing attempts.
2. Cloud-based deep models for high-confidence verification.
3. Behavioral analytics to flag anomalies in user interaction patterns.
4. Adversarially trained ASR models to maintain robustness against perturbations.

This layered approach raises the bar for attackers, forcing them to overcome multiple independent defenses simultaneously.

6.3.2 Balancing Security and Usability

The multi-layered paradigm must also carefully manage false positives and latency. Overly aggressive detectors may reject genuine users or introduce delays, undermining the very convenience that makes voice appealing as an interface. Successful defense architectures will need to incorporate adaptive thresholds, risk-based authentication, and user feedback loops to balance protection with seamless interaction. This echoes the broader challenge of designing metrics-based trade-offs between usability and security (Braz et al., 2007), which must now be reinterpreted in the context of speech-driven interfaces.

6.3.3 Integration into the Ecosystem

A broader implication of multi-layered defense is that security must be considered across the entire speech technology ecosystem—from hardware microphones that capture signals, through edge devices and network transmission, to cloud-based recognition services. Each stage presents opportunities for both attack and defense. Future efforts should focus on end-to-end resilience, ensuring that countermeasures are not isolated patches but part of a holistic design philosophy.

6.4 Conclusion: Security as an Integrated Design Principle

6.4.1 Moving Beyond Afterthoughts

Historically, security in speech HCI has often been added reactively after vulnerabilities emerge. That reactive posture is unsustainable when adversaries innovate as quickly as defenders. Long-term resilience requires treating security as a first-class design principle, embedded from requirements and architecture through implementation and maintenance.

6.4.2 Toward Trustworthy Voice Interfaces

A trustworthy voice interface is not one that is impervious to every attack—such a standard is likely unattainable—but one that is resilient, adaptive, and transparent. Trustworthy systems should degrade gracefully under stress, surface uncertainty to users when appropriate, and continuously evolve in response to new threats. Equally important, they must prioritize the user experience: minimizing disruption, preserving privacy, and fostering confidence in everyday interactions. Trustworthiness also includes ethical and social responsibilities, such as preventing surveillance misuse and ensuring equitable access across languages, dialects, and accents.

6.4.3 Research and Practice Priorities

To realize this vision, the field should pursue focused, actionable priorities:

- Build detectors that generalize beyond known datasets and attack patterns.
- Design lightweight systems that run efficiently on edge devices.
- Harness self-supervised and online learning to adapt to emerging threats.
- Adopt multi-layered, end-to-end defenses across the whole speech pipeline.
- Embed ethics and transparency into design and deployment to protect user rights and cultivate trust.

6.4.4 Final Reflection

Advances in naturalness and accuracy will only reach their full societal value if they are paired with built-in security. Security must cease to be an auxiliary fix and instead become integral to the engineering, evaluation, and productization of voice technologies. By embracing security as a design cornerstone—balancing resilience, efficiency, adaptability, and ethical responsibility—we can develop voice interfaces that are not only powerful, but trustworthy and sustainable.

REFERENCES

Abdullah, H., Warren, K., Bindschaedler, V., Papernot, N., & Traynor, P. (2021, May). Sok: The faults in our asrs: An overview of attacks against automatic speech recognition and speaker identification systems. In *2021 IEEE symposium on security and privacy (SP)* (pp. 730-747). IEEE.

Abou El Houda, Z. (2024). Cyber threat actors review: examining the tactics and motivations of adversaries in the cyber landscape. In *Cyber Security for Next-Generation Computing Technologies* (pp. 84–101). CRC Press.

Al Amin, M. A. R., Shetty, S., Njilla, L., Tosh, D. K., & Kamhoua, C. (2019). Attacker capability based dynamic deception model for large-scale networks. *EAI Endorsed Transactions on Security and Safety, 6*(21).

Alqudah, A. M., & Moussavi, Z. (2025). A Review of Deep Learning for Biomedical Signals: Current Applications, Advancements, Future Prospects, Interpretation, and Challenges. *Computers, Materials & Continua, 83*(3), 3753–3841. DOI: 10.32604/cmc.2025.063643

Ametefe, D. S., Sarnin, S. S., Ali, D. M., Ametefe, G. D., John, D., & Hussin, N. (2025). Advancements and challenges in fingerprint presentation attack detection: A systematic literature review. *Neural Computing & Applications, 37*(4), 1797–1819. DOI: 10.1007/s00521-024-10423-8

Austin, M. L. (2024). *Audiovisual Alterity: Representing Ourselves and Others in Music Videos*. Oxford University Press. DOI: 10.1093/oso/9780190277789.001.0001

Bateman, J. (2022). *Deepfakes and synthetic media in the financial system: Assessing threat scenarios*. Carnegie Endowment for International Peace.

Ben Othmane, L., Ranchal, R., Fernando, R., Bhargava, B., & Bodden, E. (2015). Incorporating attacker capabilities in risk estimation and mitigation. *Computers & Security, 51*, 41–61. DOI: 10.1016/j.cose.2015.03.001

Braz, C., Seffah, A., & M'Raihi, D. (2007, September). Designing a trade-off between usability and security: a metrics based-model. In *IFIP Conference on human-computer interaction* (pp. 114-126). Berlin, Heidelberg: Springer Berlin Heidelberg. DOI: 10.1007/978-3-540-74800-7_9

Calvo, R. A., & Peters, D. (2014). *Positive computing: technology for wellbeing and human potential*. MIT press. DOI: 10.7551/mitpress/9764.001.0001

Chen, S., Ren, K., Piao, S., Wang, C., Wang, Q., Weng, J., . . . Mohaisen, A. (2017, June). You can hear but you cannot steal: Defending against voice impersonation attacks on smartphones. In *2017 IEEE 37th international conference on distributed computing systems (ICDCS)* (pp. 183-195). IEEE.

Cross, C., & Gillett, R. (2020). Exploiting trust for financial gain: An overview of business email compromise (BEC) fraud. *Journal of Financial Crime*, *27*(3), 871–884. DOI: 10.1108/JFC-02-2020-0026

Danylov, V. (2024). OPEN SOURCE AND PROPRIETARY SOFTWARE FOR AUDIO DEEPFAKES AND VOICE CLONING: GROWTH AREAS, PAIN POINTS, FUTURE INFLUENCE. *Baltic Journal of Legal and Social Sciences*, (1), 105–113. DOI: 10.30525/2592-8813-2024-1-11

Desai, S., Black, A. W., Yegnanarayana, B., & Prahallad, K. (2010). Spectral mapping using artificial neural networks for voice conversion. *IEEE Transactions on Audio, Speech, and Language Processing*, *18*(5), 954–964. DOI: 10.1109/TASL.2010.2047683

Du, X., Zhang, Q., Zhu, J., & Liu, X. (2024). Adaptive unified defense framework for tackling adversarial audio attacks. *Artificial Intelligence Review*, *57*(8), 218. DOI: 10.1007/s10462-024-10863-7

Emara, T., Hassan, E., Trinh, T., Li, G., & Saber, A. (Eds.). (2025b). *The Role of Artificial Intelligence in Advancing Applied Life Sciences*. IGI Global Scientific Publishing., DOI: 10.4018/979-8-3693-9208-9

Emara, T. Z., Ashraf, R., Saber, A., Trinh, T., & Awad, W. (2025c). A data processing algorithm to approximate big stream data analysis. In *2nd IEEE International Conference on Machine Intelligence and Smart Innovation (ICMISI 2025)*. DOI: 10.1109/ICMISI65108.2025.11115782

Emara, T. Z., Hassan, E., Elbedwehy, S., & Saber, A. (2025a). A Historical Perspective on Artificial Intelligence in Applied Life Sciences. In *The Role of Artificial Intelligence in Advancing Applied Life Sciences* (pp. 49–86). IGI Global Scientific Publishing. DOI: 10.4018/979-8-3693-9208-9.ch002

Emara, T. Z., & Huang, J. Z. (2019a). A distributed data management system to support large-scale data analysis. *Journal of Systems and Software*, *148*, 105–115. DOI: 10.1016/j.jss.2018.11.007

Emara, T. Z., & Huang, J. Z. (2019b). RRPlib: A spark library for representing HDFS blocks as a set of random sample data blocks. *Science of Computer Programming*, *184*, 102301. DOI: 10.1016/j.scico.2019.102301

Emara, T. Z., & Huang, J. Z. (2020). Distributed data strategies to support large-scale data analysis across geo-distributed data centers. *IEEE Access : Practical Innovations, Open Solutions*, *8*, 178526–178538. DOI: 10.1109/ACCESS.2020.3027675

Emara, T. Z., Trinh, T., & Huang, J. Z. (2023). Geographically distributed data management to support large-scale data analysis. *Scientific Reports*, *13*(1), 17783. Advance online publication. DOI: 10.1038/s41598-023-44789-x PMID: 37853092

Esmaeilpour, M., Cardinal, P., & Koerich, A. L. (2019). A robust approach for securing audio classification against adversarial attacks. *IEEE Transactions on Information Forensics and Security*, *15*, 2147–2159. DOI: 10.1109/TIFS.2019.2956591

Feng, T., Hebbar, R., Mehlman, N., Shi, X., Kommineni, A., & Narayanan, S. (2023). A review of speech-centric trustworthy machine learning: Privacy, safety, and fairness. *APSIPA Transactions on Signal and Information Processing*, *12*(3). Advance online publication. DOI: 10.1561/116.00000084

Firc, A., Malinka, K., & Hanáček, P. (2023). Deepfakes as a threat to a speaker and facial recognition: An overview of tools and attack vectors. *Heliyon*, *9*(4), e15090. DOI: 10.1016/j.heliyon.2023.e15090 PMID: 37089334

Hassan, E., Saber, A., Abd El-Hafeez, T., Medhat, T., & Shams, M. Y. (2025a). Enhanced dysarthria detection in cerebral palsy and ALS patients using WaveNet and CNN-BiLSTM models: A comparative study with model interpretability. *Biomedical Signal Processing and Control*, *110*, 108128. DOI: 10.1016/j.bspc.2025.108128

Hassan, E., Saber, A., Alqahtani, O., El-Rashidy, N., & Elbedwehy, S. (2025b). An innovative approach to advanced voice classification of sacred Quranic recitations through multimodal fusion. *Egyptian Informatics Journal*, *30*, 100640. DOI: 10.1016/j.eij.2025.100640

Hassan, E., Saber, A., El-kenawy, E. S. M., Bhatnagar, R., & Shams, M. Y. (2024, August). Early detection of black fungus using deep learning models for efficient medical diagnosis. In *2024 International Conference on Emerging Techniques in Computational Intelligence (ICETCI)* (pp. 426-431). IEEE. DOI: 10.1109/ICETCI62771.2024.10704103

Hassan, E., Saber, A., Emara, T., & Elbedwehy, S. (2025c). Enhanced Monkeypox Skin Lesion Classification Using Pooling-Based Vision Transformer Architecture. In *The Role of Artificial Intelligence in Advancing Applied Life Sciences* (pp. 291–306). IGI Global Scientific Publishing. DOI: 10.4018/979-8-3693-9208-9.ch010

Jampala, R., Kola, D. S., Gummadi, A. N., Bhavanam, M., & Pannerselvam, I. R. (2024, January). The evolution of voice assistants: From text-to-speech to conversational ai. In *2024 2nd International Conference on Intelligent Data Communication Technologies and Internet of Things (IDCIoT)* (pp. 1332-1338). IEEE.

Jayakannan, S. M.Sai Manoj Jayakannan. (2025). Securing Voice-Based Financial Authentication in the Era of AI Voice Cloning: Challenges, Vulnerabilities, and Counter-Measures. *Journal of Computer Science and Technology Studies*, *7*(4), 515–520. DOI: 10.32996/jcsts.2025.7.4.60

Kafayat, S. (2025). Deepfakes' Challenge to International Politics: Sowing Political Discord. *Annals of Human and Social Sciences*, *6*(2), 318–326.

Kons, Z., Shechtman, S., Sorin, A., Hoory, R., Rabinovitz, C., & Morais, E. D. S. (2018, December). Neural TTS voice conversion. In *2018 IEEE Spoken Language Technology Workshop (SLT)* (pp. 290-296). IEEE. DOI: 10.1109/SLT.2018.8639550

LaLone, C. A., Ankley, G. T., Belanger, S. E., Embry, M. R., Hodges, G., Knapen, D., Munn, S., Perkins, E. J., Rudd, M. A., Villeneuve, D. L., Whelan, M., Willett, C., Zhang, X., & Hecker, M. (2017). Advancing the adverse outcome pathway framework—An international horizon scanning approach. *Environmental Toxicology and Chemistry*, *36*(6), 1411–1421. DOI: 10.1002/etc.3805 PMID: 28543973

Lin, L. S. (2025). Examining the role of deepfake technology in organized fraud: Legal, security, and governance challenges. *Frontiers in Law*, *4*, 6–17. DOI: 10.6000/2817-2302.2025.04.02

Liu, S., & Manocha, D. (2022). *Sound synthesis, propagation, and rendering*. Morgan & Claypool Publishers. DOI: 10.1007/978-3-031-79214-4

Mubarak, R., Alsboui, T., Alshaikh, O., Inuwa-Dutse, I., Khan, S., & Parkinson, S. (2023). A survey on the detection and impacts of deepfakes in visual, audio, and textual formats. *IEEE Access : Practical Innovations, Open Solutions*, *11*, 144497–144529. DOI: 10.1109/ACCESS.2023.3344653

Mukhtar, H. (2025). Artificial intelligence techniques for human-machine interaction. In *Artificial Intelligence and Multimodal Signal Processing in Human-Machine Interaction* (pp. 19–42). Academic Press. DOI: 10.1016/B978-0-443-29150-0.00010-X

Neekhara, P. (2019). *Blind Spots of Neural Sequence Models*. University of California.

Neekhara, P., Hussain, S., Pandey, P., Dubnov, S., McAuley, J., & Koushanfar, F. (2019). Universal adversarial perturbations for speech recognition systems. *arXiv preprint arXiv:1905.03828*. DOI: 10.21437/Interspeech.2019-1353

NguyenDuc. H., VuThi, K., NguyenDinhVi, D., Emara, T. Z., & Trinh, T. (2025). A hybrid feature selection paradigm for high-dimensional data. In H. A. Le Thi, H. M. Le, & Q. T. Nguyen (Eds.), *Advances in Data Science and Optimization of Complex Systems* (pp. 239–250). Springer Nature Switzerland. https://doi.org/DOI: 10.1007/978-3-032-00267-9_22

Orynbay, L., Razakhova, B., Peer, P., Meden, B., & Emeršič, Ž. (2024). Recent advances in synthesis and interaction of speech, text, and vision. *Electronics (Basel), 13*(9), 1726. DOI: 10.3390/electronics13091726

Pradhan, S., Sun, W., Baig, G., & Qiu, L. (2019). Combating replay attacks against voice assistants. *Proceedings of the ACM on Interactive, Mobile, Wearable and Ubiquitous Technologies, 3*(3), 1–26. DOI: 10.1145/3351258

Rich, M. S. (2023). Cyberpsychology: A longitudinal analysis of cyber adversarial tactics and techniques. *Analytics, 2*(3), 618–655. DOI: 10.3390/analytics2030035

Saber, A., Al-Zoghby, A. M., & Elmougy, S. (2018). Big-data aggregating, linking, integrating and representing using semantic web technologies. In Hassanien, A. E., Bhatnagar, R., & Taha, A. (Eds.), *International Conference on Advanced Machine Learning Technologies and Applications* (pp. 331–342). Cham: Springer International Publishing. DOI: 10.1007/978-3-319-74690-6_33

Saber, A., Emara, T., Elbedwehy, S., & Hassan, E. (2025a). A novel approach for breast cancer detection using a Nesterov accelerated adam optimizer with an attention mechanism. *Scientific Reports, 15*(1), 27065. DOI: 10.1038/s41598-025-12070-y PMID: 40715330

Saber, A., Hassan, E., Elbedwehy, S., Awad, W. A., & Emara, T. Z. (2025b). Leveraging ensemble convolutional neural networks and metaheuristic strategies for advanced kidney disease screening and classification. *Scientific Reports, 15*(1), 12487. DOI: 10.1038/s41598-025-93950-1 PMID: 40216822

Saber, A., Hussien, A. G., Awad, W. A., Mahmoud, A., & Allakany, A. (2023). Adapting the pre-trained convolutional neural networks to improve the anomaly detection and classification in mammographic images. *Scientific Reports, 13*(1), 14877. DOI: 10.1038/s41598-023-41633-0 PMID: 37689757

Saber, A., Sakr, M., Abo-Seida, O. M., & Keshk, A. (2021b). Automated breast cancer detection and classification techniques–a survey. In *2021 International Mobile, Intelligent, and Ubiquitous Computing Conference (MIUCC)* (pp. 200-207). IEEE. DOI: 10.1109/MIUCC52538.2021.9447655

Saber, A., Sakr, M., Abou-Seida, O., & Keshk, A. (2021a). A novel transfer-learning model for automatic detection and classification of breast cancer based deep CNN. *Kafrelsheikh Journal of Information Sciences*, *2*(1), 1–9. DOI: 10.21608/kjis.2021.192207

Sakr, M., Saber, A. M., Abo-Seida, O., & Keshk, A. (2020). Machine learning for breast cancer classification using k-star algorithm. *Applied Mathematics & Information Sciences*, *14*(5), 855–863. DOI: 10.18576/amis/140513

Singh, R. P., Dash, R., & Mohapatra, R. K. (2026). Unveiling explainability in face anti-spoofing: Hybrid feature extraction with XAI-guided feature aggregation. *Pattern Recognition*, *169*, 111905. DOI: 10.1016/j.patcog.2025.111905

Subasi, A., Qaisar, S. M., & Nisar, H. (Eds.). (2024). *Artificial Intelligence and Multimodal Signal Processing in Human-Machine Interaction*. Elsevier.

Talaei Khoei, T., Ould Slimane, H., & Kaabouch, N. (2023). Deep learning: Systematic review, models, challenges, and research directions. *Neural Computing & Applications*, *35*(31), 23103–23124. DOI: 10.1007/s00521-023-08957-4

Tan, H., Wang, L., Zhang, H., Zhang, J., Shafiq, M., & Gu, Z. (2022). Adversarial attack and defense strategies of speaker recognition systems: A survey. *Electronics (Basel)*, *11*(14), 2183. DOI: 10.3390/electronics11142183

Trinh, T., Duc, L. P., Tran, C. T., Duy, T. T., & Emara, T. Z. (2022). A new stratified block model to process large-scale data for a small cluster. In *Lecture Notes on Data Engineering and Communications Technologies* (Vol. 124, pp. 253–263). Springer., DOI: 10.1007/978-3-030-97610-1_21

Trinh, T., Nguyen, N., Wu, D., Huang, J. Z., & Emara, T. Z. (2019). A new location-based topic model for event attendees recommendation. In *2019 IEEE-RIVF International Conference on Computing and Communication Technologies (RIVF)* (pp. 106–111). https://doi.org/DOI: 10.1109/RIVF.2019.8713716

TrinhHuy., T., Trinh, T., NguyenViet, H., Emara, T. Z., & VuongThi, N. (2025). Event scale prediction in event-based social networks. In *11th EAI International Conference on Industrial Networks and Intelligent Systems*, Da Nang, Vietnam.

Veesa, S., & Singh, M. (2025). Deep learning countermeasures for detecting replay speech attacks: A review. *International Journal of Speech Technology*, *28*(1), 39–51. DOI: 10.1007/s10772-024-10163-z

Villalba, J., & Lleida, E. (2011, October). Preventing replay attacks on speaker verification systems. In *2011 Carnahan Conference on Security Technology* (pp. 1-8). IEEE. DOI: 10.1109/CCST.2011.6095943

VuThi., K., VuongThi, N., NguyenXuan, H., Emara, T. Z., & Trinh, T. (2024). Feature selection based on top frequency. In Nguyen Thi Dieu Linh, M. A., Nguyen, N. L. A., & Dawson, L. K. Y. (Eds.), *Proceedings of the International Conference on Intelligent Systems and Networks* (pp. 58–65). Springer Nature Singapore. https://doi.org/DOI: 10.1007/978-981-97-5504-2_7

Wei, C., Salloum, S., Emara, T. Z., Zhang, X., Huang, J. Z., & He, Y. (2018). A Two-Stage Data Processing Algorithm to Generate Random Sample Partitions for Big Data Analysis. In Luo, M., & Zhang, L.-J. (Eds.), *Cloud Computing—CLOUD 2018* (Vol. 10967, pp. 347–364). Springer International Publishing., DOI: 10.1007/978-3-319-94295-7_24

Yuan, X., Chen, Y., Zhao, Y., Long, Y., Liu, X., Chen, K., . . . Gunter, C. A. (2018). {CommanderSong}: A systematic approach for practical adversarial voice recognition. In *27th USENIX security symposium (USENIX security 18)* (pp. 49-64).

Zhang, X., Zheng, X., & Mao, W. (2021). Adversarial perturbation defense on deep neural networks. *ACM Computing Surveys*, *54*(8), 1–36.

Zhang, Y., Song, Y., Liang, J., Bai, K., & Yang, Q. (2020, August). Two sides of the same coin: White-box and black-box attacks for transfer learning. In *Proceedings of the 26th ACM SIGKDD international conference on knowledge discovery & data mining* (pp. 2989-2997). DOI: 10.1145/3394486.3403349

Zhang, Z., Yang, E., & Fang, S. (2021, December). Commandergabble: A universal attack against asr systems leveraging fast speech. In *Proceedings of the 37th Annual Computer Security Applications Conference* (pp. 720-731). DOI: 10.1145/3485832.3485892

Zong, W. (2023). Adversarial Examples and Trojan Attacks in Automatic Speech Recognition Systems.

Chapter 10

The Double-Edged Sword: Evaluating the Climate Impact of Speech Processing Technologies

Abeer Saber
https://orcid.org/0000-0002-9261-0927
Information Technology Department, Faculty of Computers and Artificial Intelligence, Damietta University, Egypt

Samar Elbedwehy
Faculty of Artificial Intelligence, Kafrelsheikh University, Egypt

Esraa Hassan
Faculty of Artificial Intelligence, Kafrelsheikh University, Egypt

Tamer Emara
https://orcid.org/0000-0001-6730-9449
Information Technology Department, Faculty of Computers and Artificial Intelligence, Damietta University, Egypt

ABSTRACT

Speech artificial intelligence has become central to digital life, yet its carbon footprint is substantial. Training large-scale models requires high-performance computing, driving electricity demand and greenhouse gas emissions. While inference is lighter per task, billions of daily interactions on smartphones, smart speakers, and call centers magnify energy use. Indirect impacts include data centers, global networking, and device manufacturing, contributing embodied carbon and e-waste, worsened by always-listening devices and rapid hardware turnover. Uneven renewable energy adoption across regions deepens inequalities. To align with the Sustainable

DOI: 10.4018/979-8-3373-3048-8.ch010

Development Goals, sustainable speech processing advances lightweight architectures, pruning, quantization, and hardware-software co-optimization. Strategies such as green data centers, edge deployment, and lifecycle assessment reflect a circular economy perspective, framing responsible AI as vital for balancing innovation, accessibility, and environmental stewardship.

1. INTRODUCTION

1.1. The Proliferation of Speech Processing

In recent years, speech processing has evolved from a niche research area into a central component of digital technologies, reshaping how humans interact with machines and with one another. Speech processing refers broadly to the set of computational techniques that enable machines to analyze, recognize, generate, and respond to human speech (Hassan et al., 2025a). With the rapid advancement of deep learning, vast datasets, and scalable computing infrastructure, speech technologies are no longer confined to laboratories—they are embedded in smartphones, vehicles, call centers, healthcare devices, and smart home systems. This proliferation marks a turning point in human-computer interaction, with profound social, economic, and cultural implications (Kashef et al., 2021).

At the core of this expansion lies automatic speech recognition (ASR), which enables machines to transcribe spoken language into text (Hassan et al., 2025b). ASR systems are now capable of handling diverse accents, noisy environments, and multilingual input with unprecedented accuracy. Parallel advances in text-to-speech (TTS) have allowed machines to generate natural, expressive voices that are indistinguishable from human speech. Together, these technologies power virtual assistants like Siri, Alexa, and Google Assistant, which have become integral to daily routines—from setting reminders and playing music to controlling appliances and retrieving information (Todericiu, 2025).

The spread of speech processing extends well beyond consumer convenience. In business contexts, automated voice systems streamline customer service by handling routine queries, reducing costs, and ensuring availability. In healthcare, speech interfaces assist clinicians by transcribing notes, supporting hands-free operation of medical devices, and improving accessibility for patients with visual or motor impairments. Education has also benefited, with language learning platforms leveraging speech recognition to provide real-time feedback on pronunciation and fluency, thereby personalizing learning experiences (Elhadad et al., 2024).

Global adoption is driven by two reinforcing forces: technological capability and market demand. On the technical side, the availability of massive speech datasets and cloud-based computing platforms has enabled companies to train increasingly complex models with billions of parameters. On the demand side, users increasingly expect seamless, hands-free interaction, especially in mobile and connected environments. The convergence of these trends has resulted in speech interfaces becoming a default feature rather than a novelty.

However, proliferation also raises challenges. Privacy concerns loom large, particularly with always-listening devices that continuously capture audio data (Malkin et al., 2019). The concentration of speech technology development in a handful of corporations leads to questions of control, accessibility, and linguistic diversity. Many widely used systems still underperform for low-resource languages, dialects, and speakers with atypical vocal characteristics, risking digital exclusion for significant populations. Moreover, the widespread deployment of large speech models carries hidden environmental costs due to the energy-intensive nature of training and inference.

Cultural impacts are equally significant. Speech technologies influence patterns of communication and reshape expectations of immediacy and responsiveness. They also contribute to the globalization of certain languages, particularly English, while potentially marginalizing others. At the same time, speech processing offers opportunities for revitalizing endangered languages by creating digital tools for preservation, documentation, and everyday use.

The trajectory of proliferation suggests that speech interfaces will continue to expand into emerging domains. In automotive systems, voice control is becoming standard for navigation and infotainment. In workplace collaboration, real-time transcription and translation tools are breaking down communication barriers across borders. In entertainment, synthetic voices are beginning to alter creative industries, from audiobooks to film dubbing. The integration of speech processing with artificial intelligence more broadly—such as conversational agents with reasoning abilities—promises to blur the line between tool and companion.

Ultimately, the proliferation of speech processing reflects both technological innovation and societal transformation. It signals a shift toward more natural, intuitive interaction between humans and machines, but it also compels critical reflection on issues of equity, privacy, sustainability, and cultural diversity. As speech technologies become ubiquitous, their design and governance will play a decisive role in shaping the future of digital communication.

1.2. Climate Change as a Grand Challenge

Climate change stands as one of the most pressing grand challenges of the 21st century, encompassing not only environmental degradation but also profound social, economic, and political consequences (Iqbal & Ghauri, 2011). Unlike many localized crises, climate change is a global phenomenon, transcending borders and affecting every ecosystem, community, and industry. Its complexity lies in the interwoven causes—ranging from fossil fuel consumption and deforestation to agricultural practices and industrial processes—and in the wide-ranging impacts, which include rising global temperatures, melting ice caps, sea-level rise, and increasing frequency of extreme weather events. Addressing climate change therefore requires coordinated action across disciplines, sectors, and nations, making it a quintessential grand challenge for humanity (Campbell-Lendrum et al., 2023).

The urgency of the issue is underscored by scientific consensus. Reports from the Intergovernmental Panel on Climate Change (IPCC) consistently show that human activities have already warmed the planet by more than 1°C above pre-industrial levels, with devastating consequences for biodiversity, food security, and human health. Left unchecked, global warming threatens to destabilize natural systems that regulate water, carbon, and energy cycles, pushing them beyond thresholds of resilience (Allen et al., 2019). These tipping points, once crossed, may trigger irreversible changes such as the collapse of coral reefs, large-scale forest dieback, or the accelerated melting of polar ice sheets.

Climate change also exemplifies a grand challenge because of its far-reaching socio-economic dimensions. It disproportionately affects vulnerable populations, particularly in developing countries, where limited resources constrain adaptation strategies. Rising sea levels threaten small island nations, while prolonged droughts jeopardize agricultural livelihoods in regions already facing food insecurity. Beyond immediate impacts, climate change has cascading effects on migration, geopolitical stability, and economic development, making it not only an environmental concern but also a humanitarian and security issue.

Despite its gravity, climate change is a challenge that can be addressed through innovation, collaboration, and systemic transformation. Technological advances are opening new pathways for mitigation and adaptation. Renewable energy technologies such as solar, wind, and hydropower are increasingly cost-competitive with fossil fuels, while innovations in energy storage, smart grids, and carbon capture hold promise for decarbonizing the energy system. At the same time, advances in agriculture—such as precision farming, sustainable land use, and alternative proteins—can reduce emissions while ensuring food security (Goniewicz et al., 2025). Urban planning and green infrastructure provide additional avenues for reducing vulnerabilities to climate-related hazards.

However, technology alone is insufficient. Climate change demands coordinated policy frameworks and global cooperation. International agreements such as the Paris Accord represent milestones in collective action, but implementation gaps remain wide. Effective responses require integrating climate considerations into economic planning, trade, education, and public health. Crucially, solutions must be equitable, ensuring that transitions to low-carbon economies do not exacerbate inequalities or leave marginalized communities behind.

Another defining aspect of climate change as a grand challenge is its ethical dimension. Decisions about energy use, land management, and industrial production raise questions of intergenerational justice: how can present societies meet their needs without compromising the ability of future generations to thrive? This moral imperative amplifies the urgency of action, highlighting the responsibility of today's leaders, businesses, and citizens to pursue sustainable development pathways (Page, 2006).

Looking ahead, addressing climate change requires a shift in mindset—from viewing it solely as an environmental problem to recognizing it as a systemic challenge that touches all aspects of life. The transition toward a sustainable future involves not only technological breakthroughs but also cultural change, political will, and the reimagining of economic growth. If tackled effectively, the fight against climate change could catalyze innovations that improve human well-being, create resilient societies, and foster global solidarity (Lehtonen et al., 2018).

In this sense, climate change is both a threat and an opportunity: a test of humanity's capacity for cooperation, creativity, and foresight. By framing it as a grand challenge, we acknowledge its complexity and scale, but also affirm our collective ability to confront it with determination and shared purpose.

1.3. Connecting Computation to Carbon: The Purpose of this Chapter

In the digital age, computation has become a defining feature of modern life, enabling breakthroughs in science, communication, healthcare, finance, and countless other sectors. Yet beneath the surface of every algorithm, data center, and device lies a material reality: computation consumes energy, and energy consumption is tied to carbon emissions. As digital systems grow in scale and complexity, their environmental footprint expands correspondingly. The purpose of this chapter is to make explicit the often-overlooked connection between computation and carbon, and to frame this relationship as a critical consideration in the design, deployment, and governance of emerging technologies.

The link between computation and carbon is neither straightforward nor uniform. On one hand, digital technologies have the potential to reduce emissions by optimizing energy systems, improving supply chains, and enabling climate modeling. On the other hand, the infrastructure that supports computation—from data centers and network hardware to end-user devices—requires electricity, materials, and cooling resources that generate significant greenhouse gas emissions. This tension is particularly evident in high-performance computing, artificial intelligence, and blockchain systems, where the scale of computation has grown exponentially. By focusing on speech processing as a case study, this chapter aims to demonstrate how even seemingly lightweight digital interactions—such as asking a virtual assistant to set a timer—are underpinned by extensive computational and environmental processes.

Understanding computation's carbon impact requires moving beyond abstract efficiency metrics to a holistic perspective that considers lifecycle costs. Training a large-scale AI model, for example, may emit as much carbon as the lifetime emissions of multiple cars. However, emissions do not end once a model is trained; the billions of daily inferences performed across global networks compound the environmental cost. Similarly, the hardware enabling computation—from microchips to servers—carries embodied carbon from mining, manufacturing, and distribution. This chapter's purpose is to foreground these hidden dimensions of digital systems, making their carbon intensity visible and measurable.

At the same time, connecting computation to carbon is not only about quantification but also about accountability and opportunity. Who bears responsibility for the emissions of digital systems—the companies building the infrastructure, the governments enabling electricity grids, or the consumers using devices? How can we design computational practices that minimize harm while still advancing innovation? By addressing these questions, this chapter situates computation within broader debates on sustainability, ethics, and equity.

The chapter also highlights emerging responses that align computation with climate goals. Sustainable computing initiatives are beginning to emphasize energy-efficient algorithms, low-power hardware design, and carbon-aware scheduling in data centers. Some companies are experimenting with renewable-powered infrastructures, while researchers propose techniques such as model pruning, quantization, and distillation to reduce the resource intensity of AI systems. Beyond technical measures, interdisciplinary approaches that bridge computer science, policy, and environmental studies are essential for ensuring that computation contributes positively to global sustainability efforts.

By articulating the connection between computation and carbon, this chapter serves several purposes. First, it raises awareness among researchers, practitioners, and policymakers about the environmental costs hidden in digital systems. Second, it provides conceptual tools for analyzing these costs, helping readers think critically about efficiency claims, lifecycle impacts, and trade-offs. Third, it outlines pathways toward more sustainable forms of computation, emphasizing that the digital future need not be environmentally destructive if guided by intentional design and governance.

Ultimately, the purpose of this chapter is to reposition computation within the larger story of climate change. Digital technologies cannot be treated as immaterial or exempt from ecological realities; they are deeply entangled with carbon flows and planetary limits. Recognizing this connection is the first step toward reimagining computation as part of the solution rather than part of the problem.

2. THE ANATOMY OF SPEECH PROCESSING: A COMPUTATIONAL WORKLOAD

Speech processing has become a defining application area for artificial intelligence (Emara et al., 2025a; Sakr et al., 2020), powering voice assistants, automated transcription services, call center automation, and countless other tools that are now embedded in daily life. While these technologies often appear seamless to the user, they rely on complex computational pipelines that demand substantial resources. Understanding the anatomy of speech processing as a computational workload helps clarify where energy is consumed, why certain tasks are more resource-intensive than others, and how the proliferation of these systems translates into significant environmental impacts.

2.1. Key Technologies (ASR, TTS, etc.)

Modern speech processing systems rest on several core technologies. Automatic Speech Recognition (ASR) converts spoken language into written text by mapping raw audio signals into phonetic, lexical, and semantic representations. Current state-of-the-art ASR relies on deep neural networks such as transformers, which require vast amounts of training data and computing power to achieve high accuracy across accents, dialects, and noisy environments (Saber et al., 2023; Saber et al., 2021; Hassan et al., 2024; Hassan et al., 2025c; Bhatnagar et al., 2024; Saber et al., 2025a, Saber et al., 2025b).

Text-to-Speech (TTS) performs the reverse operation, transforming text into natural-sounding speech. Advances in neural TTS models, including waveform generation techniques like WaveNet and neural vocoders, have enabled machines to produce highly expressive, human-like voices. These models require significant computation during training but must also deliver efficient real-time performance during inference (Kaur & Singh, 2023).

Additional technologies include speaker recognition (identifying who is speaking), speech enhancement (denoising or separating audio sources), and dialogue systems that integrate ASR and TTS with natural language understanding. Collectively, these components form the backbone of speech-enabled applications and illustrate the breadth of computational processes involved.

2.2. The Training Bottleneck: Energy-Hungry Model Development

Training is the most resource-intensive stage of speech AI development. To achieve state-of-the-art performance, models are trained on thousands of hours of labeled audio paired with text transcripts. This requires distributed training across specialized hardware, such as GPUs or TPUs, often running for weeks at a time. The energy demands of this process are immense, not only because of the raw computation required but also due to the cooling, redundancy, and networking overheads in large-scale data centres (Emara et al., 2025b; Saber et al., 2018; Emara & Huang, 2020).

The "training bottleneck" arises from the escalating size of models. With billions of parameters, speech models achieve improved accuracy and generalization but at dramatically higher computational costs. Studies have shown that training a single large ASR or TTS model can emit carbon dioxide equivalent to that produced by several cars over their lifetimes. Moreover, training is not a one-time activity; models are frequently retrained or fine-tuned to adapt to new domains, languages, or features, multiplying their energy footprint. This bottleneck highlights the tension between accuracy gains and sustainability (Gogireddy & Smithesh, 2024).

2.3. The Inference Challenge: Billions of Tiny Tasks

While training consumes large amounts of energy over relatively short periods, inference presents a different challenge: massive scale. Every voice command issued to a smart speaker, every transcription request, and every synthetic voice response requires an inference computation. Individually, these tasks may be small, often taking milliseconds and consuming minimal energy. However, when multiplied by billions of daily interactions worldwide, the cumulative demand becomes enormous (Chakravarty, 2024).

Inference workloads also differ in their distribution. Whereas training is concentrated in centralized data centers, inference occurs both in the cloud and on devices at the network edge. Cloud-based inference requires constant data transmission, adding networking and server-side energy costs, while on-device inference must be optimized for limited battery life and hardware constraints. Striking a balance between cloud and edge processing is therefore a key design consideration with direct implications for carbon emissions (Ye et al., 2024).

The inference challenge underscores a paradox: the convenience of voice interfaces depends on the rapid execution of countless micro-tasks, yet the aggregated environmental footprint of these tasks is far from negligible. As speech processing continues to proliferate across consumer and enterprise applications, inference efficiency becomes as critical as reducing training costs.

3. THE DIRECT FOOTPRINT: ENERGY CONSUMPTION AND CARBON EMISSIONS

3.1. Data Centers and the Energy Mix

Data centers are the physical backbone of modern speech processing. Every spoken query to a virtual assistant, every transcription service, and every generated synthetic voice ultimately routes through racks of servers in highly specialized facilities. These data centers deliver the computation, storage, and networking necessary for training and deploying speech AI, but they also represent a major source of energy demand and carbon emissions. To understand the direct footprint of speech AI, it is essential to examine how data centers operate and the energy sources that power them (Chen, 2025; Emara et al., 2023).

A modern data center houses thousands of servers, each running on CPUs, GPUs, or TPUs that process AI workloads. These servers consume electricity not only for computation but also for memory, storage, and data transfer. In addition, data centers require robust cooling systems to prevent overheating; in some facilities, cooling can account for up to 40% of total energy consumption. The **Power Usage Effectiveness (PUE)** metric is commonly used to evaluate efficiency, where a value closer to 1.0 indicates less overhead for cooling and infrastructure. Hyperscale providers like Google and Microsoft often report PUEs near 1.1, but smaller or older facilities may operate closer to 1.5 or higher, meaning a significant fraction of consumed electricity never reaches the processors performing speech tasks (Zhang et al., 2021).

The carbon footprint of these operations depends heavily on the **energy mix**—the proportion of electricity sourced from fossil fuels versus renewables. For example, training an ASR model in a data center powered largely by coal-based electricity results in significantly higher carbon emissions compared to training in a region rich in wind or solar power. Geographic disparities play a major role: a model trained in the United States Midwest, where fossil fuels still dominate, may carry a much higher carbon cost than one trained in Scandinavia, where hydroelectric and wind power are abundant (Zhang et al., 2014; Chen & Li, 2022).

Major cloud providers have pledged to transition toward carbon neutrality or 100% renewable energy, but progress is uneven. Some offset their emissions through renewable energy credits, while others directly invest in new wind and solar farms. However, offsets do not eliminate emissions in real time, and electricity grids remain constrained by storage and distribution challenges. For speech AI workloads, this means that the same model may have a vastly different carbon footprint depending on where and when it is trained or deployed.

Another key dimension is **scalability**. As speech AI services proliferate, demand for data center capacity grows. Billions of inference requests per day multiply the energy burden, pushing operators to expand facilities worldwide. This growth creates a feedback loop: more services drive more data center expansion, which drives higher global electricity demand. In some regions, large data centers have already strained local grids, leading to debates about energy justice and community-level environmental impacts (Chen et al., 2025; Ngata et al., 2025).

In sum, data centers and their energy mix form the foundation of the direct footprint of speech AI. The efficiency of the infrastructure, the source of electricity, and the global distribution of facilities all combine to determine how much carbon is emitted for each hour of model training and each second of speech inference. Understanding this relationship is crucial for designing sustainable pathways for the future of speech processing.

3.2. Measuring Carbon Emissions in AI (CO2e)

Understanding the carbon footprint of speech AI requires more than tracking electricity bills; it involves translating complex computational activity into standardized measures of environmental impact. The most widely used unit is **CO_2 equivalent (CO_2e)**, which expresses all greenhouse gas emissions—including methane and nitrous oxide—in terms of the amount of carbon dioxide that would produce the same warming effect. This metric allows researchers, policymakers, and industry leaders to compare the climate impact of different technologies on a common scale.

The process of estimating CO_2e in AI typically follows three steps: (1) measure energy consumption, (2) account for infrastructure overhead, and (3) convert energy into emissions using local carbon intensity values. Energy consumption is measured in kilowatt-hours (kWh), often estimated from GPU/TPU utilization logs or power meters installed in data centers. For training a speech recognition or synthesis model, this involves recording the number of devices used, their average power draw, and the total runtime. The raw figure, however, is incomplete because servers rarely operate in isolation. Cooling, networking, and storage also consume electricity. This is where the **Power Usage Effectiveness (PUE)** factor comes in, scaling raw device consumption to account for additional facility overhead (Luccioni et al., 2023; Jegham et al., 2025).

Once total energy use is estimated, it is multiplied by the **carbon intensity** of the electricity grid supplying the data center. Carbon intensity is expressed as kilograms of CO_2e per kWh and varies dramatically by region. For instance, grids relying heavily on coal may emit over 900 g CO_2e/kWh, while grids dominated by hydropower may fall below 50 g CO_2e/kWh. This variability means that the exact same model, trained with identical hardware and code, can produce an order of magnitude more or fewer emissions depending on geographic location.

Interdisciplinary research demonstrates that AI can simultaneously advance domain applications while addressing sustainability, as shown in applied life sciences (Emara et al., 2025c). Recent research has attempted to standardize this measurement. Tools such as the Machine Learning Emissions Calculator (Lacoste et al., 2019) and frameworks like Green Algorithms (Lannelongue et al., 2021) allow developers to estimate CO_2e directly from logs of cloud resource usage. Other open-source packages, such as eco2AI, provide additional methods for tracking the emissions of machine learning workloads (Boeva et al., 2022). Some cloud providers also integrate sustainability dashboards that report emissions by project or workload, though methodologies differ and transparency remains inconsistent. In parallel, organizations such as the Green Software Foundation have proposed standardized reporting through the Software Carbon Intensity (SCI) specification (Green Software Foundation, 2023). Academic studies frequently report emissions in CO_2e per training run, enabling comparisons across model architectures, datasets, or optimization strategies.

Importantly, measuring carbon emissions in AI is not limited to training. Inference, though smaller per instance, represents a massive ongoing footprint because billions of queries accumulate daily (Li, Samsi, Gadepally, & Tiwari, 2023). To capture this, researchers measure the average energy cost per inference and multiply it by expected usage volumes. This requires careful modeling, as speech applications often combine multiple components—ASR, natural language understanding, and TTS—each with its own power profile.

Another challenge is embodied emissions, which refer to the carbon released during the manufacturing, transportation, and disposal of hardware such as GPUs and servers. These emissions are often excluded from operational accounting but can be substantial when amortized over the lifetime of a device (Teehan & Kandlikar, 2013). Incorporating embodied carbon makes measurement more comprehensive but also more complex, as supply chain data is less transparent.

Ultimately, CO_2e provides a unifying framework for understanding the environmental costs of speech AI. By translating abstract kilowatt-hours into climate impact, CO_2e enables meaningful comparisons across technologies and informs strategies for mitigation. Yet, accurate measurement remains uneven, with gaps in transparency, standardization, and accounting for lifecycle costs. Closing these gaps is critical if sustainable speech processing is to move from aspiration to practice.

3.3. Case Studies: Estimating the Footprint of a Large Speech Model

While abstract metrics such as CO_2e provide a framework for understanding AI's climate impact, the discussion becomes more tangible when applied to real-world examples. Case studies of large speech models illustrate the scale of energy consumption and emissions involved, highlighting both the challenges and opportunities for sustainable design.

Consider a state-of-the-art Automatic Speech Recognition (ASR) model built on a transformer architecture. Training such a model often requires thousands of hours of speech-text pairs and runs on dozens or even hundreds of GPUs or TPUs. Parcollet et al. (2021) quantified the energy and carbon footprint of training end-to-end speech models, showing that training can require hundreds of thousands of GPU hours, leading to emissions in the tens of metric tons of CO_2e depending on carbon intensity. Assuming an average GPU consumption of 300 watts, training that draws 90 megawatt-hours (MWh) in a region with a carbon intensity of 400 g CO_2e/kWh would result in about 36 metric tons of CO_2e—roughly equivalent to the annual carbon footprint of five average European residents.

A second case involves neural Text-to-Speech (TTS) systems, which rely heavily on vocoder models such as WaveNet or HiFi-GAN. Training a high-quality TTS model for multi-speaker, multilingual scenarios can require several hundred thousand iterations across large datasets. Although less computationally expensive than giant ASR models, TTS training still incurs significant costs when scaled across multiple voices or styles. Industry reports suggest that fine-tuning synthetic voices for global markets can produce emissions on the order of several tons of CO_2e per model, even before deployment (Faiz et al., 2023).

Inference workloads amplify these numbers. For example, Li et al. (2023) demonstrated that inference at scale can represent a larger share of lifetime emissions than training, since billions of queries accumulate daily. Imagine a popular virtual assistant handling 10 billion queries per day worldwide: if each query involves ASR, a dialogue system, and TTS, the cumulative daily energy usage could scale into the tens of MWh. Over a year, this may add up to hundreds of GWh—comparable to the annual electricity consumption of a small city. Even modest inefficiencies at the per-query level, when multiplied billions of times, produce enormous carbon costs.

Case studies also reveal the importance of geographic context. Training or inference in renewable-rich regions, such as Nordic countries, can reduce emissions by as much as 80% compared to coal-dependent regions (Lannelongue et al., 2020). Similarly, deploying inference close to users through edge computing can reduce latency and transmission energy costs, though this introduces trade-offs such as shorter hardware lifecycles and smaller model capacity (Kulkarni et al., 2025).

Another instructive example comes from the development of multilingual speech models. Instead of training and deploying separate systems for each language, researchers are increasingly training massive models capable of handling dozens of languages simultaneously. While computationally expensive, case studies suggest that such consolidation may reduce global emissions by avoiding redundant training across markets (Parcollet et al., 2021).

These case studies highlight two key insights. First, the carbon footprint of large speech models is not hypothetical—it is measurable and significant, comparable to the emissions of entire households or small communities. Second, design and deployment choices matter: where, how, and at what scale speech models are trained and used can shift their footprint by orders of magnitude. By learning from such examples, the field can better balance the pursuit of performance with the imperative of sustainability.

4. THE INDIRECT IMPACT: SYSTEMIC EFFECTS AND BEHAVIORAL CHANGES

4.1. Negative Rebound Effects and E-Waste

While the direct energy footprint of speech AI is significant, an equally important part of the sustainability conversation lies in its indirect or systemic impacts. These impacts emerge not only from the immediate computation but also from how speech technologies shape user behavior, market dynamics, and material consumption. Two of the most pressing indirect issues are rebound effects and electronic waste (e-waste).

The rebound effect refers to situations where efficiency gains in a technology lead to increased overall consumption, offsetting environmental benefits. In the context of AI, efficiency improvements often trigger Jevons-style rebound effects, where lower costs and improved usability encourage greater adoption and usage (Luccioni, 2025; Gillingham, Rapson, & Wagner, 2015). For speech AI, improved accuracy and lower latency make voice interfaces more appealing and accessible, encouraging users to rely on them for a wider array of tasks. For example, voice assistants that once handled simple commands like setting alarms are now used for shopping, entertainment, and controlling home devices. Each additional task may seem trivial, but at scale, billions of extra interactions multiply into large increases in total computational demand. Thus, efficiency improvements in ASR or TTS often paradoxically raise aggregate energy use.

Rebound effects are not limited to individual behaviors. At the enterprise level, call centers adopting speech analytics to automate transcription and sentiment analysis may expand the scope of monitoring, recording, and analyzing calls, vastly increasing data storage and processing requirements. Similarly, media companies deploying synthetic voice technologies may generate more content—multilingual audiobooks, podcasts, and personalized advertisements—because production costs are lower.

While beneficial for business and accessibility, these shifts inflate overall digital workloads, reinforcing demand for more computational resources (Luccioni, 2025).

Alongside rebound effects, e-waste presents a growing sustainability concern. The proliferation of always-listening devices—smart speakers, earbuds, smartphones, and IoT gadgets—creates material footprints that extend well beyond operational energy use. Manufacturing these devices requires rare earth metals, plastics, and complex supply chains, each associated with mining, emissions, and environmental degradation. The short upgrade cycles typical of consumer electronics exacerbate the issue: devices become obsolete quickly due to hardware limitations or discontinued software support, contributing to a mounting global e-waste crisis (Quinto, 2025).

Speech AI specifically intensifies this problem in two ways. First, the demand for low-latency, on-device inference has driven rapid hardware innovation in digital signal processors (DSPs) and AI accelerators, encouraging frequent hardware refreshes. Second, the integration of voice assistants into everyday appliances—from refrigerators to cars—means that speech-enabled hardware is no longer a luxury but an expected standard. When these devices reach the end of their life, they add to a waste stream that is difficult to recycle due to proprietary components and mixed materials. Improper disposal often leads to hazardous chemical leakage, while informal recycling in low-income regions exposes workers to toxic substances (World Health Organization [WHO], 2024). Moreover, the embodied carbon of producing new devices—emissions generated during extraction, manufacturing, and shipping—is effectively wasted when devices are discarded prematurely.

Taken together, rebound effects and e-waste demonstrate that the indirect impacts of speech AI extend far beyond the walls of data centers. By stimulating greater demand and accelerating device turnover, speech technologies risk undermining the very efficiency gains that researchers and engineers work hard to achieve. Addressing these challenges requires not just technical solutions but also systemic interventions—such as circular economy practices, extended device lifecycles, and responsible consumption models—that align speech AI with broader goals of environmental sustainability.

4.2. Positive Potential: Speech AI for Environmental Mitigation and Optimization

While much of the sustainability debate around speech AI focuses on its costs, it is equally important to consider its positive potential. The same technologies that contribute to rising computational and material demand can also be redirected toward addressing environmental challenges, optimizing energy systems, and promoting sustainable behaviors. By reframing speech AI not just as a consumer convenience but as a tool for climate action, we can explore how it may become part of the solution rather than solely part of the problem.

One promising application lies in energy management and optimization. Voice-controlled systems integrated into smart homes can guide users toward energy-efficient behaviors. For example, a smart speaker connected to a home energy management system can remind residents to switch off lights, reduce thermostat settings, or shift appliance use to off-peak times when the grid is cleaner. Unlike traditional interfaces, speech-based interaction lowers the barrier for user engagement, making sustainability more intuitive and accessible. Empirical work on conversational agents shows they can increase awareness and support efficiency through dialogue and feedback (Sanguinetti & Atzori, 2024).

At a broader scale, speech AI can support grid balancing and demand response programs. Utilities increasingly rely on user participation to stabilize renewable-heavy grids, and voice interfaces can simplify participation by allowing households to opt into energy-saving modes with simple commands. By making complex systems conversationally accessible, speech AI can facilitate smoother adoption of clean energy policies and practices.

Another area of impact is sustainable mobility. Speech interfaces in electric vehicles (EVs) or public transportation apps can encourage eco-friendly travel by helping users plan efficient routes, monitor charging behaviors, or receive reminders about alternative modes of transport. For example, eco-routing navigation algorithms have been shown to reduce EV energy consumption significantly—up to **51%** in some study settings—by choosing routes that optimize for ramps, road type, and traffic conditions (Wu et al., 2020).

Speech AI also offers value in environmental education and citizen engagement. Conversational systems can disseminate information about climate risks, recycling practices, or sustainable consumption in ways that feel more personal and engaging than static websites. In workplaces, voice-based training systems could guide employees through energy-efficient practices, reducing operational footprints across sectors. For regions with low literacy rates, voice-based education systems could democratize access to climate knowledge, amplifying awareness where it is most needed.

Another underexplored dimension is scientific and operational support for environmental monitoring. Speech-enabled assistants can help field researchers log observations, annotate ecological data, or control instruments hands-free, improving efficiency and safety in remote environments. Similarly, emergency response teams can use voice-based systems to coordinate more effectively during climate-related disasters, from floods to wildfires, where rapid communication and accessibility are critical.

However, realizing these positive potentials depends on careful design and deployment. If speech AI for sustainability relies on energy-intensive cloud models, the environmental benefits could be offset by the computational costs. Thus, integrating speech processing with low-power edge computing and renewable-powered infrastructures becomes essential to maximize net gains. Moreover, human-centered design is critical—voice assistants must provide actionable, trustworthy, and context-sensitive advice to truly influence behavior.

In short, while speech AI currently amplifies environmental burdens through rebound effects and e-waste, it also holds genuine promise as a lever for mitigation and optimization. Whether it tips the scales positively depends not on the technology alone, but on the intentionality of its application. If aligned with sustainability goals, speech AI could transition from a passive consumer interface to an active agent in accelerating the green transition.

4.3. Analyzing the Net Effect

Understanding the sustainability of speech AI requires not just listing its positive and negative dimensions but also analyzing the balance between them. The central question is whether the energy and material costs of deploying speech technologies are outweighed by the efficiencies, optimizations, and behavioral shifts they can promote. This kind of analysis is complex, involving technical, social, and systemic considerations.

On the negative side, the evidence is clear: speech AI consumes large amounts of energy during training and inference, and it contributes to the broader e-waste crisis through accelerated device turnover. The rebound effect compounds these issues, as greater efficiency and accessibility lead to more frequent use. Luccioni, Strubell, and Crawford (2025) examine Jevons' Paradox in AI contexts, arguing that efficiency gains may paradoxically spur increased consumption, especially when usage becomes cheaper or more accessible. Also, life-cycle assessments show that manufacturing and disposal stages of hardware (e.g., GPUs or TPUs) contribute significantly to environmental impact even apart from energy consumption during use (Falk et al., 2025; Schneider et al., 2025).

On the positive side, speech AI can act as an enabler of sustainability. By simplifying participation in energy-saving programs, nudging consumers toward eco-friendly choices, and supporting climate education, it can produce indirect savings that might offset its footprint. For example, Google's measurement of AI inference workloads (for Gemini Apps) reports that per-prompt energy and emissions have dropped significantly over time, owing to both software and hardware efficiency improvements (Elsworth et al., 2025). If voice-controlled energy systems reduce household consumption even by a small percentage across millions of homes, the collective carbon savings could rival or exceed emissions from large-scale model training. Similarly, speech-enabled route optimization has demonstrated measurable fuel and emissions reductions in mobility studies.

The challenge lies in quantifying these trade-offs. Unlike direct emissions, which can be estimated through logged energy use, device utilization, and grid carbon intensity, indirect benefits are harder to measure. Behavioral changes are influenced by cultural context, user motivation, and system design, making outcomes less predictable. Moreover, the benefits are often diffuse and long-term, while the costs are immediate and concentrated in data centers and manufacturing.

Another layer of complexity is the distribution of impacts. The carbon footprint of training a speech model might be concentrated in one region, while its benefits — such as improved energy management or education — are spread globally. This raises questions of equity: who bears the environmental cost, and who enjoys the advantages? If most large-scale training occurs in fossil-fuel-heavy regions, but efficiency gains accrue in renewable-rich regions, the global balance may not favor sustainability.

Frameworks such as life-cycle assessment (LCA) and net impact modelling offer ways forward. An LCA of speech AI would account not only for computational energy but also for hardware production, infrastructure, and disposal. Recent studies present comprehensive LCAs for AI hardware and model training—e.g. the cradle-to-grave environmental impacts of GenAI training using Nvidia A100 GPUs, and the emissions from all stages of hardware lifecycles for modern accelerators (Falk et al., 2025; Schneider et al., 2025). These studies suggest that while speech AI has significant environmental costs, its benefits are not negligible, and that in favorable scenarios (efficient hardware, renewable energy, behavior change) the net impact can tilt positive.

Ultimately, the net effect depends on choices made today. If the industry prioritizes performance at any cost, rebound effects and e-waste will dominate, tipping the balance negative. If, however, speech AI is aligned with sustainability strategies — through efficient models, renewable-powered deployment, and applications targeting climate action — its indirect benefits could outweigh its costs. The task for researchers, policymakers, and industry leaders is to ensure that the scales tip in the right direction.

5. TOWARDS SUSTAINABLE SPEECH PROCESSING: METRICS AND EVALUATION

The rapid progress of speech processing technologies has brought significant societal and economic benefits, but it has also raised pressing concerns about energy consumption and environmental impact. Traditional evaluations of speech models have largely focused on accuracy-based measures such as word error rate (WER), perplexity, or signal-to-noise robustness. While these metrics are important for ensuring functional reliability, they fail to capture the broader costs of model training, deployment, and maintenance. Sustainable speech processing therefore demands a paradigm shift in how systems are measured and compared, such that efficiency, energy use, and carbon footprint are considered alongside performance metrics to paint a holistic picture of a system's true value (Parcollet et al., 2021; Green Algorithms Study, Lannelongue et al., 2020).

This requires developing standardized frameworks that integrate environmental dimensions into model evaluation. For instance, reporting energy consumed per training epoch, CO_2-equivalent emissions per inference, or throughput per watt provides insight into the ecological efficiency of algorithms. Such metrics can complement accuracy, allowing developers to balance performance with sustainability. Importantly, metrics should be transparent and reproducible across different computational infrastructures, enabling fair comparisons between research groups and industrial actors. The recent works by Özcan et al. (2025) and Sánchez-Mompó et al. (2025) provide examples of simulation-based and empirical pipelines that benchmark energy consumption and carbon emissions under controlled conditions.

By embedding sustainability into evaluation protocols, the speech processing community can shift incentives away from mere performance maximization and toward more responsible innovation. This transition not only reduces ecological harm but also encourages scalable solutions that are more accessible to resource-constrained researchers, ensuring that progress in speech AI is both environmentally sustainable and socially equitable.

5.1. Beyond Accuracy: Efficiency Metrics for Green Speech AI

In speech AI, accuracy-driven benchmarks have historically dominated, with improvements often measured in small reductions of error rates. However, these gains can come at disproportionately high energy costs, particularly when scaling up to billion-parameter models. To move toward greener systems, efficiency-oriented metrics must complement traditional accuracy indicators. These include computational efficiency (e.g., FLOPs per inference), energy efficiency (joules per utterance), and memory footprint. By adopting such measures, researchers can directly assess how well a system balances resource use against output quality (Lannelongue et al., 2020).

A key metric is energy-per-task, which quantifies the electricity required to complete a specific speech task such as transcription or speaker identification. This can be normalized by accuracy to yield measures like "energy per correctly transcribed word," making trade-offs explicit. Another important dimension is hardware-aware benchmarking, which evaluates performance across different devices—ranging from high-performance GPUs to edge processors in mobile devices—thereby capturing real-world deployment constraints. Furthermore, latency and throughput metrics highlight the efficiency of models under interactive conditions, where power draw directly affects user experience and sustainability. MLPerf Power, for example, provides a benchmarking methodology that collects reproducible measurements from diverse systems (Jegham et al., 2025; MLPerf Power Consortium, 2024).

The incorporation of efficiency metrics not only benefits the environment but also democratizes research. Lightweight models with lower energy demands can be developed and deployed in regions with limited computational resources, promoting inclusivity in global AI development. Ultimately, the integration of such efficiency-oriented evaluation practices will guide the field away from accuracy-at-all-costs toward models that are genuinely optimized for both performance and sustainability.

5.2. Principles of Carbon Accounting for Model Development

Carbon accounting provides a systematic method for quantifying the greenhouse gas (GHG) emissions associated with model training, fine-tuning, and deployment. In the context of speech AI, this process involves calculating the energy consumed by computational resources and converting it into CO_2-equivalent emissions based on the carbon intensity of the energy source. Proper carbon accounting enables researchers and organizations to identify the environmental cost of their models and to implement strategies for reduction. Tools like *Green Algorithms* provide frameworks for doing this calculation in a standardized and transparent way, accounting for hardware type, computation time, memory, and facility efficiency (Lannelongue et al., 2020; OECD, 2022).

Several principles should guide effective carbon accounting in speech processing. First is transparency: energy use, training time, and hardware specifications should be reported alongside accuracy metrics in publications. This allows for reproducibility and fair comparison. Second is granularity: emissions should be tracked not only at the training stage but also during hyperparameter tuning, inference, and system updates, as these stages often account for a substantial share of total emissions (Jegham et al., 2025; OECD, 2022). Third is localization: carbon intensity varies significantly depending on where computation occurs, with renewable-heavy grids producing lower emissions than coal-dependent ones. Thus, location-aware reporting is essential.

Additionally, adopting life-cycle analysis (LCA) principles ensures that the broader infrastructure costs—such as data center cooling, storage, and hardware production—are factored into sustainability evaluations (OECD, 2022). By institutionalizing these principles, the community can align model development practices with global climate goals. Carbon accounting is not merely an academic exercise but a tool for accountability and action, encouraging greener energy choices, efficiency improvements, and responsible scaling of speech AI technologies.

5.3. Benchmarking for Sustainability

Benchmarking is critical for driving progress in speech processing, but existing benchmarks primarily reward performance improvements without considering sustainability. To foster greener innovation, sustainability-oriented benchmarks must be established that evaluate models holistically across accuracy, efficiency, and environmental impact. These benchmarks can provide standardized baselines against which both academic and industrial efforts are measured, reshaping incentives and promoting environmentally conscious research.

A sustainable benchmarking framework would integrate multiple dimensions. Performance metrics (e.g., WER, robustness to noise) remain essential but must be complemented by efficiency indicators such as energy consumption per inference, FLOPs, and latency under real-world conditions. In addition, carbon footprint estimates should be incorporated, allowing comparisons of emissions across different training setups and deployment environments. Work such as *How Hungry is AI?* demonstrates how operational footprint per prompt or inference can be evaluated with environmental multipliers and hardware configuration estimations to rank models (Jegham et al., 2025). Meanwhile, MLPerf Power shows how energy efficiency benchmarking across many systems and scales can surface green trade-offs.

To ensure fairness, benchmarks must be designed with accessibility and inclusivity in mind. Open-source datasets, transparent reporting protocols, and standardized measurement tools should be made widely available to reduce barriers for resource-limited researchers. Furthermore, sustainability benchmarks can encourage innovation in model compression, efficient architectures, and hardware-aware optimization, all of which directly contribute to greener AI.

By embedding sustainability into benchmarking practices, the speech processing community can establish new norms where ecological considerations are as central as accuracy. This reorientation will accelerate the development of models that are not only state-of-the-art in performance but also aligned with the urgent need for environmental stewardship.

6. MITIGATION STRATEGIES AND FUTURE DIRECTIONS

6.1. Algorithmic Innovations for Efficiency

Algorithmic innovation is one of the most effective strategies for reducing the environmental footprint of speech AI. Techniques such as pruning, quantization, and knowledge distillation allow researchers to shrink model size without significant loss in accuracy, thereby lowering both training and inference costs. For example, pruning and quantization reduced deep speech enhancement models to just 10% of their original size while maintaining acceptable performance (Wu et al., 2019). Similarly, pruning and quantizing self-supervised speech models have shown that recognition accuracy can remain robust under noisy, real-world conditions, even on resource-constrained devices (Pimentel et al., 2023).

Beyond compression, parameter-efficient fine-tuning methods and low-rank factorization cut computational requirements while enabling rapid adaptation to new domains or languages. Feature selection techniques remain critical for reducing dimensionality and improving efficiency (NguyenDuc et al., 2025; VuThi et al., 2024). Training strategies such as adaptive learning rates, early stopping, and progressive training further reduce wasted computation by minimizing unnecessary epochs. Multitask and transfer learning approaches also enhance efficiency by enabling models to share representations across tasks, lowering the need to train separate models for each application. Importantly, algorithmic efficiency not only supports sustainability but also reduces costs, scales to edge devices, and democratizes speech AI development globally. Block-based models also play an important role in efficient processing of large-scale data (Trinh et al., 2019; Trinh et al., 2022).

6.2. Hardware and Infrastructure Choices

Hardware and infrastructure decisions are equally critical in shaping the carbon footprint of speech processing. Specialized accelerators such as TPUs or low-power AI chips are often more energy-efficient than general-purpose GPUs, offering higher throughput per watt. For deployment, edge computing reduces reliance on constant cloud communication, cutting both latency and the emissions associated with large data centers. Adaptive mechanisms for reducing power consumption in communication systems can serve as inspiration for sustainable AI deployment (Emara, 2016; Emara, 2018; Emara et al., 2014).

At the infrastructure level, strategies such as carbon-aware scheduling can significantly reduce emissions. For instance, distributed scheduling schemes that align workloads with periods or regions of high renewable energy availability have been shown to cut both energy use and CO_2 output across multi-cloud environments (STET,

2024). Such approaches demonstrate that intelligent scheduling is as impactful as algorithmic innovation in reducing environmental costs.

Furthermore, broader supply chain concerns—including hardware recycling, repairability, and lifecycle emissions—must be considered. Without addressing the embodied carbon in devices and infrastructure, even efficient deployments risk contributing to long-term environmental harm. Aligning efficient algorithms with sustainable hardware and renewable-powered infrastructure thus represents a holistic path to reducing the environmental impact of speech AI.

6.3. Policy and Carbon-Aware Development Practices

Technical progress alone cannot ensure sustainable speech AI; organizational practices and policy frameworks are equally essential. Transparency is a foundational principle: reporting energy use, emissions, and hardware configurations alongside performance metrics should become standard in academic and industrial publications. Such disclosure supports reproducibility and accountability.

Policy interventions can accelerate this shift. Proposals have emphasized mandatory reporting of data center energy use, inclusion of AI-specific emission disclosures, and the adoption of Scope-1, Scope-2, and Scope-3 emissions reporting (Institute for Global Policy, 2024). Governments can further incentivize renewable-powered data centers through subsidies or tax benefits, while academic conferences and journals can require carbon and efficiency metrics in research submissions, setting new transparency norms.

At the organizational level, adopting carbon-aware development practices is key. These include scheduling compute-intensive tasks during low-carbon hours, selecting cloud regions powered by renewables, and offsetting unavoidable emissions with verified carbon credits. More broadly, a cultural shift is required where success in speech AI is measured not only by accuracy but also by sustainability performance. By integrating technical, infrastructural, and policy measures, the speech AI community can advance innovation while aligning with global climate goals.

7. CONCLUSION AND CALL TO ACTION

7.1. Summary of the Balance of Impacts

Speech processing technologies sit at a crossroads of opportunity and responsibility. On one hand, they enable powerful applications—from assistive technologies for individuals with disabilities to more natural human-computer interaction—that can drive social and economic progress (Strubell et al., 2019). On the other hand, the increasing reliance on large-scale models carries significant environmental costs, particularly in terms of energy use and carbon emissions (Patterson et al., 2021). The challenge, therefore, lies in balancing these dual realities.

While accuracy-driven advances have long defined progress in speech AI, sustainability metrics reveal that unchecked scaling is not viable. Encouragingly, evidence shows that efficiency-oriented innovations, hardware optimization, and policy interventions can mitigate many of these impacts (Henderson et al., 2020). The balance is achievable: performance and sustainability need not be mutually exclusive. Instead, reframing evaluation criteria and development practices ensures that both dimensions advance together.

The critical takeaway is that sustainable speech AI is not about sacrificing innovation but about redefining progress to include ecological responsibility. By treating efficiency, carbon reduction, and social inclusivity as integral design goals, the field can continue to deliver transformative technologies without deepening climate burdens.

7.2. The Role of the Research Community in Leading Sustainable AI

The research community occupies a unique position of influence in shaping the trajectory of speech AI. By setting benchmarks, publishing standards, and defining evaluation criteria, researchers establish the norms that industry often follows (Schwartz et al., 2020). This places a responsibility on the community to integrate sustainability into its core practices. Academic conferences, for example, can mandate the reporting of energy use and carbon footprint alongside accuracy results, ensuring that ecological impacts are visible in the scholarly record (Anthony et al., 2020). Applications of efficient computational methods across networking and event prediction further highlight the broader role of AI in resource optimization (Emara & Huang, 2019a; Emara & Huang, 2019b; TrinhHuy et al., 2025; Wei et al., 2018).

Beyond reporting, researchers can lead by designing efficient algorithms, open-sourcing lightweight models, and sharing tools for measuring emissions, thereby democratizing access to sustainable practices (Lannelongue et al., 2021). Collaboration across disciplines—computer science, energy studies, and policy research—can also foster comprehensive solutions that address both technical and systemic challenges.

Importantly, early-career researchers and students can shape the cultural shift by prioritizing projects that combine innovation with environmental stewardship. As sustainability becomes an expectation rather than an afterthought, the research community can inspire industry to follow suit. By actively promoting transparency, efficiency, and accountability, researchers not only advance the frontiers of speech

AI but also ensure that these advances align with the urgent global imperative of combating climate change.

7.3. Final Thoughts

The pursuit of sustainable speech AI is not a marginal concern but a defining challenge for the future of artificial intelligence. The sector's rapid growth presents both risks and opportunities: unchecked scaling may intensify ecological harm, while responsible innovation can transform speech technologies into tools that advance human progress without deepening the climate crisis.

Ultimately, the path forward requires more than isolated actions—it demands a collective commitment. Developers must prioritize algorithmic efficiency, organizations must adopt transparent carbon accounting, policymakers must incentivize renewable-powered infrastructure, and researchers must redefine benchmarks to reflect ecological responsibility. Each actor has a role to play, and progress will depend on coordinated efforts across the ecosystem.

This call to action emphasizes that sustainability and technological advancement are not mutually exclusive. On the contrary, they are interdependent: only by embedding environmental considerations into the fabric of AI development can speech processing achieve long-term scalability and global impact. By embracing this vision, the speech AI community can ensure its contributions are not only groundbreaking but also sustainable for generations to come.

REFERENCES

Allen, M., Antwi-Agyei, P., Aragon-Durand, F., Babiker, M., Bertoldi, P., Bind, M., & Brown, S.. (2019). *Technical Summary: Global warming of 1.5 C. An IPCC Special Report on the impacts of global warming of 1.5 C above pre-industrial levels and related global greenhouse gas emission pathways, in the context of strengthening the global response to the threat of climate change, sustainable development, and efforts to eradicate poverty*. IPCC.

Anthony, L. F. W., Kanding, B., & Selvan, R. (2020). Carbontracker: Tracking and predicting the carbon footprint of training deep learning models. *arXiv preprint arXiv:2007.03051*. https://arxiv.org/abs/2007.03051

Bhatnagar, R., Hassan, E., Saber, A., Shams, M. Y., & Elbedwehy, S. (2024). Enhanced Vision Transformer with Lion Optimizer for Accurate Classification of Monkeypox Skin Images. In 2024 4th International Conference on Technological Advancements in Computational Sciences (ICTACS) (pp. 1897–1902). IEEE. https://doi.org/DOI: 10.1109/ICTACS62700.2024.10840567

Boeva, V., Anikin, A., & Petrov, D. (2022). eco2AI: Carbon emissions tracking of machine learning models as the first step towards sustainable AI. *arXiv*. https://doi.org//arXiv.2208.00406DOI: 10.48550

Campbell-Lendrum, D., Neville, T., Schweizer, C., & Neira, M. (2023). Climate change and health: Three grand challenges. *Nature Medicine*, *29*(7), 1631–1638. DOI: 10.1038/s41591-023-02438-w PMID: 37464036

Chakravarty, A. (2024). Deep Learning Models in Speech Recognition: Measuring GPU Energy Consumption, Impact of Noise and Model Quantization for Edge Deployment. (arXiv preprint arXiv:2405.01004). https://doi.org//arXiv.2405.01004DOI: 10.48550

Chen, H., & Li, D. (2022). Current status and challenges for liquid-cooled data centers. *Frontiers in Energy Research*, *10*, 952680. Advance online publication. DOI: 10.3389/fenrg.2022.952680

Chen, S. (2025). Data centres will use twice as much energy by 2030 - driven by AI. *Nature*. Advance online publication. DOI: 10.1038/d41586-025-01113-z PMID: 40211075

Chen, X., Wang, X., Colacelli, A., Lee, M., & Xie, L. (2025). *Electricity demand and grid impacts of AI data centers: Challenges and prospects* [Preprint]. arXiv. https://doi.org//arXiv.2509.07218DOI: 10.48550

Elhadad, A., Hamad, S., Elfiky, N., Alanazi, F., Taloba, A. I., & El-Aziz, R. M. A. (2024). Advancing Healthcare: Intelligent Speech Technology for Transcription, Disease Diagnosis, and Interactive Control of Medical Equipment in Smart Hospitals. *AI*, *5*(4), 2497–2517. DOI: 10.3390/ai5040121

Elsworth, C., Huang, K., Patterson, D., Schneider, I., Sedivy, R., Goodman, S., Townsend, B., Ranganathan, P., Dean, J., Vahdat, A., Gomes, B., & Manyika, J. (2025). *Measuring the environmental impact of delivering AI at Google scale*. arXiv. https://arxiv.org/abs/2508.15734

Emara, T. (2018). Adaptive Power-Saving Mechanism for VoIP Over WiMAX Based on Artificial Neural Network. In Waluyo, A. B. (Ed.), *Algorithms, Methods, and Applications in Mobile Computing and Communications* (pp. 158–177). IGI Global., DOI: 10.4018/978-1-5225-5693-0.ch007

Emara, T., Hassan, E., Trinh, T., Li, G., & Saber, A. (Eds.). (2025c). *The Role of Artificial Intelligence in Advancing Applied Life Sciences*. IGI Global Scientific Publishing., DOI: 10.4018/979-8-3693-9208-9

Emara, T. Z. (2016). Maximizing Power Saving for VoIP over WiMAX Systems. *International Journal of Mobile Computing and Multimedia Communications*, *7*(1), 32–40. DOI: 10.4018/IJMCMC.2016010103

Emara, T. Z., Ashraf, R., Saber, A., Trinh, T., & Awad, W. A. (2025b). A Data Processing Algorithm to Approximate Big Stream Data Analysis. In *2025 International Conference on Machine Intelligence and Smart Innovation (ICMISI)* (pp. 247–250). IEEE. https://doi.org/DOI: 10.1109/ICMISI65108.2025.11115782

Emara, T. Z., Hassan, E., Elbedwehy, S., & Saber, A. (2025a). A Historical Perspective on Artificial Intelligence in Applied Life Sciences. In *The Role of Artificial Intelligence in Advancing Applied Life Sciences* (pp. 49–86). IGI Global Scientific Publishing., DOI: 10.4018/979-8-3693-9208-9.ch002

Emara, T. Z., & Huang, J. Z. (2019a). A distributed data management system to support large-scale data analysis. *Journal of Systems and Software*, *148*, 105–115. DOI: 10.1016/j.jss.2018.11.007

Emara, T. Z., & Huang, J. Z. (2019b). RRPlib: A spark library for representing HDFS blocks as a set of random sample data blocks. *Science of Computer Programming*, *184*, 102301. DOI: 10.1016/j.scico.2019.102301

Emara, T. Z., & Huang, J. Z. (2020). Distributed Data Strategies to Support Large-Scale Data Analysis Across Geo-Distributed Data Centers. *IEEE Access : Practical Innovations, Open Solutions*, *8*, 178526–178538. DOI: 10.1109/ACCESS.2020.3027675

Emara, T. Z., Saleh, A. I., & Arafat, H. (2014). Power saving mechanism for VoIP services over WiMAX systems. *Wireless Networks*, *20*(5), 975–985. DOI: 10.1007/s11276-013-0650-5

Emara, T. Z., Trinh, T., & Huang, J. Z. (2023). Geographically distributed data management to support large-scale data analysis. *Scientific Reports*, *13*(1), 17783. Advance online publication. DOI: 10.1038/s41598-023-44789-x PMID: 37853092

Faiz, A., Kaneda, S., Wang, R., Osi, R., Sharma, P., Chen, F., & Jiang, L. (2023). *LLMCarbon: Modeling the end-to-end carbon footprint of large language models* [Preprint]. arXiv. https://doi.org//arXiv.2309.14393DOI: 10.48550

Falk, S., Ekchajzer, D., Pirson, T., Lees-Perasso, E., Wattiez, A., Biber-Freudenberger, L., Luccioni, S., & van Wynsberghe, A. (2025). More than carbon: Cradle-to-grave environmental impacts of GenAI training on the Nvidia A100 GPU. arXiv. https://arxiv.org/abs/2509.00093

Gillingham, K., Rapson, D. S., & Wagner, G. (2015). The rebound effect and energy efficiency policy. *Review of Environmental Economics and Policy*, *10*(1), 68–88. https://environment.yale.edu/gillingham/GillinghamRapsonWagner_Rebound.pdf. DOI: 10.1093/reep/rev017

Gogireddy, Y. R., & Smithesh, C. (2024). Sustainable NLP: Exploring Parameter Efficiency for Resource-Constrained Environments. [JCET]. *Journal of Computer Engineering and Technology*, *7*(1). Advance online publication. DOI: 10.51731/jcet.2024.0102

Goniewicz, K., Burkle, F. M., & Khorram-Manesh, A. (2025). Transforming global public health: Climate collaboration, political challenges, and systemic change. *Journal of Infection and Public Health*, *18*(1), 102615. DOI: 10.1016/j.jiph.2024.102615 PMID: 39644717

Green Software Foundation. (2023). *Software Carbon Intensity (SCI) Specification*. Green Software Foundation. https://sci.greensoftware.foundation

Hassan, E., Saber, A., Abd El-Hafeez, T., Medhat, T., & Shams, M. Y. (2025a). Enhanced dysarthria detection in cerebral palsy and ALS patients using WaveNet and CNN-BiLSTM models: A comparative study with model interpretability. *Biomedical Signal Processing and Control*, *110*, 108128. DOI: 10.1016/j.bspc.2025.108128

Hassan, E., Saber, A., Alqahtani, O., El-Rashidy, N., & Elbedwehy, S. (2025b). An innovative approach to advanced voice classification of sacred Quranic recitations through multimodal fusion. *Egyptian Informatics Journal*, *30*(2), 100640. DOI: 10.1016/j.eij.2025.100640

Hassan, E., Saber, A., El-kenawy, E. M., Bhatnagar, R., & Shams, M. Y. (2024). Early detection of black fungus using deep learning models for efficient medical diagnosis. In *2024 International Conference on Emerging Techniques in Computational Intelligence (ICETCI)* (pp. 426–431). IEEE. https://doi.org/DOI: 10.1109/ICETCI62771.2024.10704103

Hassan, E., Saber, A., El-Sappagh, S., & El-Rashidy, N. (2025c). Optimized ensemble deep learning approach for accurate breast cancer diagnosis using transfer learning and grey wolf optimization. *Evolving Systems*, *16*(2), 59. DOI: 10.1007/s12530-025-09686-w

Henderson, P., Hu, J., Romoff, J., Brunskill, E., Jurafsky, D., & Pineau, J. (2020). Towards the systematic reporting of the energy and carbon footprints of machine learning. *Journal of Machine Learning Research*, *21*(248), 1–43. http://jmlr.org/papers/v21/20-312.html. DOI: 10.4337/9781845424718

Institute for Global Policy. (2024). *Greening AI: A policy agenda for the artificial intelligence and energy revolutions*. Tony Blair Institute for Global Change. https://institute.global/insights/climate-and-energy/greening-ai-a-policy-agenda-for-the-artificial-intelligence-and-energy-revolutions

Iqbal, B. A., & Ghauri, F. N. (2011). Climate change: The biggest challenge in 21st century. *Mediterranean Journal of Social Sciences*, *2*(6), 41. DOI: 10.5901/mjss.2011.v2n6p41

Jegham, N., Abdelatti, M., Elmoubarki, L., & Hendawi, A. (2025). *How Hungry is AI? Benchmarking Energy, Water, and Carbon Footprint of LLM Inference* [Preprint]. arXiv. https://doi.org//arXiv.2505.09598DOI: 10.48550

Jegham, N., Abdelatti, M., Elmoubarki, L., & Hendawi, A. (2025). *How Hungry is AI? Benchmarking Energy, Water, and Carbon Footprint of LLM Inference*. arXiv. https://doi.org//arXiv.2505.09598DOI: 10.48550

Kashef, M., Visvizi, A., & Troisi, O. (2021). Smart city as a smart service system: Human-computer interaction and smart city surveillance systems. *Computers in Human Behavior*, *124*, 106923. DOI: 10.1016/j.chb.2021.106923

Kaur, N., & Singh, P. (2023). Conventional and contemporary approaches used in text to speech synthesis: A review. *Artificial Intelligence Review*, *56*(7), 5837–5880. DOI: 10.1007/s10462-022-10315-0

Kulkarni, A., El Bahri, J., Lorraine, J., Kann, K., Callison-Burch, C., & Schwartz, R. (2025). *Assessing the dual challenges of automatic speech recognition: Bias and sustainability* [Preprint]. arXiv. https://doi.org//arXiv.2503.00907DOI: 10.48550

Lacoste, A., Luccioni, A. S., Schmidt, V., & Dandres, T. (2019). Quantifying the carbon emissions of machine learning. *arXiv*. https://doi.org//arXiv.1910.09700DOI: 10.48550

Lannelongue, L., Grealey, J., & Inouye, M. (2020). *Green algorithms: Quantifying the carbon footprint of computation* [Preprint]. arXiv. https://doi.org//arXiv.2007.07610DOI: 10.48550

Lannelongue, L., Grealey, J., & Inouye, M. (2020). *Green Algorithms: Quantifying the carbon footprint of computation* [Preprint]. arXiv. https://doi.org//arXiv.2007.07610DOI: 10.48550

Lannelongue, L., Grealey, J., & Inouye, M. (2020). *Green Algorithms: Quantifying the carbon footprint of computation* [Preprint]. arXiv. https://doi.org//arXiv.2007.07610DOI: 10.48550

Lannelongue, L., Grealey, J., & Inouye, M. (2021). Green algorithms: Quantifying the carbon footprint of computation. *Advancement of Science*, *8*(12), 2100707. DOI: 10.1002/advs.202100707 PMID: 34194954

Lannelongue, L., Grealey, J., & Inouye, M. (2021). Green algorithms: Quantifying the carbon footprint of computation. *Advancement of Science*, *8*(12), 2100707. DOI: 10.1002/advs.202100707 PMID: 34194954

Lehtonen, A., Salonen, A. O., & Cantell, H. (2018). Climate change education: A new approach for a world of wicked problems. In *Sustainability, human well-being, and the future of education* (pp. 339–374). Springer International Publishing., DOI: 10.1007/978-3-319-78092-4_21

Li, B., Samsi, S., Gadepally, V., & Tiwari, D. (2023). *Clover: Toward Sustainable AI with Carbon-Aware Machine Learning Inference Service* [Preprint]. arXiv. / arXiv.2304.09781DOI: 10.1145/3581784.3607034

Li, B., Samsi, S., Gadepally, V., & Tiwari, D. (2023). *Clover: Toward sustainable AI with carbon-aware machine learning inference service* [Preprint]. arXiv. /arXiv.2304.09781DOI: 10.1145/3581784.3607034

Luccioni, A. (2025). From efficiency gains to rebound effects: The problem of Jevons' paradox in AI. In *Proceedings of the 2025 ACM Conference on Fairness, Accountability, and Transparency* (pp. 1–12). ACM. DOI: 10.1145/3715275.3732007

Luccioni, A. S., Strubell, E., & Crawford, K. (2025). From efficiency gains to rebound effects: The problem of Jevons' Paradox in AI's polarized environmental debate. In *Proceedings of the 2025 ACM Conference on Fairness, Accountability, and Transparency* (FAccT '25). ACM. DOI: 10.1145/3715275.3732007

Luccioni, A. S., Viguier, S., & Ligozat, A.-L. (2023). Estimating the Carbon Footprint of BLOOM, a 176B Parameter Language Model. *Journal of Machine Learning Research*, *24*, 1–15.

Malkin, N., Egelman, S., & Wagner, D. (2019). Privacy controls for always-listening devices. In *Proceedings of the New Security Paradigms Workshop* (pp. 78–91). https://doi.org/DOI: 10.1145/3368860.3368867

MLPerf Power Consortium. (2024). *MLPerf Power: Benchmarking the energy efficiency of ML systems at all scales* [Preprint]. arXiv. https://doi.org//arXiv.2410.12032DOI: 10.48550

Ngata, W., Bashir, N., Westerlaken, M., Liote, L., Chandio, Y., & Olivetti, E. (2025). *The Cloud Next Door: Investigating the Environmental and Socioeconomic Strain of Datacenters on Local Communities* [Preprint]. arXiv. /arXiv.2506.03367DOI: 10.1145/3715335.3736324

OECD. (2022). *Measuring the Environmental Impacts of AI Compute and Applications: The AI Footprint*. OECD Digital Economy Papers. https://www.oecd.org/content/dam/oecd/en/publications/reports/2022/11/measuring-the-environmental-impacts-of-artificial-intelligence-compute-and-applications_3dddded5/7babf571-en.pdf

Özcan, M., Wiesner, P., Weiß, P., & Kao, O. (2025). Quantifying the Energy Consumption and Carbon Emissions of LLM Inference via Simulations [Preprint]. https://doi.org//arXiv.2507.11417DOI: 10.48550

Page, E. A. (2006). Climate change, justice and future generations. In *Climate Change, Justice and Future Generations*. Edward Elgar Publishing. DOI: 10.4337/9781845424718

Parcollet, T., & Ravanelli, M. (2021). The Energy and Carbon Footprint of Training End-to-End Speech Recognizers. *Interspeech*, *2021*, 4583–4587. https://www.isca-archive.org/interspeech_2021/parcollet21_interspeech.pdf. DOI: 10.21437/Interspeech.2021-456

Parcollet, T., Yao, K., Ichikawa, Y., Wang, B., Szymanski, M., Karande, V., & Watanabe, S. (2021). The energy and carbon footprint of training end-to-end speech models. [ISCA.]. *Proceedings of Interspeech*, *2021*, 4353–4357.

Patterson, D., Gonzalez, J., Le, Q., Liang, C., Munguia, L. M., Rothchild, D., . . . Dean, J. (2021). Carbon emissions and large neural network training. *arXiv preprint arXiv:2104.10350*. https://arxiv.org/abs/2104.10350

Pimentel, A., Guimarães, H., Avila, A. R., Rezagholizadeh, M., & Falk, T. H. (2023). *On the impact of quantization and pruning of self-supervised speech models for downstream speech recognition tasks "in-the-Wild"*. arXiv. https://arxiv.org/abs/2309.14462

Quinto, S. (2025). Exploring the e-waste crisis: Strategies for sustainable management. *Sustainability, 10*(2), 72. DOI: 10.3390/su10020072

Saber, A., Al-Zoghby, A. M., & Elmougy, S. (2018). Big-data aggregating, linking, integrating and representing using semantic web technologies. In *International Conference on Advanced Machine Learning Technologies and Applications* (pp. 331–342). Springer International Publishing. https://doi.org/DOI: 10.1007/978-3-319-74690-6_33

Saber, A., Emara, T., Elbedwehy, S., & Hassan, E. (2025a). A novel approach for breast cancer detection using a Nesterov accelerated adam optimizer with an attention mechanism. *Scientific Reports, 15*(1), 27065. DOI: 10.1038/s41598-025-12070-y PMID: 40715330

Saber, A., Hassan, E., Elbedwehy, S., Awad, W. A., & Emara, T. Z. (2025b). Leveraging ensemble convolutional neural networks and metaheuristic strategies for advanced kidney disease screening and classification. *Scientific Reports, 15*(1), 12487. DOI: 10.1038/s41598-025-93950-1 PMID: 40216822

Saber, A., Hussien, A. G., Awad, W. A., Mahmoud, A., & Allakany, A. (2023). Adapting the pre-trained convolutional neural networks to improve the anomaly detection and classification in mammographic images. *Scientific Reports, 13*(1), 14877. DOI: 10.1038/s41598-023-41633-0 PMID: 37689757

Saber, A., Sakr, M., Abo-Seida, O. M., & Keshk, A. (2021). *Automated breast cancer detection and classification techniques–a survey. In 2021 International Mobile, Intelligent, and Ubiquitous Computing Conference (MIUCC)*. IEEE., DOI: 10.1109/MIUCC52538.2021.9562725

Sakr, M., Saber, A., Abo-Seida, O. M., & Keshk, A. (2020). Machine learning for breast cancer classification using k-star algorithm. *Applied Mathematics & Information Sciences, 14*(5), 855–863. DOI: 10.18576/amis/140513

Sánchez-Mompó, A., Mavromatis, I., Li, P., Katsaros, K., & Khan, A. (2025). Green MLOps to Green GenOps: An Empirical Study of Energy Consumption in Discriminative and Generative AI Operations. *Information (Basel), 16*(4), 281. DOI: 10.3390/info16040281

Sanguinetti, M., & Atzori, M. (2024). Conversational agents for energy awareness and efficiency: A survey. *Electronics (Basel), 13*(2), 401. DOI: 10.3390/electronics13020401

Schneider, I., Xu, H., Benecke, S., Patterson, D., Huang, K., Ranganathan, P., & Elsworth, C. (2025). Life-Cycle Emissions of AI Hardware: A Cradle-to-Grave Approach and Generational Trends. arXiv. https://arxiv.org/abs/2502.01671

Schwartz, R., Dodge, J., Smith, N. A., & Etzioni, O. (2020). Green AI. *Communications of the ACM, 63*(12), 54–63. DOI: 10.1145/3381831

Science and Technology for Energy Transition Review (STET). (2024). *Energy and carbon-aware distributed machine learning tasks scheduling scheme for the multi-renewable energy-based edge-cloud continuum.* https://www.stet-review.org/articles/stet/abs/2024/01/stet20240197/stet20240197.html

Strubell, E., Ganesh, A., & McCallum, A. (2019). Energy and policy considerations for deep learning in NLP. *Proceedings of the 57th Annual Meeting of the Association for Computational Linguistics*, 3645–3650. DOI: 10.18653/v1/P19-1355

Teehan, P., & Kandlikar, M. (2013). Comparing embodied greenhouse gas emissions of modern computing and electronics products. *Environmental Science & Technology, 47*(9), 3997–4003. DOI: 10.1021/es303012r PMID: 23458212

Todericiu, I. A. (2025). Virtual Assistants: A Review of the Next Frontier in AI Interaction. Acta Universitatis Sapientiae. *Informatica (Vilnius), 17*(1), 1–13. DOI: 10.2478/ausi-2025-0001

Trinh, T., Duc, L. P., Tran, C. T., Duy, T. T., & Emara, T. Z. (2022). A New Stratified Block Model to Process Large-Scale Data for a Small Cluster. In *Lecture Notes on Data Engineering and Communications Technologies* (Vol. 124, pp. 253–263). Springer Science and Business Media Deutschland GmbH., DOI: 10.1007/978-3-030-97610-1_21

Trinh, T., Nguyen, N., Wu, D., Huang, J. Z., & Emara, T. Z. (2019). A New Location-Based Topic Model for Event Attendees Recommendation. In *2019 IEEE-RIVF International Conference on Computing and Communication Technologies (RIVF)* (pp. 106–111). DOI: 10.1109/RIVF.2019.8713716

Wei, C., Salloum, S., Emara, T. Z., Zhang, X., Huang, J. Z., & He, Y. (2018). A Two-Stage Data Processing Algorithm to Generate Random Sample Partitions for Big Data Analysis. In Luo, M., & Zhang, L.-J. (Eds.), *Cloud Computing—CLOUD 2018* (Vol. 10967, pp. 347–364). Springer International Publishing., DOI: 10.1007/978-3-319-94295-7_24

World Health Organization. (2024, October 1). *Electronic waste (e-waste).* WHO. https://www.who.int/news-room/fact-sheets/detail/electronic-waste-%28e-waste%29

Wu, G., Boriboonsomsin, K., & Barth, M. J. (2020, August 21). Eco-Routing Navigation System for Electric Vehicles [Preprint]. arXiv. https://arxiv.org/abs/2008.09674

Wu, J.-Y., Yu, C., Fu, S.-W., Liu, C.-T., Chien, S.-Y., & Tsao, Y. (2019). *Increasing compactness of deep learning based speech enhancement models with parameter pruning and quantization techniques.* arXiv. https://arxiv.org/abs/1906.01078

Ye, Z., Gao, W., Hu, Q., Sun, P., Wang, X., Luo, Y., Zhang, T., & Wen, Y. (2024). Deep learning workload scheduling in gpu datacenters: A survey. *ACM Computing Surveys, 56*(6), 1–38. DOI: 10.1145/3638757

Zhang, H., Shao, S., Xu, H., Zou, H., & Tian, C. (2014). Free cooling of data centers: A review. *Renewable & Sustainable Energy Reviews, 35*, 171–182. DOI: 10.1016/j.rser.2014.04.017

Zhang, Q., Meng, Z., Hong, X., Zhan, Y., Liu, J., Dong, J., Bai, T., Niu, J., & Deen, M. J. (2021). A survey on data center cooling systems: Technology, power consumption modeling and control strategy optimization. *Journal of Systems Architecture, 119*, 102253. DOI: 10.1016/j.sysarc.2021.102253

Compilation of References

Abdullah, H., Warren, K., Bindschaedler, V., Papernot, N., & Traynor, P. (2021, May). Sok: The faults in our asrs: An overview of attacks against automatic speech recognition and speaker identification systems. In *2021 IEEE symposium on security and privacy (SP)* (pp. 730-747). IEEE.

Abdul, Z. K., & Al-Talabani, A. K. (2022). Mel frequency cepstral coefficient and its applications: A review. *IEEE Access : Practical Innovations, Open Solutions, 10*, 122136–122158. DOI: 10.1109/ACCESS.2022.3223444

Abou El Houda, Z. (2024). Cyber threat actors review: examining the tactics and motivations of adversaries in the cyber landscape. In *Cyber Security for Next-Generation Computing Technologies* (pp. 84–101). CRC Press.

Adewumi, T., Liwicki, F., & Liwicki, M. (2022). State-of-the-Art in Open-Domain Conversational AI: A Survey. *Information (Basel), 13*(6), 298. Advance online publication. DOI: 10.3390/info13060298

Afouras, T., Chung, J. S., & Zisserman, A. (2018). LRS3-TED: A large-scale dataset for visual speech recognition. *arXiv preprint* arXiv:1809.00496.

Agrawal, R., & Pandey, N. (2024). Developing Rapport between Humans and Machines: Emotionally Intelligent AI Assistants. *International Journal for Research in Applied Science and Engineering Technology, 12*(3), 1473–1480. DOI: 10.22214/ijraset.2024.59015

Ahanger, T. A., Dahan, F., Tariq, U., & Ullah, I. (2023). Quantum Inspired Task Optimization for IoT Edge Fog Computing Environment. *Mathematics, 11*(1), 156. Advance online publication. DOI: 10.3390/math11010156

Aiken, M., & Park, M. (2020). A Comparison of two Multilingual Meeting Systems. *International Journal of Computers and Technology, 20*, 38–44. DOI: 10.24297/ijct.v20i.8636

Akinpelu, S., & Viriri, S. (2023). Speech emotion classification using attention based network and regularized feature selection. *Scientific Reports*, *13*(1), 11990. Advance online publication. DOI: 10.1038/s41598-023-38868-2 PMID: 37491423

Al Amin, M. A. R., Shetty, S., Njilla, L., Tosh, D. K., & Kamhoua, C. (2019). Attacker capability based dynamic deception model for large-scale networks. *EAI Endorsed Transactions on Security and Safety, 6*(21).

Alabed, A., Javornik, A., Gregory-Smith, D., & Casey, R. (2024). More than just a chat: A taxonomy of consumers' relationships with conversational AI agents and their well-being implications. *European Journal of Marketing*, *58*(2), 373–409. Advance online publication. DOI: 10.1108/EJM-01-2023-0037

Albahri, A., Lech, M., & Cheng, E. (2015). Effect of Speech Compression on the Automatic Recognition of Emotions. *International Journal of Signal Processing Systems*, *4*(1). Advance online publication. DOI: 10.12720/ijsps.4.1.55-61

Alghifari, M. F., Gunawan, T. S., & Kartiwi, M. (2018). Speech emotion recognition using deep feedforward neural network. *Indonesian Journal of Electrical Engineering and Computer Science*, *10*(2), 554–561. DOI: 10.11591/ijeecs.v10.i2.pp554-561

Alias, F., & Munne, N. (2010). Reliable pitch marking of affective speech at peaks or valleys using restricted dynamic programming. *IEEE Transactions on Multimedia*, *12*(6), 481–489. DOI: 10.1109/TMM.2010.2051873

Ali, Y. M., Noorsal, E., Mokhtar, N. F., Saad, S. Z. M., Abdullah, M. H., & Chin, L. C. (2022). Speech-based gender recognition using linear prediction and mel-frequency cepstral coefficients. *Indonesian Journal of Electrical Engineering and Computer Science*, *28*(2), 753. DOI: 10.11591/ijeecs.v28.i2.pp753-761

Allen, M., Antwi-Agyei, P., Aragon-Durand, F., Babiker, M., Bertoldi, P., Bind, M., & Brown, S.. (2019). *Technical Summary: Global warming of 1.5 C. An IPCC Special Report on the impacts of global warming of 1.5 C above pre-industrial levels and related global greenhouse gas emission pathways, in the context of strengthening the global response to the threat of climate change, sustainable development, and efforts to eradicate poverty*. IPCC.

Alnuaim, A. A., Zakariah, M., Shashidhar, C., Hatamleh, W. A., Tarazi, H., Shukla, P. K., & Ratna, R. (2022). Speaker gender recognition based on deep neural networks and ResNet50. *Wireless Communications and Mobile Computing*, *2022*(1), 1–13. DOI: 10.1155/2022/4444388

Aloufi, R., Haddadi, H., & Boyle, D. (2020). Privacy-preserving Voice Analysis via Disentangled Representations. *CCSW 2020 - Proceedings of the 2020 ACM SIGSAC Conference on Cloud Computing Security Workshop*, 1–14. DOI: 10.1145/3411495.3421355

Aloufi, R., Haddadi, H., & Boyle, D. (2021). A tandem framework balancing privacy and security for voice user interfaces. *Proceedings on Privacy Enhancing Technologies. Privacy Enhancing Technologies Symposium*, *2021*(3), 163–183.

Al-Qaderi, M. K., & Rad, A. B. (2018). A multi-modal person recognition system for social robots. *Applied Sciences (Basel, Switzerland)*, *8*(3), 387. Advance online publication. DOI: 10.3390/app8030387

Alqudah, A. M., & Moussavi, Z. (2025). A Review of Deep Learning for Biomedical Signals: Current Applications, Advancements, Future Prospects, Interpretation, and Challenges. *Computers, Materials & Continua*, *83*(3), 3753–3841. DOI: 10.32604/cmc.2025.063643

Alwarafy, A., Al-Thelaya, K. A., Abdallah, M., Schneider, J., & Hamdi, M. (2021). A Survey on Security and Privacy Issues in Edge-Computing-Assisted Internet of Things. *IEEE Internet of Things Journal*, *8*(6), 4004–4022. DOI: 10.1109/JIOT.2020.3015432

Ametefe, D. S., Sarnin, S. S., Ali, D. M., Ametefe, G. D., John, D., & Hussin, N. (2025). Advancements and challenges in fingerprint presentation attack detection: A systematic literature review. *Neural Computing & Applications*, *37*(4), 1797–1819. DOI: 10.1007/s00521-024-10423-8

Amodei, D., Ananthanarayanan, S., Anubhai, R., Bai, J., Battenberg, E., Case, C., & Zhu, Z. (2016). Deep speech 2: End-to-end speech recognition in English and Mandarin. In *Proceedings of the International Conference on Machine Learning* (pp. 173–182).

Anthony, L. F. W., Kanding, B., & Selvan, R. (2020). Carbontracker: Tracking and predicting the carbon footprint of training deep learning models. *arXiv preprint arXiv:2007.03051*. https://arxiv.org/abs/2007.03051

Arpita, H. D., Ryan, A. A., Hossain, M. F., Rahman, M. S., Sajjad, M., & Prova, N. N. I. (2024). Exploring bengali speech for gender classification: Machine learning and deep learning approaches. *Bulletin of Electrical Engineering and Informatics*, *14*(1), 328–337. DOI: 10.11591/eei.v14i1.8146

Arrieta, A. B., Del Ser, J., Bennetot, A., Tabik, S., Barbado, A., García, S., Molina, D., Benjamins, R., Chatila, R., & Herrera, F. (2019). Explainable Artificial Intelligence (XAI): Concepts, Taxonomies, Opportunities and Challenges toward Responsible AI. *ArXiv*. https://arxiv.org/abs/1910.10045

Austin, M. L. (2024). *Audiovisual Alterity: Representing Ourselves and Others in Music Videos*. Oxford University Press. DOI: 10.1093/oso/9780190277789.001.0001

Averbukh, V. L. (2020). Evolution of human computer interaction. *Science and Vision Journal (SV-Journal), 5*(11). Retrieved from https://sv-journal.org/2020-5/11/en.pdf

Baabdullah, A. M. (2024). Generative conversational AI agent for managerial practices: The role of IQ dimensions, novelty seeking and ethical concerns. *Technological Forecasting and Social Change, 198*, 122951. Advance online publication. DOI: 10.1016/j.techfore.2023.122951

Babu, A., Raoul, E., Kassahun, G., Dufour, I., Mandal, D., & Thuau, D. (2024). Programmable Polymeric-Interface for Voiceprint Biometrics. *Advanced Materials Technologies, 9*(4), 2301551. Advance online publication. DOI: 10.1002/admt.202301551

Baevski, A., Zhou, H., Mohamed, A., & Auli, M. (2020). wav2vec 2.0: A framework for self-supervised learning of speech representations. *Advances in Neural Information Processing Systems, 33*, 12449–12460.

Bakeer, A. (2024). An integrated system for accessible summarization of web search results for the blind and visually impaired. *Benha Journal of Applied Sciences, 9*(3), 1–12. Retrieved from https://bjas.journals.ekb.eg/article_366402_7a09f443daf633fb66ae72b552be5e22.pdf

Barhoumi, C., & BenAyed, Y. (2025). Real-time speech emotion recognition using deep learning and data augmentation. *Artificial Intelligence Review, 58*(2), 49. Advance online publication. DOI: 10.1007/s10462-024-11065-x

Bateman, J. (2022). *Deepfakes and synthetic media in the financial system: Assessing threat scenarios*. Carnegie Endowment for International Peace.

Bellegarda, J. R. (2013). Spoken language understanding for natural interaction: The Siri experience. In *Proceedings of the Workshop on Language Resources, Human Assessment and Intelligent Assistant*.

Ben Othmane, L., Ranchal, R., Fernando, R., Bhargava, B., & Bodden, E. (2015). Incorporating attacker capabilities in risk estimation and mitigation. *Computers & Security, 51*, 41–61. DOI: 10.1016/j.cose.2015.03.001

Bender, E. M., Gebru, T., McMillan-Major, A., & Shmitchell, S. (2021). On the dangers of stochastic parrots: Can language models be too big? In *Proceedings of the 2021 ACM Conference on Fairness, Accountability, and Transparency*. https://doi.org/DOI: 10.1145/3442188.3445922

Bhatnagar, R., Hassan, E., Saber, A., Shams, M. Y., & Elbedwehy, S. (2024). Enhanced Vision Transformer with Lion Optimizer for Accurate Classification of Monkeypox Skin Images. In 2024 4th International Conference on Technological Advancements in Computational Sciences (ICTACS) (pp. 1897–1902). IEEE. https://doi.org/DOI: 10.1109/ICTACS62700.2024.10840567

Bhatt, S., & Sharma, S. (2024). Quantum Cryptography Using Blockchain for 6G Enabled Internet of Vehicles. In 2024 1st International Conference on Advanced Computing and Emerging Technologies (ACET), 1–6. https://doi.org/DOI: 10.1109/ACET61898.2024.10730580

Bhatt, S., Sharma, S., & Bhadula, S. (2024). NeuroAI: Emerging Artificial Intelligence and Image Processing Techniques in Neuroscience for Enhanced Medical Diagnosis of Brain Tumor. In 2024 First International Conference on Pioneering Developments in Computer Science & Digital Technologies (IC2SDT), 204–209. https://doi.org/DOI: 10.1109/IC2SDT62152.2024.10696499

Bigioi, D., Morales, T., Pandey, A., Fowley, F., Corcoran, P., & Carson-Berndsen, J. (2022, August). Sign2Speech: A novel Sign Language to speech synthesis pipeline. *24th Irish Machine Vision and Image Processing Conference*. DOI: 10.56541/CTDH7516

Billa, J. (2018, September). ISI ASR system for the low resource speech recognition challenge for Indian languages. *Interspeech*, •••, 2018. DOI: 10.21437/Interspeech.2018-2473

Blümel, J. H., Zaki, M., & Bohné, T. (2024). Personal touch in digital customer service: A conceptual framework of relational personalization for conversational AI. *Journal of Service Theory and Practice*, *34*(1), 33–65. Advance online publication. DOI: 10.1108/JSTP-03-2023-0098

Bora, B., Emanet, A. E., Elmaci, E., Kandaz, D., & Uçar, M. K.BORA. (2023). Hybrid AI-based Voice Authentication. *Turkish Journal of Forecasting*, *07*(2), 17–22. DOI: 10.34110/forecasting.1260073

Brave, S., Nass, C., & Hutchinson, K. (2005). Computers that care: Investigating the effects of orientation of emotion exhibited by an embodied computer agent. *International Journal of Human-Computer Studies*, *62*(2), 161–178. DOI: 10.1016/j.ijhcs.2004.11.002

Braz, C., Seffah, A., & M'Raihi, D. (2007, September). Designing a trade-off between usability and security: a metrics based-model. In *IFIP Conference on human-computer interaction* (pp. 114-126). Berlin, Heidelberg: Springer Berlin Heidelberg. DOI: 10.1007/978-3-540-74800-7_9

Bunt, H., & Petukhova, V. (2023). Semantic and pragmatic precision in conversational AI systems. *Frontiers in Artificial Intelligence*, *6*, 896729. Advance online publication. DOI: 10.3389/frai.2023.896729 PMID: 37064296

Busso, C., Bulut, M., Lee, C. C., Kazemzadeh, A., Mower, E., Kim, S., Chang, J. N., Lee, S., & Narayanan, S. S. (2008). IEMOCAP: Interactive emotional dyadic motion capture database. *Language Resources and Evaluation*, *42*(4), 335–359. DOI: 10.1007/s10579-008-9076-6

Calvo, R. A., & Peters, D. (2014). *Positive computing: technology for wellbeing and human potential*. MIT press. DOI: 10.7551/mitpress/9764.001.0001

Cambria, E., Das, D., Bandyopadhyay, S., & Feraco, A. (2017). Affective computing and sentiment analysis: A practical guide to sentiment analysis. IEEE, 1-10. DOI: 10.1007/978-3-319-55394-8

Campbell-Lendrum, D., Neville, T., Schweizer, C., & Neira, M. (2023). Climate change and health: Three grand challenges. *Nature Medicine*, *29*(7), 1631–1638. DOI: 10.1038/s41591-023-02438-w PMID: 37464036

Carvalho, G., Cabral, B., Pereira, V., & Bernardino, J. (2021). Edge computing: Current trends, research challenges and future directions. *Computing*, *103*(5), 993–1023. DOI: 10.1007/s00607-020-00896-5

Chandrakala, C. B., Bhardwaj, R., & Pujari, C. (2024). An intent recognition pipeline for conversational AI. *International Journal of Information Technology : an Official Journal of Bharati Vidyapeeth's Institute of Computer Applications and Management*, *16*(2), 731–743. Advance online publication. DOI: 10.1007/s41870-023-01642-8

Chandra, S., Shirish, A., & Srivastava, S. C. (2022). To Be or Not to Be ...Human? Theorizing the Role of Human-Like Competencies in Conversational Artificial Intelligence Agents. *Journal of Management Information Systems*, *39*(4), 969–1005. Advance online publication. DOI: 10.1080/07421222.2022.2127441

Chang, Y., Liu, Z., & Guo, Y. (2024). WorldScribe: Towards context-aware live visual descriptions. *arXiv preprint arXiv:2408.06627*. /arXiv.2408.06627DOI: 10.1145/3654777.3676375

Chatterjee, J., & Dethlefs, N. (2023). This new conversational AI model can be your friend, philosopher, and guide. and even your worst enemy. In *Patterns* (Vol. 4, Issue 1). DOI: 10.1016/j.patter.2022.100676

Chaudhary, S., & Sharma, D. K. (2018). Gender identification based on voice signal characteristics. *ICACCCN: 2018 International Conference on Advances in Computing, Communication Control and Networking*, 869–874. https://doi.org/DOI: 10.1109/ICACCCN.2018.8748676

Chen, S., Ren, K., Piao, S., Wang, C., Wang, Q., Weng, J., . . . Mohaisen, A. (2017, June). You can hear but you cannot steal: Defending against voice impersonation attacks on smartphones. In *2017 IEEE 37th international conference on distributed computing systems (ICDCS)* (pp. 183-195). IEEE.

Chen, H., & Li, D. (2022). Current status and challenges for liquid-cooled data centers. *Frontiers in Energy Research*, *10*, 952680. Advance online publication. DOI: 10.3389/fenrg.2022.952680

Chen, S. (2025). Data centres will use twice as much energy by 2030 - driven by AI. *Nature*. Advance online publication. DOI: 10.1038/d41586-025-01113-z PMID: 40211075

Chen, Y. Y., Lin, Y. H., Hu, Y. C., Hsia, C. H., Lian, Y. A., & Jhong, S. Y. (2022). Distributed Real-Time Object Detection Based on Edge-Cloud Collaboration for Smart Video Surveillance Applications. *IEEE Access : Practical Innovations, Open Solutions*, *10*, 93745–93759. DOI: 10.1109/ACCESS.2022.3203053

Choobbasti, A. J., Gholamian Mohammad Erfan and Vaheb, A., & Safavi, S. (2018, December). JSpeech: A Multi-Lingual Conversational Speech Corpus. 2018 IEEE Spoken Language Technology Workshop (SLT). DOI: 10.1109/SLT.2018.8639658

Chow, Y. W., Susilo, W., Li, Y., Li, N., & Nguyen, C. (2023). Visualization and Cybersecurity in the Metaverse: A Survey. *Journal of Imaging*, *9*(1), 11. DOI: 10.3390/jimaging9010011 PMID: 36662109

Church, K. W., & Gale, W. A. (1991). Probability scoring for spelling correction. *Statistics and Computing*, *1*(2), 93–103. DOI: 10.1007/BF01889984

Clark, L. (2019). Mapping perceptions of humanness in intelligent personal assistant interaction. [Unpublished manuscript].

Conneau, A., Baevski, A., Collobert, R., Mohamed, A., & Auli, M. (2021, August). Unsupervised cross-lingual representation learning for speech recognition. *Interspeech*, •••, 2021. DOI: 10.21437/Interspeech.2021-329

Cooper, S., Di Fava, A., Vivas, C., Marchionni, L., & Ferro, F. (2020). ARI: The social assistive robot and companion. In 2020 29th IEEE International Conference on Robot and Human Interactive Communication (RO-MAN), 745-751. IEEE.

Cross, C., & Gillett, R. (2020). Exploiting trust for financial gain: An overview of business email compromise (BEC) fraud. *Journal of Financial Crime*, *27*(3), 871–884. DOI: 10.1108/JFC-02-2020-0026

Cui, J., Kingsbury, B., Ramabhadran, B., Sethy, A., Audhkhasi, K., Cui, X., Kislal, E., Mangu, L., Nussbaum-Thom, M., Picheny, M., Tüske, Z., Golik, P., Schluter, R., Ney, H., Gales, M. J. F., Knill, K. M., Ragni, A., Wang, H., & Woodland, P. (2016). Multilingual representations for low resource speech recognition and keyword search. *2015 IEEE Workshop on Automatic Speech Recognition and Understanding, ASRU 2015 - Proceedings*, 259–266. DOI: 10.1109/ASRU.2015.7404803

da Silva, D. A., Louro, H. D. B., Goncalves, G. S., Marques, J. C., Dias, L. A. V., da Cunha, A. M., & Tasinaffo, P. M. (2021). Could a conversational ai identify offensive language?†. *Information (Basel)*, *12*(10), 418. Advance online publication. DOI: 10.3390/info12100418

Dalvi, A., Mittal, A., Dhingra, B., & Zaheer, M. (2017). TextBugger: Rich text error modeling for robust NLP. In *Proceedings of the ACL Workshop on Robustness in NLP* (pp. 52–60).

Damiano, L., Dumouchel, P., & Lehmann, H. (2015). Towards human-robot affective co-evolution: Overcoming oppositions in constructing emotions and empathy. *International Journal of Social Robotics*, *7*(1), 7–18. DOI: 10.1007/s12369-014-0258-7

Danylov, V. (2024). Open source and proprietary software for audio deepfakes and voice cloning: Growth areas, pain points, future influence. *Bjlss*, *1*(1), 105–113. DOI: 10.30525/2592-8813-2024-1-11

Das, M. N., Pratyush Ranjan Mohapatra, P. R., & Rao, P. S. Dr. (2022). Implementation of human voice-based gender classification using deep learning convolutional neural network. *TURCOMAT: Turkish Journal of Computer and Mathematics Education. 13*(03), 55–68. https://doi.org/DOI: 10.17762/turcomat.v13i03.12837

Dasawat, S. S., & Sharma, S. (2024). Edge Intelligence Enabled Secured Digital Transformation in Internet of Autonomous Vehicles. In 2024 12th International Conference on Internet of Everything, Microwave, Embedded, Communication and Networks (IEMECON), 1–6. https://doi.org/DOI: 10.1109/IEMECON62401.2024.10846320

Davis, M. H. (1983). Measuring individual differences in empathy: Evidence for a multidimensional approach. *Journal of Personality and Social Psychology*, *44*(1), 113–126. DOI: 10.1037/0022-3514.44.1.113

De Carolis, B., Ferilli, S., & Palestra, G. (2017). Simulating empathic behavior in a social assistive robot. *Multimedia Tools and Applications*, *76*(4), 5073–5094. DOI: 10.1007/s11042-016-3797-0

De Schutter, H., & Song, S. (2023). Immigrant linguistic justice: The lay of the land. *Metaphilosophy*, *54*(5), 575–582. DOI: 10.1111/meta.12661

Denby, B., Csapó, T. G., & Wand, M. (2023). Future speech interfaces with sensors and machine intelligence. *Sensors (Basel)*, *23*(3), 1234. PMID: 36850569

Desai, S., Black, A. W., Yegnanarayana, B., & Prahallad, K. (2010). Spectral mapping using artificial neural networks for voice conversion. *IEEE Transactions on Audio, Speech, and Language Processing*, *18*(5), 954–964. DOI: 10.1109/TASL.2010.2047683

Devlin, J., Chang, M.-W., Lee, K., & Toutanova, K. (2019). BERT: Pre-training of deep bidirectional transformers for language understanding. In *Proceedings of the 2019 Conference of the North American Chapter of the Association for Computational Linguistics: Human Language Technologies* (pp. 4171–4186). Association for Computational Linguistics. https://doi.org/DOI: 10.18653/v1/N19-1423

Dey, S., Sahidullah, M., & Saha, G. (2022). An overview of Indian spoken language recognition from machine learning perspective. ACM Trans. Asian Low-Resour. *Lang. Inf. Process.*, *21*(6), 1–45.

Ding, Z., Ji, Y., Gan, Y., Wang, Y., & Xia, Y. (2024). Current status and trends of technology, methods, and applications of Human–Computer Intelligent Interaction (HCII): A bibliometric research. *Multimedia Tools and Applications*, *83*(27), 69111–69144. DOI: 10.1007/s11042-023-18096-6

Diwan, A., Vaideeswaran, R., Shah, S., Singh, A., Raghavan, S., Khare, S., Unni, V., Vyas, S., Rajpuria, A., Yarra, C., Mittal, A., Ghosh, P. K., Jyothi, P., Bali, K., Seshadri, V., Sitaram, S., Bharadwaj, S., Nanavati Jai and Nanavati, R., Sankaranarayanan, K., … Abraham, B. (2021). Multilingual and code-switching ASR challenges for low resource Indian languages. ArXiv [Cs.CL].

Dokania, H., & Chattaraj, N. (2022). An assistive interface protocol for communication between visually and hearing-speech impaired persons in internet platform. *Disability and Rehabilitation. Assistive Technology*, *19*(1), 233–246. DOI: 10.1080/17483107.2022.2078898 PMID: 35618260

Du, X., Zhang, Q., Zhu, J., & Liu, X. (2024). Adaptive unified defense framework for tackling adversarial audio attacks. *Artificial Intelligence Review*, *57*(8), 218. DOI: 10.1007/s10462-024-10863-7

Eisenberg, N., & Morris, A. S. (2001). The origins and social significance of empathy-related responding: A review of empathy and moral development: Implications for caring and justice. *Social Justice Research*, *14*(1), 95–120. DOI: 10.1023/A:1012579805721

Eisenstein, J. (2013). What to do about bad language on the internet. In *Proceedings of NAACL-HLT* (pp. 359–369).

Elhadad, A., Hamad, S., Elfiky, N., Alanazi, F., Taloba, A. I., & El-Aziz, R. M. A. (2024). Advancing Healthcare: Intelligent Speech Technology for Transcription, Disease Diagnosis, and Interactive Control of Medical Equipment in Smart Hospitals. *AI*, *5*(4), 2497–2517. DOI: 10.3390/ai5040121

Elsworth, C., Huang, K., Patterson, D., Schneider, I., Sedivy, R., Goodman, S., Townsend, B., Ranganathan, P., Dean, J., Vahdat, A., Gomes, B., & Manyika, J. (2025). *Measuring the environmental impact of delivering AI at Google scale*. arXiv. https://arxiv.org/abs/2508.15734

Emara, T. (2018). Adaptive Power-Saving Mechanism for VoIP Over WiMAX Based on Artificial Neural Network. In Waluyo, A. B. (Ed.), *Algorithms, Methods, and Applications in Mobile Computing and Communications* (pp. 158–177). IGI Global., DOI: 10.4018/978-1-5225-5693-0.ch007

Emara, T. Z. (2016). Maximizing Power Saving for VoIP over WiMAX Systems. *International Journal of Mobile Computing and Multimedia Communications*, *7*(1), 32–40. DOI: 10.4018/IJMCMC.2016010103

Emara, T. Z., Ashraf, R., Saber, A., Trinh, T., & Awad, W. (2025c). A Data Processing Algorithm to Approximate Big Stream Data Analysis. In *2nd IEEE International Conference on Machine Intelligence and Smart Innovation (ICMISI 2025)*. DOI: 10.1109/ICMISI65108.2025.11115782

Emara, T. Z., Hassan, E., Elbedwehy, S., & Saber, A. (2025). A historical perspective on Artificial Intelligence in applied life sciences. In *Advances in Computational Intelligence and Robotics* (pp. 49–86). IGI Global., DOI: 10.4018/979-8-3693-9208-9.ch002

Emara, T. Z., & Huang, J. Z. (2019a). A distributed data management system to support large-scale data analysis. *Journal of Systems and Software*, *148*, 105–115. DOI: 10.1016/j.jss.2018.11.007

Emara, T. Z., & Huang, J. Z. (2019b). RRPlib: A spark library for representing HDFS blocks as a set of random sample data blocks. *Science of Computer Programming, 184*, 102301. DOI: 10.1016/j.scico.2019.102301

Emara, T. Z., & Huang, J. Z. (2020). Distributed Data Strategies to Support Large-Scale Data Analysis Across Geo-Distributed Data Centers. *IEEE Access : Practical Innovations, Open Solutions, 8*, 178526–178538. DOI: 10.1109/ACCESS.2020.3027675

Emara, T. Z., Saleh, A. I., & Arafat, H. (2014). Power saving mechanism for VoIP services over WiMAX systems. *Wireless Networks, 20*(5), 975–985. DOI: 10.1007/s11276-013-0650-5

Emara, T. Z., Trinh, T., & Huang, J. Z. (2023). Geographically distributed data management to support large-scale data analysis. *Scientific Reports, 13*(1), 17783. Advance online publication. DOI: 10.1038/s41598-023-44789-x PMID: 37853092

Emara, T., Hassan, E., Trinh, T., Li, G., & Saber, A. (Eds.). (2025b). *The Role of Artificial Intelligence in Advancing Applied Life Sciences*. IGI Global Scientific Publishing., DOI: 10.4018/979-8-3693-9208-9

Erol, B. A., Majumdar, A., Benavidez, P., Rad, P., Choo, K. R., & Jamshidi, M. (2019). Toward artificial emotional intelligence for cooperative social human-machine interaction. *IEEE Transactions on Computational Social Systems, 7*(1), 234–246. DOI: 10.1109/TCSS.2019.2922593

Ertam, F. (2019). An effective gender recognition approach using voice data via deeper LSTM networks. *Applied Acoustics, 156*, 351–358. DOI: 10.1016/j.apacoust.2019.07.033

Esmaeilpour, M., Cardinal, P., & Koerich, A. L. (2019). A robust approach for securing audio classification against adversarial attacks. *IEEE Transactions on Information Forensics and Security, 15*, 2147–2159. DOI: 10.1109/TIFS.2019.2956591

Failasofah, F., Mukminin, A., Masbirorotni, M., Abrar, M., Fajaryani, N., Fortunasari, F., Hidayat, M., & Habibi, A. (2022). Culture, language, and multilingual education: Bordón Rev. *Pedagog., 74*(3), 121–137.

Falk, S., Ekchajzer, D., Pirson, T., Lees-Perasso, E., Wattiez, A., Biber-Freudenberger, L., Luccioni, S., & van Wynsberghe, A. (2025). More than carbon: Cradle-to-grave environmental impacts of GenAI training on the Nvidia A100 GPU. arXiv. https://arxiv.org/abs/2509.00093

Fantaye, T. G., Yu, J., & Hailu, T. T. (2020). Investigation of automatic speech recognition systems via the multilingual deep neural network modeling methods for a very low-resource language, chaha. *J. Sign. Inf. Process., 11*(01), 1–21. DOI: 10.4236/jsip.2020.111001

Farooq, U., Iqbal, M. A., & Nazir, S. (2011). A glance into the future of human-computer interaction.

Feng, T., Hebbar, R., Mehlman, N., Shi, X., Kommineni, A., & Narayanan, S. (2023). A review of speech-centric trustworthy machine learning: Privacy, safety, and fairness. *APSIPA Transactions on Signal and Information Processing*, *12*(3). Advance online publication. DOI: 10.1561/116.00000084

Firc, A., Malinka, K., & Hanáček, P. (2023). Deepfakes as a threat to a speaker and facial recognition: An overview of tools and attack vectors. *Heliyon*, *9*(4), e15090. DOI: 10.1016/j.heliyon.2023.e15090 PMID: 37089334

Fu, T., Gao, S., Zhao, X., Wen, J. rong, & Yan, R. (2022). Learning towards conversational AI: A survey. *AI Open, 3*. DOI: 10.1016/j.aiopen.2022.02.001

Fuad, A., & Al-Yahya, M. (2022). Recent Developments in Arabic Conversational AI: A Literature Review. In *IEEE Access* (Vol. 10). DOI: 10.1109/ACCESS.2022.3155521

Gao, J., Galley, M., & Li, L. (2018). Neural approaches to conversational AI. *ACL 2018 - 56th Annual Meeting of the Association for Computational Linguistics, Proceedings of the Conference Tutorial Abstracts*. DOI: 10.18653/v1/P18-5002

Gao, J., Galley, M., & Li, L. (2019). Neural approaches to conversational AI. *Foundations and Trends in Information Retrieval*, *13*(2–3), 127–298. Advance online publication. DOI: 10.1561/1500000074

Garcia Valencia, O. A., Suppadungsuk, S., Thongprayoon, C., Miao, J., Tangpanithandee, S., Craici, I. M., & Cheungpasitporn, W. (2023). Ethical implications of chatbot utilization in nephrology. *Journal of Personalized Medicine*, *13*(9), 1363. DOI: 10.3390/jpm13091363 PMID: 37763131

GeeksforGeeks. (2025). Natural language processing (NLP) pipeline. https://www.geeksforgeeks.org/natural-language-processing-nlp-pipeline/

Gillingham, K., Rapson, D. S., & Wagner, G. (2015). The rebound effect and energy efficiency policy. *Review of Environmental Economics and Policy*, *10*(1), 68–88. https://environment.yale.edu/gillingham/GillinghamRapsonWagner_Rebound.pdf. DOI: 10.1093/reep/rev017

Gkinko, L., & Elbanna, A. (2023a). Designing trust: The formation of employees' trust in conversational AI in the digital workplace. *Journal of Business Research, 158*, 113707. Advance online publication. DOI: 10.1016/j.jbusres.2023.113707

Gkinko, L., & Elbanna, A. (2023b). The appropriation of conversational AI in the workplace: A taxonomy of AI chatbot users. *International Journal of Information Management, 69*, 102568. Advance online publication. DOI: 10.1016/j.ijinfomgt.2022.102568

Glint, T., Mittal, B., Sharma, S., Ronak, A. Q., Goud, A., Kasture, N., Momin, Z., Krishna, A., & Mekie, J. (2025). AxLaM: Energy-efficient accelerator design for language models for edge computing. *Philosophical Transactions. Series A, Mathematical, Physical, and Engineering Sciences, 383*(2288), 20230395. DOI: 10.1098/rsta.2023.0395 PMID: 39815979

Go, A., Bhayani, R., & Huang, L. (2009). Twitter sentiment classification using distant supervision. *CS224N Project Report, Stanford.*

Gogireddy, Y. R., & Smithesh, C. (2024). Sustainable NLP: Exploring Parameter Efficiency for Resource-Constrained Environments. [JCET]. *Journal of Computer Engineering and Technology, 7*(1). Advance online publication. DOI: 10.51731/jcet.2024.0102

Goldwater, S., Jurafsky, D., & Manning, C. D. (2010). Which words are hard to recognize? Prosodic, lexical, and disfluency factors that increase speech recognition error rates. *Speech Communication, 52*(3), 181–200. DOI: 10.1016/j.specom.2009.10.001

Goniewicz, K., Burkle, F. M., & Khorram-Manesh, A. (2025). Transforming global public health: Climate collaboration, political challenges, and systemic change. *Journal of Infection and Public Health, 18*(1), 102615. DOI: 10.1016/j.jiph.2024.102615 PMID: 39644717

Green Software Foundation. (2023). *Software Carbon Intensity (SCI) Specification.* Green Software Foundation. https://sci.greensoftware.foundation

Grimes, G. M., Schuetzler, R. M., & Giboney, J. S. (2021). Mental models and expectation violations in conversational AI interactions. *Decision Support Systems, 144*, 113515. Advance online publication. DOI: 10.1016/j.dss.2021.113515

Grudin, J. (2017). A moving target — The evolution of human-computer interaction. In *Handbook of Human-Computer Interaction* (3rd ed.). Microsoft Research., Retrieved from https://www.microsoft.com/en-us/research/wp-content/uploads/2017/01/HCIhandbook3rd.pdf

Hadidi, R., Cao, J., Ryoo, M. S., & Kim, H. (2020). Toward collaborative inferencing of deep neural networks on internet-of-things devices. *IEEE Internet of Things Journal, 7*(6), 4950–4960. DOI: 10.1109/JIOT.2020.2972000

Han, B., & Baldwin, T. (2011). Lexical normalisation of short text messages: Makn sens a# twitter. In *Proceedings of the 49th Annual Meeting of the Association for Computational Linguistics* (pp. 368–378).

Hassan, E., Saber, A., Abd El-Hafeez, T., Medhat, T., & Shams, M. Y. (2025a). Enhanced dysarthria detection in cerebral palsy and ALS patients using WaveNet and CNN-BiLSTM models: A comparative study with model interpretability. *Biomedical Signal Processing and Control, 110*, 108128. DOI: 10.1016/j.bspc.2025.108128

Hassan, E., Saber, A., Alqahtani, O., El-Rashidy, N., & Elbedwehy, S. (2025b). An innovative approach to advanced voice classification of sacred Quranic recitations through multimodal fusion. *Egyptian Informatics Journal, 30*, 100640. DOI: 10.1016/j.eij.2025.100640

Hassan, E., Saber, A., El-kenawy, E. S. M., Bhatnagar, R., & Shams, M. Y. (2024, August). Early detection of black fungus using deep learning models for efficient medical diagnosis. In *2024 International Conference on Emerging Techniques in Computational Intelligence (ICETCI)* (pp. 426-431). IEEE. DOI: 10.1109/ICETCI62771.2024.10704103

Hassan, E., Saber, A., El-Sappagh, S., & El-Rashidy, N. (2025c). Optimized ensemble deep learning approach for accurate breast cancer diagnosis using transfer learning and grey wolf optimization. *Evolving Systems, 16*(2), 59. DOI: 10.1007/s12530-025-09686-w

Hassija, V., Chakrabarti, A., Singh, A., Chamola, V., & Sikdar, B. (2023). Unleashing the Potential of Conversational AI: Amplifying Chat-GPT's Capabilities and Tackling Technical Hurdles. *IEEE Access : Practical Innovations, Open Solutions, 11*, 143657–143682. Advance online publication. DOI: 10.1109/ACCESS.2023.3339553

Henderson, P., Hu, J., Romoff, J., Brunskill, E., Jurafsky, D., & Pineau, J. (2020). Towards the systematic reporting of the energy and carbon footprints of machine learning. *Journal of Machine Learning Research, 21*(248), 1–43. http://jmlr.org/papers/v21/20-312.html. DOI: 10.4337/9781845424718

Hinton, G., Deng, L., Yu, D., Dahl, G. E., Mohamed, A. R., Jaitly, N., Senior, A., Vanhoucke, V., Nguyen, P., Sainath, T., & Kingsbury, B. (2012). Deep neural networks for acoustic modeling in speech recognition: The shared views of four research groups. *IEEE Signal Processing Magazine, 29*(6), 82–97. DOI: 10.1109/MSP.2012.2205597

Hirose, K. (2018). Voice and speech synthesis—highlighting the control of prosody. In S. Frühholz & P. Belin (Eds.), The Oxford Handbook of Voice Perception (pp. 756–776). Oxford University Press.

Hsu, T. C., Abelson, H., & Van Brummelen, J. (2022). The Effects on Secondary School Students of Applying Experiential Learning to the Conversational AI Learning Curriculum. *International Review of Research in Open and Distance Learning*, *23*(1), 82–103. Advance online publication. DOI: 10.19173/irrodl.v22i4.5474

Huang, G., & Gorin, A., & Gauvain Jean-Luc and Lamel, L. (2016, March). Machine translation based data augmentation for Cantonese keyword spotting. 2016 IEEE International Conference on Acoustics, Speech and Signal Processing (ICASSP). DOI: 10.1109/ICASSP.2016.7472833

Hu, P., Lu, Y., & Gong, Y. (2021). Dual humanness and trust in conversational AI: A person-centered approach. *Computers in Human Behavior*, *119*, 106727. Advance online publication. DOI: 10.1016/j.chb.2021.106727

Hu, Z., LingHu, K., Yu, H., & Liao, C. (2023). Speech emotion recognition based on attention MCNN combined with gender information. *IEEE Access : Practical Innovations, Open Solutions*, *11*, 50285–50294. DOI: 10.1109/ACCESS.2023.3278106

HWANG. S., Seo, T., Kim, Y., & Oh, H. (2024). Metaverse Counseling: Transforming Depression Care With AI Digital Humans in Virtual Realms. Research Square. DOI: 10.21203/rs.3.rs-4244666/v1

IBM. (2024). What is NLP (natural language processing)? https://www.ibm.com/topics/natural-language-processing

Iles, J., & Edmondson, W. (2024, March). FEATURE DRIVEN FORMANT SYNTHESIS. Speech and Hearing.

Institute for Global Policy. (2024). *Greening AI: A policy agenda for the artificial intelligence and energy revolutions*. Tony Blair Institute for Global Change. https://institute.global/insights/climate-and-energy/greening-ai-a-policy-agenda-for-the-artificial-intelligence-and-energy-revolutions

Iqbal, B. A., & Ghauri, F. N. (2011). Climate change: The biggest challenge in 21st century. *Mediterranean Journal of Social Sciences*, *2*(6), 41. DOI: 10.5901/mjss.2011.v2n6p41

Jahangir, R., Teh, Y. W., Memon, N. A., Mujtaba, G., Zareei, M., Ishtiaq, U., Akhtar, M. Z., & Ali, I. (2020). Text-independent speaker identification through feature fusion and deep neural network. *IEEE Access : Practical Innovations, Open Solutions*, *8*, 32187–32202. DOI: 10.1109/ACCESS.2020.2973541

Jaleel, H. Q., Stephan, J. J., & Naji, S. A. (2022). Gender identification from speech recognition using machine learning techniques and convolutional neural networks. *Webology, 19*(1), 1666–1688. DOI: 10.14704/WEB/V19I1/WEB19112

James, F., Rayner, M., & Hockey, B. A. (2000). Accuracy, coverage, and speed: What do they mean to users? Koenecke, A., Nam, A., Lake, E., Nudell, J., Quartey, M., Mengesha, Z., ... & Goel, S. (2020). Racial disparities in automated speech recognition. *Proceedings of the National Academy of Sciences of the United States of America, 117*(14), 7684–7689.

Jampala, R., Kola, D. S., Gummadi, A. N., Bhavanam, M., & Pannerselvam, I. R. (2024, January). The evolution of voice assistants: From text-to-speech to conversational ai. In *2024 2nd International Conference on Intelligent Data Communication Technologies and Internet of Things (IDCIoT)* (pp. 1332-1338). IEEE.

Jayakannan, S. M.Sai Manoj Jayakannan. (2025). Securing Voice-Based Financial Authentication in the Era of AI Voice Cloning: Challenges, Vulnerabilities, and Counter-Measures. *Journal of Computer Science and Technology Studies, 7*(4), 515–520. DOI: 10.32996/jcsts.2025.7.4.60

Ji, H., Han, I., & Ko, Y. (2023). A systematic review of conversational AI in language education: focusing on the collaboration with human teachers. In *Journal of Research on Technology in Education* (Vol. 55, Issue 1). DOI: 10.1080/15391523.2022.2142873

Jiang, X., Paulmann, S., Robin, J., & Pell, M. D. (2015). More than accuracy: Nonverbal dialects modulate the time course of vocal emotion recognition across cultures. *Journal of Experimental Psychology. Human Perception and Performance, 41*(3), 597–612. DOI: 10.1037/xhp0000043 PMID: 25775176

Jiao, X., Yin, Y., Shang, L., Jiang, X., Chen, X., Li, L., Wang, F., & Liu, Q. (2019). TinyBERT: Distilling BERT for Natural Language Understanding. *ArXiv*. https://arxiv.org/abs/1909.10351

Jindal, I., Li, Y., Brahma, S., & Zhu, H. (2020). CLAR: A cross-lingual argument regularizer for semantic role labeling. Findings of the Association for Computational Linguistics: EMNLP 2020.

Jin, Y., Hu, G., Chen, H., Miao, D., Hu, L., & Zhao, C. (2023). Cross-Modal Distillation for Speaker Recognition. *Proceedings of the 37th AAAI Conference on Artificial Intelligence, AAAI 2023, 37*, 12977–12985. DOI: 10.1609/aaai.v37i11.26525

Joshi, A., Dabre, R., Kanojia, D., Li, Z., Zhan, H., Haffari, G., & Dippold, D. (2025). Natural language processing for dialects of a language: A survey. *ACM Computing Surveys, 57*(6), 1–37. DOI: 10.1145/3712060

Joshi, P., & Patki, R. (2015). Implementation of Voice User Interface using Speech Recognition. *International Journal of Computer Applications*, *124*(10), 37–42. DOI: 10.5120/ijca2015905633

Journal, I. (2024). A Review on Speech-to-Text. *Interantional Journal of Scientific Research in Engineering and Management*, *08*(03), 1–13. DOI: 10.55041/IJSREM29004

Jurafsky, D., & Martin, J. H. (2023). *Speech and language processing* (3rd ed.). Pearson.

Kabir, A., Ahmad, M. A., Aliyu, A. A., Abdulkadir, S., & Muazu, A. A. (2025). A deep learning model for gender recognition using voice data. *TheScientificWorldJournal*, *20*(1), 137–141. DOI: 10.4314/swj.v20i1.18

Kafayat, S. (2025). Deepfakes' Challenge to International Politics: Sowing Political Discord. *Annals of Human and Social Sciences*, *6*(2), 318–326.

Kandoi, R., Dixit, D., Tyagi, M., & Yadav, R. S. (2024). Conversational AI. *International Journal for Research in Applied Science and Engineering Technology*, *12*(3), 769–775. Advance online publication. DOI: 10.22214/ijraset.2024.58787

Karpov, A. A., & Yusupov, R. M. (2018). Multimodal interfaces of Human–Computer Interaction. *Herald of the Russian Academy of Sciences*, *88*(1), 67–74. DOI: 10.1134/S1019331618010094

Kashef, M., Visvizi, A., & Troisi, O. (2021). Smart city as a smart service system: Human-computer interaction and smart city surveillance systems. *Computers in Human Behavior*, *124*, 106923. DOI: 10.1016/j.chb.2021.106923

Kasula, A. J. (2016). Olowalu Review: Developing identity through translanguaging in a multilingual literary magazine. *Colombian Applied Linguistics Journal*, *18*(2), 109. DOI: 10.14483/calj.v18n2.10014

Kaur, D., Singh, B., & Rani, S. (2023). Cyber security in the metaverse. *Handbook of Research on AI-Based Technologies and Applications in the Era of the Metaverse*, 418–435. DOI: 10.4018/978-1-6684-8851-5.ch023

Kaur, G., Srivastava, M., & Kumar, A. (2018). Genetic algorithm for combined speaker and speech recognition using deep neural networks. *Journal of Telecommunications and Information Technology*, *2*(2018), 23–31. DOI: 10.26636/jtit.2018.119617

Kaur, N., & Singh, P. (2023). Conventional and contemporary approaches used in text to speech synthesis: A review. *Artificial Intelligence Review*, *56*(7), 5837–5880. DOI: 10.1007/s10462-022-10315-0

Khalil, R. A., Jones, E., Babar, M. I., Jan, T., Zafar, M. H., & Alhussain, T. (2019). Speech Emotion Recognition Using Deep Learning Techniques: A Review. *IEEE Access : Practical Innovations, Open Solutions*, *7*, 117327–117345. DOI: 10.1109/ACCESS.2019.2936124

Khanjani, Z., Jeddi, E. M., Hekmati, I., Khalilzade, S., Etemadi Nia, M., Andalib, M., & Ashrafian, P. (2015). Comparison of cognitive empathy, emotional empathy, and social functioning in different age groups. *Australian Psychologist*, *50*(1), 80–85. DOI: 10.1111/ap.12099

Khanjani, Z., Watson, G., & Janeja, V. P. (2022). Audio deepfakes: A survey. *Frontiers in Big Data*, *5*, 1001063. DOI: 10.3389/fdata.2022.1001063 PMID: 36700137

Kharumnuid, B., Kharmuti, S. L., & Thingbaijam, L. (2024). *The Evolution of Edge Computing in a Data-Driven World*. Int Res J Adv Engg MGT., DOI: 10.47392/IRJAEM.2024.0477

Khatri, C., Venkatesh, A., Hedayatnia, B., Ram, A., Gabriel, R., & Prasad, R. (2018). Alexa prize-state of the art in conversational AI. *AI Magazine*, *39*(3), 40–55. Advance online publication. DOI: 10.1609/aimag.v39i3.2810

Kiwanuka, F., & Shafik, W. (2025). Nursing as a Lingua Franca for Artificial Intelligence in Patients' Care Trajectories: Where Are We Headed? *Nursing Research*, *74*(3), 170. DOI: 10.1097/NNR.0000000000000799 PMID: 40266973

Kobayashi, T. (2015). Prosody control and variation enhancement techniques for HMM-based expressive speech synthesis. In *Speech Prosody in Speech Synthesis: Modeling and generation of prosody for high quality and flexible speech synthesis* (pp. 203–213). Springer Berlin Heidelberg. DOI: 10.1007/978-3-662-45258-5_14

Koenecke, A., Nam, A., Lake, E., Nudell, J., Quartey, M., Mengesha, Z., Toups, C., Rickford, J. R., Jurafsky, D., & Goel, S. (2020). Racial disparities in automated speech recognition. *Proceedings of the National Academy of Sciences of the United States of America*, *117*(14), 7684–7689. DOI: 10.1073/pnas.1915768117 PMID: 32205437

Kons, Z., Shechtman, S., Sorin, A., Hoory, R., Rabinovitz, C., & Morais, E. D. S. (2018, December). Neural TTS voice conversion. In *2018 IEEE Spoken Language Technology Workshop (SLT)* (pp. 290-296). IEEE. DOI: 10.1109/SLT.2018.8639550

Kotian, A. L., & Nandipi, R. (2024). A systematic review on human and computer interaction. In *Proceedings of the 2024 2nd International Conference on Advanced Computing and Communication Engineering*. DOI: 10.1109/IDCIoT59759.2024.10467622

Krulatz, A., & Iversen, J. (2020). Building inclusive language classroom spaces through multilingual writing practices for newly-arrived students in Norway. *Scandinavian Journal of Educational Research*, *64*(3), 372–388. DOI: 10.1080/00313831.2018.1557741

Kulkarni, A., Tokareva, A., Qureshi, R., & Couceiro, M. (2024). The balancing act: Unmasking and alleviating ASR biases in Portuguese.

Kulkarni, C. S. (2023). The Evolution of Large Language Models in Natural Language Understanding. *Journal of Artificial Intelligence. Machine Learning and Data Science*, *1*(4), 49–53. DOI: 10.51219/JAIMLD/chinmay-shripad-kulkarni/28

Kumar, A., & Shankar, A. (2024). Will metaverse revolutionize retail banking? Understanding user acceptance towards metaverse banking. *International Journal of Retail & Distribution Management*, *52*(6), 629–646. DOI: 10.1108/IJRDM-06-2023-0396

Kumar, M. G., Kuriakose, J., Thyagachandran, A., Kumar, A., Seth, A., Prasad, L. V. S. V. D., Jaiswal, S., Prakash, A., & Murthy, H. A. (2021). Dual Script E2E Framework for Multilingual and Code-Switching ASR. *Proceedings of the Annual Conference of the International Speech Communication Association. Interspeech*, *1*, 381–385. DOI: 10.21437/Interspeech.2021-978

Kumar, P. R., & Rajagopalan, S. (2023). Light Weight Native Edge Load Balancers for Edge Load Balancing. *Green Intelligent Systems and Applications*, *3*(1), 48–55. DOI: 10.53623/gisa.v3i1.256

Kurian, N. (2023). AI's empathy gap: The risks of conversational Artificial Intelligence for young children's well being and key ethical considerations for early childhood education and care. *Contemporary Issues in Early Childhood*. Advance online publication. DOI: 10.1177/14639491231206004

Kwasny, D., & Hemmerling, D. (2021). Gender and age estimation methods based on speech using deep neural networks. *Sensors (Basel)*, *21*(14), 4785. DOI: 10.3390/s21144785 PMID: 34300525

Lai, H. Y., Hu, C. C., Wen, C. H., Wu, J. H., Pai, N. S., Yeh, C. Y., & Lin, C. H. (2024). Mel-scale frequency extraction and classification of Dialect-Speech signals with 1D CNN based classifier for gender and region recognition. *IEEE Access : Practical Innovations, Open Solutions*, *12*, 102962–102976. DOI: 10.1109/ACCESS.2024.3430296

LaLone, C. A., Ankley, G. T., Belanger, S. E., Embry, M. R., Hodges, G., Knapen, D., Munn, S., Perkins, E. J., Rudd, M. A., Villeneuve, D. L., Whelan, M., Willett, C., Zhang, X., & Hecker, M. (2017). Advancing the adverse outcome pathway framework—An international horizon scanning approach. *Environmental Toxicology and Chemistry, 36*(6), 1411–1421. DOI: 10.1002/etc.3805 PMID: 28543973

Landay, J. A., Oliver, N., & Song, J. (2019). Conversational User Interfaces and Interactions. *IEEE Pervasive Computing, 18*(2), 8–9. DOI: 10.1109/MPRV.2019.2921176

Lannelongue, L., Grealey, J., & Inouye, M. (2021). Green algorithms: Quantifying the carbon footprint of computation. *Advancement of Science, 8*(12), 2100707. DOI: 10.1002/advs.202100707 PMID: 34194954

Latif, S., Qadir, J., & Bilal, M. (2019). Unsupervised Adversarial Domain Adaptation for Cross-Lingual Speech Emotion Recognition. *2019 8th International Conference on Affective Computing and Intelligent Interaction, ACII 2019*. DOI: 10.1109/ACII.2019.8925513

Latif, S., Qadir, J., Qayyum, A., Usama, M., & Younis, S. (2021). Speech Technology for Healthcare: Opportunities, Challenges, and State of the Art. *IEEE Reviews in Biomedical Engineering, 14*, 342–356. DOI: 10.1109/RBME.2020.3006860 PMID: 32746367

Lee, H.-S., & Shim, H.-S. (2023). Study on the Design of a ChatGPT-Based Metaverse Platform Model. *Korea Industrial Technology Convergence Society, 28*(2), 131–136. DOI: 10.29279/jitr.2023.28.2.131

Lee, A., Gong, H., Duquenne, P.-A., Schwenk, H., Chen, P.-J., Wang, C., Popuri, S., Adi, Y., Pino, J., Gu, J., & Hsu, W.-N. (2022). Textless Speech-to-Speech Translation on Real Data. *Proceedings of the 2022 Conference of the North American of the Association for Computational Linguistics: Human Technologies.*

Le, H., Barbier, F., Nguyen, H., Tomashenko, N., Mdhaffar, S., Gahbiche, S. G., Lecouteux, B., Schwab, D., & Estève, Y. (2021). ON-TRAC' systems for the IWSLT 2021 low-resource speech translation and multilingual speech translation shared tasks. *Proceedings of the 18th International Conference on Spoken Translation (IWSLT 2021)*. DOI: 10.18653/v1/2021.iwslt-1.20

Lehtonen, A., Salonen, A. O., & Cantell, H. (2018). Climate change education: A new approach for a world of wicked problems. In *Sustainability, human well-being, and the future of education* (pp. 339–374). Springer International Publishing., DOI: 10.1007/978-3-319-78092-4_21

Leite, I., Pereira, A., Mascarenhas, S., Martinho, C., Prada, R., & Paiva, A. (2013). The influence of empathy in human-robot relations. *International Journal of Human-Computer Studies*, *71*(3), 250–260. DOI: 10.1016/j.ijhcs.2012.09.005

Lemon, O. (2022). Conversational AI for multi-agent communication in Natural Language. *AI Communications*, *35*(4), 295–308. Advance online publication. DOI: 10.3233/AIC-220147

Leschanowsky, A., Popp, B., & Peters, N. (2023). Debiasing Strategies for Conversational AI: Improving Privacy and Security Decision-Making. *Digital Society : Ethics, Socio-Legal and Governance of Digital Technology*, *2*(3), 34. Advance online publication. DOI: 10.1007/s44206-023-00062-2

Li, B., Samsi, S., Gadepally, V., & Tiwari, D. (2023). *Clover: Toward Sustainable AI with Carbon-Aware Machine Learning Inference Service* [Preprint]. arXiv. / arXiv.2304.09781DOI: 10.1145/3581784.3607034

Liang, L. (2025). *Research on Real-Time Image Processing System Combining Convolutional Neural Network and Edge Computing*. DOI: 10.1117/12.3059980

Liang, S., Wu, H., Zhen, L., Hua, Q., Garg, S., Kaddoum, G., Hassan, M. M., & Yu, K. (2022). Edge YOLO: Real-Time Intelligent Object Detection System Based on Edge-Cloud Cooperation in Autonomous Vehicles. *IEEE Transactions on Intelligent Transportation Systems*, *23*(12), 25345–25360. DOI: 10.1109/TITS.2022.3158253

Lin, L. S. (2025). Examining the role of deepfake technology in organized fraud: Legal, security, and governance challenges. *Frontiers in Law*, *4*, 6–17. DOI: 10.6000/2817-2302.2025.04.02

Li, S., Ding, C., Lu, X., Shen, P., Kawahara, T., & Kawai, H. (2019, September). End-to-end articulatory attribute modeling for low-resource multilingual speech recognition. *Interspeech*, •••, 2019. DOI: 10.21437/Interspeech.2019-2092

Liu, S., & Manocha, D. (2022). *Sound synthesis, propagation, and rendering*. Morgan & Claypool Publishers. DOI: 10.1007/978-3-031-79214-4

Livieris, I. E., Pintelas, E., & Pintelas, P. (2019). Gender recognition by voice using an improved Self-Labeled algorithm. *Machine Learning and Knowledge Extraction*, *1*(1), 492–503. DOI: 10.3390/make1010030

Lovely, F. P., & Wicaksana, A. (2021). Rule-based lip-syncing algorithm for virtual character in voice chatbot. *Telkomnika*, *19*(5), 1517–1528. DOI: 10.12928/telkomnika.v19i5.19824

Luccioni, A. (2025). From efficiency gains to rebound effects: The problem of Jevons' paradox in AI. In *Proceedings of the 2025 ACM Conference on Fairness, Accountability, and Transparency* (pp. 1–12). ACM. DOI: 10.1145/3715275.3732007

Luccioni, A. S., Viguier, S., & Ligozat, A.-L. (2023). Estimating the Carbon Footprint of BLOOM, a 176B Parameter Language Model. *Journal of Machine Learning Research, 24*, 1–15.

Lu, R., Wei, R., & Zhang, J. (2024). Human-computer interaction based on speech recognition. *Applied and Computational Engineering, 36*(1), 102–110. DOI: 10.54254/2755-2721/36/20230429

Lv, Z., Poiesi, F., Dong, Q., Lloret, J., & Song, H. (2022). Deep Learning for intelligent Human–Computer Interaction. *Applied Sciences (Basel, Switzerland), 12*(22), 11457. DOI: 10.3390/app122211457

Lyu, K.-M., Lyu, R.-Y., & Chang, H.-T. (2024). Real-time multilingual speech recognition and speaker diarization system based on Whisper segmentation. *PeerJ. Computer Science, 10*, e1973. DOI: 10.7717/peerj-cs.1973 PMID: 38660177

M. K., A. H. K., & Aithal, P. S. (2024). Implementation of Voice Biometric System in the Banking Sector. *International Journal of Applied Engineering and Management Letters*, 120–127. DOI: 10.47992/IJAEML.2581.7000.0217

Malbos, E., Chichery, N., Borwell, B., Weindel, G., Molitor, J., Einig-Iscain, M., Seimandi, J., & Lançon, C. (2025). Virtual Reality and Relaxation for the Treatment of Generalized Anxiety Disorder: A Randomized Comparative Study with Standard Intervention. *Journal of Clinical Medicine, 14*(4), 1351. Advance online publication. DOI: 10.3390/jcm14041351 PMID: 40004880

Malinowska, J. K. (2022). Can I feel your pain? The biological and socio-cognitive factors shaping people's empathy with social robots. *International Journal of Social Robotics, 14*(2), 341–355. DOI: 10.1007/s12369-021-00787-5

Malkin, N., Egelman, S., & Wagner, D. (2019). Privacy controls for always-listening devices. In *Proceedings of the New Security Paradigms Workshop* (pp. 78–91). https://doi.org/DOI: 10.1145/3368860.3368867

Mamyrbayev, O., Kydyrbekova, A., Alimhan, K., Oralbekova, D., Zhumazhanov, B., & Nuranbayeva, B. (2021). Development of Security Systems Using Dnn and I & X-Vector Classifiers. *Eastern-European Journal of Enterprise Technologies, 4*(9–112), 32–45. DOI: 10.15587/1729-4061.2021.239186

Mamyrbayev, O., Toleu, A., Tolegen, G., & Mekebayev, N. (2020). Neural architectures for gender detection and speaker identification. *Cogent Engineering*, *7*(1), 1727168. DOI: 10.1080/23311916.2020.1727168

Manic, M. (2023). An Impact Analysis of Conversational AI on Marketing Processes. *Bulletin of the Transilvania University of Brasov. Series V, Economic Sciences*, 23–28. Advance online publication. DOI: 10.31926/but.es.2023.16.65.1.3

Marchisio, A., Hanif, M. A., Khalid, F., Plastiras, G., Kyrkou, C., Theocharides, T., & Shafique, M. (2019). Deep Learning for Edge Computing: Current Trends, Cross-Layer Optimizations, and Open Research Challenges. *Proceedings of IEEE Computer Society Annual Symposium on VLSI, ISVLSI, 2019-July*, 553–559. DOI: 10.1109/ISVLSI.2019.00105

Mathur, V., Dadu, T., & Aggarwal, S. (2024). Evaluating neural networks' ability to generalize against adversarial attacks in cross-lingual settings. *Applied Sciences (Basel, Switzerland)*, *14*(13), 5440. DOI: 10.3390/app14135440

Ma, Y., & Tang, Y. (2024). The Intelligibility Benefits of Modern Computer-Synthesized Speech for Normal-Hearing and Hearing-Impaired Listeners in Non-Ideal Listening Conditions. *Journal of Otorhinolaryngology, Hearing and Balance Medicine*, *5*(1), 5. DOI: 10.3390/ohbm5010005

McKeown, K., Cole, R., Hirschman, L., Atlas, L., et al. (1995). The challenge of spoken language systems: Research directions for the nineties. [Report].

Milvus. (2025). How does speech recognition integrate with natural language processing (NLP)? https://milvus.io/

Miner, A. S., Shah, N., Bullock, K. D., Arnow, B. A., Bailenson, J., & Hancock, J. (2019). Key Considerations for Incorporating Conversational AI in Psychotherapy. *Frontiers in Psychiatry*, *10*, 746. Advance online publication. DOI: 10.3389/fpsyt.2019.00746 PMID: 31681047

Modupe, O. T., Otitoola, A. A., Oladapo, O. J., Abiona, O. O., Oyeniran, O. C., Adewusi, A. O., Komolafe, A. M., & Obijuru, A. (2024). Reviewing the Transformational Impact of Edge Computing on Real-Time Data Processing and Analytics. *Computer Science & It Research Journal*, *5*(3), 693–702. DOI: 10.51594/csitrj.v5i3.929

Mohsin, M. A., Shahrouzi, S. N., & Perera, D. G. (2024). Composing Efficient Computational Models for Real-Time Processing on Next-Generation Edge-Computing Platforms. *IEEE Access : Practical Innovations, Open Solutions*, *12*, 24905–24932. DOI: 10.1109/ACCESS.2024.3365652

Moore, R. K. (2019). Talking with robots: Opportunities and challenges.

Mubarak, R., Alsboui, T., Alshaikh, O., Inuwa-Dutse, I., Khan, S., & Parkinson, S. (2023). A survey on the detection and impacts of deepfakes in visual, audio, and textual formats. *IEEE Access : Practical Innovations, Open Solutions, 11*, 144497–144529. DOI: 10.1109/ACCESS.2023.3344653

Mukhtar, H. (2025). Artificial intelligence techniques for human-machine interaction. In *Artificial Intelligence and Multimodal Signal Processing in Human-Machine Interaction* (pp. 19–42). Academic Press. DOI: 10.1016/B978-0-443-29150-0.00010-X

Mulfari, D., Carnevale, L., & Villari, M. (2023). Toward a lightweight ASR solution for atypical speech on the edge. Future Generations Computer Systems: FGCS, 149, 455–463. DOI: 10.1016/j.future.2023.08.002

Mustaquim, M. (2013). Use of human speech for inclusive games design.

Mystakidis, S. (2022). *Metaverse*. Encyclopedia., DOI: 10.3390/encyclopedia2010031

Nadworny, B. A. (1988). A user interface management system for voice I/O applications.

Nainan, S., & Kulkarni, V. H. (2024). *Multimodal Speaker Recognition using voice and lip movement with decision and feature level fusion*. DOI: 10.21203/rs.3.rs-2960709/v1

Nass, C., & Brave, S. (2005). *Wired for speech: How voice activates and advances the human-computer relationship*. MIT Press.

Nautsch, A., Jasserand, C., Kindt, E., Todisco, M., Trancoso, I., & Evans, N. (2019). The GDPR & Speech data: Reflections of legal and technology communities, first steps towards a common understanding. *Proceedings of the Annual Conference of the International Speech Communication Association, INTERSPEECH, 2019-Septe*, 3695–3699. DOI: 10.21437/Interspeech.2019-2647

Naviy, L., Sh. Ualikhanov Kokshetau State University Kokshetau Republic of Kazakhstan, Zhussupbekova Gulsara G and Stukalenko, N. M., Zhakhina, B. B., Baimanova, L. S., & Kukubaeva, A. K. (2020). Development of communication and speech skills of students in the process of education. J. Intellect. Disabil. -. *Diagn. Treat.*, *8*(3), 437–442.

Neekhara, P., Hussain, S., Pandey, P., Dubnov, S., McAuley, J., & Koushanfar, F. (2019). Universal adversarial perturbations for speech recognition systems. *arXiv preprint arXiv:1905.03828*. DOI: 10.21437/Interspeech.2019-1353

Neekhara, P. (2019). *Blind Spots of Neural Sequence Models*. University of California.

Nekvinda, T., & Dušek, O. (2020a). *One Model, Many Languages: Meta-Learning for Multilingual Text-to-Speech.* /arxiv.2008.00768DOI: 10.21437/Interspeech.2020-2679

Ngata, W., Bashir, N., Westerlaken, M., Liote, L., Chandio, Y., & Olivetti, E. (2025). *The Cloud Next Door: Investigating the Environmental and Socioeconomic Strain of Datacenters on Local Communities* [Preprint]. arXiv. /arXiv.2506.03367DOI: 10.1145/3715335.3736324

NguyenDuc. H., VuThi, K., NguyenDinhVi, D., Emara, T. Z., & Trinh, T. (2025). A hybrid feature selection paradigm for high-dimensional data. In H. A. Le Thi, H. M. Le, & Q. T. Nguyen (Eds.), *Advances in Data Science and Optimization of Complex Systems* (pp. 239–250). Springer Nature Switzerland. https://doi.org/DOI: 10.1007/978-3-032-00267-9_22

Nguyen, L. M., Nayak, S., & Coler, M. (2023, January). Improving luxembourgish speech recognition with cross-lingual speech representations. *2022 IEEE Spoken Language Technology Workshop (SLT).* DOI: 10.1109/SLT54892.2023.10022706

Ng, Y. L. (2024). Exploring the association between use of conversational artificial intelligence and social capital: Survey evidence from Hong Kong. *New Media & Society*, *26*(3), 1429–1444. Advance online publication. DOI: 10.1177/14614448221074047

Nilep, C. (2006). " Code Switching " in Sociocultural Linguistics. *Colorado Research in Linguistics, 19*(June), 1–22. https://doi.org/DOI: 10.31235/osf.io/jfecn

Norvig, P. (2007). How to write a spelling corrector. http://norvig.com/spell correct .html

OECD. (2022). *Measuring the Environmental Impacts of AI Compute and Applications: The AI Footprint.* OECD Digital Economy Papers. https://www.oecd.org/content/dam/oecd/en/publications/reports/2022/11/measuring-the-environmental-impacts-of-artificial-intelligence-compute-and-applications_3dddded5/7babf571-en.pdf

Oh, C., Kim, C., & Park, K. (2023). Building robust Korean speech recognition model by fine-tuning large pretrained model. *Phon. Speech Sci.*, *15*(3), 75–82. DOI: 10.13064/KSSS.2023.15.3.075

Olaniyan, R., & Maheswaran, M. (2022). A Fast Edge-Based Synchronizer for Tasks in Real-Time Artificial Intelligence Applications. *IEEE Internet of Things Journal*, *9*(5), 3825–3837. DOI: 10.1109/JIOT.2021.3100295

Oluwaniyi, P. S. D., Azuka, D. B. F., Ojo, P. S. G., Dr Festus Sunday Smart Oloda, Jekayinfa, D. J. O., & Okwuosa, D. S. O. (2024). Effect of bilingual instructional method in the academic achievement of Junior Secondary School students in mathematics. Er, 10(2), 27–33.

Ooi, K. B., Tan, G. W. H., Aw, E. C. X., Cham, T. H., Dwivedi, Y. K., Dwivedi, R., Hughes, L., Kar, A. K., Loh, X. M., Mogaji, E., Phau, I., & Sharma, A. (2023). Banking in the metaverse: A new frontier for financial institutions. *International Journal of Bank Marketing*, *41*(7), 1829–1846. DOI: 10.1108/IJBM-03-2023-0168

Orynbay, L., Razakhova, B., Peer, P., Meden, B., & Emeršič, Ž. (2024). Recent advances in synthesis and interaction of speech, text, and vision. *Electronics (Basel)*, *13*(9), 1726. DOI: 10.3390/electronics13091726

Paiva, A., Leite, I., Boukricha, H., & Wachsmuth, I. (2017). Empathy in virtual agents and robots: A survey. [TiiS]. *ACM Transactions on Interactive Intelligent Systems*, *7*(3), 1–40. DOI: 10.1145/2912150

Panda, S. P. (2017). Automated speech recognition system in advancement of human-computer interaction. *Proceedings of the International Conference on Computing Methodologies and Communication, ICCMC 2017, 2018-Janua*, 302–306. DOI: 10.1109/ICCMC.2017.8282696

Pandey, C., Sharma, S., & Bhadula, S. (2024). Artificial Intelligence Technique in Next Generation Healthcare Systems. In *2024 IEEE International Conference on Communication, Computing and Signal Processing (IICCCS)*, 1–6. https://doi.org/ DOI: 10.1109/IICCCS61609.2024.10763570

Parcollet, T., & Ravanelli, M. (2021). The Energy and Carbon Footprint of Training End-to-End Speech Recognizers. *Interspeech*, *2021*, 4583–4587. https://www.isca-archive.org/interspeech_2021/parcollet21_interspeech.pdf. DOI: 10.21437/Interspeech.2021-456

Parcollet, T., Yao, K., Ichikawa, Y., Wang, B., Szymanski, M., Karande, V., & Watanabe, S. (2021). The energy and carbon footprint of training end-to-end speech models. [ISCA.]. *Proceedings of Interspeech*, *2021*, 4353–4357.

Park, S., & Whang, M. (2022). Empathy in human-robot interaction: Designing for social robots. *International Journal of Environmental Research and Public Health*, *19*(3), 1889. DOI: 10.3390/ijerph19031889 PMID: 35162909

Passanante, A., Pertwee, E., Lin, L., Lee, K. Y., Wu, J. T., & Larson, H. J. (2023). Conversational AI and Vaccine Communication: Systematic Review of the Evidence. In *Journal of Medical Internet Research* (Vol. 25, Issue 1). DOI: 10.2196/42758

Patel, T., Huang, H. H., & Lin, D. (2022). Private and scalable voice-based services using federated learning. *Proceedings on Privacy Enhancing Technologies. Privacy Enhancing Technologies Symposium, 2022*(2), 202–222.

Patra, G. K., Kuraku, C., Konkimalla, S., Boddapati, V. N., & Sarisa, M. (2023). *Voice Classification in AI: Harnessing Machine Learning for Enhanced Speech Recognition*. Global Research and Development Journals., DOI: 10.70179/GRD-JEV09I110003

Patterson, D., Gonzalez, J., Le, Q., Liang, C., Munguia, L. M., Rothchild, D., . . . Dean, J. (2021). Carbon emissions and large neural network training. *arXiv preprint arXiv:2104.10350*. https://arxiv.org/abs/2104.10350

Peña-Acuña, B., & Rubio-Alcalá, F. D. (2024). Ethical approach to the use of immersive technologies. Advance about digitalisation of multilingual programs in the EHEA. *Frontiers in Virtual Reality*, •••, 5.

Peng, J., Wang, Y., Li, B., Guo, Y., Wang, H., Fang, Y., & Yu, K. (2025). A survey on Speech Large Language Models for understanding. Retrieved from https://arxiv .org/abs/2410.18908 DOI: 10.36227/techrxiv.175321809.95815200/v1

Pérez-Rosas, V., Min, D. J., & Mihalcea, R. (2021). Evaluating automatic speech recognition quality and its impact on counselor utterance coding. In *Proceedings of the Seventh Workshop on Computational Linguistics and Clinical Psychology (CLPsych).*

Pfeiffer, J., Piccinno, F., Nicosia Massimo and Wang, X., Reid, M., & Ruder, S. (2023). MmT5: Modular multilingual pre-training solves source language hallucinations. Findings of the Association for Computational Linguistics: EMNLP 2023, 1978–2008.

Pham, N.-Q., Nguyen, T. N., Ha, T.-L., Stüker, S., Waibel, A., & He, D. (2021). Multilingual Speech Translation KIT @ IWSLT2021. *Proceedings of the 18th International Conference on Spoken Translation (IWSLT 2021).*

Pimentel, A., Guimarães, H., Avila, A. R., Rezagholizadeh, M., & Falk, T. H. (2023). *On the impact of quantization and pruning of self-supervised speech models for downstream speech recognition tasks "in-the-Wild"*. arXiv. https://arxiv.org/abs/ 2309.14462

Polkosky, M. D. (2005). *Toward a social-cognitive psychology of speech technology: Affective responses to speech-based e-service* (Doctoral dissertation, University of South Florida).

Ponnusamy, P., Ghias, A. R., Yi, Y., Yao, B., Guo, C., & Sarikaya, R. (2021). Feedback-based self-learning in large-scale conversational AI agents. *AI Magazine*, *42*(4), 43–56. Advance online publication. DOI: 10.1609/aaai.12025

Pradhan, S., Sun, W., Baig, G., & Qiu, L. (2019). Combating replay attacks against voice assistants. *Proceedings of the ACM on Interactive, Mobile, Wearable and Ubiquitous Technologies*, *3*(3), 1–26. DOI: 10.1145/3351258

Prakash, A., Leela Thomas, A., Umesh, S., & Murthy, A. (2019a). *H.* Building Multilingual End-to-End Speech Synthesisers for Indian Languages., DOI: 10.21437/SSW.2019-35

Preston, S. D., & De Waal, F. B. M. (2002). Empathy: Its ultimate and proximate bases. *Behavioral and Brain Sciences*, *25*(1), 1–20. DOI: 10.1017/S0140525X02000018 PMID: 12625087

Qawaqneh, Z., Mallouh, A. A., & Barkana, B. D. (2017). Deep neural network framework and transformed MFCCs for speaker's age and gender classification. *Knowledge-Based Systems*, *115*, 5–14. DOI: 10.1016/j.knosys.2016.10.008

Qian, J., Du, H., Hou, J., Chen, L., Jung, T., & Li, X. Y. (2018). Hidebehind: Enjoy voice input with voiceprint unclonability and anonymity. *SenSys 2018 - Proceedings of the 16th Conference on Embedded Networked Sensor Systems*, 82–94. DOI: 10.1145/3274783.3274855

Quinto, S. (2025). Exploring the e-waste crisis: Strategies for sustainable management. *Sustainability*, *10*(2), 72. DOI: 10.3390/su10020072

R, M. K. S., Pitale, O., & Malapati, A. (2023). Leveraging Multi-Task Learning in Code-Switched Setting. Research Square. DOI: 10.21203/rs.3.rs-3328574/v1

Raaijmakers, S., Cremers, A., Krahmer, E., & Westera, M. (2023). Editorial: Conversational AI. In *Frontiers in Artificial Intelligence* (Vol. 6). DOI: 10.3389/frai.2023.1203910

Rabiner, L. R. (1989). A tutorial on hidden Markov models and selected applications in speech recognition. *Proceedings of the IEEE*, *77*(2), 257–286. DOI: 10.1109/5.18626

Rao, M., Raju, A., Dheram, P., Bui, B., & Rastrow, A. (2020). Speech to semantics: Improve ASR and NLU jointly via all-neural interfaces. *arXiv preprint arXiv:2008.06173*. /arXiv.2008.06173DOI: 10.21437/Interspeech.2020-2976

Rawat, R., Goyal, H. R., & Sharma, S. (2024). Hofstede's Cultural Dimension Driven Artificial Narrow Intelligence IDFIS for Industry 5.0 Empowered Digital Society. *Recent Patents on Engineering*, *19*. Advance online publication. DOI: 10.2174/0118722121334543241001050846

Ray, P. P. (2023). Benchmarking, ethical alignment, and evaluation framework for conversational AI: Advancing responsible development of ChatGPT. *BenchCouncil Transactions on Benchmarks. Standards and Evaluations*, *3*(3), 100136. Advance online publication. DOI: 10.1016/j.tbench.2023.100136

Rich, M. S. (2023). Cyberpsychology: A longitudinal analysis of cyber adversarial tactics and techniques. *Analytics*, *2*(3), 618–655. DOI: 10.3390/analytics2030035

Roper, A., Wilson, S., Neate, T., & Marshall, J. (2019). Speech and language.

Ruder, S., Vulić, I., & Søgaard, A. (2019). A survey of cross-lingual word embedding models. *Journal of Artificial Intelligence Research*, *65*, 569–631. DOI: 10.1613/jair.1.11640

Saber, A., Sakr, M., Abo-Seida, O. M., & Keshk, A. (2021b). Automated breast cancer detection and classification techniques–a survey. In *2021 International Mobile, Intelligent, and Ubiquitous Computing Conference (MIUCC)* (pp. 200-207). IEEE. DOI: 10.1109/MIUCC52538.2021.9447655

Saber, A., Al-Zoghby, A. M., & Elmougy, S. (2018). Big-data aggregating, linking, integrating and representing using semantic web technologies. In Hassanien, A. E., Bhatnagar, R., & Taha, A. (Eds.), *International Conference on Advanced Machine Learning Technologies and Applications* (pp. 331–342). Cham: Springer International Publishing. DOI: 10.1007/978-3-319-74690-6_33

Saber, A., Emara, T., Elbedwehy, S., & Hassan, E. (2025a). A novel approach for breast cancer detection using a Nesterov accelerated adam optimizer with an attention mechanism. *Scientific Reports*, *15*(1), 27065. DOI: 10.1038/s41598-025-12070-y PMID: 40715330

Saber, A., Hassan, E., Elbedwehy, S., Awad, W. A., & Emara, T. Z. (2025b). Leveraging ensemble convolutional neural networks and metaheuristic strategies for advanced kidney disease screening and classification. *Scientific Reports*, *15*(1), 12487. DOI: 10.1038/s41598-025-93950-1 PMID: 40216822

Saber, A., Hussien, A. G., Awad, W. A., Mahmoud, A., & Allakany, A. (2023). Adapting the pre-trained convolutional neural networks to improve the anomaly detection and classification in mammographic images. *Scientific Reports*, *13*(1), 14877. DOI: 10.1038/s41598-023-41633-0 PMID: 37689757

Saber, A., Sakr, M., Abo-Seida, O. M., & Keshk, A. (2021). *Automated breast cancer detection and classification techniques–a survey. In 2021 International Mobile, Intelligent, and Ubiquitous Computing Conference (MIUCC).* IEEE., DOI: 10.1109/MIUCC52538.2021.9562725

Saber, A., Sakr, M., Abou-Seida, O., & Keshk, A. (2021a). A novel transfer-learning model for automatic detection and classification of breast cancer based deep CNN. *Kafrelsheikh Journal of Information Sciences*, *2*(1), 1–9. DOI: 10.21608/kjis.2021.192207

Saka, A. B., Oyedele, L. O., Akanbi, L. A., Ganiyu, S. A., Chan, D. W. M., & Bello, S. A. (2023). Conversational artificial intelligence in the AEC industry: A review of present status, challenges and opportunities. In *Advanced Engineering Informatics* (Vol. 55). DOI: 10.1016/j.aei.2022.101869

Sakr, M., Saber, A. M., Abo-Seida, O., & Keshk, A. (2020). Machine learning for breast cancer classification using k-star algorithm. *Applied Mathematics & Information Sciences*, *14*(5), 855–863. DOI: 10.18576/amis/140513

Sánchez-Mompó, A., Mavromatis, I., Li, P., Katsaros, K., & Khan, A. (2025). Green MLOps to Green GenOps: An Empirical Study of Energy Consumption in Discriminative and Generative AI Operations. *Information (Basel)*, *16*(4), 281. DOI: 10.3390/info16040281

Sanguinetti, M., & Atzori, M. (2024). Conversational agents for energy awareness and efficiency: A survey. *Electronics (Basel)*, *13*(2), 401. DOI: 10.3390/electronics13020401

Sanh, V., Debut, L., Chaumond, J., & Wolf, T. (2019). DistilBERT, a distilled version of BERT: Smaller, faster, cheaper and lighter. *ArXiv*. https://arxiv.org/abs/1910.01108

Sarker, A. (2017). Contextual sentiment analysis in social media text. *Information Processing & Management*, *53*(1), 227–239. DOI: 10.1016/j.ipm.2016.07.003

Satyasree, E., & al, . (2023). Edge AI for Real-Time Video Analytics in Surveillance Systems. *International Journal on Recent and Innovation Trends in Computing and Communication*, *11*(10), 2269–2275. DOI: 10.17762/ijritcc.v11i10.8947

Schneider, I., Xu, H., Benecke, S., Patterson, D., Huang, K., Ranganathan, P., & Elsworth, C. (2025). Life-Cycle Emissions of AI Hardware: A Cradle-to-Grave Approach and Generational Trends. arXiv. https://arxiv.org/abs/2502.01671

Schwartz, R., Dodge, J., Smith, N. A., & Etzioni, O. (2020). Green AI. *Communications of the ACM*, *63*(12), 54–63. DOI: 10.1145/3381831

Science and Technology for Energy Transition Review (STET). (2024). *Energy and carbon-aware distributed machine learning tasks scheduling scheme for the multi-renewable energy-based edge-cloud continuum.* https://www.stet-review.org/articles/stet/abs/2024/01/stet20240197/stet20240197.html

Sears, A., & Young, M. (2003). Physical disabilities and computing technologies: An analysis of impairments. In Sears, A., & Jacko, J. A. (Eds.), *The human-computer interaction handbook* (pp. 482–503). L. Erlbaum Associates.

Seki, H., Hori, T., Watanabe, S., Le Roux, J., & Hershey, J. R. (2019). End-to-end multilingual multi-speaker speech recognition. *Proceedings of the Annual Conference of the International Speech Communication Association, INTERSPEECH, 2019-Septe*, 3755–3759. DOI: 10.21437/Interspeech.2019-3038

Selvarani, P., Kamalanaban, E., Azarudeen, H. M., Kumar, M. M., & Kavibharathi, K. (2025). Textual interaction framework for assistive computing. In CRC Press eBooks (pp. 598–604). https://doi.org/DOI: 10.1201/9781003559139-89

Seminck, O. (2023). Conversational AI: Dialogue Systems, Conversational Agents, and Chatbots by Michael McTear. *Computational Linguistics*, *49*(1), 257–259. Advance online publication. DOI: 10.1162/coli_r_00470

Shafik, W. (2023). Introduction to ChatGPT. In *Advanced Applications of Generative AI and Natural Language Processing Models*. DOI: 10.4018/979-8-3693-0502-7.ch001

Shafik, W. (2024). Artificial Intelligence and Internet of Things Roles in Sustainable Next-Generation Manufacturing. In *Sustainable Innovation for Industry 6.0* (pp. 207–239). IGI Global., DOI: 10.4018/979-8-3693-3140-8.ch012

Shanthamallappa, M., Puttegowda, K., Hullahalli Nannappa, N. K., & Vasudeva Rao, S. K. (2024). Robust automatic speech recognition using wavelet-based adaptive wavelet thresholding: A review. *SN Computer Science*, *5*(2), 248. DOI: 10.1007/s42979-023-02491-9

Sharma, M., & Sarma, K. K. (2015). Soft-Computational Techniques and Spectro-Temporal Features for Telephonic Speech Recognition. In *IGI Global* (pp. 161–189). DOI: 10.4018/978-1-4666-9474-3.ch006

Sharma, S., Gautam, A., & Tyagi, R. (2024). Artificial Intelligence and Cyber Security Driven Social Innovations in Digital Adventure Tourism. In 2024 First International Conference on Pioneering Developments in Computer Science & Digital Technologies (IC2SDT), 1–6. https://doi.org/DOI: 10.1109/IC2SDT62152.2024.10696759

Sharma, S., Tomar, M., & Tyagi, R. (2024). Federated learning enabled secure air transport and tourism system. 2022 13th International Conference on Computing Communication and Networking Technologies (ICCCNT), 1–6. https://doi.org/DOI: 10.1109/ICCCNT61001.2024.10724849

Sharma, S., Tyagi, R., & Mohan, S. (2024). Generative Artificial Intelligence-Enabled climate change and Deep-Sea food webs. In Advances in environmental engineering and green technologies book series (pp. 199–224). https://doi.org/DOI: 10.4018/979-8-3693-6670-7.ch009

Sharma, S., Tyagi, R., & Mohan, S. (2025). Artificial intelligence and optimized computational modelling against climate crisis. In Elsevier eBooks (pp. 1–14). https://doi.org/DOI: 10.1016/B978-0-443-21905-4.00006-7

Sharma, R., Anil, K., & Kumar, V. (2021). A hybrid sentiment analysis model for social media text. *Social Network Analysis and Mining*, *11*(1), 56–66. DOI: 10.1007/s13278-021-00731-1

Singh, S., & Beniwal, H. (2022). A survey on near-human conversational agents. In *Journal of King Saud University - Computer and Information Sciences* (Vol. 34, Issue 10). DOI: 10.1016/j.jksuci.2021.10.013

Singhal, A., & Sharma, D. K. (2023a). Precision value, error rate and accuracy of human gender identification based on randomized voice signals datasets. *International Journal of Intelligent Engineering and Systems*, *16*(4), 348–361. DOI: 10.22266/ijies2023.0831.28

Singhal, A., & Sharma, D. K. (2023b). *Low resource language analysis using deep learning algorithm for gender classification.* ACM Transactions on Asian and Low-Resource Language Information Processing., DOI: 10.1145/3614427

Singhal, A., & Sharma, D. K. (2024). Comprehensive analysis of gender classification accuracy across varied geographic regions through the application of deep learning algorithms to speech signals. *Computer Systems Science and Engineering*, *48*(3), 609–625. DOI: 10.32604/csse.2023.046730

Singh, R. P., Dash, R., & Mohapatra, R. K. (2026). Unveiling explainability in face anti-spoofing: Hybrid feature extraction with XAI-guided feature aggregation. *Pattern Recognition*, *169*, 111905. DOI: 10.1016/j.patcog.2025.111905

Siriwardhana, S., Weerasekera, R., Wen, E., Kaluarachchi, T., Rana, R., & Nanayakkara, S. (2023). Improving the Domain Adaptation of Retrieval Augmented Generation (RAG) Models for Open Domain Question Answering. *Transactions of the Association for Computational Linguistics*, *11*, 1–17. DOI: 10.1162/tacl_a_00530

Skjuve, M., Brandtzaeg, P. B., & Følstad, A. (2024). Why do people use ChatGPT? Exploring user motivations for generative conversational AI. *First Monday*, *29*(1). Advance online publication. DOI: 10.5210/fm.v29i1.13541

So, C., Khvan, A., & Choi, W. (2023). Natural conversations with a virtual being: How user experience with a current conversational AI model compares to expectations. *Computer Animation and Virtual Worlds*, *34*(6), e2149. Advance online publication. DOI: 10.1002/cav.2149

Son, G., Kwon, S., & Park, N. (2019). Gender classification based on the non-lexical cues of emergency calls with recurrent neural networks (RNN). *Symmetry*, *11*(4), 525. DOI: 10.3390/sym11040525

Sonie, O., Chakraborty, A., & Mullick, A. (2022). concept2code: Deep Reinforcement Learning for Conversational AI. *Proceedings of the ACM SIGKDD International Conference on Knowledge Discovery and Data Mining*. DOI: 10.1145/3534678.3542635

Steichen, B., & Freund, L. (2015, April). Supporting the modern polyglot. *Proceedings of the 33rd Annual ACM Conference on Human in Computing Systems*.

Strubell, E., Ganesh, A., & McCallum, A. (2019). Energy and policy considerations for deep learning in NLP. In *Proceedings of ACL 2019* (pp. 3645–3650). https://doi.org/DOI: 10.18653/v1/P19-1355

Sudarshan, B. (2018). High Protection Voice Identification based Bank Locker Security System with Live Image Authentication. *International Journal for Research in Applied Science and Engineering Technology*, *6*(6), 401–406. DOI: 10.22214/ijraset.2018.6062

Suh, S., & An, P. (2022). Leveraging Generative Conversational AI to Develop a Creative Learning Environment for Computational Thinking. *International Conference on Intelligent User Interfaces, Proceedings IUI*. DOI: 10.1145/3490100.3516473

Sumon, R. I., Uddin, S. M. I., Akter, S., Mozumder, M. A. I., Khan, M. O., & Kim, H. C. (2024). Natural Language Processing Influence on Digital Socialization and Linguistic Interactions in the Integration of the Metaverse in Regular Social Life. *Electronics (Basel)*, *13*(7), 1331. Advance online publication. DOI: 10.3390/electronics13071331

Sun, L., Wang, Z., Jiang, J., Kim, Y., Joo, B., Zheng, S., Lee, S., Yu, W. J., Kong, B. S., & Yang, H. (2021). In-sensor reservoir computing for language learning via two-dimensional memristors. *Science Advances*, *7*(20), eabg1455. Advance online publication. DOI: 10.1126/sciadv.abg1455 PMID: 33990331

Surendran, A., Murali, R., & Babu, R. K. R. (2020). Conversational AI - A Retrieval Based Chatbot Conversational AI. *EasyChair Preprint, 4020*.

Suresh Babu, C. V., & Akshara, P. M. (2024). Revolutionizing Conversational AI: Unleashing the Power of ChatGPT-Based Applications in Generative AI and Natural Language Processing. In A. Obaid, B. Bhushan, M. S., & S. Rajest (Eds.), Advanced Applications of Generative AI and Natural Language Processing Models (pp. 228-248). IGI Global. DOI: 10.4018/979-8-3693-0502-7.ch011

Suresh Babu, C. V., & Suruthi, G. (2024). Unravelling the Evolution of Generative AI in Communication Education: A Historical Journey Into Human-Machine Communication. In Elmoudden, S., & Wrench, J. (Eds.), *The Role of Generative AI in the Communication Classroom* (pp. 55–71). IGI Global., DOI: 10.4018/979-8-3693-0831-8.ch003

Suresh, H., & Guttag, J. (2019). A framework for understanding unintended consequences of machine learning. *Big Data*, *7*(2), 59–79. DOI: 10.1089/big.2016.0150

Suresh, H., & Guttag, J. V. (2019). *A Framework for Understanding Sources of Harm throughout the Machine Learning Life Cycle*. ArXiv., DOI: 10.1145/3465416.3483305

Swanger, D. (1993). The arts, empathy, and Aristotle. *Journal of Aesthetic Education*, *27*(1), 41–49. DOI: 10.2307/3333340

Taha, T. M., Messaoud, Z. B., & Frikha, M. (2024). Convolutional neural network architectures for gender, emotional detection from speech and speaker diarization. *International Journal of Interactive Mobile Technologies*, *18*(03), 88–103. DOI: 10.3991/ijim.v18i03.43013

Tahir, S., Shah, S. A., & Abu Khalaf, J. (2023). Artificial Empathy Classification: A survey of deep learning techniques, datasets, and evaluation scales. arXiv.

Talaei Khoei, T., Ould Slimane, H., & Kaabouch, N. (2023). Deep learning: Systematic review, models, challenges, and research directions. *Neural Computing & Applications*, *35*(31), 23103–23124. DOI: 10.1007/s00521-023-08957-4

Tamrakar, S. R., & Silpasuwanchai, C. (2022). Comparative evaluation of transformer-based Nepali language models. In *Research Square*. DOI: 10.21203/rs.3.rs-2289743/v1

Tan, X., Qin, T., Soong, F., & Liu, T.-Y. (2021). A survey on neural speech synthesis. *arXiv preprint arXiv:2106.15561*. https://doi.org//arXiv.2106.15561DOI: 10.48550

Tan, H., Wang, L., Zhang, H., Zhang, J., Shafiq, M., & Gu, Z. (2022). Adversarial attack and defense strategies of speaker recognition systems: A survey. *Electronics (Basel), 11*(14), 2183. DOI: 10.3390/electronics11142183

Tan, S., & Joty, S. (2021). Code-mixing on sesame street: Dawn of the adversarial polyglots. *Proceedings of the 2021 Conference of the North American of the Association for Computational Linguistics: Human Technologies.*

Tao, R., Das, R. K., & Li, H. (2020). Audio-visual speaker recognition with a cross-modal discriminative network. *Proceedings of the Annual Conference of the International Speech Communication Association, INTERSPEECH, 2020-Octob*, 2242–2246. DOI: 10.21437/Interspeech.2020-1814

Tay, Y., Dehghani, M., Bahri, D., & Metzler, D. (2020). Efficient Transformers: A Survey. *ArXiv*. https://arxiv.org/abs/2009.06732

Teehan, P., & Kandlikar, M. (2013). Comparing embodied greenhouse gas emissions of modern computing and electronics products. *Environmental Science & Technology, 47*(9), 3997–4003. DOI: 10.1021/es303012r PMID: 23458212

Thieme, A. H., Zheng, Y., Machiraju, G., Sadee, C., Mittermaier, M., Gertler, M., Salinas, J. L., Srinivasan, K., Gyawali, P., Carrillo-Perez, F., Capodici, A., Uhlig, M., Habenicht, D., Löser, A., Kohler, M., Schuessler, M., Kaul, D., Gollrad, J., Ma, J., & Gevaert, O. (2023). A deep-learning algorithm to classify skin lesions from mpox virus infection. *Nature Medicine, 29*(3), 738–747. DOI: 10.1038/s41591-023-02225-7 PMID: 36864252

Thomas, J., Arya, L., Hussain, M., & Prasanna, S. R. M. (2023). Speech Act Theory and Ethics of Speech Processing as Distinct Stages: the ethics of collecting, contextualizing and the releasing of (speech) data. *2023 IEEE International Symposium on Ethics in Engineering, Science, and Technology (ETHICS)*, 1–10. DOI: 10.1109/ETHICS57328.2023.10154932

Tian, J., Li, Y., Chen, W., Xiao, L., He, H., & Jin, Y. (2021). Diagnosing the First-Order Logical Reasoning Ability through LogicNLI. *EMNLP 2021 - 2021 Conference on Empirical Methods in Natural Language Processing, Proceedings*, 3738–3747. DOI: 10.18653/v1/2021.emnlp-main.303

Todericiu, I. A. (2025). Virtual Assistants: A Review of the Next Frontier in AI Interaction. Acta Universitatis Sapientiae. *Informatica (Vilnius), 17*(1), 1–13. DOI: 10.2478/ausi-2025-0001

Tomashenko, N., Srivastava, B. M. L., Wang, X., Vincent, E., Nautsch, A., Yamagishi, J., Evans, N., Patino, J., Bonastre, J. F., Noé, P. G., & Todisco, M. (2020). Introducing the VoicePrivacy initiative. *Proceedings of the Annual Conference of the International Speech Communication Association, INTERSPEECH, 2020-Octob*, 1693–1697. DOI: 10.21437/Interspeech.2020-1333

Tran, M., & Soleymani, M. (2023). A Speech Representation Anonymization Framework via Selective Noise Perturbation. *ICASSP, IEEE International Conference on Acoustics, Speech and Signal Processing - Proceedings, 2023-June*. DOI: 10.1109/ICASSP49357.2023.10095173

TrinhHuy., T., Trinh, T., NguyenViet, H., Emara, T. Z., & VuongThi, N. (2025). Event scale prediction in event-based social networks. 11th EAI International Conference on Industrial Networks and Intelligent Systems, Da Nang, Vietnam.

TrinhHuy., T., Trinh, T., NguyenViet, H., Emara, T. Z., & VuongThi, N. (2025). Event scale prediction in event-based social networks. In *11th EAI International Conference on Industrial Networks and Intelligent Systems*, Da Nang, Vietnam.

Trinh, T., Duc, L. P., Tran, C. T., Duy, T. T., & Emara, T. Z. (2022). A New Stratified Block Model to Process Large-Scale Data for a Small Cluster. In *Lecture Notes on Data Engineering and Communications Technologies* (Vol. 124, pp. 253–263). Springer Science and Business Media Deutschland GmbH., DOI: 10.1007/978-3-030-97610-1_21

Trinh, T., Nguyen, N., Wu, D., Huang, J. Z., & Emara, T. Z. (2019). A New Location-Based Topic Model for Event Attendees Recommendation. In *2019 IEEE-RIVF International Conference on Computing and Communication Technologies (RIVF)* (pp. 106–111). DOI: 10.1109/RIVF.2019.8713716

Tschopp, M., Gieselmann, M., & Sassenberg, K. (2023). Servant by Default? How Humans Perceive Their Relationship With Conversational AI. *Cyberpsychology (Brno)*, *17*(3). Advance online publication. DOI: 10.5817/CP2023-3-9

Tsur, O., & Rappoport, A. (2010). Don't let me be misunderstood: Misinterpretation of emoticon structure in sentiment analysis. In *Proceedings of the Fourth International Conference on Weblogs and Social Media* (pp. 396–399).

Tukur, M., Schneider, J., Househ, M., Dokoro, A. H., Ismail, U. I., Dawaki, M., & Agus, M. (2023). The metaverse digital environments: A scoping review of the challenges, privacy and security issues. *Frontiers in Big Data*, *6*, 1301812. Advance online publication. DOI: 10.3389/fdata.2023.1301812 PMID: 38074486

Turcian, D., & Stoicu-Tivadar, V. (2024). Speech Emotion Recognition Using openSMILE and GPT 3.5 Transformer. *Studies in Health Technology and Informatics*, *316*, 924–928. DOI: 10.3233/SHTI240562 PMID: 39176943

Tursunov, A., Mustaqeem, , Choeh, J. Y., & Kwon, S. (2021). Age and gender recognition using a convolutional neural network with a specially designed multi-attention module through speech spectrograms. *Sensors (Basel)*, *21*(17), 5892. DOI: 10.3390/s21175892 PMID: 34502785

Uddin, M. A., Pathan, R. K., Hossain, M. S., & Biswas, M. (2021). Gender and region detection from human voice using the three-layer feature extraction method with 1D CNN. *Journal of Information and Telecommunication*, *6*(1), 27–42. DOI: 10.1080/24751839.2021.1983318

Ullah, R., Asif, M., Shah, W. A., Anjam, F., Ullah, I., Khurshaid, T., Wuttisittikulkij, L., Shah, S., Ali, S. M., & Alibakhshikenari, M. (2023). Speech Emotion Recognition Using Convolution Neural Networks and Multi-Head Convolutional Transformer. *Sensors (Basel)*, *23*(13), 6212. Advance online publication. DOI: 10.3390/s23136212 PMID: 37448062

Vaghefi, S. A., Stammbach, D., Muccione, V., Bingler, J., Ni, J., Kraus, M., Allen, S., Colesanti-Senni, C., Wekhof, T., Schimanski, T., Gostlow, G., Yu, T., Wang, Q., Webersinke, N., Huggel, C., & Leippold, M. (2023). ChatClimate: Grounding conversational AI in climate science. *Communications Earth & Environment*, *4*(1), 480. Advance online publication. DOI: 10.1038/s43247-023-01084-x

Valliappan, I., Kaipa, R., & Karuppali, S. (2023). Exploring the attitudes and practices among student clinicians in India on multilingual issues in the field of speech-language pathology. *CoDAS*, *35*(6), e20220249. DOI: 10.1590/2317-1782/20232022249en PMID: 37672414

Van Pinxteren, M. M. E., Pluymaekers, M., Lemmink, J., & Krispin, A. (2023). Effects of communication style on relational outcomes in interactions between customers and embodied conversational agents. *Psychology and Marketing*, *40*(5), 938–953. DOI: 10.1002/mar.21792

Varitimiadis, S., Kotis, K., Pittou, D., & Konstantakis, G. (2021). Graph-based conversational ai: Towards a distributed and collaborative multi-chatbot approach for museums. In *Applied Sciences (Switzerland)* (Vol. 11, Issue 19). DOI: 10.3390/app11199160

Veesa, S., & Singh, M. (2025). Deep learning countermeasures for detecting replay speech attacks: A review. *International Journal of Speech Technology*, *28*(1), 39–51. DOI: 10.1007/s10772-024-10163-z

Vilares, D., Gómez-Rodr\'\iguez, C., & Alonso, M. A. (2016). One model, two languages: training bilingual parsers with harmonized treebanks. Proceedings of the 54th Annual Meeting of the Association for Computational Linguistics (Volume 2: Short Papers). DOI: 10.18653/v1/P16-2069

Villalba, J., & Lleida, E. (2011, October). Preventing replay attacks on speaker verification systems. In *2011 Carnahan Conference on Security Technology* (pp. 1-8). IEEE. DOI: 10.1109/CCST.2011.6095943

VuThi., K., VuongThi, N., NguyenXuan, H., Emara, T. Z., & Trinh, T. (2024). Feature Selection Based on Top Frequency. In M. and N. L. A. and L. K. Y. Nguyen Thi Dieu Linh and Dawson (Eds.), Proceedings of the International Conference on Intelligent Systems and Networks (pp. 58–65). Springer Nature Singapore. https://doi.org/DOI: 10.1007/978-981-97-5504-2_7

Wahde, M., & Virgolin, M. (2023). DAISY: An Implementation of Five Core Principles for Transparent and Accountable Conversational AI. *International Journal of Human-Computer Interaction*, *39*(9), 1856–1873. Advance online publication. DOI: 10.1080/10447318.2022.2081762

Waller, A. (1989). Implementing linguistic text anticipation in a writing device for the disabled.

Wallis, P. (2021). Introducing the Talk Markup Language (TalkML): Adding a little social intelligence to industrial speech interfaces.

Wang, Y., Shafik, W., Seong, J. T., Al Mutairi, A., SidAhmed Mustafa, M., & Mouhamed, M. R. (2023). Service delay and optimization of the energy efficiency of a system in fog-enabled smart cities. *Alexandria Engineering Journal*, *84*, 112–125. Advance online publication. DOI: 10.1016/j.aej.2023.10.034

Wei, C., Salloum, S., Emara, T. Z., Zhang, X., Huang, J. Z., & He, Y. (2018). A Two-Stage Data Processing Algorithm to Generate Random Sample Partitions for Big Data Analysis. In Luo, M., & Zhang, L.-J. (Eds.), *Cloud Computing—CLOUD 2018* (Vol. 10967, pp. 347–364). Springer International Publishing., DOI: 10.1007/978-3-319-94295-7_24

Weng, F., & Lee, H. (2016). Robust spoken language understanding: Using alignment and correction models. *IEEE/ACM Transactions on Audio, Speech, and Language Processing*, *24*(12), 2115–2126. DOI: 10.1109/TASLP.2016.2608500

Wijonarko, P., & Zahra, A. (2022). Spoken language identification on 4 Indonesian local languages using deep learning. *Bulletin of Electrical Engineering and Informatics*, *11*(6), 3288–3293. DOI: 10.11591/eei.v11i6.4166

Williams, J., Fong, J., Cooper, E., & Yamagishi, J. (2021a). *Exploring Disentanglement with Multilingual and Monolingual VQ-VAE*. 124–129. DOI: 10.21437/SSW.2021-22

Wolf, T., Debut, L., Sanh, V., Chaumond, J., Delangue, C., Moi, A., Cistac, P., Rault, T., Louf, R., Funtowicz, M., Davison, J., Shleifer, S., Von Platen, P., Ma, C., Jernite, Y., Plu, J., Xu, C., Le Scao, T., Gugger, S., . . . Rush, A. M. (2020). Transformers: State-of-the-Art Natural Language Processing. *EMNLP 2020 - Conference on Empirical Methods in Natural Language Processing, Proceedings of Systems Demonstrations*, 38–45. DOI: 10.18653/v1/2020.emnlp-demos.6

Woolf, B. P. (2010). *Building intelligent interactive tutors: Student-centered strategies for revolutionizing e-learning*. Morgan Kaufmann.

World Health Organization. (2024, October 1). *Electronic waste (e-waste)*. WHO. https://www.who.int/news-room/fact-sheets/detail/electronic-waste-%28e-waste%29

Woubie, A., & Bäckström, T. (2021a).. . *Federated Learning for Privacy Preserving On-Device Speaker Recognition, 1–5*, 1–5. Advance online publication. DOI: 10.21437/SPSC.2021-1

Wu, C. S., Hoi, S., Socher, R., & Xiong, C. (2020). TOD-BERT: Pre-trained natural language understanding for task-oriented dialogue. *EMNLP 2020 - 2020 Conference on Empirical Methods in Natural Language Processing, Proceedings of the Conference*, 917–929. DOI: 10.18653/v1/2020.emnlp-main.66

Wu, P., Liang, P. P., Shi, J., Salakhutdinov, R., Watanabe, S., & Morency, L. P. (2021). Understanding the Tradeoffs in Client-side Privacy for Downstream Speech Tasks. *2021 Asia-Pacific Signal and Information Processing Association Annual Summit and Conference, APSIPA ASC 2021 - Proceedings*, 841–848. DOI: 10.48550/arxiv.2101.08919

Wu, G., Boriboonsomsin, K., & Barth, M. J. (2020, August 21). Eco-Routing Navigation System for Electric Vehicles [Preprint]. arXiv. https://arxiv.org/abs/2008.09674

Wu, J.-Y., Yu, C., Fu, S.-W., Liu, C.-T., Chien, S.-Y., & Tsao, Y. (2019). *Increasing compactness of deep learning based speech enhancement models with parameter pruning and quantization techniques*. arXiv. https://arxiv.org/abs/1906.01078

Wu, S. (2024). Speech Recognition Interaction Control Method for Smart Home Based on Natural Language Processing. *International Journal of Product Development, 28*(4), 10067949. Advance online publication. DOI: 10.1504/IJPD.2024.10067949

Wu, T. W., Su, R., & Juang, B. H. (2021). A context-aware hierarchical BERT fusion network for multi-turn dialog act detection. *Proceedings of the Annual Conference of the International Speech Communication Association. Interspeech, 5*, 3891–3895. DOI: 10.21437/Interspeech.2021-95

Yang, R., Li, L., Gan, W., Chen, Z., & Qi, Z. (2023). The Human-Centric Metaverse: A Survey. *ACM Web Conference 2023 - Companion of the World Wide Web Conference, WWW 2023*, 1296–1306. DOI: 10.1145/3543873.3587593

Yang, Y., & Bao, W. (2023). Application of Human-Computer Interaction Technology in remote language learning platform. *International Journal of Human-Computer Interaction*, •••, 1–11. DOI: 10.1080/10447318.2023.2194709

Yao, J., Wang, Q., Lei, Y., Guo, P., Xie, L., Wang, N., & Liu, J. (2022). Distinguishable Speaker Anonymization Based on Formant and Fundamental Frequency Scaling. *ArXiv, 2023-June*. DOI: 10.1109/ICASSP49357.2023.10095120

Yao, Y., Liang, T., Feng, R., Shi, K., Yu, J., Wang, W., & Li, J. (2024). SR-TTS: A rhyme-based end-to-end speech synthesis system. *Frontiers in Neurorobotics*, *18*, 1322312. Advance online publication. DOI: 10.3389/fnbot.2024.1322312 PMID: 38476267

Yasmin, G., Das, A. K., Nayak, J., Vimal, S., & Dutta, S. (2022b). Retracted Article: A rough set theory and deep learning-based predictive system for gender recognition using audio speech. *Soft Computing*, *28*(S2, Suppl 2), 453. DOI: 10.1007/s00500-022-07074-z

Ye, F., & Yang, J. (2021). A deep neural network model for speaker identification. *Applied Sciences (Basel, Switzerland)*, *11*(8), 3603. DOI: 10.3390/app11083603

Ye, Z., Gao, W., Hu, Q., Sun, P., Wang, X., Luo, Y., Zhang, T., & Wen, Y. (2024). Deep learning workload scheduling in gpu datacenters: A survey. *ACM Computing Surveys*, *56*(6), 1–38. DOI: 10.1145/3638757

Yousefpour, A., Fung, C., Nguyen, T., Kadiyala, K., Jalali, F., Niakanlahiji, A., Kong, J., & Jue, J. P. (2019). All one needs to know about fog computing and related edge computing paradigms: A complete survey. *Journal of Systems Architecture*, *98*, 289–330. DOI: 10.1016/j.sysarc.2019.02.009

Yuan, F., Yin, J., Yu, W., Liu, Y., Guo, C., & Wu, J. (2021). ASR error correction for improving spoken language understanding with contextual information. In *ICASSP 2021 – 2021 IEEE International Conference on Acoustics, Speech and Signal Processing* (pp. 7363–7367). IEEE. https://doi.org/DOI: 10.1109/ICASSP39728.2021.9414309

Yuan, X., Chen, Y., Zhao, Y., Long, Y., Liu, X., Chen, K., . . . Gunter, C. A. (2018). {CommanderSong}: A systematic approach for practical adversarial voice recognition. In *27th USENIX security symposium (USENIX security 18)* (pp. 49-64).

Yusnita, M. A., Hafiz, A. M., Fadzilah, M. N., Zulhanip, A. Z., & Idris, M. (2017). Automatic gender recognition using linear prediction coefficients and artificial neural network on speech signal. *7th IEEE International Conference on Control System, Computing and Engineering*, 372–377. https://doi.org/DOI: 10.1109/ICCSCE.2017.8284437

Zhang, H., Shao, S., Xu, H., Zou, H., & Tian, C. (2014). Free cooling of data centers: A review. *Renewable & Sustainable Energy Reviews*, *35*, 171–182. DOI: 10.1016/j.rser.2014.04.017

Zhang, K., Meng, X., Yan, X., Ji, J., Liu, J., Niu, E., Xu, H., Liu, D., Wang, J., & Wang, X., gao, J., Wang, Y., Shao, C., Wang, W., Li, J., Zheng, M., Yang, Y., & Tang, Y.-D. (. (2024). Revolutionizing Healthcare: The Transformative Impact of LLMs in Medicine (Preprint). *Journal of Medical Internet Research*, *27*, e59069. DOI: 10.2196/59069 PMID: 39773666

Zhang, Q., Meng, Z., Hong, X., Zhan, Y., Liu, J., Dong, J., Bai, T., Niu, J., & Deen, M. J. (2021). A survey on data center cooling systems: Technology, power consumption modeling and control strategy optimization. *Journal of Systems Architecture*, *119*, 102253. DOI: 10.1016/j.sysarc.2021.102253

Zhang, X., Chen, Y., Hu, L., & Wang, Y. (2022). The metaverse in education: Definition, framework, features, potential applications, challenges, and future research topics. *Frontiers in Psychology*, *13*, 1016300. Advance online publication. DOI: 10.3389/fpsyg.2022.1016300 PMID: 36304866

Zhang, X., Zheng, X., & Mao, W. (2021). Adversarial perturbation defense on deep neural networks. *ACM Computing Surveys*, *54*(8), 1–36.

Zhang, Y., Song, Y., Liang, J., Bai, K., & Yang, Q. (2020, August). Two sides of the same coin: White-box and black-box attacks for transfer learning. In *Proceedings of the 26th ACM SIGKDD international conference on knowledge discovery & data mining* (pp. 2989-2997). DOI: 10.1145/3394486.3403349

Zhang, Y., Weiss, R. J., Zen, H., Wu, Y., Chen, Z., Skerry-Ryan, R. J., Jia, Y., Rosenberg, A., & Ramabhadran, B. (2019, September). Learning to speak fluently in a foreign language: Multilingual speech synthesis and cross-language voice cloning. *Interspeech*, •••, 2019. DOI: 10.21437/Interspeech.2019-2668

Zhang, Z., Falai, A., Sanchez, A., Angelini, O., & Yanagisawa, K. (2022). *Mix and match: An empirical study on training corpus composition for Polyglot text-to-speech*. TTS.

Zhang, Z., Yang, E., & Fang, S. (2021, December). Commandergabble: A universal attack against asr systems leveraging fast speech. In *Proceedings of the 37th Annual Computer Security Applications Conference* (pp. 720-731). DOI: 10.1145/3485832.3485892

Zhehua, Z., & Zhang, Z. (2022). Application of Intelligent Speech Synthesis Technology Assisted by Mobile Intelligent Terminal in Foreign Language Teaching. *Mathematical Problems in Engineering*, *2022*, 1–10. DOI: 10.1155/2022/9751094

Zhu, G., Liu, D., Du, Y., You, C., Zhang, J., & Huang, K. (2020). Toward an Intelligent Edge: Wireless Communication Meets Machine Learning. *IEEE Communications Magazine*, *58*(1), 19–25. DOI: 10.1109/MCOM.001.1900103

Zhu, J., Hasegawa-Johnson, M., & Sari, L. (2020). Identify speakers in cocktail parties with end-to-end attention. *Proceedings of the Annual Conference of the International Speech Communication Association, INTERSPEECH, 2020-Octob*, 3092–3096. DOI: 10.21437/Interspeech.2020-2430

Zhu, X., Li, J., Liu, Y., Ma, C., & Wang, W. (2023). A Survey on Model Compression for Large Language Models. *ArXiv*. https://arxiv.org/abs/2308.07633

Zong, J., Lee, C., Lundgard, A., Jang, J., Hajas, D., & Satyanarayan, A. (2022). Rich screen reader experiences for accessible data visualization. *Computer Graphics Forum: Journal of the European Association for Computer Graphics, 41*(3), 15–27. DOI: 10.1111/cgf.14519

Zong, W. (2023). Adversarial Examples and Trojan Attacks in Automatic Speech Recognition Systems.

About the Contributors

Abeer Saber was born in Damietta, Dumyat, Egypt, in 1992. She received the B.Sc. Degree in Computer Science and the M.Sc. Degree in Computer Science from Mansoura University, Egypt, in 2013 and 2018, respectively. She is received the Ph.D. in computer science from Menoufia University, Egypt, in 2022. She is currently a Lecturer in information technology with the Faculty of Computers and Artificial intelligence, Damietta University, Egypt. She has published many research articles in prestigious international conferences and reputable journals. She is also a reviewer for many journals. Her current research interests include big data analysis, semantic web, linked open data, Optimization, machine learning, Deep learning, bioinformatics, and IoT.

Tamer Emara holds a Ph.D. in Information and Communication Engineering from Shenzhen University, China, and is an Assistant Professor at the Faculty of Computers and Artificial Intelligence, Damietta University, Egypt. He earned his M.Sc. and B.Sc. degrees from Mansoura and Tanta Universities, respectively. Dr. Emara has received numerous awards, including the Excellent Paper Award from the Big Data Mining and Analytics journal in 2021, the Outstanding Scientific Award from the Higher Institute of Engineering and Technology Kafrelsheikh, the Shenzhen Universiade International Scholarship, and recognition as the Outstanding Doctoral Student of Shenzhen University in 2016. Dr. Emara is actively engaged in the academic community, serving as Program Committee Chair for the 2025 IEEE International Conference on Computer Science, Technology, and Engineering (ICCSTE2025) in Wuhan, China, and as General Chair for the 2024 International Conference on Artificial Intelligence and Mechanical Engineering (ICAIME2024) in Nanjing, China. He also contributes as a member of the Technical Program Committee (TPC) and Organization Committees for various conferences and serves as a reviewer for multiple journals. Dr. Emara is a senior member of the IEEE and a member of the ACM. His research interests span big data management and applications, machine learning, distributed and parallel computing, bioinformatics, and IoT.

Mohammad Sultan Mahmud (Senior Member, IEEE) received the Ph.D. degree from Shenzhen University, China, in 2023, and the master's degree from King Mongkut's University of Technology North Bangkok, Thailand, in 2014. Currently, Dr. Mahmud is a Research Fellow with the College of Computer Science and Software Engineering, Shenzhen University, China. He is one of the pioneers in the distributed clustering ensemble of big data research. Dr. Mahmud has published research articles in esteemed journals such as Information Fusion, IEEE Transactions on Big Data, Big Data Mining and Analytics, and the Journal of Big Data. He has organized a special issue on "Mixture of Experts (MoE) and Ensemble Learning for Big Data" in Information Fusion (Elsevier). His current research focuses on big data mining, distributed and parallel computing, ensemble learning, and mixture of experts.

Muhammad Azhar is the Associate Head of Department and Director of BSc-ADS programme of Applied Data Science and Assistant Professor at Hong Kong Shue Yan University, SAR, China. He is also the Director of Big Data Laboratory of HKSYU. Before joining HKSYU as an Assistant Professor in 2023, Dr. Azhar has over 11 years of experience in teaching and research in different universities and research institutes in South Korea, Mainland China and Pakistan. In addition to this, he worked in different software companies of Pakistan (Sofnix Private Limited and Turnotech Private Limited) and U.K. (Welltime Ltd.). He received his B.S. degree in Computer Science from National University of Computer and Emerging Sciences, Islamabad, Pakistan, master's degree in computer science from Sejong University, Seoul, South Korea, and the Ph.D. degree in Machine Learning and Data Mining from Shenzhen University, Shenzhen, China. He worked as a Research Professor at Chosun University, South Korea. His research interests include Data Mining, Natural Language Processing and Computer Vision through conventional machine learning and advanced deep learning techniques.

Esraa Hassan was born in Kafrelsheikh, Kafrelsheikh, Egypt, in 1992. She received a B.Sc. Degree in Computer Science and a M.Sc. Degree in Computer Science from Mansoura University, Egypt, in 2013 and 2018, respectively. She received her Ph.D. in computer science from Mansoura University, Egypt, in 2022. She is currently a lecturer at the Faculty of Artificial Intelligence, Kafrelsheikh University, Egypt. She has published many research articles in prestigious international conferences and reputable journals. She is also a reviewer for many journals. Her research interests include machine learning, deep learning, optimization, and bioinformatics.

***

Nizirwan Anwar, MT, IPM, ASEAN.Eng is a Lecturer in the Informatics Engineering Study Program, Faculty of Computer Science, Universitas Esa Unggul under the auspices of the Kemala Bangsa Education Foundation (YPKB). The author was born in the city of Bandung on July 24 1964, completed his bachelor's degree from the Physics Study Program, Faculty of Mathematics and Natural Sciences, Padjadjaran University, Bandung in 1989 and continued the Electrical Engineering Study Program, Faculty of Engineering (dh. Postgraduate Study Program) University of Indonesia, Jakarta, completing his studies in 1995, obtaining a Bachelor of Engineering Intermediate Professional (IPM) and ASEAN Engineer (ASEAN.Eng). Alhamdulillah has produced several reputable and indexed published scientific papers at national and international levels (research a categories; Internet of Things, Cryptography, Bibliometrics and Data Science). To date, he is registered as active in several professional organizations, National Lecturer BKD assessor (NIRA), as a reviewer in Arjuna accredited journals (Kemendikbud Saintek); Scientific Committe, Central Executive of the Vocational Agency BKI PII,

Muhammad Faisal, received her S.SI degree from the Department of Information Systems, STMIK Profesional, Makassar, Indonesia, at 2011, and an M.T degree from the Masters in Information Technology, Postgraduate School, Hasanuddin University, Makassar, Indonesia at 2014. Furthermore, Ph.D degree from the School and Technology Information, Doctoral Programme, Asia E University Malaysia. He is currently a lecturer and researcher at the Department of Informatics, Universitas Muhammadiyah Makassar, Indonesia. His current research interests include Mobile Programming, Data Mining, Decision Support System, Expert System, Web Applications, Image Processing, and Machine Learning.

Aishwarya Laxmi is a postgraduate in Biomedical Engineering with research interests in deep learning, speech recognition, and medical image processing. Her recent research focuses on speaker gender identification using speech signals, utilizing MFCC and LPCC feature extraction techniques in combination with CNN and LSTM models. Her academic work is centered on the application of artificial intelligence to address challenges in speech processing and medical image analysis.

Raden Teddy Iswahyudi, currently working as a Lecturer at the Undergraduate Study Program (S1) in the Informatics Engineering Study Program, Faculty of Computer Science, Esa Unggul University under the auspices of the Kemala Bangsa Education Foundation (YPKB). The author was born in Jakarta on November 10, 1975, completed his S1 education from the Electrical Engineering Study Program, Faculty of Engineering, University of Indonesia, Depok, West Java (2003) and continued his Masters Program in Computer Science, Faculty of Computer Science (formerly Postgraduate Study Program) Esa Unggul University, Jakarta (formerly DKI Jakarta) completing his studies (2023). A brief history of the author's career journey as an educator (lecturer) in implementing and devoting himself to the TriDharma of Higher Education has been 2 years - now. Alhamdulillah, he has produced several reference books; published and indexed scientific works and has a reputation (National/International), research in the field of Internet of Things (IoT), Cyber Security, Digital Transformation.

Muhabbat Jumaniyozova is working at Department of Methodology of Primary Education, Urgench State University, Urgench, Uzbekistan

Maqsuda Narboshova is working in the Department of Pedagogy and Psychology at Termez University of Economics and Service, Termez, Uzbekistan.

Ravikumar R N is an experienced educator with 11+ years of teaching in Computer Science across India and overseas. Currently an Assistant Professor at Marwadi University, Rajkot, he specializes in Advanced Java, Machine Learning, Data Science, and AI. He holds a Mini MBA from the Swiss eLearning Institute (2015), an M.E. in Computer Science Engineering from VMRF University (2013), and a B.E. from Anna University (2010). Completed PhD at Amity University, Jaipur, he is dedicated to research, professional development, and advancing education through technology.

Pappu Kumar Rai is working as Assistant Professor at Department of Computer Engineering, Marwadi University, Rajkot, India

Aarthi S is a dedicated Assistant Professor in Computer Science with over six years of teaching experience. She is currently pursuing her Ph.D. at Marwadi University, Gujarat, and holds an M.Phil. and MCA from Bharathiar University, Tamil Nadu. Throughout her academic career, Aarthi has specialized in programming languages such as C++, Java, and C, and contributed to research in recommender systems and AI-related data privacy. She has published journal articles, contributed to book chapters, and actively participated in technical workshops. Known for her student mentorship and engagement in academic events, Aarthi remains committed to fostering innovation and excellence in computer science education.

Wasswa Shafik (Member, IEEE) received a Bachelor of Science degree in information technology from Ndejje University, Uganda, a Master of Engineering degree in Information Technology (Computer and Communication Networks) from Yazd University, Iran, and a PhD in Computer Science with the School of Digital Science, Universiti Brunei Darussalam, Brunei Darussalam. He is also the Founder and Research Director of the Dig Connectivity Research Laboratory (DCRLab) after serving as a Research Associate at the Network Interconnectivity Research Laboratory at Yazd University. Prior to this, he worked as a Community Data Analyst at Population Services International (PSI-Uganda), a Community Data Officer at the Programme for Accessible Health Communication (PACE-Uganda), a Research Assistant at the Socio-Economic Data Centre (SEDC-Uganda), Uganda, an Assistant Data Officer at TechnoServe, Kampala, Uganda, and Asmaah Charity Organization as Cheif Executive Officer. He has hundreds of publications with renowned publishers. His research interests include Artificial Intelligence, Neural Networks, Computer Vision, Smart Agriculture, Digital Health, and Green Computing.

Sachin Sharma has worked as a Professor at Amity School of Engineering and Technology, Amity University, Punjab, Mohali, India since January 2025. He also worked as Associate Dean of International Affairs and Professor, Department of Computer Science and Engineering at Graphic Era Deemed to be University, Dehradun, Uttarakhand, India from February, 2018 to January 2025. He has experience of 15+ years in industry and academia. He is also Co-founder and Chief Technology officer (CTO) of IntelliNexus LLC, Arkansas, USA based company. He also worked as a Senior Systems Engineer at Belkin International, Inc., Irvine, California, USA. He received his Philosophy of Doctorate (Ph.D.) degree in Engineering Science and Systems specialization in Systems Engineering from University of Arkansas at Little Rock, USA with 4.0 out 4.0 GPA and M.S. degree in Systems engineering from University of Arkansas at Little Rock with 4.0 out 4.0 GPA. Dr. Sharma has authored/coauthored over 270+ publications in the form of books, patents, and papers in refereed journals and conference proceedings. He holds 70+ US, Indian and international patents in the area of IoT, wireless communication.

C.V. Suresh Babu is a pioneer in content development. A true entrepreneur, he founded Anniyappa Publications, a company that is highly active in publishing books related to Computer Science and Management. Dr. C.V. Suresh Babu has also ventured into SB Institute, a center for knowledge transfer. He holds a Ph.D. in Engineering Education from the National Institute of Technical Teachers Training

& Research in Chennai, along with seven master's degrees in various disciplines such as Engineering, Computer Applications, Management, Commerce, Economics, Psychology, Law, and Education. Additionally, he has UGC-NET/SET qualifications in the fields of Computer Science, Management, Commerce, and Education. Currently, Dr. C.V. Suresh Babu is a Professor in the Department of Information Technology at the School of Computing Science, Hindustan Institute of Technology and Science (Hindustan University) in Padur, Chennai, Tamil Nadu, India.

Venkat T, Professor and Head, Department of Computer Science and Engineering AI&ML, Sreenidhi Institute of Science and Technology, Hyderabad, Telangana, India.

J V P Udaya Deepika, Asst.Professor, Department of Computer Science and Engineering AI&ML, Sreenidhi Institute of Science and Technology, Hyderabad, Telangana, India.

Maryam Ahmad Usmani is working in the Department of Romano-Germanic Philology, Mamun University, Khiva, Uzbekistan

Index

A

C

D

E

F

G

H

I

L

M

N

www.ingramcontent.com/pod-product-compliance
Lightning Source LLC
LaVergne TN
LVHW080906300926
849162LV00003B/574